11.80

W9-BKW-976

6516

E
184
.A1
W5

Williams

Strangers next
door

Date Due

NO 24 '75

Strangers Next Door; Ethnic Relations In
E184.A1W5   6516

Williams, Robin Murphy
VRJC/WRIGHT LIBRARY

PRINTED IN U.S.A.

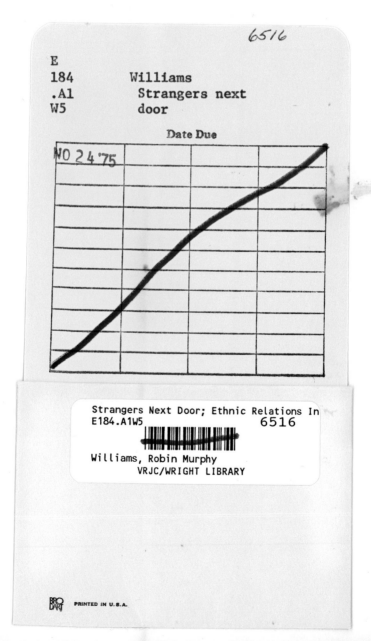

STRANGERS
Next Door

PRENTICE-HALL INTERNATIONAL, INC., LONDON
PRENTICE-HALL OF AUSTRALIA, PTY., LTD., SYDNEY
PRENTICE-HALL OF CANADA, LTD., TORONTO
PRENTICE-HALL OF INDIA (PRIVATE) LTD., NEW DELHI
PRENTICE-HALL OF JAPAN, INC., TOKYO
PRENTICE-HALL DE MEXICO, S.A., MEXICO CITY

STRANGERS
Next Door

ETHNIC RELATIONS IN AMERICAN COMMUNITIES

Robin M. Williams, Jr.

in collaboration with JOHN P. DEAN and EDWARD A. SUCHMAN

*and containing adaptations of contribu-
tions from Lois R. Dean, Robert Eichhorn,
Manet Fowler, Robert B. Johnson, Melvin
L. Kohn, Pauline Moller Mahar, Donald L.
Noel, Alphonso Pinkney, and Alice S. Rossi*

PRENTICE-HALL, INC.   Englewood Cliffs, New Jersey

VERNON REGIONAL
JUNIOR COLLEGE LIBRARY

PRENTICE-HALL SOCIOLOGY SERIES

Herbert Blumer, *Editor*

To My Parents

Current printing (last digit):

12   11   10   9   8   7   6   5

© 1964 by Prentice-Hall, Inc., Englewood Cliffs, N. J.

All rights reserved. No part of this book may be
reproduced in any form, by mimeograph or any other
means, without permission in writing from the publisher.

Library of Congress Catalog Card Number: 64-14007

Printed in the United States of America
C–85088

PREFACE

This book derives from a program of research that had its beginnings in 1948. At that time, studies were initiated in Elmira, New York, which later led to intensive research in other cities and eventually to the collection of data on a nationwide basis. Throughout the eight years of research that followed, and in a wide variety of studies, we tried to lay a basis for a better understanding of attitudes and behavior involved in relations among racial, ethnic, and religious groupings in the United States.

In the course of a long, complex, and far-flung set of research endeavors, a great many persons contributed to the work to be described here. The Cornell Studies in Intergroup Relations owed much at its inception to the encouragement of Leonard S. Cottrell, Jr., then Chairman of the Department of Sociology and Anthropology at Cornell University, and to the understanding and support of Joseph Willits and Leland C. DeVinney of the Rockefeller Foundation.

The findings in this volume are drawn in considerable part from this research program. From 1948 to 1956, under grants from the Rockefeller Foundation, a series of field studies was conducted under the general direction of John P. Dean,* Edward A. Suchman, and Robin M. Williams, Jr. In its initial phases, the program was closely involved in cooperative field work with the 1948 Voting Study in Elmira, and Dean and Suchman contributed to the final report of that study.†

Several academic generations of graduate students gained their research apprenticeships and carried out their own research for dissertations within the program. During the decade spanned by the Cornell Studies, the various persons who engaged in the research made hundreds of presentations

---

* Deceased.

† Bernard R. Berelson, Paul F. Lazarsfeld, and William N. McPhee; *Voting* (Chicago: University of Chicago Press, 1954).

to professional meetings, to intergroup agencies and conferences, and to civic groups. Meanwhile, a growing roster of publications marked the continuous effort to master the accumulations of data and to communicate to wider audiences. A list of the publications which emerged follows this preface.

It is always difficult to gauge the influence of a research program of this type. Outcomes of such a sustained series of research endeavors are varied, numerous, and often subtle. Certainly in this study the experiences of the senior staff were infused into their teaching and into the entire spectrum of their professional activities. We believe that the consequences were of substantial benefit to their academic and civic contributions.

The main object of the studies, however, was knowledge, not education nor social reform. Although we saw no reason for shying away from applied research, we did not set out to solve problems or to induce social change. Nevertheless, some positive changes did occur in the daily life of the communities studied merely as a consequence of the fact that a research group was known to be making a study. The effects were modest, but we believe that intensive research on subjects involving social tension and controversy can be conducted in a scientific spirit, not only without disruptive consequences but also with tangible positive contributions. In Elmira we think there were observable contributions to increased clarity in local public action and to constructive developments in the relations among the racial and ethnic segments that make up the pluralistic balance of many American communities. Consultation services provided by members of the research staff to governmental and civic organizations appear to have encouraged the use of research data as a component in responsible decisions concerning public policy in the United States.

We would like to thank the usually patient, and often warm and helpful, people who allowed themselves to be interviewed in the Cornell Studies, and we are appreciative, in a way, of those who were unfriendly, too. All of them helped us to learn. We realize, after some of the sting has gone, that such people as the overbearing newspaper editor in one community who threatened to run us out of town revealed things we could not have learned by any easier or more pleasant route. The essential task that now lies ahead is to bring together in some manageable synthesis the fruits of a decade's research—our own and that of others—on intergroup relations in the United States.

R. M. W., JR.

I. *Books*

1. John P. Dean and Alex Rosen, *A Manual of Intergroup Relations.* Chicago: University of Chicago Press, 1955.
2. Edward A. Suchman, John P. Dean, and Robin M. Williams, Jr., with the assistance of Morris Rosenberg, Lois Dean, and Robert Johnson, *Desegregation: Some Propositions and Research Suggestions.* New York: Anti-Defamation League of B'nai B'rith, 1958.
3. Robin M. Williams, Jr. and Margaret W. Ryan (eds.), *Schools in Transition.* Chapel Hill, N. C.: University of North Carolina Press, 1954.

II. *Articles, and Chapters in Books*

1. E. Martinez and E. Suchman, "Letters from America and the 1948 Elections in Italy," *Public Opinion Quarterly,* Spring, 1950.
2. J. Greenblum and L. I. Pearlin, "Vertical Mobility and Prejudice: A Socio-Psychological Analysis," in R. Bendis and S. M. Lipset (eds.), *Class, Status and Power,* pp. 480-81. New York: Free Press of Glencoe, Inc., 1953.
3. Robin M. Williams, Jr., "Review and Assessment of Research on Race and Culture Conflict," *Conference on Research in Human Relations.* Rockefeller Foundation, 1953 (Processed).
4. John P. Dean and Edward A. Suchman, Chapters on "Social Institutions" and "Political Institutions," in Bernard R. Berelson, Paul F. Lazarsfeld, and William N. McPhee, *Voting.* Chicago: University of Chicago Press, 1954.
5. Edward A. Suchman and Herbert Menzel. "The Interplay of Demographic and Psychological Variables in the Analysis of Voting Surveys," in Paul F. Lazarsfeld and Morris Rosenberg (eds.), *The Language of Social Research,* pp. 148-55. New York: Free Press of Glencoe, Inc., 1954.
6. John P. Dean, "Patterns of Socialization and Association Between Jews and Non-Jews," *Jewish Social Studies,* XVII, No. 3 (July, 1955), 247-68.
7. Bernard C. Rosen, "Conflicting Group Membership: A Study of Parent-Peer Group Cross-Pressures," *American Sociological Review,* XX, No. 2 (April, 1955), 155-61.
8. Melvin L. Kohn and Robin M. Williams, Jr., "Situational Patterning in Intergroup Relations," *American Sociological Review,* XXI (April, 1956), 164-74.

---

* As noted, the primary studies were conducted under grants from the Rockefeller Foundation. The various publications appropriately note other sources of financial support.

9. Robin M. Williams, Jr., Burton R. Fisher, and Irving L. Janis, "Educational Desegregation as a Context for Basic Social Science Research," *American Sociological Review,* XXI (October, 1956), 577-83.

10. Robin M. Williams, Jr., "Religion, Value-Orientations, and Intergroup Conflict," *The Journal of Social Issues,* XII (1956), 12-20.

11. Robin M. Williams, Jr., "Unity and Diversity in Modern America," *Social Forces,* XXXVI (October, 1957), 1-8.

12. Robert B. Johnson, "Negro Reactions to Minority Group Status," in Milton L. Barron, *American Minorities,* pp. 192-212. New York: Alfred A. Knopf, Inc., 1957.

13. Robin M. Williams, Jr., "Racial and Cultural Relations," in Joseph B. Gittler (ed.), *Review of Sociology: Analysis of a Decade.* New York: John Wiley & Sons, Inc., 1957.

14. Bernard C. Rosen, "Minority Group in Transition": A Study of Adolescent Religious Conviction and Conduct," in Marshall Sklare (ed.), *The Jews: Social Patterns of an American Group,* pp. 336-47. New York: The Free Press of Glencoe, 1958.

15. John P. Dean, "Jewish Participation in the Life of Middle-Sized American Communities," in *Ibid.,* pp. 304-20.

16. Robin M. Williams, Jr., "Continuity and Change in Sociological Study," *American Sociological Review,* XXIII, No. 4 (December, 1958), 619-33 (especially pp. 624-27).

17. Richard L. Simpson, "Negro-Jewish Prejudice: Authoritarianism and Social Variables as Correlates," *Social Problems,* VII, No. 2 (Fall, 1959), 138-46.

18. Peter I. Rose, "Small-Town Jews and Their Neighbours in the United States," *The Jewish Journal of Sociology* (England), III, No. 2 (December, 1961), 1-18.

19. Alphonso Pinkney, "The Quantitative Factor in Prejudice," *Sociology and Social Research,* XLVII, No. 2 (January, 1963), 161-68.

20. Edward A. Suchman and John P. Dean, "Intergroup Contact and Prejudice," in Alvin W. Gouldner and Helen P. Gouldner, *Modern Sociology,* pp. 280-84. New York: Harcourt, Brace & World, Inc., 1963.

III.   *Theses (Cornell University Library, Ithaca, N. Y.)*

1. Caterina Edda Elena Martinez, *The Influence of Italian-Americans on the 1948 Elections in Italy: A Study of Immigrant Pressures upon the Homeland* (1949). M.A. thesis.

2. Bernard Carl Rosen, *Religion, Reference Group Theory and Group Identification* (1952). Ph.D. thesis.

3. Richard Leo Simpson, *Factors in the Attitudes of Two Minority Groups Toward Each Other* (1952). M.A. thesis.

 4. Melvin Lester Kohn, *Analysis of Situational Patterning in Intergroup Relations* (1952). Ph.D. thesis.

 5. Leila Calhoun Deasy, *Social Mobility in Northtown* (1953). Ph.D. thesis.

 6. Robert Lee Eichhorn, *Patterns of Segregation, Discrimination and Interracial Conflict: Analysis of a Nationwide Survey of Intergroup Practices* (1954). Ph.D. thesis.

 7. Pauline Moller Maher, *Dimensions of Personality as Related to Dimensions of Prejudice in a Survey of a Northeastern City* (1955). Ph.D. thesis.

 8. Robert Burgette Johnson, *The Nature of the Minority Community: Internal Structure, Reactions, Leadership and Action* (1955). Ph.D. thesis.

 9. Peter Isaac Rose, *The Exemption Mechanism: A Conceptual Analysis* (1957). M.A. thesis.

10. Lionel S. Lewis, *Discrimination and Insulation: An Intercommunity Comparison* (1959). M.A. thesis.

11. Peter Isaac Rose, *Strangers in Their Midst: A Sociological Study of the Small-Town Jew and His Neighbors* (1959). Ph.D. thesis.

12. Donald L. Noel, *Correlates of Anti-White Prejudice: Attitudes of Negroes in Four American Cities* (1961). Ph.D. thesis.

13. Alphonso Pinkney, *The Anatomy of Prejudice: Majority Group Attitudes Toward Minorities in Selected American Cities* (1961). Ph.D. thesis.

ACKNOWLEDGMENTS

The original research program upon which this book is founded was a collaborative endeavor in all aspects of the work, from initial planning to final analysis of data.

In addition to the collaborators listed on the title page, many other persons made substantial contributions. We are grateful to all of them. Special mention must be made of the long period of highly competent and helpful assistance given by Mrs. Mildred S. Essick to the field research in Elmira. Also deserving special mention for his part in interviewing and observation is Mr. Martin Keavin. Crucial advice and help were freely given by Mr. Howard Coleman and Mr. Lewis H. Stark, Jr.

In Elmira, the research was immeasurably aided by an Advisory Committee, initially composed of the following persons: Dr. William Pott (Chairman), Mr. James L. Burke, Mrs. Leslie D. Clute, Mrs. Laura Hailstork, Mr. Leon Hogg, Miss Alice Magenis, Mr. David Sheehan, Rev. John Sterns, Mr. Josef Stein, Professor Raymond B. Stevens, Hon. Emory Strachen, Mr. Merle Thompson, Mr. Peter Whitcher, and Mr. Charles Winding.

Among the Cornell graduate students who participated in the field work special thanks go to Gloria May, who, as a Sigmund Livingston Fellow (1949-50), studied the life of Negro adolescents in Elmira and endured the severities of being a participant observer in situations of racial discrimination. Similar appreciation is due to Bernard C. Rosen for his work, also as a Sigmund Livingston Fellow (1950-51), in a study of religious beliefs and practices among Jewish adolescents. Research assistance was given by H. David Kirk, Sadie Yancey, Norman Hilmar, David Kallen, Harley Frank, Thomas Matthews, Roger Baldwin, Richard Simpson, William Evan, and Jessie Cohen.

Indispensable help and advice were given on many occasions by Alex Rosen, then Director of the Jewish Community Center in Elmira. Rosen later collaborated with John P. Dean to write *A Manual of Intergroup Relations*.

A special acknowledgment is due to Manet Fowler, who performed the task of initially organizing into a single manuscript much of the accumulation of research memoranda, notes, tabulations, and field reports that had filled the files by the end of the program of field studies. Her draft has been heavily utilized in the writing of this book.

I deeply appreciate the helpfulness of Mr. Alfred W. Goodyear and Mrs. Ilene McGrath of the Prentice-Hall staff, and of Mrs. Robin Brancato who copyedited the manuscript.

For skillful and patient secretarial assistance I am greatly indebted to Mrs. Anne Tower of the Center for Advanced Study in the Behavioral Sciences (Stanford, California); to Mrs. Kathryn Harrison of Menlo Park, California; and to Mrs. Margaret Anagnost and Miss Ellen Cunningham, Department of Sociology, Cornell University. Major administrative and secretarial tasks for several years were ably performed by Mrs. Katherine Riegger of Cornell.

To the hundreds of interviewers, observers, and respondents in many communities goes our appreciation for making possible the collection of the basic data.

Completion of the book was made possible by an academic year at the Center for Advanced Study in the Behavioral Sciences and by a Senior Postdoctoral Fellowship from the National Science Foundation.

We acknowledge with appreciation the permission of authors and publishers to quote materials, as indicated by footnote citations in the text. Separate acknowledgement is due to UNESCO for permission to quote from the *International Social Science Bulletin*.

CONTENTS

CHAPTER 1

WHERE WE STAND:
AN INTRODUCTION

From the earliest records to those of our day, human history reveals that men have always regarded themselves as members of particular groups or societies and have always distinguished themselves from persons belonging to other groups and societies. Although unlike groups have sometimes lived in a state of peaceful coexistence, the historical story of man is often dominated by the chronicles of national, religious, racial, and class conflict. In the fifth and fourth centuries B.C. the Greeks of the city-states regarded peoples who did not speak Greek as "babblers" who were different, inferior, and often hateful. Long before the voyages of discovery Europe had come to know the ravages of internecine religious and class strife. When European expansion brought explorers and settlers in contact with new peoples, doctrines of racial superiority and inferiority developed and were eagerly accepted. Subsequent economic and political rivalries and half-understood biological discoveries have contributed to man's distrust of groups other than his own.

The twentieth century has been marked by two world wars and hundreds of smaller conflicts, all in the space of less than fifty years. The decrease in traveling time between distant places and the increased technological potentialities for destruction make it essential for us to find out all we can about group relationships—and about prejudice, hostility, and conflict.

It is particularly vital that the citizens of the United States understand their own society in relation to the rest of the world. The heterogeneity that has made this country distinctive has also introduced social strains. The United States has been torn apart by civil war caused partially by racial strife, it has known religious conflict, and it has a complex history of ethnic tensions. Though there is no doubt that Americans have a common core culture, its unifying influence does not always prevail against racial, religious, and ethnic differences. Then too, our domestic difficulties are sharply watched by other peoples the world over. Domestic discord and conflict already have occasioned doubts and criticisms of our leadership and example among the uncommitted nations.

At this point in history throughout the world colonialism is dying, and new nations are emerging. In this country intergroup relations are being radically affected by forces of change. Cultural differences based on nationality no longer have their former importance. With some exceptions religious intolerance has diminished. And despite the long struggle ahead, racial discrimination and segregation have been reduced. In the decades ahead the success or failure of relationships among and between ethnic, religious, and racial groupings will profoundly influence the character of American and world society.

AN ORIENTATION FOR THE READER

This book is a combination of the findings of the Cornell Studies in Intergroup Relations and an interpretation of the studies in the light of what is currently known and theorized by specialists in this field. General discussions of ethnocentrism and prejudice are followed by specific data accumulated in the studies. Definitions of terms and other background information have been provided when necessary.

The book is intended to be objective, relevant to the subject, and balanced with regard to the general and the specific. The studies on which this volume is based were planned and carried out with the intention of objectivity, and the primary task in writing the book has been to describe, to analyze, and to understand, rather than to evaluate. An attempt has been made to form generalizations that are as widely applicable as possible without being too speculative. Specific data are cited as examples that support generalizations.

The reader of this book has an opportunity to view in proper perspective the results presented here. A look at past history may often explain motives for the behavior and attitudes of interviewees recorded in the book. The reader should also consider that these findings have been gathered from specific locations at a specific point in time, and that attitudes and behavior are ever changing.

CHAPTER 2

A DESCRIPTION
OF THE STUDIES

When the researchers of the Cornell Studies in Intergroup Relations began their work in Elmira, New York, in 1948, they could not foresee that the research would lead them on to many more cities over the next eight years. Numerous problems in securing and interpreting the data were faced by the researchers, and only after solving one problem at a time were we able to determine the final direction of the studies.

THE ORIGINAL RESEARCH PLAN

The original plan of research called for a three-year study of intergroup relations in a middle-sized industrial community in upstate New York. The plan called for a broad descriptive study of the community structure, especially of those aspects most closely related to the life of the ethnic, religious, and racial groups. Sample surveys were to focus on attitudes and behavior directly involved in intergroup relations. Quasi-experimental analyses were to be applied in situations of change in ethnic relations within the community.

The laboratory community that was initially selected, and from which came more data than from any other single community, was Elmira, New York. In order to emphasize the more general and universal aspects of our data rather than local uniqueness, we gave pseudonyms to the towns surveyed most intensively. Therefore, Elmira will usually be referred to hereafter as Hometown.[1] After our study in Hometown was under way we had the opportunity to secure much valuable information from the 1948 Voting Study's opinion surveys.[2]

THE SCOPE WIDENS

By early 1950 it seemed essential to inquire into communities other than Hometown. The idea was growing that attitudes and behavior in Hometown might be less universal than we had thought. It seemed feasible to develop survey methods that would enable us to develop quickly and economically crucial information on basic intergroup patterns in a number of other cities. Furthermore, once it had become widely known in Hometown that our study was in progress, even the widespread pretesting of the kind needed for our local studies held considerable hazard to the larger research program. We decided to find at first just one other appropriate town for the pretesting work.

Our expansion soon took us to not one but five trial communities, each of about the same general size-class: Auburn, Poughkeepsie, and New Rochelle, New York; Norwalk, Connecticut; and Lancaster, Pennsylvania. In these cities it was possible in a short time to secure a large body of essential facts about the local pattern of segregation and discrimination. Interviews with informed leaders were cross-checked against one another, using a twenty-five page inventory. Interviewing was continued until discrepancies were eliminated and essential data were simply being repeated without any new information developing.

During the first three years of the program (1948-1951), the field re-

---

[1] Steubenville, Ohio is referred to as Steelville; Bakersfield, California as Valley City; and Savannah, Georgia as Southport. These were the four cities most intensively analyzed.

[2] The 1948 Voting Study, headed by Bernard Berelson, Paul Lazarsfeld, and W. McPhee and sponsored by more than a dozen philanthropic and business organizations, was focused on Elmira so that Cornell Studies interviewers could gather voting data along with information about ethnic attitudes and behavior. The Voting Study data revealed much about the majority and minority groups of the community. Thus the same data were useful to both studies. The results of the Voting Study have been published in *Voting* (Chicago: University of Chicago Press, 1954).

search staff made such reconnaissance surveys in twenty cities, widely
scattered across the United States. In three of these communities, only informal impressions were gathered: Los Angeles, California; Flandreau,
North Dakota; and Claxton, Georgia. Techniques were developed by which
it was possible in the remaining cities to secure in a relatively short time a
systematic inventory and diagnosis of local patterns of segregation, discrimination, conflict, and interaction-action programs. Complete inventories
of such data were secured in the following cities: Ashland, Kentucky; Auburn, New York; Bakersfield, California; Chester, Pennsylvania; Elmira,
New York; Lancaster, Pennsylvania; Montclair, New Jersey; New Rochelle,
New York; Norwalk, Connecticut; Phoenix, Arizona; Poughkeepsie, New
York; Sault Ste Marie, Minnesota; Savannah, Georgia; Sioux Falls, South
Dakota; Steubenville, Ohio; Tucson, Arizona; and Weirton, West Virginia.

Our intensive studies, then, were conducted in Hometown, Steelville,
Valley City, and Southport. In these four cities we conducted sample surveys, carried out many intensive interviews, and made numerous detailed
observations. The other twenty cities provided checks upon representative-
ness of our findings and supplied many clues for interpretation of the more
intensive studies.

Choosing the cities

For our intensive surveys we sought cities large enough to provide a complex urban context for intergroup relations and to reveal the impersonal
impact of political and economic processes upon local minorities. At the
same time, we wanted each city to be small enough to permit concrete
visualization of all its major organizations and social areas and detailed
knowledge of its leadership structure. We hoped each would be stable
enough to reveal a clearly defined set of dominant attitudes and practices,
yet fluid enough to exhibit significant social change.

Typicality

How typical were the cities we studied intensively? They were not precisely representative of intergroup relations in the United States, or in the
regions in which they were located, or even in other cities of the same size
in nearby areas. However, neither were they unique, and it is reasonable
to believe that they reflected a great many features common to other communities of similar size and population composition in the regions in which
they were situated. We can, therefore, generalize beyond the samples.[3] On
the other hand, the field experiences taught the basic lesson that local situations were endlessly varied and often difficult to explain by any obvious

---

[3] *Ibid.,* p. 4.

social conditions. By discovering that a condition in Southport, for example, did not necessarily exist in Tucson or Weirton, we learned our lesson of caution. However, the main findings did prove to be widely relevant in American industrial cities of small to middle size in the Northeast, Border States, Deep South, and Far West in the mid-twentieth century. It is on this basis of informal estimate of rational credibility that we wish to present the data.

The character of the cities

All four communities studied intensively were industrial areas, with populations ranging from about 40,000 to about 120,000 at the time of the surveys. Each had a predominantly working-class population. None was a satellite or appendage of a larger metropolitan complex. Each, however, was linked with many other urban centers through good transportation and communication facilities. Because of their different geographical locations and historical developments, however, the major industries of each differed considerably.

Each city had at least two distinct ethnic minorities, one of which was Negro. Gradually, the non-Negro minorities utilized freely most of the public facilities. For example, integration of white and non-Negro ethnic minori-. ties in the public schools was accepted practice, with the exception of one Mexican-American school in Valley City. As a rule, Jews participated in the general life of the community; they served in important municipal positions. This was not the case with Negroes. With isolated exceptions, they were excluded from the general affairs of the community. Treatment of Mexican-Americans was similar to that of Negroes.

In each city the Negro minority was more rigidly segregated than were other ethnic groups. Southport provided the clearest example of caste for its Negro inhabitants. While Negroes did not participate fully in all aspects of community life in any city studied, only in this Deep South city were Negroes relegated to certain aspects of community life by law. The extent to which Negroes were the objects of racial segregation in public facilities varied from total segregation in Southport to virtually no official segregation in Hometown. Steelville and Valley City, like Hometown, were situated in states with laws that prohibited segregation and discrimination in most public facilities; but there were many public facilities in these two cities that Negroes did not use because experience had demonstrated that difficulty would be likely to result if they did.

Southport was roughly comparable to Valley City in size, as was Hometown to Steelville. However, in Valley City there were many diverse cultural and racial minorities, most of which were of fairly recent origin. In Southport the largest ethnic minority (Negro) had lived there as a separate community since the Civil War. Valley City was a loosely structured community, whereas Southport was an old, highly stratified city, tending to stress tradition. In terms of general social relations, Hometown and Steelville appeared to be somewhat more formal than Valley City but less so than Southport. In our samples, the extent of ethnic tolerance in a city seemed to parallel roughly the lack of rigidity in social structure generally.

These comparative community studies showed immense variation from one locality to another, even within the same general region of the country, in the details of local attitudes and practices. We found that thoroughly accepted rights of Negroes in Hometown might be controversial issues in city X and unheard-of breaches of custom in city Y. Moreover, acceptable intergroup activity might vary even within the same urban area. For example, one movie theater would be for whites only, another would be integrated, and a third would be sometimes one and sometimes the other. Some practices seemed firmly rooted in long-established attitudes and customs; others seemed, on the surface at any rate, to be arbitrary.

The national survey

From one community we had been led into twenty. These twenty, in their great variation, seemed to call imperatively for some better estimate of the range of variability and of the prevalence of these differing conditions we were observing. Even while the first reconnaissance surveys were being studied, we decided to seek certain limited data from a nation-wide sample of cities. To make field visits to hundreds of cities in all parts of the country would have been prohibitively expensive in money and time. A workable alternative was found in an elaborate mail survey. An initial list of informants for all cities of 10,000 population or more was built up through inquiries at the national headquarters of organizations dealing with intergroup relations. A greatly expanded sample was then developed through voluminous correspondence in which each cooperating informant named other persons in the city who were well-informed concerning local intergroup relations. Wherever possible, informants were drawn from every major racial and ethnic group in the city. Each informant filled out a detailed Intergroup Relations Inventory that asked primarily questions of fact,[4] not questions about the informant's attitudes. Each return was checked for completeness and consistency. As multiple reports accumulated for each city, any discrepancies or disagreements were reported back to each respondent, with a request for clarification. In this tedious manner, a body of

---

[4] We asked, for example, the number of Negro policemen, teachers, firemen; whether there were Jewish members in certain types of clubs; whether there had been any racial rioting during the past year; whether Negroes were represented in the various professions; practices concerning service for Negroes in restaurants.

reliable information was constructed for some 248 cities. The coverage extended to all cities of over 100,000 population, with progressively smaller proportions in each successive category of size, down to and including cities of under 25,000 population.

Thus, one line of development of the research was to extend its geographic range and social representation. On the whole, the results of this survey were gratifyingly consistent. Not only was there substantial agreement among different informants in the same community; the findings of the quick reconnaissance field surveys, wherever they were made, tended to agree with the results of the mail questionnaire. We felt that in broad outline we now could describe the national patterns of segregation and discrimination in a meaningful way.[5]

The next step was to extend the house-to-house interview surveys to a few communities in several different parts of the nation. The search for comparison and replication led to intensive surveys of samples of adults in Steelville, Valley City, and Southport. We also secured data on high school youths in Hometown, Steelville, Weirton, and Phoenix.

For convenient reference, Table 2.1 presents the inventory of the main samples studied by means of local questionnaire surveys. The volume of available data from these studies is so great that we shall have to pick and choose only a part for actual presentation in this book. Wherever data are presented to support a conclusion, we shall note any contradictory evidence from any of the surveys.

The Direction Is Established

As data were gathered, it became obvious that there was often a discrepancy between the attitudes and the behavior of the subjects. This impression of ours was corroborated by the studies of Joseph Lohman, William Bradbury, and associates, who were at that time assembling data on segregation in Washington, D.C.[6] We interpreted their findings to mean: (1) that conventionalized operating practices in segregation and other forms of discrimination are sometimes maintained by small groups of power holders without strong support from the total community; (2) that a change in operating practices (either legal or administrative) will often be accepted by persons whose initial attitudes would have indicated strong resistance; (3) that discriminatory behavior by the same individuals is highly variable from one situation to another.

---

[5] A comprehensive analysis of these data may be found in Robert L. Eichhorn, "Patterns of Segregation, Discrimination, and Interracial Conflict: Analysis of a Nationwide Survey of Intergroup Practices" (Ph.D. thesis, Cornell University, 1954).

[6] J. D. Lohman, *Segregation in the Nation's Capital,* National Committee on Segregation in the Nation's Capital (Chicago, 1949).

Table 2.1

Number of respondents in each of the main sample surveys in cities
included in the Cornell studies.

Cities Surveyed	Majority-group (white gentiles)		Negroes		Jews		Mexican-Americans	
	Adults	Youths	Adults	Youths	Adults	Youths	Adults	Youths
Hometown (Elmira, N.Y.)	529*	2,307	150	100	150	50	—	
Steelville (Steubenville, Ohio)	288	501† 630‡	140	147	67	—	—	
Riverton (Weirton, W. Va.)	—	475	—	96	—	—	—	
Valley City (Bakersfield, Calif.)	319	—	227	—	—	—	131	
Southport (Savannah, Ga.)	294§	—	288		—	—	—	
Phoenix ⌠1952 (Phoenix, Ariz.) ⌡1954	— —	428 175	— —	262 160	— —	— —	— —	215 70
Totals	1,430	4,516	805	765	217	50	131	285

*Does not include an additional sample of 150 Italian-American persons studied in 1949.
 The main sample, originally 529 cases, was surveyed as a panel on six occasions.
†Protestant.
‡Catholic.
§Original sample of 354 reduced for analysis.

Both studies, for example, showed cases of an individual's dutifully testifying to popular stereotypes and negative sentiments without ever allowing
these negative feelings to affect his actual interactions with the group he
claimed to dislike. Our greatest problem was, then, whether to focus our
study on (1) data related to institutional structures in communities and
the operating practices of these institutions, (2) data related to the attitudes
and opinions of our sample of the adult population, or (3) the relationship
of attitudes and behavior. We decided to study, for the first time in detail,
the relationship between (a) prejudice, personality, and cultural stereotypes
and (b) discriminating behavior and actual contact situations between unlike groups. Our major methods of securing data on the relationship between attitudes and behavior were house-to-house interviews and direct
observations of contact situations.

HOW DATA WERE GATHERED

House-to-house interviews

A survey administered in Hometown from May to July, 1949, was later
revised and refined for use in several other communities. The cross section

interviewed in Hometown included 529 majority-group respondents, 150 Negroes, 150 Jews, and 150 Italian-Americans. Interviewers were usually local people who had had previous experience in interviewing and who were trained by the field staff of the Cornell Studies. In the case of samples of the Negro and Jewish population, the interviewers were of the same racial or religious background as the respondents.

Defining groups

The adult majority-group population sampled in the communities was simply those persons left after defining the minority-group populations that were themselves to be the objects of special studies. It was the white gentile population, excluding Jews, Negroes, and, in Valley City, Mexican-Americans. Although for various other research purposes a more homogeneous majority-group (for example, white native-born Protestants of native parentage) might have been defined, the residual definition seemed desirable for a program of studies that explored primarily Jewish-gentile and white-Negro attitudes and behavior. Occasionally, however, we made more refined distinctions by subdividing the majority-group—for example, by religious denomination.

In general, it was not difficult to define a minority population by relying upon the commonly accepted local definitions, crude and simple as this method may seem. That is, "Negroes" were all persons so regarded by themselves and by other persons who clearly were themselves Negro. "Jews" were persons who regarded themselves as Jewish and were so regarded by others.

Sampling

Sampling varied in details from one survey to another, with the most elaborate design and the greatest amount of checking employed in the Hometown panel. In all instances, however, procedures were employed that gave reasonable assurance that each household within the geographic community would have an equal likelihood of being included and that each eligible adult respondent would similarly be given an equal chance to be included in the sample. Refusal rates were acceptably low in all surveys, and refusals together with not-at-homes and other dropouts never amounted to more than about 8 per cent, and often were as low as 4 to 5 per cent.

What we asked

Majority-group respondents were asked about their contacts with Negroes, Jews, and Italian-Americans at work, in their neighborhoods, in organizations, and in their social groups. In every instance in which respondents had contacts with ethnic group members, we inquired whether they felt differently towards these persons and whether any personal friendships had been formed with them. If the respondent had not yet had contact with, say, Negroes, in one of the aforementioned situations, he was asked to predict his probable reaction to them.

Direct observations of contact situations

As soon as the direction of our studies was established we realized that we would have to observe the interaction of majority and minority groups and interview the participants about their feelings in these situations. It was not easy to find contact situations that would provide fruitful data. The contacts that were easy to observe—in stores, on buses—were too casual and transitory for analysis. And the more significant, more personal contacts were more difficult for the observer to find. The solution to this problem came through those members of our staff who were themselves members of a minority group. For example, we were able to study the effects of such situations as a Negro staff member's making a speech before a Business and Professional Women's Club, a Negro girl's being invited to join the American Association of University Women, and a Negro girl's attendance at a party given by her white friends at college. Furthermore, Negro and Jewish staff members actively tested out local discriminatory codes. (The results of these studies are reported in Chapter 9.) Occasionally we arranged situations involving these staff members that were calculated to draw a response from interactors and onlookers.[7]

Whenever possible in these cases we returned later to recanvass the scene and to interview as many of the key participants as we could. Our participant-observers and Negro stimulus-participants not only recorded in chronological order all that had taken place, but they also filled out forms that were designed to record in specific detail the participant-observers' observations and interpretations of what had taken place. The success of these efforts to comprehend interaction in intergroup situations created increasing confidence in our new methods. All told, we studied forty-three major situations in Hometown.

Other ways in which we attempted to gain information on intergroup contacts in Hometown were:

1. We started having some members of the Negro community keep a log of their contacts with whites.

2. We mapped a mixed neighborhood and started interviewing all house-

---

[7] For example, we cultivated the friendship of the bartender in a tavern known not to serve Negroes. When we arranged for a Negro field worker to meet us there one day, he was served reluctantly but without discourtesy. (See Chapter 9.)

wives on their contacts with white and Negro neighbors (who were also being interviewed).

3. We looked up the places of employment of Negro panel members who had contact with whites on the job, in order to interview their work associates.

4. We made an orderly canvass of the mixed white-Negro area every afternoon to observe situations among playing children.

The complete chronological list of our research efforts appears in Appendix A.

How Data Were Handled

Objectivity

Our survey data consist of answers given by persons who were interviewed, usually in their own homes, by interviewers who did not divulge their own opinions. Interviewers maintained a friendly but noncommittal attitude and asked the prepared questions in a prescribed way. Through selection of interviewers and through instruction and supervised practice we tried to develop careful and objective recording. Similar precautions were employed in the observation of field situations. Whenever diffuse observations gave sufficient clues to permit the design of a systematic survey or an observational experiment, we moved as rapidly as possible into the collection of standardized data suitable for statistical treatment. Whenever the tabulations raised perplexing questions of interpretation, we tried to get back into the community, again observing and interviewing. There was continuous interplay between the IBM tabulations and the naturalist's notebook.

Interpretation of data

It is neither necessary nor appropriate in this book to enter into an extended discourse on methodology or techniques of analysis. For the most part, we shall analyze the survey data by relatively straightforward cross tabulations and relatively simple statistical tests. We make extensive use of multiple-item scores that approximate the Guttman-type attitude scale, but we rarely have enough items for an ideal scale, and our claims for this procedure are rather limited. Were we now beginning afresh, we would at some points wish to try some of the newer approaches to data-analysis. But, given the data actually collected, for most of our hypotheses the less elaborate procedures are workable and suitable.

One basic point in the logic of analysis will appear so frequently that it must be made explicit. Some data refer to the *same* individual at two or more points in time. These data make it possible to analyze, for example, changes in degree of prejudice and degree of frequency of interaction with ethnic outgroup members from Time 1 to Time 2. Estimates can be derived of the relative magnitude of the effects associated with changes in interaction versus those associated with changes in prejudice. Together with the individual's testimony concerning changes in his own attitudes and behavior, in relation to other happenings in his personal life and his associations with others, these data constitute relatively strong evidence for inferring causal relationships.

For the most part, however, we will be working with information gathered at a single point in time. With our fairly large samples, reliable descriptions can be developed of the prevalence of various attitudes and patterns of behavior in the several communities. From the same basic data, analysis can show how each item of information is related to any other—how attitudes are associated; how prejudice varies among persons classified by sex, age, education, occupation, and so on; how prejudice is associated with frequency of outgroup contact.

Reliability and validity

The reliability and validity of the data compare favorably with those typically found in other well-controlled surveys and field studies by professional research organizations. Certain techniques of eliciting and recording data (for example, in the situational diagnosis discussed in Chapter 8) went well beyond the usual research practice at the time. Another strength of the Cornell Studies came from the replication of types of studies and of specific scales and items in different population groupings and in different communities. Other advantages derived from amassing a large amount of different kinds of information on various aspects of intergroup relations in the same community. It permitted many cross checks on the reliability of reporting and the validity of conclusions. It also aided immensely in interpreting each separate finding in the light of a known context of other facts. Finally, in the special case of Hometown, it was possible to develop a basic panel of respondents who were interviewed repeatedly over a period of eight years.

Limitations and advantages

Nevertheless, there are still many limitations and defects in the available data. Most obvious, perhaps, is the absence of any truly experimental studies. Whenever possible, we carried out semicontrolled field trials, but these could not properly be called experiments. A second limitation derives from the difficulty of directly relating, for a whole community, the attitudes expressed in interviews to the attitudes and behavior of the same persons in actual situations.

We probably carried out an unnecessarily large number of direct observations and open-ended interviews, for we were sensitive in our community studies to the advocates of an anthropological approach who insisted that much concrete familiarity with the community was essential to the effective design, later, of systematic surveys. In this book we need little direct use of these background materials. They have, however, furnished an essential context for many detailed interpretations of survey data; and they have strengthened the reliability of the data themselves. Because of an intimate firsthand acquaintance with the communities, we know that the survey responses are meaningfully consistent with other, directly observed behavior. In other instances, we are able to judge the typical or atypical character of an observed episode by referring to a statistical regularity in a sample of the entire population, for example, the frequency of contact with Negroes in organizations.

Most of the data used systematically in the subsequent chapters are derived from probability samples of adults and youths in one or more communities. Before turning to the major substantive problems of the research, in Chapter 3, we wish to comment briefly on one other major point of research technique and methodology.

Responses to questions that require a person to report on his own feelings and beliefs are affected by two major factors other than those feelings and beliefs themselves. One is the factor of social desirability, that is, the respondent's awareness of the general social evaluation of what he is reporting. (Thus, just as people are likely to be reluctant to report bad things about themselves, so are they likely to be reluctant to express socially disapproved attitudes.) Second, responses are affected by the respondent's generalized tendency toward acquiescence, that is, his inclination to agree with suggestions or to give the answers he thinks are expected, or, on the contrary, to reject whatever is presented to him almost without regard to its manifest content. These two factors give trouble in personality tests, for example, when they conceal or distort facts or feelings important to know.

Fortunately these factors are not so serious when the responses concern social, public attitudes. Undoubtedly many people in our surveys disagreed with statements of prejudice presented to them by our interviewers because they felt that it was not socially approved to have the suggested attitudes. And surely some others accepted stereotypes and statements of prejudice, not out of conviction or strong feeling, but only as a matter of acquiescence in a conventional response. Nevertheless, these responses do represent an important social reality: If a respondent is so easily swayed in an interview situation, which is permissive, friendly, relatively nonthreatening, and temporary, he probably will be similarly susceptible to the more powerful social pressures often encountered in ordinary daily life. If his attitudes are really strong and clear, he will resist the implicit blandishments and pressures sufficiently to state his own position. Both private and public attitudes are real. The important thing is to be clear which is which and what the fact means for a particular purpose of analysis.

Remaining considerations of technique and method will be discussed when this becomes necessary to the understanding of particular data. Let us now turn to the major problems to which all this research was addressed.

CHAPTER 3

ETHNOCENTRISM

Ethnocentrism, says William Graham Sumner, is that ". . . view of things in which one's own group is the center of everything, and all others are scaled and rated with reference to it." [1] It is a fact that men classify their fellows in a variety of ways and react to others as members of social categories. What is the nature of these groups that men form? How do they form them, and why? What is the nature of ethnocentric feelings, and how strong are they? The answers to these questions will constitute the main part of this chapter. We will also consider, in the final pages of this chapter, whether ethnocentrism necessarily results in prejudice.

THE FORMING OF GROUPS

Terminology

The word "group" is used in everyday parlance to refer to anything from a crowd at Yankee Stadium to the members of a family. Although we too

---

[1] *Folkways* (Boston: Ginn & Company, 1906), p. 13.

may find it convenient to employ the term "group" in our discussion of inter-group relations, it is necessary to understand that there are actually many kinds of groups, which vary from one another in cohesiveness and social significance and which should technically be referred to by some term other than "group." The category of least social importance is the *aggregate,* a collection of human individuals having no relationships among themselves other than those that are intrinsic in occupying geographic space in some proximity. As the distinctiveness, unity, and internal organization of the aggregate increases, we may want to recognize it as a *social category,* then as a *collectivity,* then as a *group,* and finally as a *society.* The social category is exemplified by an occupational grouping or a social class, where there is only a vague sense of membership and very rudimentary capacity for any sort of concerted collective action. A fully developed collectivity, on the other hand, is a *people,* and is characterized by 1) a distinctive culture; 2) tests or criteria of membership; 3) a set of constitutive norms regulating social relations both within the collectivity and with outsiders; 4) an aware-ness of a distinct identity by both members and nonmembers; 5) obligations of solidarity, such as enforced requirements to help members in need and to resist derogation by outsiders; and 6) a high capacity for continued ac-tion by the collectivity on behalf of its members or of itself as a unit. In its most comprehensive development such a collectivity may become a poten-tially self-sufficient society, able to meet all internal needs from its own re-sources and to perpetuate itself as a functioning system from generation to generation.

The term "group," then, when used most accurately, refers to a special case of a small-scale collectivity. What traditionally have been called "mi-nority groups" are either social categories or collectivities. However, so long as it is clear from the context what kind of collection of individuals is meant, we will freely use the term "group" (or the compromise term "group-ing" when we wish to stress the loose, aggregative quality of some part of the population).

How socially significant groups form

How do aggregates become collectivities? There undoubtedly are several different major sets of processes. One important general sequence, illus-trated by the cases of American Negroes and many immigrant populations, is approximately as follows:

1. By reason of any one of many historical circumstances, there is an initial categorization of persons considered to have some important charac-teristic in common—for example, they are slaves, newcomers, foreigners, or heathens. An identifying set of symbols is found that gives the category high social visibility: skin color, food habits, religious rites.

2. Persons in the category are typically found (or, are believed to be found) in occupations or other social roles that are recognizably different from those typically associated with persons in one or more other social categories: trade, money lending, domestic service, landlordism.

3. As a consequence of their distinctive social roles, persons in the given ethnic category will develop additional relatively distinctive interests, beliefs, values, and specific modes of behavior.

4. These differences will render more distinct, reinforce, and elaborate the initial definition of the social category.

5. As a consequence of all these developments, the like-circumstanced members of the social category will come increasingly to have a sense of common identity, which will tend to increase their within-category inter-action and to reduce their contacts with outsiders. This closure of inter-action will increase the tendency of outsiders to treat them as a unit, and this tendency, in turn, will enhance the new collectivity's cultural distinc-tiveness and social separateness.

6. If, however, the collectivity so formed is part of and is economically and politically dependent upon a larger social system, it will not become a completely closed social system. Its members must maintain relationships with members of other collectivities and social categories within the same total society.

7. If some other collectivity, or set of collectivities, is economically and politically dominant, the new subordinate collectivity will be forced to ac-cept the dominant grouping's rules of the game. It will be forced into a largely one-way adaptation to a common set of constitutive norms that will regulate the necessary relations between the two groupings. In other words, the subordinates have to accept some of the culture of the superordinate grouping, especially the basic rules of the game for vital dealings with the members of the dominant collectivity.

Groups of greatest social significance

Although there are numerous social categories that have social impor-tance (such as enlisted men, union workers, women), the groups that are of greatest social significance and those in which students of intergroup re-lations are most interested are those collectivities that have racial, ethnic, and religious distinctions. It is within the ethnic grouping that all individuals form their first relationships, their deepest dependencies, and the most im-portant bases of emotional ambivalence.

Why we are ethnocentric

All individuals need group belongingness and group anchorage. Without stable relationships to other persons, without some group ties, the individual

VERNON REGIONAL
JUNIOR COLLEGE LIBRARY

becomes insecure, anxious, and uncertain of his identity. In order to receive the emotional support of the group (that is, the family group, the neighborhood or school peer group) the individual must heed the opinions of other group members. In the homogeneous family group he learns definite codes for behavior within the group and for behavior towards other groups. The child discovers very early that agreement with group opinions and codes is rewarding. He learns that the teachings of one's parents and close associates are helpful in getting what he wants and avoiding what he does not want. To the extent to which the child finds the instruction of elders and peers reliable for achieving rewarding results, he learns to give credence to their opinions. The child's need is great for relationships of trust that mediate reality to him. And through group attachments and loyalties he learns also of group antipathies and conflicts. He perceives groups, then, as social units in which he can expect security and love or danger and negative emotional experience.

Secure identity as a member of an ingroup is not a free good, contrary to some first appearances, but is only to be had at a price. Often one must have already established credentials of other group memberships and of personal qualities and achievements. Furthermore, maintenance of a clear, full, and secure identity within the ingroup requires conformity to group norms. More exactly, the price of one's group identity is responsible reciprocity with other members, a reciprocity defined by mutually accepted norms.

The overlapping of groups

Particularly in our complex society, most individuals are members of more than one group. The child, aware at first only of his membership in a kinship group, slowly becomes conscious of other memberships. Piaget reports that only at the age of ten to eleven were the children he studied capable of understanding that they could be members of both a locality and a nation, and of understanding what a nation is.[2] By adulthood then, the individual is aware of a plurality of group memberships that help him identify himself. The person is rare in urban America today who feels a clear and strong sense of identification with one and only one grouping or segment of the community and nation. The typical individual is a member of many ingroups (groups of intimate belonging; "we-groups") and may relate

---

[2] J. Piaget and Anne-Marie Weil, "The Development in Children of the Idea of the Homeland and of Relations with Other Countries," *International Social Science Bulletin,* III, No. 3 (Autumn, 1951), 561-78: ". . . the feeling and the very idea of the homeland are by no means the first or even early elements in the child's make-up, but are a relatively late development in the normal child, who does not appear to be drawn inevitably towards patriotic sociocentricity." (p. 562)

himself to many other reference groups (those that matter to him, and upon whose opinions he relies).

It is difficult to realize fully the enormous significance of alternative group memberships. If the individual can belong to only one group, that group inevitably becomes all-important to him. In it all his satisfactions are found and are controlled and limited. It encompasses and constricts all his experiences. However, totalistic character of group membership diminishes in complex and fluid societies.[3] The growth of alternative possibilities of group membership and group reference depends upon the number and variety of distinctive groupings, but the sheer multiplication of groupings is far from the whole story. Changes in the criteria of membership are accentuated by changes in the functions of groups and by shifts in the alignments among and between groups. The characteristics that actually are statistically typical of a grouping or category at one time cease to be typical later.

A specific example of ethnocentrism

The following description of the upper-income, socially elite residents of Hometown will illustrate how similarities in occupation, income, background, ethnic origins, and style of life can cement a collection of individuals into a sociopsychological unity.[4]

> Among the socially elite of Hometown there is not a single Negro, Jewish, or Italian-American person. Members of the elite are native born of native-born parents. Most of them were born in Hometown, have inherited high social prestige, and form a self-chosen "village" within the city. Catholics are rare in the inner circles, although some Catholic adherents are found in peripheral circles. Elite members are overwhelmingly members of prestigeful Protestant churches and are Republicans in politics. Family background is a crucial factor in acceptance into the elite. The wrong ethnic background is automatically enough to insure exclusion. The elite grouping is difficult to enter and difficult to leave. Once in, a family is relinquished with reluctance, and much deviant behavior may be tolerated in the interests of group loyalty, exclusiveness, and protective secrecy against outsiders. Within the stratum most adults know, or know a great deal about, most of the others. And at least so far as the women are concerned, neither friendship, informal social participation, nor membership in clubs is sought outside these groups of like-circumstanced and mutually acquainted persons.

So far as members of the elite stratum are concerned, Hometown is not a city of some 50,000 socially significant persons, but is rather a series of overlapping primary groups among fewer than 200 families.

---

[3] Of course we recognize that multigroup societies can be engulfed by political totalitarianism, which enforces a new kind of all-encompassing membership.

[4] This description is based on Leila Calhoun Deasy's *Social Mobility in Northtown* (Unpublished Ph.D. thesis, Cornell University, 1953). Data were gathered from interviews with 126 women who clearly were members of the local upper stratum.

ETHNOCENTRIC FEELINGS

Positive ethnocentrism

What are the components of the sentiments of ethnocentrism? George Peter Murdock says, "Always the 'we-group' and its codes are exalted, while 'other groups' and their ways are viewed with suspicion, hostility and contempt." [5] It is true that satisfaction with one's own group (Oog) sometimes is accompanied by negative feelings toward other groups, but for the moment let us examine the attitude that ethnocentric groups have toward themselves. The most important are:

1. A belief in the unique value of Oog.
2. Satisfaction with membership in Oog.
3. Solidarity, loyalty, or cooperation with regard to Oog.
4. Preference for association with members of Oog.
5. Belief in the rightness of Oog's relationships with other groups.

The attitudes toward other groups that often accompany the five sentiments just mentioned are:

1. Judging other groups by Oog's standards.
2. Belief that Oog is superior to other groups, in all ways or in some ways.
3. Ignorance of other groups.
4. Lack of interest in other groups.
5. Hostility towards other groups.

Negative ethnocentrism

It is not true, as is often assumed, that every group, people, or society considers itself superior in some generalized sense to all others or even to most others. There are many well-documented instances in which positive loyalty to the ingroup goes along with some appreciation of outgroup values and practices. One's own group does provide the norms for judging other groups, and in various particular ways an outgroup may be seen as superior. For instance, a tribe that prides itself upon its skill in the building of boats can recognize that the products of another tribe represent superior craftsmanship. This admission need not result in a general devaluation of Oog; it is negative ethnocentrism only in its admission of specific points of inferiority. One still retains one's ingroup standards and a basic adherence to its values. [6]

---

[5] "Ethnocentrism," *Encyclopedia of the Social Sciences,* V, 613.

[6] Cf. Marc J. Swartz, "Negative Ethnocentrism," *The Journal of Conflict Resolution,* V, No. 1 (March, 1961), 75-81.

Yet, the phenomena of self-hatred and self-deprecation of one's own membership group are common and must be taken into account. History is replete with voluntary exiles, expatriates, outgroup emulators, social climbers, renegades, and traitors. Also, the dominant attitude in a whole people can be one of accepting at least some of the low evaluations of outsiders. Peter A. Munch has given a fascinating account of such attitudes among the inhabitants of the remote island of Tristan da Cahuna.[7] Among the villagers in southern Italy whose amoral familism has been described by Edward C. Banfield, the desire to emigrate, the awareness of poverty, and the deprecation of the local society are evident.[8] Other examples can be found, as in numerous instances of tribal peoples overwhelmed by conquest and subordinated to technologically advanced rulers. But the most important manifestations of negative sentiments toward the individual's own membership group occur in subordinated minority groups that are objects of prejudice and discrimination. (This negative ethnocentrism will be discussed further in Chapter 8.)

Does Positive Ethnocentrism Necessarily Result in Prejudice?

Whether strong negative feelings toward an outgroup always develop along with positive feelings of ethnocentrism is a question that has been explored in numerous studies. On the one hand we have Mary Ellen Goodman's study of Negro and white children, which showed that racial preferences were associated with hostility in only a minority of cases.[9] On the other hand, William Graham Sumner is usually singled out among American sociologists as favoring the idea that ingroup solidarity is related to outgroup hostility. What he says, however, is somewhat ambiguous: "The relationship of comradeship and peace in the we-group and that of hostility and war toward others-groups are correlative to each other." [10] Sumner was thinking primarily of preliterate groups with relatively clear boundaries in situations in which threat and counterthreat affected the group as a whole. Even so, his statement bears the marks of caution: he says "are correlative" rather than "necessarily occur together." The consensus of studies, however, seems to be that continued interaction between culturally distinctive peoples need not result in conflict. One group may be assimilated by another, or there are even rare examples of sustained contacts between two

---

[7] *Sociology of Tristan Da Cahuna* (Oslo, Norway: Det Norske Videnskaps-Akademi: I Kommisjon Hos Jacob Dywab, 1945).

[8] *The Moral Basis of a Backward Society* (New York: Free Press of Glencoe, Inc., 1958).

[9] Mary Ellen Goodman, *Race Awareness in Young Children* (New York: Collier Books, 1964).

[10] *Folkways*, p. 12.

endogamous and ethnocentric peoples with little conflict and little or no assimilation of one culture to the other.[11] Such accommodative relations seem to rest upon an economic interdependence that is mutually advantageous and essentially noncompetitive. Much more common, unfortunately, are asymmetrical relations in which cultural differences become signals for discriminating behavior by members of a more powerful collectivity.[12]

Whether or not prejudice results is dependent on such complicated factors as 1) the nature of the social system of which the groups are a part, 2) the extent to which one group is a threat (economically or otherwise) to the other, and 3) the degree of understanding or misunderstanding of one group towards another. Other significant factors that will be discussed in subsequent chapters are the personality structures and dynamics of individuals within the groups.

The nature of the social system

When ethnic distinctions have been built into the cultural definitions and the norms of routine behavior in a social system, prejudiced attitudes and discriminatory behavior will be characteristic of normal personalities in that system. The manifestation of prejudice is not necessarily a symptom of unusual psychological needs or of neurotic or psychotic tendencies. When prejudice is normal in a society its manifestations are found among the respectable members of the population who are most firmly embedded in and committed to the legitimate organizations and conventional behavior characteristic of that social system. (Conversely, as shown by the findings in Southport, low prejudice is found most often among persons who are most likely to be free from the most constrained adherence to the general conventions of the community.) That is, when ethnic differences are the result of deeply rooted historical cleavages, it is usual for prejudice to accompany ethnocentrism.

Threat

If for any reason two clearly distinguished social categories or collectivities are so situated in a society that their members frequently come into competition, the likelihood is high that negative stereotyping (a common variety of prejudice) will reinforce a sense of difference and that hostile attitudes will tend to restrict interaction and/or cause conflict. Whether the

---

[11] The case usually cited as an example has been described by E. J. Lindgren, "An Example of Culture Contact without Conflict," *American Anthropologist,* XV, No. 5 (October–December, 1938), 605-21. See also: John Gillin, "Race Relations Without Conflict: A Guatemalan Town," *American Journal of Sociology,* LIII, No. 5 (March 1948), 337-43.

[12] Cf. Hilda Kuper, *Indian People in Natal* (Pietermartzburg: University of Natal Press, 1960).

competition is economic, political, sexual, or for prestige, if one group perceives another as a threat, prejudice results. A central implication of Rokeach's extensive résumé of research on dogmatism is that a closed belief system is a consequence of threat.[13] It is implied by this formulation that the greater the threat: (1) the more rigid the belief system that develops in response, (2) the more intense the affects supporting the beliefs, and (3) the more punitive the sanctions against disbelief.

Certain individuals and segments of the population will be so located in the social structure as to be especially likely to attach the meaning of threat, injury, deprivation, or punishment to the presence and behavior of one or more ethnic groups. Concretely, this most often means economic competition. For example, a white union member on strike sees "his" job taken by a Negro; a Protestant businessman believes his profits are reduced by the competition offered by a Jewish merchant. Or the so-called realistic threat may be noneconomic, such as when legislation thought to have been passed at the public behest of Catholic spokesmen confronts the Protestant with legal restrictions on dissemination of birth-control information or materials. Another example might be the Mexican-American father who is deeply concerned with the preservation of customary roles of women and fears the example set for his daughters by Anglo-American schoolmates.

When two ethnocentric groups come into a mutually threatening relationship, the stage for group conflict is fully set.[14] Short of the cycle of threat-hostility-threat that is the classical prelude to group conflict—from gang fights, to riots, to global wars—we can observe a quieter prejudice, stabilized in systems of preferential ranking and preferential social access and personal association.

Understanding and misunderstanding

The notion that understanding will always lead to the reduction of prejudice and/or the diminution of conflict has limitations that are often overlooked, ignored, or underestimated. Deadly enemies often understand one another all too well. Conversely, some groups manage to live together in a state of uneasy but tolerable accommodation when an accurate and detailed knowledge of each other's real sentiments and intentions would precipitate severe conflict. Understanding will reduce antipathy and the likelihood of conflict only if the groups like or respect what they discover by understanding each other or if one group finds that the threat posed by the other, though real, is not so severe, unalterable, or immediate as previously believed.

---

[13] Milton Rokeach, *The Open and Closed Mind: Investigations into the Nature of Belief Systems and Personality Systems* (New York: Basic Books, Inc., 1960).

[14] H. M. Blalock, Jr., "A Power Analysis of Racial Discrimination," *Social Forces,* XXXIX, No. 1 (October, 1960), 58.

When persons feel themselves to be members of a group and identify themselves with that group's corporate views or policies in competition with another group, they necessarily find it difficult to comprehend the other group's position. An ingenious experiment by Blake and Manton [15] suggests that under these conditions a loss in competition leads to hostility both toward impartial judges and toward the winning group, ". . . with feelings expressed that the decision was completely unjustified in the light of the 'evidence.' " Even though the members of the competing groups reported that they understood the competitor's views as well as they understood those of their own group, they, in fact, did not. In all groups, the members knew their own group's position best and were inclined toward distortion in their comprehension of the other group's position.

Misunderstanding another group's beliefs and values. Many observers, noting the relative unimportance of skin color biologically—and the failure of scientific studies to produce significant evidence of genetically determined racial differences in intelligence—have been puzzled to observe that many individuals persist in exhibiting prejudice towards those with physical racial characteristics. In studies done by Rokeach it has been revealed that prejudice may not be a result of the fact that the other person is of a different racial category, national origin, or religious group affiliation but a result of the prejudiced person's assuming that the other individual's beliefs and values are incongruent with his own.[16] He found that white students both in the North and in the South prefer a Negro with similar beliefs to a white person with different beliefs. But in most situations many white persons would take it for granted that the Negro person did differ from them in basic ways. Thus misunderstanding or lack of knowledge of the outgroup frequently results in prejudice.

Possibly one can now see why a wide range of concepts and types of data must be dealt with in order to begin to understand the causes and the nature of prejudice. Intergroup behavior involves three great systems of human social action: the culture, the social system, and the personality system. Accordingly, we need to study cultural content—"stereotypes," beliefs, and evaluations; and we need to study personality as related to cultural content and to social interaction. We must analyze interaction both in terms of general patterns of intergroup contact and in terms of specific situations. And even while we deal with each of these sets of factors, we must remember that they all are simultaneously engaged in those person-to-person communications that are conceived by the participants to have an intergroup character.

---

[15] Robert R. Blake and Jane Srygley Manton, "Comprehension of Own and of Outgroup Positions under Intergroup Competition," *Journal of Conflict Resolution,* V, No. 3 (September, 1961), 309.

[16] Rokeach, *The Open and Closed Mind.*

We shall begin with a general discussion of the kinds of prejudice that exist. We shall then examine the manifestations of prejudice—social-distance feelings and stereotypes. In this discussion of manifestations we will begin to see how a cultural heritage defines the social objects for prejudices. When we have described basic patterns of prejudice, we shall look at who the prejudiced are.

CHAPTER 4

WHEN ETHNOCENTRISM
BECOMES PREJUDICE

THE MANY FACES OF PREJUDICE

Prejudice is a broad concept having no clear meanings until we give meanings to it. As a general rule the term should always be understood in the specific context in which it is used. There are positive and negative prejudices (though in literature dealing with intergroup relations negative prejudice, or prejudice *against* some group, is nearly always implied). And although a prejudice is always a prejudgment, prejudgments may be based on direct experience or on second-hand experience. Prejudices may be very important to the persons who hold them, or they may be peripheral to the main concerns of the prejudiced. (The term used here to refer to an important form of peripheral prejudice is "disengaged prejudice," which will be further explained subsequently.) Also, prejudices may be highly specific toward a particular outgroup or generalized toward all outgroups. Prejudices may be primarily cognitive (stereotyping), affective (attraction or aversion), or evaluative (for example, attitudes toward questions of public policy concerning racial minorities). Mention of all these varieties will be made elsewhere in this book. We begin, however, with a look at two aspects of prejudice, social-distance feelings and stereotypes—two results of ethnocentrism that are inert but potentially active.

Manifestations of Prejudice

Social-distance feelings

Social-distance feelings are feelings of unwillingness among members of a group to accept or approve a given degree of intimacy in interaction with a member of an outgroup. Specific aspects of social-distance feelings are: 1) feelings of group difference, 2) dislike of the outgroup, 3) feelings of inappropriateness, 4) fear of anticipated reactions of the ingroup, 5) aversion to and fear of anticipated responses of the outgroup, 6) generalized feelings of shyness or discomfort regarding unfamiliar social situations.

Source of social-distance feelings. It has already been mentioned that the individual learns norms of appropriate behavior toward his own group and toward outgroups from the primary groups in which he has membership. Social-distance feelings, then, may reflect the individual's conformity to the expectations and demands of his ingroup rather than his attitudes toward members of the outgroup. All other things being the same, both his acceptance of the norms and his actual conformity with them will be the more likely, the more he has a positive desire to associate with and be approved by the members of his group. His conformity, by the same token, will be a way of avoiding negative sanctions, including disapproval.[1]

How the Cornell Studies measured social-distance feelings. The measures of social-distance feelings in our studies came from questions asking whether the respondent would ever find it a little distasteful to come into various kinds of social contact with persons in named social categories—Negro, Jew, Mexican, and so on. An actual example is:

Do you think you would ever find it a little distasteful:
 to eat at the same table with a _____*?*
 to dance with a _____*?*

---

[1] An individual may thus abide by a definition of social distance without being actively hostile toward the excluded group. Cf. Michael Banton's comment on British attitudes: "When people say that others of their acquaintance would dislike working with a coloured man, or having one as a neighbour, or visitor, they are saying that this would be contrary to the group's norms of conduct, *not* that each one of these people, individually, is unfavourably disposed. . . . The maintenance of social distance is customary; it is not necessarily actuated by prejudice." [*White and Coloured: The behaviour of British people toward coloured immigrants* (New Brunswick, New Jersey: Rutgers University Press, 1960), p. 113.]

to go to a party and find that most of the people there were
_____ *s?*

to have a _____ *person marry someone in your family?*

In such questions the emphasis inevitably conveyed to the respondent is not
so much upon selective self-chosen association with particular individuals
but upon the ethnic category as an undifferentiated anonymous grouping.
In other words, the form of the questions themselves suggests an assumed
set of differences between ingroup and outgroup.[2] Even a very mild sense
of vague difference could be enough, for example, to induce a non-Jewish
person to agree that he would find it a little distasteful to go to a party and
find that most of the people were Jewish. A high distasteful score, therefore, does not necessarily reflect a high degree of active disliking or hostility,
although in fact it usually does indicate some negative feeling. It is in part
an index of feelings of social appropriateness—of intergroup etiquette. If
the generally accepted norm among friends and acquaintances in the local
area is to maintain ethnic and racial homogeneity in informal social gatherings, then the idea of finding oneself at a party at which most of the people
are Negro suggests awkwardness, being out of place, stumbling into a social
error. Clearly then, as was mentioned previously, the individual in this
awkward situation is likely to be affected not only by his own reaction to
his behavior, but also to the expected reactions of other ingroup persons,
by imagined responses of disapproval, withdrawal, rebuff, or other negative
expressions on the part of outgroup members, and by generalized norms of
reserve and social propriety and generalized feelings of shyness or discomfort in any social contacts, especially those which are new and not well
understood.

Variations in the findings. We found marked differences in what was
thought to be appropriate behavior from one city to another, from one
school to another within the same city, and from the more insulated to the
less insulated students within the same school. In the case of dancing with
Negroes, 45 per cent of the white students found it unpleasant in one school
in Hometown, 89 per cent in another school in Steelville (See Table 4.1).
Similarly in the case of going to a party and finding that most of the people
are Jewish, the variation in finding this experience unpleasant was 35 per
cent to 55 per cent. There was even variation from one grade in the same
high school to another, depending upon the setting. At the time when the
questionnaires were filled in by the students, the eleventh grade in Hometown Southside High School had several outstanding Negro students, one
of whom held a high leadership position in the school. Among those white

---

[2] This point was made early in our analysis by Alice S. Rossi.

Table 4.1

Variations in social-distance attitudes of youths in different social settings
(Catholic youth).

	Have contact with Negro in school	Have no contact with Negro in school
	(Per cent finding it distasteful to dance with Negro)	
Hometown		
Southside High School	45% (213)	57% (44)
Catholic High School	70% (20)	60% (117)
Hometown Free Academy	70% (489)	88% (25)
Steelville		
Catholic Central	77% (322)	84% (96)
Steelville High School	89% (104)	† (8)
Weirton		
Riverton High School	*	76% (130)

*Segregated schools.
†Too few cases.

	Have contact with Jew in school	Have no contact with Jew in school
	(Per cent finding it distasteful to go to party and find most people Jewish)	
Hometown		
Southside High School	39% (236)	51% (33)
Catholic High School	*	42% (105)
Hometown Free Academy	39% (477)	55% (44)
Steelville		
Catholic Central	–	55% (383)
Steelville High School	35% (113)	*

*Too few cases.

students in this grade having a Negro friend, there was a strikingly small number who found it unpleasant to dance with a Negro.

Conceptions of inappropriateness also vary considerably with the specific situation. To obtain insight concerning this situational variability, respondents in the cross sections were asked the following series of questions:

1. *Imagine you are in one of the restaurants where you often eat in town. A young, well-dressed Negro man comes in and sits down to have dinner and is refused service because of his race. Would you approve or disapprove of his not being served?*

2. *Now suppose that, instead of leaving, the Negro customer complains to the manager, and the manager says: "Look, fellow, I like your kind of people and I'd be glad to serve you, but my customers object. Be a good sport and try some place else, will you?" Would you approve or disapprove?*

3. *Now suppose a well-known doctor who overhears the conversa-*
tion between the manager and the Negro says: "I think you
should serve this gentleman. He's entitled to service just like the
rest of us. I think you're wrong about how your customers feel.
This is America, you know, and we want to see that all people
get treated fairly. If you don't serve him, you'll lose my trade for
good." So the manager agrees to serve the Negro. Would you
approve or disapprove?

If we divide the sample of persons into four groups on a ranking of general prejudice from most prejudiced to least prejudiced, we find that the
proportion approving initially of the Negro being served ranges from 80
per cent among the most prejudiced to 93 per cent among the least prejudiced. But when those who approved of the restaurant serving the Negro
were confronted with situation 2, 75 per cent of the most prejudiced, 66
per cent of the medium-high prejudiced, 57 per cent of the medium-low
prejudiced, and 52 per cent of the least-prejudiced were persuaded to give
up their nondiscriminatory position. (See Table 4.2.) Furthermore, when
the persons who approved of the manager's plea were confronted with situation 3, 54 per cent of the most prejudiced, 80 per cent and 82 per cent of
the medium-prejudiced groups, and 70 per cent of the least prejudiced
were persuaded to approve of the Negro's being served. The data here suggest that it is easier to induce a person to shift his position concerning a discrimination situation when that position is in conflict with his basic attitudinal set. More important, perhaps, is the fact that, regardless of position
taken, one-half of all respondents were quickly persuaded to change their
position. And nearly one-half (47 per cent) of the group that initially disapproved of the Negro's not being served changed their position twice as
the interviewer modified the hypothetical circumstances of the situation. The
very considerable inconsistency of both the more and less prejudiced in
modifying their initial positions supports the view that disengaged prejudice
(peripheral, "rote" expressions of common attitudes [3]) is highly variable
from one social situation to another.

Variability in the expression of prejudice occurs not only in connection
with the details of the situation, but also in connection with the context in
which the interactive behavior is perceived. Consider, for example, the
matter of Negroes trying on clothes in a white department store. In our
Southport study, we asked about this situation in three different places in

---

[3] This term, used here to refer to prejudice that is expressed without direct reference to an immediate real intergroup situation, is suggested by the way gears engage
and disengage each other in the driving mechanism of a machine.

Table 4.2

Modifying conception of what is appropriate (Adults, Hometown).

	General Prejudice Score			
	High	Medium-High	Medium-Low	Low
Total respondents	(86)	(98)	(120)	(83)
Number of respondents who initially disapproved of Negro not being served	80% (69)	89% (87)	94% (113)	93% (77)
Per cent of above who were talked out of nondiscriminating position by manager's plea	75%	66%	57%	52%
Number who approved of manager's plea asking Negro to go somewhere else	(68)	(64)	(71)	(44)
Per cent who approved manager's agreeing to serve Negro after doctor's plea	54%	80%	82%	70%
Per cent of those initially disapproving of Negro not being served who changed their position twice as the circumstances were modified (47%)	34%	54%	49%	38%

the questionnaire. Respondents were asked if they would find it distasteful "to try on clothes that had been tried on by a Negro." Only 17 per cent of the 328 respondents said they would *not* find it distasteful. We also inquired if Negroes should have the right to try on clothes in white department stores. Sixty-five per cent thought that Negroes should have the right. Respondents were also asked to suppose that a Negro was trying on some clothes in a department store where they were shopping and were asked whether they approved or disapproved. Eighty per cent said they approved. These three questions formed a scale meeting Guttman criteria (scalability = 0.82).[4] Actually, as a matter of normal, routine practice, Negroes do try on clothes in white department stores in Southport.

Apparently if an interactive situation is posed in terms of a situation that

---

[4] The methods of scaling attitudes and opinions developed by Louis Guttman are set forth in Samuel A. Stouffer *et al., Measurement and Prediction,* Vol. 4 of *Studies in Social Psychology in World War II* (Princeton, N. J.: Princeton University Press, 1950). For a brief description see William J. Goode and Paul K. Hatt, *Methods in Social Research* (New York: McGraw-Hill Book Company, 1952).

actually exists, the approval is most likely to be forthcoming. Furthermore, putting the question in terms of rights, thus incorporating the American Creed in the question, called forth fewer prejudiced responses than stating the question in highly personal terms.

Where the social definition is highly explicit, there may be unanimity regardless of the context of the question. With regard to residential segregation in Southport, only 4 per cent of the 327 respondents would not find it distasteful to have a Negro family living next door, 3 per cent thought Negroes should have the right to live in the same neighborhoods with whites, and 3 per cent approved of Negroes living in mixed neighborhoods with whites. In Hometown, where conceptions of social appropriateness are less explicit, 57 per cent of the 394 respondents said they would find it distasteful to eat at the same table with a Negro, but 71 per cent approved of Negroes eating in white restaurants. Again, the more personal context called forth the more negative reaction.

What "others" will think. The connection between the social-distance feelings of any particular individual and the social atmosphere of his group

Table 4.3

Relation between individual's personal definition of social appropriateness and the definition of his family and friends (Hometown).

	If one of your social group danced with a Negro boy or girl at one of the school dances, how do you think the rest of your friends would feel about it?	
	Approve or make no difference	Disapprove
	(Per cent finding it unpleasant to dance with a Negro)	
How do you think your family would feel about it if you were to dance with a Negro boy or girl?		
Approve or make no difference	25% (455)	58% (48)
Disapprove	70% (164)	90% (229)

setting is reflected in the high correlation between an individual's personal feelings about dancing with a Negro and how he thinks his family and friends feel about it. (See Table 4.3.) Undoubtedly the individual to some degree simply attributes his own attitudes to others, but he also often correctly reports the real feelings of others in his own social circles. The field interviews emphasized how very much individuals tend to see their own behavior through the eyes of the significant other persons with whom they associate. How comfortable or uncomfortable a person feels when dancing with a Negro depends heavily on how he thinks it appears to his friends. In a prejudiced environment, the stares and gossiping that may accompany such a situation when most of the onlookers disapprove are almost certain to stir up feelings of discomfort in the participant.

Furthermore, social-distance feelings appear to reflect the reactions of parents and friends just as much as or more than they reflect the experience of fairly close social contacts with Negroes. Even if one has invited a Negro fellow student to one's home, or has engaged with him in some social activity, one is still likely to find it unpleasant to dance with a Negro if one thinks his family or friends would disapprove. (See Table 4.4.)

Table 4.4

Relation between previous social contact with Negroes and judgment of friends' reactions (Hometown).

	Has invited a Negro home	Has not invited a Negro home, but has done something social with a Negro	Has done neither
	(Per cent finding it unpleasant to dance with a Negro)		
How do you think your friends would feel if you were to dance with a Negro boy or girl?			
Approve	11% (18)	34% (50)	32% (66)
Make no difference	28% (69)	37% (134)	40% (290)
Disapprove	59% (22)	88% (59)	82% (142)
How do you think your family would feel if you were to dance with a Negro boy or girl?			
Approve	9% (22)	18% (33)	26% (46)
Make no difference	21% (58)	33% (116)	29% (229)
Disapprove	67% (30)	81% (90)	79% (217)

These social definitions of appropriateness are undoubtedly affected by the nature of the ingroup. Among high school youth in Phoenix, for example, members of large and loosely knit cliques were less likely to find eating with a Negro unpleasant than were members of a small closely knit clique. Boy-and-girl cliques were more likely to manifest social-distance reaction than were one-sex cliques. (See Table 4.5.)

No matter how the components of social-distance feelings become merged in any given social environment, they appear to represent a clear cut attitude scale. That is, almost all the people who find it distasteful to dance with a Negro also would find it distasteful to go to a party and find that most of the people were Negro, and to have a Negro marry someone in their family.

Table 4.5

Relationship between nature of ingroup and attitudes towards outgroup.

	Large Clique		Small Clique	
	Meet fewer than 25 times per month	Meet more often than 25 times per month	Meet fewer than 25 times per month	Meet more often than 25 times per month
	(Per cent finding it unpleasant to eat with a Negro)			
Belong to:				
All-boy cliques	15% (27)	45% (36)	38% (29)	48% (31)
All-girl cliques	36% (22)	*	43% (30)	43% (23)
Mixed cliques	33% (72)	49% (61)	62% (26)	74% (23)

*Too few cases.

If a person would find only two of these situations distasteful, we can be reasonably sure that the two would be the party situation and having a Negro marry someone in the family. In the case of social distance, then, it clearly makes sense to speak of more prejudiced and less prejudiced individuals. Respondents can be meaningfully placed at appropriate points on a social-distance scale.

Stereotypes

What they are and how they emerge. Along with social-distance feelings, stereotypes are one of the most common manifestations of prejudice. Stereotypes are labels or identities we assign to people that show what we believe these persons are like and how we think they will behave. Human beings, particularly when they feel little interest in individuals within a class of objects or people, tend to ignore the perceptible differences among these objects or people and tend to view all members of the class as being the same. Gouldner says of group members' forming stereotypes:

> . . . (1) They observe or impute to a person certain characteristics.
> . . . (2) These observed or imputed characteristics are then related to and interpreted in terms of a set of culturally prescribed *categories* which have been learned during the course of socialization. Conversely, the culturally learned categories focus attention upon certain aspects of the individuals behavior and appearance. (3) In this manner the individual is "pigeonholed"; that is, he is held to be a certain "type" of person, a teacher, Negro, boy, man, or woman. The process . . . can be called the assignment of a "social identity." The types or categories to which he has been assigned *are* his social identities.[5]

---

[5] Alvin W. Gouldner, "Cosmopolitans and Locals: Toward an Analysis of Latent Social Roles—I," *Administrative Science Quarterly,* II, No. 3 (December, 1957), 283.

Thus stereotypes need not be based on direct sensory experience with the stereotyped object. An individual may describe the alleged characteristics of a group without ever having observed the members of that category.

Their function with regard to culture, personality, and society. Stereotypes constitute a part of culture, a part of an organized aggregate of shared symbols, beliefs, and values. Considered as part of a system of prejudice, stereotypes are operative in defining both the objects of action and the evaluative standards applied to social objects. Indeed, the maintenance of established stereotypes over long periods of time is possible partly because there are systems of action primarily devoted to their maintenance.[6] These systems range from processes of inculcation within the family to the incorporation of stereotypes in song and story and to societywide dissemination through media of mass communication. Stereotypes are also components of social and personality systems: as summaries of and rationalizations for past experiences, they have sociological implications; as predictions of the behavior of others they give direction to psychological energies. The function of stereotypes as far as social systems are concerned is that the sharing of stereotypes reassures the holders and helps maintain systems of group privileges and power. In situations of competition and conflict, stereotypes simplify the alignments, sharpen group boundaries, and facilitate ingroup consensus. Their function as far as the personality is concerned is to reduce cognitive dissonance,[7] affective ambivalence, or incongruity in evaluation.

On what are stereotypes based? Stereotyping, like rumor, is especially likely to thrive on the combination of interest and ignorance. Thus stereotypes emerge as distillations of the political, economic, and cultural alignments of nations as interpreted by leaders and intellectuals, especially through mass media and in reference to dramatic public events. What one person or one group believes about another is usually expressed without any immediate confrontation of evidence. Stereotypes may contain a core of truth, but the amount of truth may be very little indeed. Consider the personality stereotypes attached to personal names such as Percival or Ebenezer. How accurate are they? Is it true that red hair indicates a quick temper? If so, how much of the redhead's behavior is due to a self-fulfilling prophecy?

Does hostility cause stereotyping? Although it has sometimes been thought that stereotypes were causes rather than effects of hostility, experiments have demonstrated that if two groups having no preconceived stereo-

---

[6] After a somewhat tortuous intellectual history, cultural systems have been acknowledged as systems of action. Cf. Talcott Parsons *et al.* (eds.), *Theories of Society*, II (New York: Free Press of Glencoe, Inc., 1961), p. 964.

[7] Leon Festinger, *A Theory of Cognitive Dissonance* (New York: Harper & Row, Publishers, 1957).

types develop hostility towards one another in a situation of rivalry and conflict, each will also spontaneously develop definite negative stereotypes concerning the other.[8] Sherif showed that individuals who were initially inclined to be friendly toward one another became hostile when placed in opposing groups. Experimental situations that engaged two rival groups in competing and mutually frustrating activities led to the development of hostile attitudes and highly unfavorable stereotypes in each group toward the other group and its members.[9] The positive or negative characteristics attributed by each group to the other tended to reflect the actual functional relationships between the two.

Sherif gives partial support to the view that stereotypes are symptomatic of hostility rather than causes of it when he says, "A number of field studies and experiments indicate that if the functional relations between groups are positive, favorable attitudes are formed towards the outgroup. If the functional relationships between groups are negative, they give rise to hostile and unfavorable stereotypes in relation to the outgroup." [10]

How stereotypes perpetuate hostility. Of course, whenever real cultural differences exist between two populations living in proximity, the differences will have consequences for the interaction which develops.[11] This is quite evident, for example, in those interactions that are rendered very difficult by mutual lack of knowledge of the other's language. Other cultural differences may have important effects, even if not always so immediately obvious. Where actual differences in culture become closely associated with definite statuses and roles, many stereotypes may come to have considerable descriptive value. A system of group dominance and subordination can create conditions that reinforce stereotypes. For example, to the degree that members of a dominant group feel that the system of group relations is unjust, or to the extent that they project their own reactions to deprivation upon the subordinate group, so will they expect hostility from the subordinates.[12]

---

[8] Muzafer Sherif, "Superordinate Goals in the Reduction of Intergroup Conflict," *American Journal of Sociology,* LXVIII, No. 4 (January, 1958), 349-56.

[9] ". . . At the same time there was an increase in in-group solidarity and cooperativeness." (*Ibid.,* p. 353.)

[10] *Ibid.,* p. 351. See also, Gerhart Saenger and Samuel Flowerman, "Stereotypes and Prejudicial Attitudes," *Human Relations,* VII, No. 2 (May, 1954), 217-38.

[11] Cf. Sydney Collins, *Coloured Minorities in Britain* (London: Lutterworth Press, 1957), p. 201: "One of the main hindrances to the absorption of members of the Moslem community into British society is the distinct cultural character of the former. These cultural differences are crystallized by the foreign languages spoken, especially where Arabic is concerned, since emphasis is placed on its religious value."

[12] Cf. John Dollard, *Caste and Class in a Southern Town* (New York: Harper & Row, Publishers, 1937), p. 294: "The expectation of hostility from the Negro caste and the use of every incident to confirm this stereotype are tremendously important in Southerntown." (Cf. also pp. 315ff.)

The expected hostility, since it may at any time be expressed in aggressive behavior, is perceived as a standing threat. A typical group response to this sense of threat is to insist upon rigid patterns of segregation, deference, and discrimination. These patterns, of course, perpetuate the closed cycle just described.

Stability of stereotypes. Stereotypes are petrified expectations that are relatively unyielding to social change. They are usually more or less impervious to new evidence that is incongruent with their content.[13] Experimental evidence, indeed, indicates that persons most readily learn materials that are in agreement with or supportive of their own attitudes concerning intergroup issues. When people were given the task of learning statements, those who favored racial segregation learned plausible prosegregation statements and implausible antisegregation statements much more rapidly than they did plausible antisegregation and implausible prosegregation statements. Persons opposed to segregation showed the corresponding reverse tendencies.[14] Resistance to alteration through new information or evaluation is characteristic of stereotypes.

However, under the impact of unusual and momentous events, stereotypes can be shattered and reformed. Stereotypes sometimes are altered radically and dramatically within a relatively short period of time. The American stereotype of Japan and the Japanese people changed from that of the Madame Butterfly era to World War II's image of a cruel and treacherous people, then back again to a benign image of industry, cleanliness, modernism, and friendliness as actual relations between the nations changed. Between 1942 and 1948, the stereotypes of Americans held in several European countries changed drastically to an emphasis on unfavorable characteristics. Such rapid and massive changes run far beyond any corresponding change in knowledge of the typical, actual personal characteristics of individuals when functioning "at home" within national groups.[15]

Stereotypes in a larger setting. Stereotypes are usually embedded in a larger set of ideas and beliefs about the nature of man and society and, indeed, of the universe. Arising in some collective historical experience, initial generalizations about the characteristics and behavior of outgroups are sometimes reshaped and reworked in relation to these comprehensive beliefs. An illustration of this point is the ante-bellum development of justi-

---

[13] Stereotypes thus tend to be found as parts of closed systems of belief. See Rokeach, *The Open and the Closed Mind*, p. 33.

[14] E. E. Jones and R. Kohler, "The Effects of Plausibility on the Learning of Controversial Statements," *Journal of Abnormal and Social Psychology*, LVII, No. 3 (November, 1958), 315-20.

[15] William Buchanan, "Stereotypes and Tensions as Revealed by the UNESCO International Poll," *International Social Science Bulletin*, III, No. 3 (Autumn, 1951), p. 526.

fications for slavery in the United States.[16] The theory of Aryan superiority promulgated during the past hundred years and culminating in the "blood and soil" doctrine of Nazi Germany is an even more remarkable case in point.[17]

Specific stereotypes. Stereotypes that refer to social categories, statuses, groups, or collectivities are usually stated in terms of qualities (traits, properties, characteristics) conceived as if somehow inherent in the objects: Americans are materialistic; Italians are excitable; Orientals are inscrutable; professors are absent-minded; women are flighty; white people are cruel. Such imputations of qualities very easily become expectations of behavior; and these stereotypes have the same overgeneralized and rigid character as those of physical appearance or psychological states.[18]

Negative stereotypes used by majority-group members in the United States to stigmatize outgroups usually are the reversed images of dominant positive traits. The epithet of laziness reflects the value of industriousness. Ignorance contrasts with the virtues of competence, education, self-improvement. Dishonesty is the opposite of upright, moral, fair dealings. "Sexually loose" is the antithesis of Puritan reserve. "Loud and noisy" is the converse of the ideals of public decorum, the strict control of impulse, the taboos against giving in to emotion. Even the stereotype of the "power of the Catholic Church" acquires much of its negative resonance from some Protestant views of the church as a man-made vehicle of religious expression.

Examples of agree-disagree items that the Cornell students used to elicit information about the acceptance and rejection of stereotypes were:

1. *Generally speaking, Negroes are lazy and ignorant.*
2. *Although some Jews are honest, in general Jews are dishonest in their business dealings.*

Exemption. Stereotypes normally cause the prejudiced individual to place outgroup members in particular categories. But occasionally the individual meets an outgroup member who doesn't fit the stereotype, in which case he simply calls him an exception rather than altering or eliminating his stereo-

---

[16] Religious, political, and quasi-biological philosophies were all involved. Only very rarely could slavery be totally defended. Cf. Eric John Dingwall, *Racial Pride and Prejudice* (London: Watts & Company, 1946), p. 220.

[17] Nor do such master-stereotypes easily disappear. Persistence of anti-Jewish stereotypes in Western Germany a quarter-century after Hitler's rise to power has been found in a study of 1,200 elementary and secondary school children; H. E. Wolf, "Sozialpsychologische Untersuchung der Vorurteile gegen 'Neger' und 'Juden' bei Ober-und Volksschülern," *Kölner Zeitschrift für Soziologie und Sozialpsychologie*, XI, No. 4 (1959), 651-65.

[18] Sydney Collins, *Coloured Minorities in Britain*, p. 126.

type. Thus, a Negro who lacks musical ability, is highly talented as a bio-chemist, is unable to dance a step, and is remarkably energetic, hard work-ing, and self-disciplined is excluded from the stereotype as an exception, as "not really" a Negro.

Prevalence. No major culture or racial division is immune to stereo-typing.[19] The prevalence of it is well illustrated by the numerous derogatory nicknames used by the members of racial or ethnic groups to refer to other racial or ethnic groups. All known racial or ethnic groups have some such derogatory names (ethnophaulisms) to refer to outgroups and their mem-bers. In fact, Palmore [20] was able to demonstrate that the rankings of vari-ous ethnic groups by white Protestant, majority-group Americans on the Bogardus social-distance scale were closely associated (Kendall's r 0.95) with the number of ethnophaulisms (as listed in the *Dictionary of American Slang*) referring to these groups. The prevalance of stereotyping is also in-dicated by the fact that it is not confined to ethnic objects alone.

Stereotypes of social categories. Stereotypes may be attached to social as well as to ethnic categories. Table 4.6 shows that stereotypes are more often applied to labor unions and businessmen than to some racial, ethnic, and religious groups. Future studies of ethnic stereotypes would profit by at-tempting to ascertain the extent of stereotyping of occupations, social or-ganizations, economic groupings, and other groups.

National stereotypes. Stereotypes of national groupings were investigated by the 1956-1957 survey of the UNESCO Institute for Social Sciences,[21] a study that supports the findings of research done in the United States alone. Based on samples from Belgium, France, Germany, and Holland, the study revealed definite stereotypes. For example: "The Germans are called hardworking, businesslike, authoritative, brutal, militaristic. The French, among other characteristics, are called gay, friendly, charming, lazy, and lighthearted, but not hardworking." [22] Self-images in each country are more favorable than are images of other nationals. Persons who had experienced foreign acquaintance and contact (as indexed by speaking a foreign lan-guage, visiting abroad, having friends or relatives from one or more of the specified countries) were less ethnocentric, manifesting high ratios of posi-tive to negative opinions of traits of the other countries being described.

---

[19] For particular instances see the references listed by Donald T. Campbell and Robert A. LeVine: "A Proposal for Cooperative Cross-Cultural Research on Ethno-centrism," *The Journal of Conflict Resolution*, V, No. 1 (March, 1961), 84, 108.

[20] Erdman B. Palmore, "Ethnophaulism and Ethnocentrism," *The American Jour-nal of Sociology*, LXVII, No. 4 (January, 1962), 442-45.

[21] Erich Reigrotski and Nels Anderson, "National Stereotypes and Foreign Con-tacts," *Public Opinion Quarterly*, XXIII, No. 4 (Winter, 1959-1960), 513-28.

[22] *Ibid.*, 520.

Table 4.6

Groupings chosen as competitively threatening.

Do you think any of these groups is trying to get ahead at the expense of people like you?

	Protestants	Catholics	Jews	Negroes	Labor Unions
Majority group					
Hometown	2%	13%	32%	10%	61%
Southport	2%	18%	22%	23%	26%
Valley City	7%	23%	29%	20%	57%
Minority group					
Hometown					
Negroes	11%	24%	46%	14%	36%
Jews	8%	25%	18%	6%	53%
Italians	6%	2%	26%	7%	50%

	Business Men	Foreign Born	Mexican	Japanese	Cases*
Majority group					
Hometown	21%	18%	†	†	(294)
Southport	12%	12%	†	†	(267)
Valley City	37%	16%	13%	15%	(94)
Minority group					
Hometown					
Negroes	45%	33%	†	†	(97)
Jews	18%	16%	†	†	(49)
Italians	43%	6%	†	†	(54)

*Percentages based only on those who named one or more groups.
 Total may exceed 100% due to multiple responses.
†Not asked.

An interesting side note, by the way, is that the total character of attitudes toward foreign nations is changed as one moves from particular known individuals to social types, to nations as wholes. In a study of the responses of British people to the United States and to Americans, it was observed that attitudes become more highly generalized (and less favorable) as the questions moved from particular persons to Americans as types, to the American people, and to the United States as a world power. By the time the British respondents were speaking of the American people as a whole, they were relying heavily on the press and literary accounts; the generalizations were more sweeping; the personal traits attributed were more blurred; and ". . . considerations of American national and international policy [began] to affect some respondent's replies, and the circle from the individual American friend to the U.S.A. as a dominant world power [was] closed." [23]

How groups see themselves. Although negative stereotypes about themselves are accepted to some extent in groupings exposed to discrimination and prejudice from some dominant grouping, persons tend to attribute virtues to themselves and negative traits to outgroups. The nine-nation UNESCO study showed that the most frequently accepted stereotypes of one's own countrymen are invariably flattering. In most of the countries, one of the three most frequently applied descriptions of the person's own countrymen included hardworking, intelligent, brave, and peace-loving; in none of the nine national samples did the three most popular terms include any of these: conceited, cruel, backward, practical, self-controlled, progressive, or domineering.[24]

THE LANGUAGE OF PREJUDICE [25]

Stereotypes are part of a whole way of talking about outgroups. This special universe of discourse has its own distinctive vocabulary, its own idiom, its own peculiar style. The derogatory epithets (and other terms expressing disparagement or awareness of group difference) which arise in most sizable ingroups that exist for any considerable period of time constitute the "language of prejudice." We may define the language of prejudice as an aggregate of words and phrases applied (accidentally or intentionally, directly or indirectly) to express contempt, derision, stereotypic assumptions, or, at least, a belief that there are generalized group differences, to another social category or to an individual because of his membership in that category.

In all the communities studied evidence was found that the language of prejudice—for Negroes and whites, Jews and gentiles, Mexicans and Anglo-Americans, and so on—acted as a cue for intergroup tension and as a barrier to effective communication between ethnic groupings. These reactions are more noticeable in smaller than in larger communities, partly because opportunity for casual intergroup contact is greater in the smaller communities where less residential segregation exists, and partly because the small proportion of ethnics and the low number of intergroup contacts

---

[23] Milton D. Graham, "An Experiment in International Attitudes Research," *International Social Science Bulletin,* III, No. 3 (Autumn, 1951), 539.

[24] William Buchanan, "Stereotypes and Tensions as Revealed by the UNESCO International Poll," 515-28. (See particularly p. 522: "There is evidently a universal tendency to appropriate the complimentary adjectives for one's own countrymen, and, by reflection of virtue, for oneself.")

[25] Another summary of the materials of this section may be found in Robert B. Johnson, "Negro Reactions to Minority Group Status," in Milton L. Barron, ed., *American Minorities* (New York: Alfred A. Knopf, Inc., 1957), pp. 192-212.

on the part of white majority-group persons result in a lack of experience in intergroup communication and a correlative lack of sophistication and insight. In the one most intensively studied instance, the most noticeable elements of the language of prejudice experienced and discussed by Hometown's Negro community might be subdivided into those that are accidental and those that are intentional on the part of whites, and into those that are indirect references and those that are direct racial references.

Accidental-indirect

Phrases pertaining to color. These phrases follow an historical tradition of equating whiteness with purity or desirability and blackness with evil. Examples are: "That's darn white of you," "free, white, and twenty-one," "He treated me white," or "Your face may be black, but your heart's as white as mine."

Disparagement of other minorities. This behavior may take the form of whites telling Negroes jokes about Jews, Italians, Catholics, etc. or confidential statements such as "you Negroes are all right with me, but it's those Jews I don't like." In some instances, the Negro's negative reaction is based on the recognition of necessity for interminority solidarity; in more instances, it is based on the Negro's recognition of the phenomenon of group prejudice and categorical thinking, even though it refers to another minority group.

Accidental-direct

Racial testimonials. In many cases, Hometown Negroes reported that whites seek to establish rapport by making favorable categorical statements of their preference for Negroes or by making assertions that Negroes are not inferior to whites; for example, "I like Negro people," "What the hell— you're as good as I am," or the statement sometimes referred to by Negroes as the "black mammy speech": "I've loved the colored ever since I was rocked to sleep in the arms of my black mammy." Though some Negroes are aware that the testimonial is sometimes the product of a white person's guilt feelings, others feel that the ingratiating statements are employed in order to disarm and exploit the Negro, or that they are overprotesting their affection for Negroes. One Negro explained testily that "I don't like too much butter on my bread."

The racial slip. To the Negroes of Hometown, the most noticeable and disturbing of all the elements of the language of prejudice, despite its accidental nature, is the racial slip. This involves unintentional phrases in the speech of whites that carry epithets or other expressions that are disparaging of minorities, for example, "I worked like a nigger," "I jewed him down," "There's a nigger in the woodpile," or words that Negro public school youths complain are frequently employed by teachers—reference to Brazil nuts as "nigger-toes," or reference to a type of garden weed as "nigger-heads." Slips cause particular apprehension among Negroes because (1) the epithet that is used is disturbing, despite its accidental nature, (2) the Negro person is often aware of the white person's acute embarrassment when he becomes aware of the disturbing nature of what he has said, and (3) the Negro is often aware that he is expected to make a protest to the slip that he would often prefer to avoid.

Intentional-indirect

Stereotyped preconceptions of Negroes. Many Negroes know the stereotypes about them held by whites, and they express disapproval of white people who expect all Negroes to be able to dance and sing, or who assume that each Negro knows thoroughly all aspects of Negro life in the South and in Africa, or who think that each Negro knows all other Negroes, or who believe that Negroes are lazy, ignorant, and happy-go-lucky, or who believe that all Negroes are sexually immoral. This disapproval is particularly great among higher-status Negroes whose way of life is similar to that of middle-class whites, but who may partially share the white person's stereotypic view of lower-status Negroes, and resent being placed in a similar category.

Caricatures of the Negro. Negroes also express disapproval at the way Negro life is parodied in the media of communication; they often cite the examples of the former radio shows of "Amos 'n Andy" and "Beulah," the "Little Black Sambo" children's fable, and certain cinema characters. The annoyance is more extreme when in interracial contacts, they are addressed by whites in imitations of Negro dialect, parodied by white's imitations of stereotypic Negro characters, or called names drawn from derogatory stories, like "Sambo," "Nicodemus," or "Rastus." Occasionally, the attempts by proprietors of business establishments to show Negroes that their patronage is not wanted may take the form of indirect caricatures, parodies of Southern Negro speech, or addressing the Negro by stereotypic names.

Intentional-direct

Jokes, songs, and stories disparaging Negroes. Embedded in American culture are a number of so-called darky jokes, comic stories in pseudo-Negro dialect, stories ridiculing the stereotyped traits of the Negro, or songs that contain racial epithets. These are intentional to the extent that the white person is usually aware that they have racial implications; the fact that they offend some Negroes is often accidental, since the lack of interracial understanding may make the white person unaware that Negroes could take offense at what is often considered mere good fun. A few whites hold the mistaken assumption that telling a darky joke is an act of friendly recognition of the Negro, and are seriously surprised and disturbed if Negroes express objection.

Intentional use of racial epithets. Situations of interracial tension often involve purposive words of contempt on the part of whites, like "smoke," "jig," "coon," or "shine." Some Negroes have been able to recall as many as twenty of these epithets. However, as far as Negro reactions are concerned, the one most negatively evaluated term is the word "nigger"—a word so intensely disliked that the Negro press generally prints it as "n----r," regardless of the context. Its connotations, drawn largely from Southern experiences, produce in most Negroes a bitterness, anger, and occasional fury that is usually far greater in its intensity than most white persons realize. Hence, many of the actual incidents of tension and violence in interracial situations are produced through the utterance of this epithet by whites. This reaction also causes Negroes to resent less intentionally disparaging terms like "Negress," the Southern white pronunciation of Negro as "Nigra," and even the nonracial word "niggardly."

In a general sense, the language of prejudice exists because of several anti-Negro aspects of American culture that are unreflectively absorbed by many, perhaps most, American white people in the process of growing-up. A white person whose interracial contacts are rare may, then, on encountering a Negro, search through his limited store of knowledge about Negroes and make inappropriate comments; a white person may attempt to establish a joking relationship with a Negro, which is acceptable in his own informal social groups but inconsistent with the Negro's past interracial experience (for example, joking about women and sex; calling friends "boy" —an expression of friendship to many whites, but regarded by Southern-born Negroes as an expression of white contempt); a white person in attempting to indicate his lack of prejudice may accidentally employ inappropriate techniques or make slips; finally, the white person in anger or contempt may employ power words, epithets that he knows will disturb the minority-group member.

In order to test more systematically the reactions to the language of prejudice expressed by Hometown Negroes, four statements were selected to be presented to a cross section of 150 adult Hometown Negroes; the testimonial, the rapport device disparaging other minorities, the slip, and the extreme racial epithet. The responses are shown in Table 4.7.[26]

---

[26] That the reactions of Hometown's Negroes are representative of other regions is shown by the fact that the marginal figures for each of these reactions is almost identical in four cross-sectional studies of Negro adults and four studies of Negro youths in different parts of the country. For example, in these eight surveys, the Far West community had the smallest proportion of Negroes who said they got angry when a white person uses the word "nigger" (71 per cent), and the largest proportion were in the Deep South community (78 per cent).

Table 4.7

Extent of negative reaction to four elements of the language of prejudice (Negroes, Hometown).

Which of these things make you angry, which just annoy you, and which don't bother you at all?

	Makes me angry	Annoys me	Doesn't bother me
When a white person tells you how much he likes Negroes (testimonial)	9%	32%	59%
When a white person tells you how much he dislikes some other minority like Jews or Catholics (faulty rapport device, disparaging other groups)	26%	36%	38%
When a white person forgets or "slips" and uses the word "darky" (the slip)	57%	26%	17%
When a white person uses the word "nigger" (the extreme epithet)	74%	15%	11%

In addition, 44 per cent of Hometown's Negro adults said they felt uncomfortable when a white person told them: *You're as good as I am,* whereas only 23 per cent said that it made them feel good. When asked about barriers to greater contact with white people, two-thirds of the Negro adults mentioned one or more barriers. Of these, 50 per cent agreed that *I expect the white person to make a slip and say something wrong about Negroes.* Among 100 Hometown Negro youths, 43 per cent agreed with the deliberately biased statement that *When I am around white people, I am* always *expecting someone to make a slip, and say something bad about Negroes.*

Strong negative reactions to the extreme racial epithets were further documented by the 100 Hometown Negro youths who were asked: *If your white best friend slipped and called you a nigger, what would you do?* Twenty per cent of them were conflicted and unable to say what they would do. Six per cent said they would assume that the white friend didn't mean it; 13 per cent said they would ignore it, or do nothing; 2 per cent said they would sympathize with the white person; 23 per cent said they would make a vigorous verbal protest ("wise him up," "tell him to watch his tongue," "I'd resent it, and tell him so in strong words"); 24 per cent mentioned physical violence ("slap her face, but good," "I think I would find myself fighting," "I would dip my fist into his mouth," "give him a black eye," "sock him in the teeth"). One young girl said: "I would forgive."

The examples quoted here are among the more extreme cases observed. Hometown interracial relations show so little overt tension because most reactions to the language of prejudice are less intense than suggested here. Some Negroes resent certain behavior from strange whites that they would dismiss if the white person were a friend. Some show no objections at all; others, particularly the better-educated, younger, Northern-born Negroes, are likely to be more annoyed than angry at manifestations of the language of prejudice. Some have little awareness of racial differences and do not notice or negatively interpret such behavior. Nevertheless, the language of prejudice is a pervasive source of discomfort and avoidance of interracial contacts shown by many Negroes. The language of prejudice is diminishing in interracial contacts as general community norms increasingly oppose it, as the media of communication—radio, motion pictures, television, etc.— adopt nondiscriminatory standards in their handling of minority groups, and as whites and Negroes experience increasing favorable, equal-status contacts and thus gain insight, experience, and confidence.

However, Negro expectation of "slips" and epithets from the white persons with whom Negroes come into contact may be maintained at a high level, even in areas where white people have no negative framework from which to draw elements of the language of prejudice.

Our summary may be stated in this way: Prejudice on the part of majority group members results in a tendency to use certain terms and expressions that disparage minority-group members. Minority-group members in varying degrees are aware of these symbols and tend to react negatively to them, and particularly to affectively-laden outgroup epithets.

THE PREJUDICED

Every group has their own way. I'm afraid of the colored. I don't like them. They have razors and kill each other and things. Where we lived when we were first married, out of spite a woman sold her house to colored. They brought a lot of colored to Elmira. People sold their homes. They were always fighting with razors. They're ugly people. You dasn't say "colored" to them or they'll fight. I've seen people say "nigger" to them and they beat 'em up. I had no trouble with 'em. I didn't say anything to them. I feel sorry for 'em. Domineering niggers marry whites, and whites marry niggers. Their children, some are white and some are black. In Omaha they push the whites off the streets. They hold hands in a line and push you off. They call you "white trash." In Omaha, Nebraska, they have bold niggers. Course, they're not all that way. What I've seen have been.

—Prejudiced respondent

Who are the prejudiced? The next section of this chapter will be devoted to a discussion of the social correlates of prejudice. In a complex society we may suspect variations in degree of prejudice among people who live in different geographic areas, among the various socioeconomic classes and those with varying amounts of education, among people with different religious affiliations, among those who belong to different political parties and other organizations, and among those who differ with regard to age, sex, and marital status.

To analyze such variations among the majority-group people in our four communities, we shall use a standard index of one variety of ethnocentrism —feelings of reluctance or distaste concerning close social interaction with persons in outgroup ethnic categories. This index is the unidimensional (Guttman) score, already described in this chapter, concerning outgroup association in interdining, parties, dancing, and intermarriage.[27] We have already indicated that this measure reflects a complex mixture of sentiments relating to conformity, norms of social appropriateness, fear, dislike, and so on; we have further suggested that it nevertheless is a valid indicator of a scale of culturally standardized social distance between ethnic groupings.[28]

We shall begin the discussion by comparing the prevalence of prejudice among the native white Americans making up our samples in four cities in three major regions of the country, the Deep South, the Northeast, and the Far West. Then we shall proceed to an examination of the other correlates of prejudice.

The factors on which degree of prejudice depends

Geographic area. To provide some clue to regional variations in prejudice, we compare the prevalence in the samples of white gentiles in the four cities of certain stereotypes about Negroes, foreigners, Jews, and the Catholic Church. (Because the scales that are used to measure prejudice throughout are not always comparable in the four cities, it is necessary to depend upon stereotypes as single-item measures in this case.) We find that residents in Southport expressed greater antiminority prejudice than did those in any other city; those in Valley City expressed the least antiminority prejudice; and those in Hometown and Steelville fell somewhere in between (Table 4.8). So far as these data are concerned, we may say that the South is the region of the greatest antiminority prejudice, whereas the Far West is the region of least prejudice. Tables 4.9 and 4.10 illustrate regional variations in prejudice based on responses to questions of rights and questions of distastefulness.

---

[27] See pp. 29-30. Note that different items had to be used in Southport. (See also Appendix C.)

[28] The basic technique has been successfully applied in caste ranking by Pauline M. Mahar in "A Multiple Scaling Technique for Caste Ranking," *Man in India,* XXXIX, No. 2 (April-June, 1959), 127-47.

Table 4.8

Variations in acceptance of stereotypes.

	Generally speaking, Negroes are lazy or ignorant			Although some Jews are honest, generally speaking most Jews are dishonest in their business dealings		
	Agree	Disagree	Cases	Agree	Disagree	Cases
Majority group						
Hometown	45%	55%	(498)	36%	64%	(483)
Steelville	42%	58%	(276)	39%	61%	(275)
Southport	50%	50%	(331)	44%	56%	(313)
Valley City	34%	66%	(308)	27%	73%	(296)
Minority group						
Hometown						
Negroes	13%	87%	(147)	62%	38%	(129)
Jews	36%	64%	(128)	9%	91%	(144)
Italians	36%	64%	(128)	27%	73%	(128)
Steelville						
Negroes	17%	83%	(131)	65%	35%	(126)
Jews	25%	75%	(65)	–	100%	(66)
Italians	57%	43%	(72)	47%	53%	(72)
Southport						
Negroes	10%	90%	(285)	48%	52%	(263)
Valley City						
Negroes	15%	85%	(226)	50%	50%	(217)
Mexicans	12%	88%	(122)	34%	66%	(121)

However, quantitative evidence concerning regional differences in prejudice is not fully consistent. In our sample, respondents in the Far West consistently, and often significantly, manifest less prejudice toward minorities than do those in any other region. This finding illustrates the point that the prevalence of prejudice is not always a good predictor of discrimination; field observations show that discrimination against Negroes is considerably more widespread in Valley City than in Hometown, yet we find that Hometown's residents are far more willing to express prejudiced attitudes toward Negroes than are those in Valley City.

Socioeconomic status and education. In this chapter we use education as one major indicator of socioeconomic status. Social class identification and occupation are also used as indicators of socioeconomic status.

Attitudes of social distance toward Negroes—expressed aversion toward close social interaction—are less frequent among the well-educated than among the relatively uneducated. The association of low education with prejudice is found in each of the four communities, and the differences are large and statistically significant in three of them. The variation between extremes is truly impressive: the proportion reporting feelings of marked

Table 4.9

Variations in willingness to grant minorities rights.

	As you see it, are (Ethnic Group) today demanding more than they have a right to or not?		
	Yes	No	Cases
Majority group			
Hometown			
Negroes	22%	78%	(472)
Jews	34%	66%	(465)
Italians	8%	92%	(451)
Steelville			
Negroes	41%	59%	(272)
Southport			
Negroes	58%	42%	(281)
Jews	37%	63%	(239)
Valley City			
Negroes	39%	61%	(269)
Mexicans	12%	88%	(243)
Minority group			
Hometown			
Negro			
Jews	33%	67%	(113)
Whites	58%	42%	(126)
Jew			
Negroes	10%	90%	(129)
Gentiles	10%	90%	(128)
Italian			
Negroes	25%	75%	(115)
Jews	21%	79%	(115)
Steelville			
Jew			
Gentiles	14%	86%	(64)
Italian			
Negroes	56%	44%	(71)

social-distance ranges from 91 per cent among the poorly educated inhabitants of Southport to only 25 per cent among the well-educated residents living in Valley City.

Social-distance responses concerning Jews are less closely related to education, although in this case also the better-educated are less likely than the uneducated to express reluctance to accept relatively intimate social contact.

In the one community having a sizable Mexican-American population, educational level was inversely related to social-distance prejudice among Anglo-American respondents against Mexican-Americans.

In the non-Southern communities of Hometown and Valley City and in

Table 4.10

Variations in responses to questions of distastefulness.

Do you think you would ever find it a little distasteful:

	to eat at the same table with a (Ethnic)?			to go to a party and find that most of the people are (Ethnic)?		
	Yes	No	Cases	Yes	No	Cases
Majority group						
Hometown						
Negroes	50%	50%	(520)	81%	19%	(517)
Jews	9%	91%	(519)	32%	68%	(507)
Italians	7%	93%	(494)	24%	76%	(484)
Steelville						
Negroes	61%	39%	(285)	89%	11%	(284)
Jews	8%	92%	(284)	25%	75%	(281)
Southport						
Negroes	92%	8%	(350)	—	—	—
Jews	13%	87%	(343)	34%	66%	(337)
Valley City						
Negroes	51%	49%	(315)	80%	20%	(316)
Mexicans	23%	77%	(313)	57%	43%	(317)
Minority group						
Hometown						
Negro						
Jews	13%	87%	(146)	29%	71%	(142)
Whites	14%	86%	(150)	32%	68%	(145)
Jew						
Negroes	30%	70%	(141)	65%	35%	(136)
Gentiles	3%	97%	(149)	9%	91%	(147)
Italian						
Negroes	48%	52%	(141)	84%	16%	(138)
Jews	5%	95%	(142)	13%	87%	(137)
Steelville						
Negro						
Whites	12%	88%	(140)	34%	66%	(135)
Jew						
Negroes	26%	74%	(65)	79%	21%	(63)
Gentiles	—	100%	(67)	9%	91%	(67)
Italian						
Negroes	74%	26%	(77)	94%	6%	(77)
Southport						
Negro						
Jews	40%	60%	(284)	57%	43%	(280)
Whites	35%	65%	(289)	62%	38%	(284)
Valley City						
Negro						
Whites	10%	90%	(227)	23%	77%	(226)
Mexicans	7%	93%	(227)	20%	80%	(226)
Mexican						
Americans	4%	96%	(130)	9%	91%	(130)
Negroes	11%	89%	(128)	43%	57%	(127)

Southport, white persons who identified themselves as belonging to the working class were only slightly more likely than self-styled members of the middle class to express social-distance feelings toward Negroes. The differences are consistent, but are statistically significant only in Valley City. The relationship between class identification and prejudice is reversed when Jews are the object of the feelings of social distance. In the two communities for which clearly compatible data are available, the middle-class respondents are somewhat more likely than working-class persons to express feelings of social distance toward Jews.

Although none of the differences are strikingly large—the greatest is a difference of 15 per cent in the responses of Hometown's white gentiles toward Jews—the pattern is consistent with that found by most other studies. In the Hometown and Southport samples where it is possible to "control" education, the middle-class persons at each educational level are the more likely to manifest feelings of discomfort or distance toward Jews. Furthermore, the differences found are in the direction that would be predicated on the assumption that social-distance feelings are most likely at the point of greatest sensed threat from social and economic competition.

Our confidence in the interpretation just suggested would be somewhat further strengthened if we found that prejudices concerning Negroes were most frequent among white persons of low occupational position, whereas social-distance reactions toward Jews were to appear most often in the higher occupational levels. What does, in fact, obtain in our four widely separated cities? As is so often the case in the world of reality, the answer to the question is complicated, and patience is required to untangle the facts. (See Table 4.11.)

Table 4.11

Relationship of social distance toward Negroes and occupational status.

Occupational Category	Hometown (N = 314)	Valley City (N = 107)	Southport (N = 140)
High (professional, business, and allied)	61%	10%*	53%*
Medium (skilled)	76%	50%	94%
Low (semiskilled and unskilled)	83%	61%	78%

*Less than 25 cases.

It is clear that social-distance prejudice against Negroes tends to be most frequent among white persons in the less well-paid and prestigeful types of occupations.

In the case of attitudes toward social contact with Jews, comparable data are available for Hometown and Southport as we see in Table 4.12.

Table 4.12

Relationship of social distance toward Jews and occupational level of gentile respondents.

Occupational Category	Valley City (N = 314)	Southport (N = 140)
High	67%	82%*
Medium	57%	47%
Low	53%	38%

*Less than 25 cases.

Here we see a tendency for anti-Jewish responses to go along with higher occupational position.

The correlation between occupation and prejudice toward Negroes almost disappears when amount of education is held constant. However, at all educational levels the greatest frequency of social-distance prejudice against Jews is found among persons in the higher, rather than the lower, occupational categories.

Imperfect and limited as these data are, they are compatible with the supposition that prejudice reflects a sense of threat, and that white gentiles in the upper socioeconomic strata therefore are less likely to be prejudiced against Negroes and more likely to be prejudiced against Jews than their fellows in the less affluent and less educated strata.

An overwhelming majority of the studies concerned with the relationship between education and prejudice show that higher levels of education are associated with greater tolerance of ethnic minorities. This is true of the older studies [29] as well as of the more recent ones. However, a minority of studies find either no difference or even a positive association of education and prejudice.[30] Though most of the more recent studies show, as does the present research, that higher education goes with low prejudice, there are some contradictory findings. Simpson [31] shows that among Negroes in

[29] See, for example, E. B. Bolton, "Measuring Specific Attitudes Toward the Social Rights of the Negro," *Journal of Abnormal and Social Psychology*, XXXI (1937), 384-97; W. P. Chase, "Attitudes of North Carolina College Students (Women) toward the Negro," *Journal of Social Psychology*, XII (Second Half, November, 1940), 367-78; D. D. Dobra, "Education and Negro Attitudes," *Sociology and Social Research*, XVII (1932), 137-41; A. L. Porterfield, "Education and Race Attitudes," *Sociology and Social Research*, XXI, No. 6 (July-August, 1937), 538-43; V. M. Sims and J. R. Patrick, "Attitudes Toward the Negro of Northern and Southern College Students, *Journal of Social Psychology*, VII, No. 2 (May, 1936), 192-203.

[30] See, for example, G. W. Moore, "Social and Political Attitudes of Students at North Carolina State College," reported by E. L. Horowitz in *Characteristics of the American Negro*, ed. O. Klineberg (New York: Harper & Row, Publishers, 1944), p. 233; Gardner Murphy and Rensis Likert, *Public Opinion and the Individual* (New York: Harper & Row, Publishers, 1938).

[31] Richard L. Simpson, "Negro-Jewish Prejudice: Authoritarianism and Social Variables as Correlates, *Social Problems*, VII, No. 2 (Fall, 1959), 138-46.

Hometown there is no consistent or significant relationship between education and anti-Jewish prejudice. However, among Jews, education is strongly negatively related to prejudice toward Negroes. Hunt [32] finds in a study of integrated housing in Kalamazoo, Michigan, that among the whites who have Negro neighbors, those individuals with high-school education are more willing to favor mixed housing patterns than are either the college or grammar-school groups. Himelhoch[33] reports that among Jewish students at a college in New York City the ethnocentrism score of the students was significantly lower than that of their parents. This difference he attributes to extraparental influences, including those associated with college. Stouffer [34] found that higher education is associated with greater tolerance of racial differences. In a study of male students at the University of Texas, Holtzman [35] reports that students in advanced years of college tended to approve of nonsegregated schools. In their study of 341 households in North Carolina, Tumin and others [36] showed that the higher the formal education, the more favorable the attitude toward desegregation. Martin and Westie [37] found that in Indianapolis, Indiana, tolerant subjects were significantly higher in education than their more prejudiced counterparts.

Finally, in a reanalysis of data from some 26 studies, Stember [38] shows a more complex pattern: the better educated are less prejudiced toward minority groups in some ways, but in others they tend to be more prejudiced. Whether or not they appear to be more tolerant, therefore, depends upon the dimension of prejudice under consideration. For example, they are less likely to subscribe to stereotypes, but more likely to reject intimate relations with members of minority groups. In general, however, the better educated are found to be more tolerant. The evidence indicates that education has an effect on prejudice that is independent of other factors usually associated with high educational status (for example, urbanization and information level).

Insofar as occupation and antiminority prejudice is concerned, the findings are contradictory. For example, two earlier studies show that prejudice

[32] Chester L. Hunt, "Private Integrated Housing in a Medium Size Northern City," *Social Problems*, VII, No. 3 (Winter, 1959-60), 196-209.

[33] Jerome Himelhoch,"Tolerance and Personality Needs: A Study of Liberalization of Ethnic Attitudes among Minority Group College Students," *American Sociological Review*, XV, No. 1 (February, 1950), 79-88.

[34] Samuel A. Stouffer, *Communism, Conformity, and Civil Liberties* (Garden City, N. Y.: Doubleday & Company, Inc., 1955).

[35] Wayne H. Holtzman, "Attitudes of College Men Toward Non-Segregation in Texas Schools," *Public Opinion Quarterly*, XX, No. 3 (Fall, 1956), 559-69.

[36] Melvin Tumin *et al.*, "Education, Prejudice and Discrimination: A Study in Readiness for Desegregation," *American Sociological Review*, XXIII (1958), 41-49.

[37] James G. Martin and Frank R. Westie, "The Tolerant Personality," *American Sociological Review*, XXIV (1959), pp. 521-28.

[38] Charles H. Stember, *Education and Attitude Change* (New York: Institute of Human Relations Press, 1961).

toward Jews tends to be more prevalent in the upper occupational groups,[39] and two others report no occupational status differences in attitudes toward minorities.[40] Among the more recent studies, Tumin and others [41] report that high-occupation and high-income groups tend to be overrepresented in the high education-less prejudiced category. Martin and Westie [42] found that tolerant subjects show a significantly higher mean occupational status than their more prejudiced counterparts. On the other hand, Hunt [43] found that laborers were slightly more likely to favor mixed housing than those in white collar and small business occupations.

Our own data show that the well-educated, on the whole, were less ready to accept stereotypes concerning minority groups. In Hometown, for instance, respondents were asked, *As you see it, are Jews and Negroes today demanding more than they have a right to or not?* The percentages who said "yes" were:

Among those whose education was:	Jews	Negroes
Elementary school only	41	30
Some high school	32	20
High school graduate	34	22
College training	25	14

On the other hand, acceptance of the stereotype of Jews as "pushy" does not vary with educational level. Two other stereotypes of Negroes, however, illustrate the tendency for the better educated to reject gross negative images: (1) *Generally speaking, Negroes are lazy and ignorant;* (2) *Do you think Negroes today are trying to push in where they are not wanted?:*

	Percentage saying	
	"Agree" to (1)	"Yes" to (2)
Elementary	47	49
Some high school	30	43
High school graduate	31	44
College	23	23

In all four communities, the better educated tended to reject the crude negative stereotypes, although education is not related to some other types of prejudice items; for example, it is not associated with willingness to have someone in one's family marry a Jew. Other studies have shown similar results. The pattern of relationships between education and different dimensions of prejudicial attitudes is thus quite complex.

---

[39] Cf. H. H. Harlan, "Some Factors Affecting Attitudes toward Jews," American Sociological Review, VII (1942), 816-27; D. J. Levinson and R. N. Sanford, "A Scale for the Measurement of Anti-Semitism," *Journal of Psychology*, XVII (1944), 339-70.

[40] See, for example, Murphy and Likert, *Public Opinion and the Individual;* also Sims and Patrick, *op. cit.*

[41] Tumin, *et al.*, "Education, Prejudice and Discrimination," 41-49.

[42] *Op. cit.*, pp. 521-28.

[43] *Op. cit.*, p. 206.

With few exceptions, then, our findings regarding socioeconomic status and prejudice are consistent with those of other studies. This is clear for education and prejudice. The finding that there is greater prejudice toward Jews among upper occupational status individuals is consistent with results of a majority of other studies. The same is true of the finding that persons in occupations of lower status tend to express greater prejudice toward Negroes.

Religious background and participation. The relationships between prejudices or discriminatory behavior, on the one hand, and religious beliefs, attitudes, and behaviors on the other are complex, and the existing research findings are often ambiguous. Many studies have reported a higher frequency of expressed prejudice toward racial or ethnic outgroups among members of organized religious bodies than among nonmembers and, similarly, greater prevalence of such prejudices among persons who frequently attend religious services than among those who do not. On the other hand, there are studies that present data suggesting a curvilinear association between prejudice and religious activity—both the completely inactive and the highly active persons being less often prejudiced. For example, Friedrichs' study of a New Jersey town showed the highest percentages of tolerant attitudes toward Negroes among white persons with very high or very low rates of attendance at religious services, and suggests ". . . that the studies uncovering a simple inverse relationship may have failed to distinguish between those approximating the institutional norm in religious activity and those exceeding it." [44]

Clearly a first question is whether religious background or affiliation is related in any way to racial and ethnic prejudice. In the present studies, the prevalence of social-distance aversions in the various Christian groupings is so varied as to defy any easy generalization.[45] The religious group containing most social-distance feeling toward Negroes is: in Hometown, Baptist; in Valley City, Presbyterian; in Southport, Roman Catholic. As if this were not confusing enough, prejudice against close association with Jews is highest in Hometown among Baptists (again), but in Southport the greatest prevalence is among the Episcopalians. It is known that the social and cultural characteristics of members of any one of the major Protestant denominations are subject to great regional and local variations. Our data show no simple relationship between prejudice and specific religious affiliations. The great variability from one community to another in the rankings of the various denominations is impressive and

---

[44] Robert W. Friedrichs, "Christians and Residential Exclusion: an Empirical Study of a Northern Dilemma," *Journal of Social Issues*, XV, No. 4 (1959), 19.

[45] The detailed data are presented in Alphonso Pinkney, "The Anatomy of Prejudice" (Unpublished Ph.D. thesis, Cornell University, 1961), pp. 93-98.

makes us wary of attributing too much importance to the observed inter-denominational differences.

Research by other investigators has not shown a clear pattern of consistent differences in racial and ethnic prejudices among members of various religious denominations. Some deeply committed and active participants in some organized religious bodies are strong and consistent advocates of equality and integration, whereas in other instances, whole ethnicoreligious groups manifest a policy of segregation and subordination of other, racially different people.[46] Very common indeed is a third type of situation, in which the more religiously inclined have compartmentalized their ethnic attitudes and actions, apart from their religious beliefs concerning brotherhood.[47] Furthermore, denominational groups may find themselves internally divided by regional and local differences in interpretations of the implications of Christian doctrine for church policies concerning racial segregation and related issues. Dornbusch and Irle found that in the failure of Presbyterian union in 1955, the vote of Southern presbyteries against union with the Northern Presbyterians correlated +0.57 with the percentage of Negroes in the total population of the general areas in which the presbyteries were located.[48]

The relationships between religious affiliation and racial or ethnic prejudices are greatly complicated by variations in the other social and cultural characteristics of the members of different faiths and denominations. For example, in the United States, there is a tendency for the membership of the Catholic and Protestant fundamentalist groups to fall toward the lower end of the socioeconomic scale, for the Jewish population to concentrate in the middle strata, and for the prestige Protestant denominations (for example, Congregational, Episcopalian, Presbyterian) to be overrepresented in the upper strata.[49] Protestant denominations bracket the full range of class differences. Many small sects are composed almost exclusively of the very poor. In particular regions and localities, the membership of a particular faith or denomination may also have a distinctive ethnic character, for example, French-Canadian (Catholic), German (Lutheran). There are other cultural differences that may be associated with religious group identity.

---

[46] "To the Dutch-Nationalist of today, as to the Boers of the last century, racial inequality as an avowed doctrine expressed in public policy is Christian, moral, and ethically justified. . . . Apartheid does not lack so-called 'morality.' " [Eugene P. Dvorin, *Racial Separation in South Africa* (Chicago: The University of Chicago Press, 1952), p. 189.]

[47] Friedrichs, *op. cit.*, p. 22.

[48] S. M. Dornbusch and R. D. Irle, "The Failure of Presbyterian Union," *American Journal of Sociology*, LXIV, No. 4 (1959), 353-55.

[49] Cf. the summary by Michael Argyle, *Religious Behavior* (London: Routledge & Kegan Paul, Ltd., 1958), pp. 129-33.

In the United States, it seems clear that respectable status and conforming behavior are associated with involvement in organized religion.[50] In a sample of 1,126 Christian students from 13 colleges and universities, Putney and Middleton found that those subscribing to orthodox (fundamentalist) beliefs tended to be authoritarian, concerned with social status, and conservative in attitudes concerning economic and political issues.[51] In general, ". . . the highest status groups, adults possessing college degrees and adults whose family heads are professionals, have the greatest regularity of church attendance within the Protestant, Catholic, Baptist, and Methodist groups." [52] Church attendance is greater in rural areas and small towns than in the larger urban centers.[53] Although some small sects represent culturally marginal and economically depressed groups, the conventionally devout among white Christians in America are most numerous in the relatively comfortable and conservative parts of the social order.

Several studies have shown that religious affiliation and participation are positively correlated with prejudices against Negroes, Jews, and other ethnic groups.[54] Stouffer found in his nationwide samples that church attenders are more likely than persons who do not attend to be generally intolerant.[55] Holtzman found that college men who often attend church services are more likely to favor segregation than those who attend less frequently.[56] On the other hand, in another study in the South, persons who were frequent church attenders tended to fall in the low-prejudice portion of the community.[57] In some instances an apparent association between prejudice and frequency of attendance at religious services may simply reflect denominational differences.[58]

Some investigators have concluded that religious participation may reflect either mere social conventionality or genuine commitment to religious

---

[50] Bernard Lazerwitz, "Some Factors Associated with Variations in Church Attendance," *Social Forces*, XXXIX, No. 4 (May, 1961), 303-4. (See bibliographical citations on pp. 301-2.)

[51] Snell Putney and Russell Middleton, "Dimensions and Correlates of Religious Ideologies," *Social Forces*, XXXIX, No. 4 (May, 1961), 289.

[52] Lazerwitz, *op. cit.*, p. 308.

[53] G. E. Lenski, "Social Correlates of Religious Interest," *American Sociological Review*, XVIII, No. 5 (October, 1953), 533-44.

[54] T. W. Adorno, Else Frenkel-Brunswik, Daniel J. Levinson, R. Nevitt Sanford, (see Chap. 5, ftn. 8) *et al.*, *The Authoritarian Personality* (New York: Harper & Row, Publishers, 1950), pp. 210-17; M. G. Ross, *Religious Beliefs of Youth* (New York: Association Press, 1950); R. K. Goldsen *et al.*, *What College Students Think* (New York: D. Van Nostrand Co., Inc., 1960).

[55] Stouffer, *Communism, Conformity, and Civil Liberties*, pp. 140-52.

[56] Holtzman, "Attitudes of College Men toward Non-Segregation in Texas Schools," 559-69.

[57] Melvin Tumin *et al.*, "Education, Prejudice and Discrimination, 41-49.

[58] John Harding *et al.*, "Prejudice and Ethnic Relations," in *Handbook of Social Psychology*, Gardner Lindzey, ed., II (Cambridge, Mass.: Addison-Wesley Publishing Company, 1954), 1039.

values; only the latter would be expected to minimize ethnic prejudice.[59] This conclusion seems entirely sound, so far as it goes. In communities in which conventionalized ethnic prejudices are normal, the very exercise of respectable conformity may reinforce the acceptance of stereotypes and the support of a discriminatory social pattern. Under these circumstances, a man has to be a rebel or a saint, or both, to act upon a personal code of toleration, acceptance, and appreciation of group differences. The ordinary American churchgoer may find himself caught between the vaguely sensed implications of a universalistic creed and the social pressures of the status-conscious and ethnocentric community of believers. It may thus happen that the unaffiliated and the nonbelievers may be less prejudiced than the conventionally religious, although the very devout religious participants are also low in ethnic and racial prejudice.[60]

These considerations point to the possibility that there may be a curvilinear relationship between religious activity and prejudice: low prejudice among the frequent attenders and among persons who do not attend at all; greatest prejudice among persons who attend church but not frequently. The hypothesis would be that the infrequent attenders tend to be the conventionally religious persons who conform to community norms but are not much influenced by religious values such as brotherly love.

For three of our four communities, data are available on both social-distance prejudice and frequency of attendance at religious services among white Christians. The pattern of findings is generally consistent with the hypothesis just stated, although that hypothesis is not thereby proved.

Social-distance feelings toward Negroes are consistently more frequent among persons who seldom attend religious services than among either those who attend often or those who never attend. In two of the three cities (Steelville and Valley City), those who seldom attended were significantly more prejudiced toward Negroes than those who often attended. (The prejudice score for Steelville includes both anti-Negro prejudice and prejudice toward Jews.) In Southport, those who seldom attended were more prejudiced, but the difference was not significant. There is a consistent pattern in which those who seldom attended more often manifested prejudiced attitudes than those who said they never attended.[61]

In Steelville and Valley City those who often attended religious services appeared to be less prejudiced than those who seldom or never attended, whereas in Southport this was not the case. In Steelville and Valley City those individuals who seldom attended religious services were significantly more prejudiced toward Negroes than those who often attended.

---

[59] Gordon W. Allport and Bernard M. Kramer, "Some Roots of Prejudice," *Journal of Psychology*, XXII, First Half (July, 1946), 38.

[60] Argyle, *Religious Behaviour*, pp. 84-85.

[61] Cf. data in Pinkney, *op. cit.*, pp. 98-103.

Insofar as prejudice toward Jews is concerned, we found in Southport, again, that those who indicated that they seldom attended services were more prejudiced than those who either often attended or never attended. In this case, those who never attended were less prejudiced than those who often attended.

Prejudice toward Mexican-Americans follows the familiar pattern. Those who seldom attended were significantly more prejudiced toward Mexican-Americans than were those who often attended or those who never attended.

From these data it seems clear that those individuals in our sample who seldom attend religious services (that is, churchgoers who go infrequently) more often express prejudice than those who often attend or those who never attend. The findings regarding differences in prejudice for those who often attend and those who never attend are inconclusive. However, it seems fair to say from our data that within given educational levels those who often attend are consistently although slightly less prejudiced toward minority groups than those who never attend.

Political party affiliation. We have just seen glimpses of the possibility that religious participation may contain two sets of forces pulling in opposite directions: a code of humanitarianism and ethical universalism versus a code of group exclusiveness and conformity to the social *status quo.* Another angle on this matter might be provided by correlating prejudice with political party preferences. For example, is the independent in politics like the nonattender in the religious sphere? In some communities one political party tends to solicit and integrate minority groups in political affairs whereas another does not. Are there, then, any differences between Democrats and Republicans in the sample, insofar as antiminority prejudice is concerned?

In Steelville, Valley City, and Southport there was a consistently higher rate of prejudice toward Negroes, Jews, and Mexican-Americans among Democrats than among Republicans, but the differences were slight and not significant. Although the data do not permit a comparison among Republicans, Democrats, and independents in each of the four cities, such a comparison is possible in Valley City. In this case we found that independent voters were consistently less prejudiced toward Mexican-Americans and Negroes than were either Republicans or Democrats; the difference between independents and Democrats is significant in both cases.

Democrats in all the locations are slightly more prejudiced toward minorities than are Republicans; however, since the differences are not significant in any case, and since they are slight, it seems fair to say that these findings are inconclusive. However, it is clear that independent voters are less prejudiced toward minority groups in Valley City than are either Republicans or Democrats. This instance suggests the possibility that individuals who are willing to deviate from the expected patterns set by the group are more likely to be tolerant of minorities.

Organization membership. As a rule, those individuals who report membership in social, civic, and fraternal clubs or organizations less often express prejudice toward Negroes, Jews, and Mexican-Americans in all four cities. In two cases (prejudice toward Negroes in Hometown and Southport) these differences are statistically significant. In one case (Steelville) they are not significant, and in one (Valley City) they approach significance.[62]

If we hold education constant, we find that the differences that were present are greatly reduced. That is, education appears to be a better indicator of prejudice than membership in clubs and organizations.

Age. There are several plausible reasons for expecting social-distance prejudice to be positively correlated with age. But before we proceed we ought to find out whether older persons are in fact any more likely than younger persons to be prejudiced. As we look at the social-distance attitudes toward Negroes, our first impression must be that age is not a relevant condition. In only one community (Valley City) does it seem to make a difference.[63] However, in the instances of reactions to Jews and to Mexican-Americans, the younger people less often express attitudes of social distance or rejection.

The association between age and prejudice might simply reflect the influence of the higher educational level of the younger adults. But we cannot dismiss the differences in that way. When education is held constant, younger adults are still less likely than older persons to express social-distance prejudices.[64] Especially noteworthy are the consistent and rather large differences between older and younger gentile persons in attitudes toward social interaction with Jews. Persons born after 1915 or so are less likely to be prejudiced.

Sex. Are there any good grounds for expecting social-distance prejudices to be more likely among men than among women, or vice versa? It appears that a believable case can be made out, *a priori,* for either side of the argument.

On the side of greater acceptance and tolerance among males might be the greater prevalence of wide-ranging and varied social contacts outside the family. Also, it is sometimes plausibly alleged that men in our culture feel less bound by niceties of social conventions, less obligated to be conservative in their social relationships. Further, it could be argued, the contingency of unwanted amorous advances is less likely to occur or to be threatening to the man, and that men are more likely to accept certain

62 See Pinkney, *op. cit.,* pp. 106-9.

63 *Ibid.,* pp. 79-84.

64 *Ibid.*

intergroup relationships in the interests of association with and access to women of the outgroup. It is possible, in addition, that men are more likely than women, on the average, to be trained in accepting and managing functionally specific and affectively neutral relationships.

On the other hand, it may be contended that it is precisely the special role of women in our society that predisposes them to accept the kind of social contacts with outgroup members that are reflected in our social-distance measure (eating together, dancing, going to a party), at least so long as the level of intermarriage on the part of a member of one's family is not involved. For all of the emancipation of women, nurturing, protective, and humanitarian concerns, including sensitivity to personal feelings and skill in relatively intimate social relationships, are still expected to be especially their province.

And we must remember that for the men, the very same social and occupational orbits that provide occasions for intergroup contacts also frequently entail competitive relations and other potential sources of friction and threat.

The actual differences in prejudice as between the sexes in the populations studied are not great. In two of our cities, females are more likely than males to express social-distance prejudice toward Negroes; in another the reverse is the case. Only in Hometown are white women significantly more likely than white men to reject contact with Negroes as distasteful. In orientation to both Jews (two communities) and Mexican-Americans (one community), prejudices are slightly more prevalent among women than among men. Although consistent in direction, the differences are not large or statistically significant. (In general they are nevertheless maintained when education is controlled.)

The findings, therefore, are rather inconclusive. There does appear to be a slight tendency for women to manifest more often social-distance feelings toward minorities. This result could represent the outcome of strong tendencies that cancel out. A second possibility is that potentially sizable differences have been eliminated through communication and persuasion; for example, a spouse comes to accept the views of wife or husband. The lack of significant differences, finally, could mean that the prejudice-engendering forces working upon men and women are not greatly different in kind or magnitude.

Marital status. There does not seem to be a clear basis in theory for expecting differences in marital status to be associated in an unequivocal way with differences in social-distance prejudice. Of course, a variety of *ad hoc* hypotheses could be invented. One might imagine that married people would be more likely than single persons to feel aversion to close intergroup association because of fears for the social standing of the family unit, because of concern about possible threats of intermarriage of children, because of greater average age (a spurious factor), or because of greater immersion in family-connected social life. The greater freedom of single persons to engage in recreational activities and to establish casual interpersonal relationships without responsible commitments might be thought to reduce social-distance feelings toward outgroup members. On the other hand, single women might be expected to be under special pressure to limit their outgroup interaction. Persons who are divorced, separated, or widowed might emphasize social distance from Jews and Negroes either because of general misanthropy arising from frustration and deprivation, or because of restricted social opportunities, or because of basic personality difficulties.

Possible interpretations are far more plentiful than data. Comparing single with married persons, we note an irregular tendency for lower frequency of social-distance reactions to occur among the single population, but the tendency is contradicted by the Southport samples' attitudes toward Jews. (See Table 4.13.) We have no inkling as to why this may be so.

Table 4.13

Relationship between social-distance feelings and marital status.

Attitude and Marital Status	Hometown (N = 528)	Valley City (N = 319)	Southport (N = 344)
Toward Negroes	-------->		
Married	73%	48%	81%
Single	70%	24%	80%
Other	90%	61%	83%
		Toward Mexican-Americans	
Toward Jews ------------>			
Married	58%	41%	50%
Single	61%	20%	65%
Other	62%	58%	53%

These data clearly are quite inconclusive. It is a little more impressive to observe the differences between those who are either married or single and the persons who were once married (that is, are now divorced, separated, or widowed). There is a general tendency for prejudice to be more highly concentrated in the latter category. Pending direct evidence not available in these data, the most suitable hypotheses would seem to be those that would combine differences in interaction-patterns and in frustration-load and in personality difficulties to account for the observed pattern of prejudices.

Summary. The main generalizations concerning social correlates of prejudice emerging from the data are:

1. The Southern sample exhibits the greatest frequency of social-distance prejudice. The Far Western city has the largest proportion of relatively

tolerant or accepting individuals. The Northeastern and Midwestern samples fall in between.

2. Educational level is significantly associated with degree of prejudice: the higher the educational level, the less frequent are high degrees of prejudice toward Negroes, Jews, and Mexican-Americans.

3. Individuals who identify themselves with the upper class tend to be slightly more prejudiced than other white gentiles toward Jews. While the relationships between social-distance feelings toward Negroes and self-chosen class identity are not clear cut, there is some tendency for persons who say that they belong to the working class to be more likely than those who consider themselves to be upper class to maintain attitudes of aversion concerning close social contacts. In both instances, those who identify with the middle class fall in between these two categories in prejudice toward Jews and Negroes.

4. Persons who work in relatively high-status occupations tend to be more prejudiced toward Jews, whereas those in lower status occupations are the more likely to have feelings of social distance toward Negroes and Mexican-Americans.

5. There are no large or consistent differences among the various Protestant denominations nor between Protestants and Catholics in the extent of prejudice toward Jews, Negroes, or Mexican-Americans.

6. Individuals who report that they *seldom* attend religious services tend to be more prejudiced than those who report that they *often* attend *or* those who say they *never* attend. The regular churchgoers are the group showing least frequency of social-distance reactions, followed by the non-attenders, whereas it is the infrequent attenders—perhaps the "imperfectly churched" or "conventionally religious"—who are most likely to show exclusionistic prejudice. It appears, however, that the observed differences are partly due to correlated differences in education.

7. Political party affiliation or preference is not strongly related to differences in prejudice, although in the cities studied, there is a slight tendency for the greatest frequency of intolerance to appear among Democrats. Independent voters are most likely to be free of feelings of social distance toward racial and ethnic minorities.

8. Individuals who report membership in clubs and organizations tend to be consistently more tolerant of Negroes and Mexican-Americans than those who do not belong to such groups. (Organizational membership is not predictive of attitudes toward association with Jewish persons.) The apparent effects of organizational membership are confounded with, and may be largely reducible to, effects related to educational level and social class.

9. On the whole, there is a slight tendency among adults for the preva-

lence of prejudices against close social contacts with Negroes, Jews, and Mexican-Americans to be greater among older persons.

10. Females are slightly more likely than males to be prejudiced against the three minorities named.

11. Individuals who are either divorced, separated, or widowed tend to be slightly more often prejudiced than those who are married or single. No clear conclusions can be drawn from comparisons of single with married people.

In general, individuals who are closely bound to the dominant mores of the particular subgroup tend more often to be prejudiced toward minorities. Examples from our data who fit into this category are residents of the South, females, older people, and nonindependent voters. There are exceptions to this general rule. For example, it might be expected that church members who often attend religious services would be more intolerant than others, when, in fact the tendency is for them to be more tolerant. On the whole, however, it seems fair to say that individuals who are less closely bound with traditional subgroup ties appear to be more tolerant.

Tendencies of the prejudiced

Prejudiced people share certain tendencies with regard to the inconsistency and confusion of their responses, their ignorance of the true feelings of outgroup members, the degree of their guilt feelings about the treatment of minorities, and the degree to which they generalize prejudices.

Inconsistency and confusion. Christie has said that logically incompatible stereotypes may be held together because they express a common attitude or feeling.[65] Indeed, many individuals place different evaluations upon the very desirability of logical consistency in giving responses. Such differences in evaluation may be systematically associated with various social strata, educational levels, and ethnic categories. For example, there are scattered but consistent evidences that relatively uneducated Negro respondents are especially likely to agree to interview or questionnaire items, to give more inconsistent answers as between original and reversed forms of items, and to give more "don't know" or "can't answer" responses.[66]

Our firsthand interviews gave many vivid impressions of the tendency, especially in authoritarian [67] and generally hostile individuals, for various

---

[65] Richard Christie, "Authoritarianism Re-Examined," in *Studies in the Scope and Method of the Authoritarian Personality,* R. Christie and M. Jahoda, eds. (New York: The Free Press of Glencoe, Inc., 1954), p. 152.

[66] See a review of some of the evidence in Paul A. Hare, "Interview Responses: Personality or Conformity?" *Public Opinion Quarterly,* XXIV, No. 4 (Winter, 1960), 679-85.

[67] See Chapter 5. The term has been popular since the publication of *The Authoritarian Personality* in 1950 by T. W. Adorno *et al.*

stereotypes to blur and interlock. Some respondents spoke of all racial, ethnic, and religious groupings other than their own as nationalities (as, "There are a lot of different nationalities in this town, like Negroes, those Catholics, and some Greeks"). Some respondents spoke of Jews as a nationality; others talked of the Jewish race, even while referring to Negroes as a class of people.

Further seeming inconsistencies can be seen by the following survey data secured from 353 white respondents in Southport:

1. Negro youths should have an equal chance to earn a decent living.	313
2. Negroes should have a right to:	
receive the same pay as whites for the same work.	307
try on clothes in stores.	128
work side-by-side with whites at the same jobs.	105
sit in same part of buses.	30
go to same schools.	13
live in same neighborhoods.	11
3. Negroes are lazy and ignorant.	166
4. Negroes are demanding more than they have a right to.	163
5. I like Negroes.	97
6. I don't mind the idea of Negroes living in my neighborhood.	56 *
7. I don't mind Negroes in the organizations I belong to.	43
8. I dislike Negroes.	41

* Actually there were 93 families that reported that there were Negroes living within a block or two of their homes. Negro residences in Southport were not rigidly confined to a single area. Many domestic employees lived close to their employers. Under the caste-like local system, the proximity of Negroes' residences to white middle-class areas probably does not represent so great a status threat as it would in many Northern cities.

The mere listing of these responses shows how varied are each individual's attitudes toward Negroes. Obviously some of the 166 persons who subscribed to the cliché that Negroes are lazy and ignorant were nevertheless found among the 307 who indorsed Negroes' right to equal pay for the same work. Notice also the small number who were willing to admit to dislike, in comparison with the near-unanimity of support for segregation in school and neighborhood.

Finally, interviews with some of the most prejudiced residents of Hometown reveal inconsistencies and confusion about the objects of their negative feelings:

    (*About Negroes moving in*)
    I don't know. I suppose they have a perfect right to. They should be in their own section. All the Negroes should be together. I think

they'd be happier, too. White people can't help resenting them. They have their own stores, churches, and schools. They're human beings, and there are some nice good people among them. If I was colored, I'd rather be among the colored than whites. I'd feel the same about the whites as I do about them. They're mean and have awful tempers. They all fight—among their own people. You're always reading in the papers, they have tempers, pulling knives.

(*About Negroes*)

Every time the last member of a family dies around here, we're afraid they'll sell to colored. I wouldn't want them that close. The ones that pass by here are well dressed. They dress as well as we do. They mind their business, better than some whites do. My nephew lives over there. Now his wife wants to get out of there. He says it's silly. He's in radio. He's fixed things for a lot of them. He says they keep their houses and themselves just as clean as any white people. They're very neat. This apartment house over here is colored. Very neat, nice-looking, well-dressed colored come out of there. They have nice cars, but if you're driving look out! They won't slack up for you, and they'll always take the corner before you. They're arrogant.

(*About Jews*)

There are three Jewish families in _____. They are all very nice. One's a doctor, a veterinary doctor. The other two have stores. Of course they aren't like those from New York. There are types of Jews. I think when they get together they try to take things over. Like Miami Beach. There are hotels that will only take genteels (respondent's pronunciation), *and beaches where white people won't go—I mean genteels. If you travel with them, you're all right. If you're with them you get everything, but if you're not. . . .*

Ignorance of true feelings of outgroup. Members of dominant social groupings who insist upon deferential behavior from the lower orders are strongly disposed to regard the respectful behavior they require as evidence that their subordinates fully accept the system. In modern America very rarely is this self-assuring assumption correct. Probably most of the white respondents in Southport are unaware that 40 per cent of the local Negroes feel that they have more in common to discuss with a Negro in New York than with a white resident of Southport. Certainly some would show surprise if they knew that anger or annoyance at hearing the word "nigger" is reported by no less than 92 per cent of the Negroes in the city.[68] The as-

---

[68] Lionel S. Lewis, "Discrimination and Insulation" (Unpublished M.A. thesis, Cornell University, 1959), p. 31. Of Southport's Negro adults, 60 per cent see a Negro newspaper at least weekly.

sumption that minority-group members are well satisfied with their lot is often voiced, whether defensively or naïvely, by many members of dominant social groups who feel well satisfied with their own way of life. This claim does not fare well either, in confrontation with our data. As Table 4.14 and Chart 4.1 show, the frequency of satisfaction with the local community

Table 4.14

Satisfaction with local community among ethnic groupings.

We'd like to know how you feel about living in this city. How good or bad would you say it is as a place to live? Would you say very good, fairly good, not so good, or very bad?

| | Percentages of replies which said: | | | | |
	Very Good	Fairly Good	Not So Good	Very Bad	Cases
Majority group (white gentiles)					
Hometown	72%	24%	4%	*	(524)
Steelville	51%	41%	7%	1%	(287)
Southport	60%	35%	4%	1%	(352)
Valley City	71%	25%	3%	1%	(319)
Minority group					
Hometown					
Negroes	28%	64%	6%	2%	(148)
Jews	56%	43%	1%	—	(143)
Steelville					
Negroes	12%	56%	25%	7%	(139)
Jews	46%	50%	2%	2%	(65)
Southport					
Negroes	41%	54%	4%	1%	(285)
Valley City					
Negroes	26%	51%	19%	4%	(227)

*Less than 0.5 per cent.

as a place to live is lower among Jewish persons and is very much lower among Negroes than among white gentiles in the four communities surveyed.

These data indicate that, among the correlates of ethnocentrism, ignorance of the actual nature of another group can be a powerful factor in affecting relationships with that group.[69] The net effects may be either positive or negative.

Guilt feelings. Examining America's treatment of minorities, Gunnar Myrdal called the problem of the Negro in the United States the "American Dilemma." [70] How much this dilemma is experienced by different types of

---

[69] H. M. Blalock, Jr., "A Power Analysis of Racial Discrimination," *Social Forces,* XXXIX, No. 1 (October, 1960), 57.

[70] *An American Dilemma* (New York: Harper & Row, Publishers, 1944).

Chart 4.1

Proportion highly satisfied with the community as a place to live.

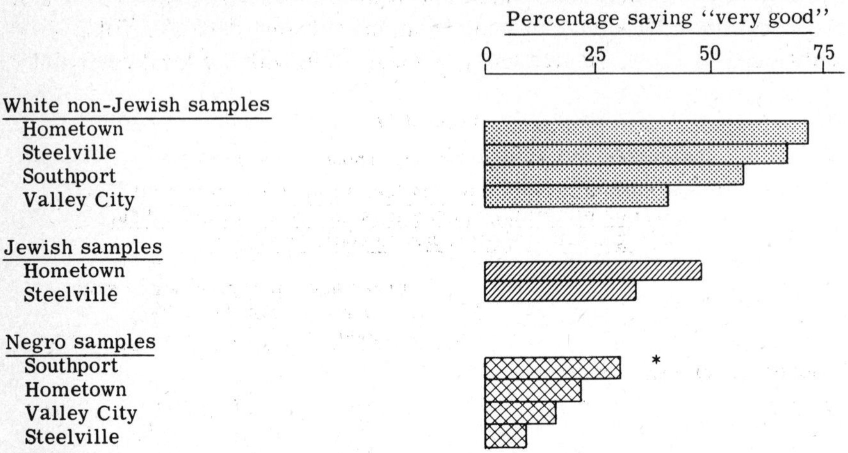

Percentage saying "very good"

*One may be reminded of the testimony of some white people in each of these cities: "Our Negro people are well satisfied here—it's just outsider agitators who cause all the trouble."

Americans as a personal reaction is difficult to determine. But in answer to a direct question: *Do you ever feel guilty about the way Negroes are treated—would you say never, sometimes, or fairly often?*, 33 per cent of a cross section of white adults in Southport said "sometimes" and 8 per cent said "often."

The people in our sample gave an overwhelming demonstration of the proverbial public expression of confidence of the white Southerner in his superior understanding of Negroes. At the level of lip-service, this confidence, even if it be defensive and mistaken, is still widespread. We asked, *Do you think that Southerners understand Negroes better than Northerners or not so well as Northerners do?* The replies:

"Better"   70 per cent

"About the same"   12 per cent

"Not so well"   9 per cent

"Do not know" or no answer   9 per cent

At the same time, our Southport respondents were willing to testify in the ratio of 2:1 that Negroes are better off in the South than in the North.

Of course, all this testimony may be defensive or overcompensatory. Short of depth interviews, which we were not in a position to conduct, we could not deal directly with this problem. Nevertheless, the survey responses give some indirect clues as to possible underlying attitudes that may be at variance to an important extent with the explicit picture of positive appraisal, optimism, and lack of guilt. Having asked about whether white people in the South feel guilty, we went on to inquire, *How about you, personally, do you ever feel guilty about the way Negroes are treated —would you say never, sometimes, or fairly often?* When responding in these specifically personal terms, 8 per cent said they feel guilty "fairly often" and another 33 per cent admitted to guilt feelings "sometimes." Can we take these responses as really indicative of guilt? It seems likely that in a Deep South city in the early 1950's there would not be many people who, in a confidential interview, would testify to guilt unless they did feel it. How many others of the 57 per cent who said they never feel guilty may have unconscious guilt we have no way of guessing.

These Southern adults are much more likely to deny feelings of guilt than are high-school youths in the far more liberal atmosphere of a Western city. In a survey of high-school students in Phoenix just two years after desegregation, the youths in the Phoenix Union High School were asked, *How often do you feel guilty about the way Negroes in the United States are treated—would you say never, sometimes, or fairly often?* The replies:

Never	16 per cent
Sometimes	64 per cent
Fairly often	20 per cent

Putting side by side the answers to the two questions about guilt asked in Southport raises the possibility that we may be dealing with pluralistic ignorance. Although the two questions are not strictly comparable, it is clear that more people admit to guilt feelings in themselves than believe that other whites feel guilty. Both estimates cannot be right, and it seems likely that the social control of opinions concerning Negro-white relations leads to underestimation by local people of the extent of doubt and uneasiness generated by the system. Such mutual ignorance of others' private feelings undoubtedly is one of the mechanisms by which imperfectly integrated social arrangements are maintained in opposition to pressures toward change.

Other kinds of defensive beliefs and systematic ignorance may work in a similar way to support the *status quo.*

Generalizing prejudice. Are there some people who more than others have a tendency to express categorically negative reactions to all minorities? We selected items that represented the different components of prejudice (for example, stereotypes, social-distance distastefuls, "dislike" items, "should-have-the-right-to" items, "approve-of" items) and tested the responses of majority-group respondents to see whether there was a single attitude toward a single minority group, when the items themselves included all the different prejudice components.[71] The results are shown in Table 4.15.

In 22 tests in three different communities with regard to prejudice toward each of three minorities, three-item scales using items from different components meet Guttman-scale criteria. This striking finding strongly suggests that there may be something that can be regarded as prejudice toward a given minority.

Is there then a general prejudice toward all the minorities taken together, not separately? To explore this question, we selected the following prejudice item used in Hometown: *On the whole, would you say that you like or dislike Negro people?* Since we substituted in a later question *Jewish people* and *Italian people,* we checked to see if the responses to these three questions fit Guttman-scale criteria. Similarly in Valley City, we tried to scale items in which respondents had been asked if they would find it distasteful to go to a party and find that most of the people were Negro, Indian, Chinese, Jewish, Mexican, or Japanese. In both instances the respondents could be ordered according to Guttman-scale criteria, thus indicating that respondents can be ranked on how much distaste they express about associating with a number of different minorities. Furthermore, there is a rank-order of minorities according to whether majority-group respondents consider association with a given minority more or less distasteful than association with the other minorities. In Valley City, the rank-order from most acceptable to least acceptable runs: [72] Jewish, Indian, Chinese, Japanese, Mexican, Negro.

When we compare respondents' feelings of distaste in the instance of different minorities in the same situation (at a party) with the number of situations they would find distasteful regarding a given minority, we find a high correlation (See Table 4.16). This indicates that the more social-

---

[71] All items in the questionnaires used in Southport, Hometown (two surveys), and Valley City were studied and arranged according to the components they were thought to index. Then groups of three items were selected to meet two criteria: each of the three items must represent a different component; and each must represent a different marginal distribution (one, 10 to 30 per cent; one, 30 to 50 per cent; and one, 60 to 90 per cent). The items were then tested to see if they met Guttman-scale criteria. Two scales were tested for each minority group in each city (except in the case of Jews in Hometown, where marginal distributions allowed only one scale). The samples were divided into respondents having contact with the minority and those not having contact, because it was felt that perhaps the prejudices of those without contact would be more disengaged—and therefore more likely to scale. The number of cases used in each test was over 100 in every instance.

[72] The rank-order among respondents in the Mexican-American and Negro cross-sections is slightly different for Mexican-Americans and quite different for Negro respondents.

VERNON REGIONAL
JUNIOR COLLEGE LIBRARY

Table 4.15

Specific prejudices toward particular minorities.

	Reproducibility	Scalability
Hometown Negro—First series of questions		
Respondents with contact	.94	.79
Respondents without contact	.96	.84
Hometown Negro—Second series of questions		
Respondents with contact	.94	.77
Respondents without contact	.97	.85
Hometown Jewish		
Respondents with contact	.92	.63
Respondents without contact	.91	.67
Southport Negro—First series of questions		
Respondents with contact	.95	.83
Respondents without contact	.94	.81
Southport Negro—Second series of questions		
Respondents with contact	.98	.92
Respondents without contact	.95	.84
Southport Jewish—First series of questions		
Respondents with contact	.92	.77
Respondents without contact	.91	.67
Southport Jewish—Second series of questions		
Respondents with contact	.98	.88
Respondents without contact	.98	.87
Valley City Negro—First series of questions		
Respondents with contact	.93	.72
Respondents without contact	.95	.77
Valley City Negro—Second series of questions		
Respondents with contact	.96	.83
Respondents without contact	.97	.87
Valley City Mexican—First series of questions		
Respondents with contact	.94	.72
Respondents without contact	.97	.87
Valley City Mexican—Second series of questions		
Respondents with contact	.97	.85
Respondents without contact	.97	.87

distance prejudice a respondent feels toward one minority, the more likely he is to extend that prejudice to a number of minorities.

Further data can be seen in Table 4.17, which illustrate the relationship in white gentile populations between a generalized expression of outgroup derogation and social-distance feelings toward specific ethnic and racial minorities. Among persons who agree that the United States "would be better off if there were not so many foreigners here," there is a high likelihood of expressed distaste for close social contacts with Negroes, Jews, and Mexican-Americans; among those who disagree, there is a much greater

Table 4.16

Generalizing prejudices.

Number of minorities with whom respondents would find it distasteful to be at a party

Number of situations respondents say would be distasteful re Mexican-Americans	4 to 6	2 to 3	None or 1
4	43	25	—
3	28	39	1
2	25	17	11
1	16	6	34
0	4	7	63
Total cases	(116)	(94)	(109)

Table 4.17

Relationship between prejudice toward foreigners and toward Negroes, Jews, and Mexican-Americans (white gentiles in four cities).

This country would be better off if there were not so many foreigners here.

	Number of Cases	Percentages expressing high social-distance feeling* toward:		
		Negroes	Jews	Mexican-Americans
Hometown				
Agree	(232)	81	72	Not applicable
Disagree	(268)	47	47	
Steelville				
Agree	(94)	82†	Not applicable	Not applicable
Disagree	(182)	62		
Valley City				
Agree	(98)	69	Not applicable	61
Disagree	(206)	29		32
Southport				
Agree	(176)	90	60	Not applicable
Disagree	(100)	65	37	

*The scale of social distance is made up of answers to these four items: "Do you think you would ever find it a little distasteful: (1) to eat at the same table with a _____? (2) to dance with a _____? (3) to go to a party and find that most of the people are _____? (4) to have a _____ marry someone in your family?" These questions were asked concerning Negroes and Jews in Hometown, and in a combined form in Steelville. In Valley City questions were asked concerning Mexican-Americans and Negroes. In Southport, it was necessary to use a different set of items referring to Negroes: "Do you think you would ever find it a little distasteful: (1) to shake hands with a Negro? (2) to sit beside a Negro on a bus? (3) to eat at the same table with a Negro? (4) to have a Negro family living next door to you?"

†Feelings toward Negroes-or-Jews.

frequency of acceptance of such social contacts. Individuals who express antipathy toward the presence of foreigners in this country are significantly more likely to express a different kind of manifest prejudice—social-distance feelings—toward these three particular minorities.

The social-distance prejudices are strongly associated with acceptance of common stereotypes. Persons who agree with the statement, *Generally speaking, Negroes are lazy and ignorant,* are more likely than those who disagree to express distaste for association with Jews [73] and Mexican-Americans. For example, in Hometown the proportions expressing high social distance toward Jews among those who accept the unfavorable stereotype of Negroes is 72 per cent, in contrast to 47 per cent among persons who reject the stereotype.

An especially interesting comparison can be made from the relationship between prejudices in two communities in the case of attitudes toward Mexican-Americans. In Valley City there are large numbers of Mexican-Americans; in Southport, none or almost none. In both Valley City and Southport, the white respondents were presented with the stereotyped statement, "Generally speaking Mexicans are shiftless and dirty," and were asked to agree or disagree with it. (Incidentally, respondents typically did not differentiate between "Mexicans" and "Mexican-Americans.") The results are shown in Table 4.18. As expected, social-distance feelings

Table 4.18

Relationship between social-distance feelings toward Negroes and attitude concerning Mexican-Americans.

Generally speaking, Mexicans are shiftless and dirty.

	Valley City	Southport
	Percentages high in social distance toward Negroes	
Agree	65 (119)	85 (134)
Disagree	39 (184)	60 (36)

toward Negroes are stronger among those respondents who accepted the stereotype of Mexicans. What is perhaps more striking is the fact that the level of both types of prejudice against both minorities is higher in Southport than in Valley City. The proportion accepting the anti-Mexican stereotype in Valley City, where Mexicans do live, is only 37 per cent, whereas in Southport, where most respondents could not have had any contact with Mexicans, the stereotype is endorsed by 79 per cent. Among both those who agree and those who disagree the proportion rejecting social contact with Negroes is higher in Southport. It seems likely that in Southport the

---

[73] Cf. E. T. Protho, "Ethnocentrism and Anti-Negro Attitudes in the Deep South," *Journal of Abnormal and Social Psychology,* XLVII (1952), 105-8.

widespread acceptance of racist stereotypes and attitudes concerning Negroes is so strong and generalized that Mexicans are readily assimilated to the negative images held concerning Negroes. Thus, there is an important degree of generalization of prejudice across minority groups and across different aspects of prejudice (social distance versus stereotypes).

Just as in the majority group, there are positive correlations in the minority group among different specific prejudices. As we shall see more specifically in Chapter 8, a considerable proportion of Negroes manifest prejudices toward white persons. For Valley City and Southport we have two sets of comparable data from 515 Negroes: (1) a three-item social-distance score concerning whites; and (2) a three-item index of prejudice toward other ethnic outgroups, consisting of (a) *This country would be better off if there were not so many foreigners here,* (b) *Generally speaking, Mexicans are shiftless and dirty,* and (c) *Do you think you would ever find it a little distasteful to go to a party and find that most of the people are Jewish?* [74] The data show a significantly frequent association of antiwhite prejudice with antiminority prejudice (P < 0.001; C = 0.31).[75]

Furthermore, Negroes who reject a variety of outgroups also tend to accept negative stereotypes and criticisms of Negroes. Prejudice generalizes to the person's own group, even when indices of authoritarianism are held constant. [76]

The very data that demonstrate this generalized aspect of prejudice also show that every particular item indexing prejudice has more than one component. A person holding negative stereotypes concerning one ethnic category will tend to stereotype all other categories, but to varying degrees. Part of the variation is attributable to different ethnic objects. Another part is attributable to the aspect of dimension—whether stereotype, liking-disliking, social distance, advocacy of civil rights, or something else.

Between stereotypes on the one side and decisions concerning concrete actions on the other, stand intervening motives, values, and beliefs. For

---

[74] P = probability that the observed result would occur by chance.

   C = contingency coefficient.

[75] These and the related data have been analyzed by Donald L. Noel in an unpublished paper, "Generalized Prejudice and Group Identification among Negroes" (1962), pp. 1-11 (personal communication from the author).

[76] Our findings do not take into account perceived similarities and differences in beliefs as between the respondents and the ethnic and racial categories to which they referred their attitudes. Rokeach has found that: ". . . with belief held constant, the greater the rejection of Negroes [by whites], the greater also the rejection of whites; the greater the rejection of gentiles (by Jewish children), the greater also the rejection of Jews. Prejudice toward a specific outgroup takes on a new significance when it is seen to be but a special case of a more general misanthropy, which often includes one's own group . . . the misanthropy . . . takes the external form of rejection only in the case of those who disagree with the misanthropist." (*The Open and Closed Mind,* p. 392)

instance, judgments of public policy about school desegregation would never be perfectly predictable from the acceptance or rejection of stereo-typed beliefs concerning Negroes. The stereotypes represent beliefs that have been learned from the teachings and examples of persons who were early objects of identification, the pressures of social conformity, the defense of vested interests, the defense of self-commitments, and so on.

Stereotyped beliefs and images tend to be unchecked by the complex considerations involved in real-life decisions. A study of attitudes toward desegregation among white males in North Carolina has shown that low-income and uneducated persons and those with no children have the highest degree of opposition to desegregation. Apart from differences in acceptance of stereotypes, persons least willing to accept desegregation seemed to lack the intervening values and perspectives which moderated the attitudes of the less resistant individuals.[77]

Prejudice: a summary. Our data, then, indicate that prejudices consist of sets of interwoven attitudes and opinions that often are not clearly formulated. Most individuals can be considered more or less prejudiced. These prejudices are expressed most frequently in situations where no minority persons are present, and, although the expression may have been precipitated by some concrete situation of intergroup relations, it is primarily a response to interaction with *ingroup* members. Unless these responses are later directed into intergroup action, they remain nonfunctional or disengaged.

Under certain circumstances, persons in authority or leadership positions will make the disengaged prejudice reactions of a number of people the basis for decisions in concrete intergroup situations. But it is often surprising, as we shall see in more detail in Chapter 9, how little the disengaged prejudice of rank-and-file individuals affects the concrete intergroup situations in which they find themselves. The generalized, disengaged prejudice may be analogous in many instances to the attitudes and opinions of a consumer about the cost of living, which may have almost no effect on his day-to-day transactions in buying goods. Disengaged prejudice may have been considered the cause of many situations in which it has actually had little to do with the course of events. This is not necessarily true of the strong, fully engaged prejudices involved in real situations.

---

[77] See Melvin M. Tumin, "Imaginary vs. Real Children: Some Southern Views on Desegregation," *School and Society,* LXXXVI, No. 2138 (October 11, 1958), 357-60.

CHAPTER 5

PERSONALITY

AND PREJUDICE

We have already seen that prejudice is a complex term. The connotations of the word personality are even more numerous and diffuse. The research using the two concepts is difficult to summarize in the form of concise and definite conclusions. The task will be eased by clarifying a few points first.

THE RELATIONSHIP BETWEEN PERSONALITY AND SOCIAL INTERACTION

The hazards of imperialism and isolationism in the behavioral sciences

So far we have treated intergroup attitudes with little acknowledgment that the attitudes are held and expressed as part of the personality systems of distinct individuals. Too easy is the tendency to conceive of individuals as ". . . interchangeable specimens of gutless creatures, devoid of sensation, perception, motivation, and emotion and innocent of susceptibility to conflict"; [1] and we were alert to this danger from the beginning of the studies. We wished, rather, to see culture, personality, and social systems as interdependent and interpenetrating, even though each could be analyzed independently.

There has been a temptation, to which many have succumbed, to interpret intergroup relations exclusively in either psychological or sociological terms and to deny the importance, even the relevance, of the other factors. It is true that theories of intergroup relations which dispense with either psychological or sociological variables are conceivable and sometimes legitimate. But the sociological theory that *denies* the relevance of psychological factors cannot connect the social and cultural systems with personality, and the purely "psychological" theory has no systematic stimulus field and no direct account of the processes of collectivities as real systems, in contrast to processes that occur in individuals.

Personality and society—two sides of the same coin?

The platitude is unquestionable that social behavior is a function both of the immediate situation of action and of the prior organization of personality. But, which particular aspects of personality remain fixed, and to what extent do others vary under specific circumstances? Some personalities are so rigidly fixed in repetitive forms of thought, feeling, and behavior as to be relatively impervious to ordinary variations in social situations. On the other hand, some personalities are highly sensitive and reactive to very fine nuances of the behavior of others. We cannot expect a useful, simple, and universal answer to the ill-advised question: is personality or social situation the more important in explaining prejudice?

Personality, as here considered, is the system of relatively enduring psychological states "carried" in an individual. Much of the patterning of perception and motivation in any personality will have derived from social experience, and nearly all of the beliefs and values will have been so derived. This does not mean that society and personality are two sides of the same coin. This cliché must be decisively rejected. Men are needful animals, and personality has forceful and urgent demands and resistances that are not fully compatible with the demands of society. Conversely, social systems are never mere plastic expressions of the desires of individuals. But personality systems and social systems do interpenetrate in the most profound way.

Hostile people. The motivational processes that constitute the dynamic aspects of personality systems always are interdependent with the cultural

---

[1] Theodore M. Newcomb, "Sociology and Psychology," in *For a Science of Social Man,* John Gillin, ed. (New York: The Macmillan Company, 1954), p. 237.

content that is "learned" largely through social interaction. For example, our community studies found many persons whose characteristic orientation to others might be termed "moralistic condemnation." This is evidenced by harsh criticism and advocacy of severe punishment for alleged deviants from the norms of right behavior. Such persons hold categorical and rigid conceptions of right and wrong conduct. Their central belief-systems derive in part from childhood learning from parents, teachers, and religious authorities. At the same time, we have observed that the psychological energy suffusing their angry, bitter, or peevish condemnations often represents an uneasy alliance between a harsh superego and the hostility deriving from the deprivations and injuries of socialization and the continuing exactations of the resulting superego functions.

Again, it is not mysterious that in intergroup relations individuals may express needs and demands that arose in family or other contexts not involving intergroup relations. Chronic rage reactions resulting from failure to solve early developmental crises in relations to parents may be inhibited in later ingroups but may erupt when a vulnerable outgroup object is available.[2] A person who feels threatened by and hostile toward every person who appears in his environment will be antagonistic toward members of minority groups; he "reserves the right to hate anyone regardless of race, creed, or national origin." And the tendency toward antagonism, so clear in its extreme degree, is equally understandable in lesser degrees. Differential readiness to react with hostility, aversion, or withdrawal in interpersonal contacts seems indisputable; individuals, then, with different personality predispositions have varying susceptibilities to prejudices and differing propensities to discriminatory and conflictful behavior toward outgroups.

Uniqueness of individuals. Individual differences in readiness to accept stereotypes, to express hostility, to discriminate, and so on, are thus to be expected. In the details of expression, and in the role of prejudice in the psychic economy of the individual, each personality must be understood as a specific, unique system. The understanding of the nuances of prejudice in a particular personality may require intensive clinical study.

People are incredibly complex in their inner life, in their perceptions, in their experiences of meaning and emotion. But they are not so complex as to prevent us from generalizing about their overt behavior in response to gross patterns of stimuli.

The learning of concepts. For present purposes we are interested in

---

[2] For example: "There is evidence that some personalities develop self-generating cycles of hate as a result of early traumatic incidents occurring which are elaborated at the Oedipal and adolescent phases of development." Harold D. Lasswell, "The Selective Effect of Personality on Political Participation," in *Studies in the Scope and Method of "The Authoritarian Personality,"* R. Christie and M. Jahoda, eds. (New York: The Free Press of Glencoe, Inc., 1954), p. 210.

conduct, that is, motivated behavior that is conceptualized and value laden. Although this conduct is influenced by physiological and other conditions, all useful definitions grant it conceptual and directional components. If the prejudice we are discussing is not sheer "reflexive" hostility, it must be a mode of personality organization. Intergroup prejudice represents a very complex and abstract conceptualization of persons.

Both prejudice and personality, then, are aspects of the processes by which behavior becomes repetitive and organized. The essence of any definition of society is that patterned conduct exists. "Every man must categorize his fellows in order to interact with them." [3]

The earliest models and mentors are few and are predictable in status: father, mother, siblings, neighborhood and school groups of peers. Since typically like marries like, socially and culturally, the child first learns from a culturally homogeneous group. The family unit is treated as a social unit, and the definition of the child by others is in terms of his status in the family. In homogeneous play groups, the child continues his education in group relations.

So, the child learns an ingroup culture, and, whatever his personality structure, he learns definite codes about when, where, how, and against whom one may legitimately, and/or with impunity, aggress. This is a crucial point at which social structure and personality must be related. For neither learning nor aggression tells the social sources of negative prejudgments and sentiment-structures nor what objects will be "selected" for prejudice and discrimination. Recent studies in Brazil, the classic land of alleged racial amity in the Americas, find a high frequency of personalities who perceive their fellows as hostile and unpredictably violent (although the actual frequency of violence is low). There appears to be a widespread tendency to project repressed hostility to others.[4] But aggression is highly controlled and generally is not directed along racial lines.

Objects must be identified before they can be loved or hated, and they are defined by concepts. The learning of concepts means, in one aspect, the learning of *classifications.* And since concepts are social products, ". . . when the child learns classifications he learns modes of response that are common to the groups in which he has membership." [5] Thus, theories that analyze prejudice in the language of personality processes need not be incompatible with those that account for it in terms of culture and social structure, provided the two are not used as exclusive approaches. Some

---

[3] Nelson N. Foote, "Identification as the Basis for a Theory of Motivation," *American Sociological Review,* XVI, No. 1 (February, 1951), 17.

[4] Bernard C. Rosen, "Socialization and Achievement Motivation in Brazil," *American Sociological Review,* XXVII, No. 5 (October, 1962), 616.

[5] Karl Schluessler and Anselm Strauss, "A Study of Concept Learning by Scale Analysis," *American Sociological Review,* XV, No. 6 (December, 1950), 752.

research questions can be handled reasonably well within the schema of personality, with little attention to cultural or social factors, for example, the relation of outgroup stereotypes to the intensity and quality of ingroup identification. Some questions can be treated with reasonable adequacy in terms of social structure, with little reference to intrapsychic variables, for example, the patterning of intermarriage in relation to assimilation and cultural sub-superordination.

Prejudice a result of personality abnormality? In the process of socialization, the developing personality acquires a sensitivity to the values and expectancies of an ingroup and learns to differentiate between that ingroup and outgroups. If the ingroup is homogeneous and the larger culture supports stereotyped conceptions of certain social categories, then "prejudice" becomes a "normal" personality component. The fanatical bigot may be neurotic or psychotic, and his prejudice may be the vehicle for dealing with deep emotional disturbance—but so may hand-washing, anti-Red crusades, claustrophobia, *ad infinitum*. If there are neurotic and nonneurotic bigots, there are also neurotic and nonneurotic people who are tolerant. The prejudice of conformity is not necessarily the active prejudicial hostility of the true bigot.[6]

Consistency of personality. We know, further, that behavior in real situations is very imperfectly predictable from test responses such as the indorsement of verbal stereotypes in an interview. If human beings tend toward self-consistency, this would be manifested when they are asked about their opinions. Such testimony is typically highly organized. But the consistency and continuity of personality are in part phenomena of values and concepts rather than of concrete behavior. Were this not so, behavior would be hopelessly rigid, for the "same" pattern of action has different meanings and carries different values in different situations.

The organized pattern of the personality may be impeccably clear and self-consistent. But we call it psychotic unless the person can accept the disturbances introduced by other personalities interacting with the individual in concrete situations. Unless paranoia is our model, we *expect* both behavioral variability and considerable looseness in the organizations of the personality as a system of values. For all these and other reasons, trait psychology is little help in this area, no more than in criminology where the net result of numerous studies is failure to demonstrate a consistent relation between specific traits and criminality.[7] The regularities that we call "personality" are not to be deduced from a fixed list of specific needs or predispositions.

---

[6] Percy Black, "White-Negro Relations: A Different Slant," *Rural Sociology,* XIV, No. 3 (September, 1949), 261-62.

[7] Karl F. Schluessler and Donald R. Cressey, "Personality Characteristics of Criminals," *American Journal of Sociology,* LV (March, 1950), 476-84.

Social responsiveness. Social action, then, is not simply an unfolding of personality traits. It is oriented to the reactions of others and their sensibilities, judgments, and feelings. Thus, social action is both more and less than the action that would follow from personality dispositions alone. It is *more* because it represents additional psychological elements and organizations of elements induced by orientation to the social object. It is *less* because some tendencies are not acted upon.

Men usually are to some degree socially responsive. Indeed, the person who is completely impervious to the demands and expectations of others is regarded as possessed, insane, sick, or criminal, monstrous, and the like. Unless a person is responsive to the demands and expectations of *some* others, regardless of his momentary impulses and moods, he does not "perform his role" in the interrelations that constitute social life.

Thus we see that persons of different personality dispositions can be induced to act in similar ways, and persons of similar personality dispositions can be moved to act in different ways, by the presence and activity of others, or even by the remembered and anticipated judgments of others. To be sure, individuals differ greatly in extent and manner of social responsiveness (and responsibility). These differences are of very great importance. But the crucial fact remains that responsiveness is a basic normative requirement that is inculcated in children from earliest days in all societies and that is continuously demanded from other people. Personality needs and social requirements do not have to coincide exactly.

Therefore a pattern of intergroup relations is not necessarily a function of the personality needs of the population, and some system different from the one that exists might be equally compatible with the personality dispositions, or at least tolerable without major changes in personality structure or function.

It follows that *extensive changes in systems of group relations do not necessarily involve extensive changes in the basic personality dispositions of the members of the society who have formerly conformed to the* status quo ante.

This conclusion may appear now to be obvious. It has not been obvious in all cases to persons who have written on the subject of change in intergroup relations. Nor have its implications been fully incorporated into either behavioral theory or social policy and public action in this field. More will be said about this subject in Chapters 8 through 10.

AUTHORITARIANISM AND ETHNOCENTRISM

All discussions of the scientific problems of personality and prejudice since 1950 have had to take into account the data and formulations of *The*

Authoritarian Personality.[8] Here we shall review that work's contentions and main findings in relation to our investigations.

The general thesis of *The Authoritarian Personality* is well known: that persons who hold negative stereotypes and attitudes concerning racial, ethnic, or religious groups other than their own tend to differ from nonprejudiced persons in a whole syndrome or cluster of personality characteristics. In particular these "authoritarian" personalities not only idealize social authority and strict discipline but also are especially likely to show general stereotypy, conventionalism, superstition, concern for social status, rigid moral judgments, a tendency to feel admiration for strength and contempt for weakness, a tendency to divide people into "good" versus "bad," repression and denial of unacceptable wishes, projection, underlying hostility and distrust of other people, and a view of the world as basically threatening, chaotic, or irrational.

Studies on frustration and aggression

Studies by several researchers of the relation of frustration to aggression early provided data congruent with the search for a personality syndrome conducive to prejudice. The problem was posed by the publication of *Frustration and Aggression* in 1939.[9] It was early established that aggressive behavior often follows, immediately or in a delayed manner, upon the experiencing of frustration; but, also, aggression does *not* occur in all instances. The frequency with which an aggressive response will be elicited and the form and direction that it will take cannot be predicted without a knowledge of variables other than the intensity of the frustrating stimulus. Dollard and his associates had originally hypothesized that the appearance of aggression would depend upon the strength of the frustrated goal-response on one hand, and the anticipated punishment for aggression on the other. It was subsequently suggested [10] that the strength of instigation to aggression toward the frustrating agent would vary with different kinds of agents. Furthermore, it was found that the arbitrary or nonarbitrary nature of the imposed frustrating situation could be a significant factor: Pastore [11] found a greater frequency of aggressive responses in arbitrary than in nonarbitrary situations.

---

[8] T. W. Adorno, Else Frenkel-Brunswik, Daniel J. Levinson, R. Nevitt Sanford, *et al.* (New York: Harper & Row, Publishers, 1950).

[9] J. Dollard, L. W. Doob, N. E. Miller, O. H. Mowrer, and R. R. Sears (New Haven, Conn.: Yale University Press, 1939).

[10] F. K. Graham, W. A. Charwat, A. S. Honig, and P. C. Weltz, "Aggression as a Function of the Attack and the Attacker," *Journal of Abnormal and Social Psychology*, XLVI, No. 4 (October, 1951), 512-20.

[11] N. Pastore, "The Role of Arbitrariness in the Frustration-Aggression Hypothesis," *Journal of Abnormal and Social Psychology*, XLVII, No. 3 (July, 1952), 728-31.

Based upon these earlier studies, Arthur R. Cohen's research [12] dealt with three major independent variables: (1) arbitrary versus nonarbitrary frustration, (2) authority figures versus peers as the frustrating agent, (3) "ideal" response ("socially acceptable or socially circumscribed") versus "what one would actually do regardless of social norms." [13] Greater frequency of aggression was indicated (1) for "actual" responses rather than "ideal"; (2) in arbitrary rather than nonarbitrary situations; (3) when the agent of frustration was a peer rather than an authority figure.

Although the conditions of the experiment, including selection of subjects, suggest caution in generalizing to other situations, the study points to the need to take into account the variables it attempted to manipulate. It seems reasonable to suppose that aggression will generally be less frequent and overt when its expression is contrary to major social norms. Likewise, it is in accord with our wider knowledge of social behavior to expect that situations of frustration that are not considered to be reasonable in terms of commonly accepted cultural standards will cause more frequent and overt aggression than will situations regarded as fair or unavoidable or normal. And the differential reactions to authority figures and to peers are expectable either on the assumption that authority figures are regarded as more likely to punish, or that they more powerfully stimulate guilt feelings, or both.

On the other hand, the rank-order in importance of the three variables in determining frequency and/or intensity of aggressive responses remains uncertain, as Cohen was careful to indicate. In particular, it appears that the experimental manipulation gave only a very weak value to the variable of authority, in comparison with the weight it often carries in "real-life" situations; the negative sanctions of the authority figures imaginable by the subjects probably could not well simulate the severity of real sanctions. In much the same way, the "arbitrariness" that might be found tolerable without increased aggression may differ between hypothetical situations of a questionnaire and the experienced situations; [14] for example, logical consistency is more likely to result in the questionnaire. Finally, the normative restraints against the expression of aggression may be much more variable—towards both extreme laxity and extreme severity—in real situations.

As experimental studies refined and qualified the preliminary ideas about

---

[12] "Social Norms, Arbitrariness of Frustration, and Status of the Agent of Frustration in the Frustration-Aggression Hypothesis," *Journal of Abnormal and Social Psychology,* LI, No. 2 (September, 1955), 222-26.

[13] *Ibid.,* 222.

[14] Cf. Philip Worchel, "Hostility: Theory and Experimental Investigation," in *Decisions, Values and Groups,* Dorothy Willner, ed. (New York: Pergamon Press, 1960): The author says on p. 255: "People accept obstacles to goal-directed behavior without aggressive behavior or any other sign of hostility when the obstacles are perceived as reasonable in terms of the individual's value system."

the connections between frustration and aggression, clarification of the basic concepts was sought in several different bodies of psychological theory.

New approaches in psychoanalysis that emphasized the need to understand ego functions also questioned the idea that aggression blindly follows frustration. As Erikson put it (in the same year *The Authoritarian Personality* was published):

> Here we must qualify . . . the statement which summarized the first impact of psychoanalytic enlightenment on this country—namely, that frustration leads to aggression. Man, in the service of a faith, can stand meaningful frustration. Rather, we should say that exploitation leads to fruitless rage: exploitation being the total social context which gives a specific frustration its devastating power. Exploitation exists where a divided function is misused by one of the partners involved in such a way that for the sake of his pseudoaggrandizement he deprives the other partner of whatever sense of identity he had achieved, of whatever faith in integrity he had approached. The loss of mutuality which characterizes such exploitation eventually destroys the common function and the exploiter himself.[15]

Furthermore, the distinction between aggression and hostility,[16] which had sometimes become blurred, was revived and sharpened in the more recent research. It was again emphasized that one may be hostile without being aggressive, or aggressive without being hostile. Hostile behavior is not merely overtly different from aggressive behavior; it is psychologically different:

> There are changes in the perception of the field, widespread physiological involvements, interference with complex learning, and an affectual component of hate . . . it is suggested that we reserve the term "aggression" to include any attempt to remove a frustration directly for the sole purpose of attaining the original goal-object. Hostility will then refer to some postulated need-condition whose primary object is injury to the frustrating agent.[17]

One gradually becomes impressed with the frequency with which aggression emerges when people are frightened, and the frequency with which hostility follows when people feel threatened by some individual or group. Our own observations would support McNeil's conclusion:

> We have come to know of the intimate connection between fear and aggression and have learned never to deal with one without the other. We have discovered that the most usual error is that of underestimating the fear component in aggressive acts.[18]

---

[15] Erik H. Erikson, *Childhood and Society* (New York: W. W. Norton & Company, Inc., 1950), p. 373.

[16] Cf. Robin M. Williams, Jr., *The Reduction of Intergroup Tensions* (New York: Social Science Research Council, 1947), pp. 42-43, 51-54.

[17] Worchel, *op. cit.,* p. 257.

[18] Elton B. McNeil, "Personal Hostility and International Aggression," *Journal of Conflict Resolution,* V, No. 3 (September, 1961), 288.

When flight is difficult, a frequent response to fear is to mobilize to attack the perceived source of threat. Insecure populations pervaded with fear are readily rendered hostile.

If we now combine our psychological and sociological insights, we can suggest a plausible scheme for describing how frustration occurs and how it can (when it does occur) lead through specific intermediary steps to chronic hostility and/or to aggressive action. Its main components are as follows:

1. There is a strong need, whether based on a particular biological drive or socially induced.

2. There are socially shared norms and values (conceptions of what is desirable) that the individual incorporates into his own personality. These are then internalized standards of what it is right to expect, what one deserves to get ("proper" rewards or punishments), what one should do or must do (rights, duties, obligations, privileges). Thus, he will have emotionally important ideas about how others should treat him and how he should treat others.

3. The person is repeatedly and persistently deprived and thwarted over a considerable period of time with regard to important needs and goal-strivings, the satisfactions of which he regards as normal and morally justifiable.

4. He feels these frustrations to be unnecessary and avoidable.

5. He perceives the deprivations and blockings as a threat to his survival and integrity; he feels them as affecting essential parts of the personality, not just peripheral desires or impulses.

6. He feels these illegitimate frustrations, constituting dangerous threats, with special force if the chronic assault, the siege of frustration, is occasionally highlighted by unpredictable episodes, irregular periods of legitimate .satisfaction, or plausible promises of a better future.

7. The individual is very likely to take action to try to reduce frustration by altering the external situation.

8. If these efforts are blocked, the person will tend to become hostile.

9. If he is hostile and finds himself prevented from effectively reducing his initial frustrations, he will very likely seek to injure, to aggress against, vulnerable social objects which he can define as (a) plausible sources of frustration or threat and (b) outside of or deviant from the main value system he accepts as ideal.

10. The result indicated in number 9, however, is one of many possible modes of response. Its probability of occurrence is affected by specific personality structure and dynamics, for example, the strength of ego controls, the individual's favored modes of defense. The intensity of hostility is im-

portant: such surging hatred may exist that almost *any* target in the immediate environment may become the object of aggression.[19]

11. The direction of hostile feelings and aggressive behavior depends upon (*a*) the cultural definition (for example, ethnic stereotypes) of vulnerable and accessible objects and (*b*) the social networks of interaction, the kinds of social sanctions in force, and the norms of social interaction.

In any case, the vicissitudes of growing up and making one's way in society impose many frustrations upon nearly everyone. Much frustration is accepted without arousal of hostility. Even when hostility is instigated, many responses to it do not take the form of aggression.[20] When aggression does occur, it is not always directed toward social objects. But there surely is much daily activation and reactivation of hostility, and much of it, in societies containing culturally identified outgroups, can take the form of prejudice. Is there then a kind (or kinds) of personality that is especially likely to be prejudiced? It was the great merit of *The Authoritarian Personality* to take this question seriously and to study it intensively.

Studies on authoritarian personalities

The study from which the book came relied for its characterizations of personality both upon intensive clinical evaluations of extreme cases of prejudiced and nonprejudiced persons, and upon larger numbers of cases in which persons responded to questionnaires containing, among many other things, the famous F-scale (Fascism-scale). The latter was the measure that many readers of the book later came to call "authoritarianism," apparently by some vague association with the title of the study. An enormous research literature quickly emerged—by the end of 1956 at least 230 publications dealt with authoritarianism.[21] These studies and those appearing since have almost invariably confirmed the existence of a significant positive association between F-scale scores and ethnic prejudice. The interpretation of this fact requires caution.

First, we must not assume that an expressed opinion necessarily reflects

---

[19] It will never do to overlook the stark actuality of hate. It is easy to ignore its well-camouflaged presence in "normal" people, and to underestimate its force even in severely "maladjusted" persons. For vivid descriptions of hostility in disturbed children, see Fritz Redl and David Wineman, *Children Who Hate* (New York: The Free Press of Glencoe, Inc., 1951).

[20] But: "Owing to their content, prevailing social prejudices would appear to be especially attractive to persons who use projection as a way of precluding the perception of their consciously unacceptable motives." [Irving Sarnoff, "Psychoanalytic Theory and Social Attitudes," *Public Opinion Quarterly*, XXIV, No. 2 (Summer, 1960), 272.]

[21] R. Christie and P. Cook, "A Guide to the Published Literature Relating to Authoritarian Personality Through 1956," *Journal of Psychology*, XLV, Second Half (April, 1958), 171-99.

deep-seated psychological trends or processes. It may be just a learned, culturally conventional response. Or it may reflect an accurate judgment of
social and psychological reality in some particular stratum or subculture
within our society.

Different psychological states are distributed in a nonrandom, patterned
way within the social system. Thus, many studies show a systematic association between socioeconomic position, no matter how measured, and various
psychological conditions or variables.[22] The large-scale Midtown Study of
mental health in New York City (using a sample of 1,660 individuals)
secured psychiatric evaluations of symptoms reported in interviews. Generalized anxiety symptoms were inferred in about three-fourths of the cases
in each level of socioeconomic status. But every other major constellation
of symptoms was found to be most prevalent in the lower classes and least
prevalent in the upper class. Among these symptom constellations were
rigidity, suspiciousness, depression, hypochondriasis, alcoholism, immatu-
rity, neurasthenia, withdrawal, and passive dependency.[23] And there is consistent evidence from a number of studies that low education tends to be
associated with authoritarian responses. For example, here are differences
in responses from persons of different educational levels as found in national samples surveyed by the National Opinion Research Center.[24]

	College (217)	High School (545)	Grammar School (504)
N =			
Agree that:			
The most important thing to teach children is absolute obedience to their parents.	35%	60%	80%
Prison is too good for sex criminals. They should be publicly whipped or worse.	18%	31%	45%
Believe that most people can be trusted.	77%	70%	52%

[22] ". . . social class has proved to be so useful a concept because it refers to more
than simply educational level, or occupational position, or any of the large number
of correlated variables. It is so useful because it captures the reality that the intricate interplay of all these variables creates different basic conditions of life at different levels of the social order. Members of different social classes, by virtue of
enjoying (or suffering) different conditions of life, come to see the world differently—to develop different conceptions of social reality, different aspirations and
hopes and fears, different conceptions of the desirable." [Melvin L. Kohn, "Social
Class and Parent-Child Relationships: An Interpretation," processed paper, National
Institute of Mental Health, Bethesda, Md. (January, 1962), pp. 1-2.]

[23] Thomas A. C. Rennie *et al.,* "Urban Life and Mental Health: Socio-Economic
Status and Mental Disorder in the Metropolis," *The American Journal of Psychiatry,*
CXIII, No. 9 (March, 1957), 834.

[24] Adapted from Hyman and Sheatsley in *Studies in the Scope and Method of
"The Authoritarian Personality,"* R. Christie and M. Jahoda, eds., p. 94.

Authoritarian beliefs, like prejudices against minority groups, are learned. They may reflect deep, irrational personality processes, but they need not in all cases. Indeed, there is the real possibility that *both* authoritarian beliefs and prejudices may be learned in the same way that we learn that the world is round (or flat, or held up on the back of a giant turtle). The association of both prejudices and personality items with formal education forces us to take seriously the possibility that widespread indoctrination, relatively independent of individual psychological needs, may account for at least a considerable part of the correlation of authoritarianism and prejudice.[25] Thus, *both* authoritarianism and prejudice may tend to be characteristic of persons in economically and socially deprived positions in the social structure. And it is indeed true that a large number of studies have consistently shown high negative correlations between authoritarianism and social status and between ethnocentrism and social status.[26]

Another important body of evidence that helps to define the relationship between authoritarian attitudes and ethnic prejudices comes from comparative studies of this relationship in different cultural settings. In our own community studies we were led, as early as 1951, to observe:

> Our general picture of the majority-group population in the communities thus far studied includes a wide range of prejudice, with true bigots at one extreme and nonprejudiced persons at the other, but with a vast middle range in which reside the "gentle people of prejudice." The great majority of prejudiced persons carry prejudice at a low temperature, and much of their discriminatory behavior reflects relatively passive conformity to taken-for-granted patterns prevalent in the social groups which give them their statuses and sense of belonging. They are not paranoid, anti-Semitic fascists, nor obsessive-compulsive fanatics. Nor are they "militant liberals," nor paragons of security and affectional capacity.[27]

Later comparisons among communities and among ethnic groups showed that a high prevalence of authoritarianism did not always go along with a high level of racial prejudice. And in the meantime, other investigators brought forward detailed evidence along the same lines. It was well established that, by any measure used, anti-Negro prejudice is much more frequent in the South than in other regions of the country. At the same time, studies of white Southerners found no evidence of a significantly greater prevalence of authoritarianism, as indicated by F-scores.[28] It was clear also

[25] Cf. *ibid.*, 108-10.
[26] Christie and Cook, "A Guide to the Published Literature Relating to Authoritarian Personality Through 1956," p. 188.
[27] Robin M. Williams, Jr., "Personality and Prejudice: Some Research Notes," paper presented at the meetings of the Eastern Sociological Society, New Haven, Conn., April, 1951, p. 8.
[28] O. Milton, "Presidential Choice and Performance on a Scale of Authoritarianism," *American Psychologist,* VII, No. 10 (October, 1952), 597-98; C. U. Smith and J. W. Prothro, "Ethnic Differences in Authoritarian Personality," *Social Forces,* XXXV, No. 4 (May, 1957), 334-38.

that the relatively low level of anti-Semitism in the South, coexisting with high prevalence of anti-Negro attitudes,[29] did not fit well with the idea that the projective hostility of authoritarians was the central element in ethnic prejudice.

Pettigrew studied four small New England towns in comparison with four small Southern towns, two in the Black Belt (38 per cent and 45 per cent Negro population) and two outside (10 per cent and 18 per cent Negro). In the two Black Belt towns, the white population much more than in the other pair of communities held negative attitudes toward Negroes and toward desegregation. But the two populations were essentially alike in F-scores, and the Southern samples were not more authoritarian than samples from four New England towns, each having less than one per cent Negro population.[30] Furthermore, there was no significant difference between Northern and Southern samples in the size of the correlations between measures of anti-Negro prejudice and the index of authoritarianism. Nor were there differences between North and South in the strong tendency for anti-Negro and anti-Jewish prejudice to be associated. In other words, in both the North and the South there is generalized antiminority prejudice, and this is associated with authoritarianism. But the socially reinforced norms of prejudice in the South are expressed by many nonauthoritarian persons who would be "unprejudiced" in the North. Noteworthy in this connection is the finding that the more tolerant Southerners tended to be deviants from dominant local social patterns—they were more often non-attenders at church, independent voters, downwardly mobile in occupational status, veterans, and relatively well educated.[31]

Since Northerners and Southerners do not differ in their apparent needs to utilize prejudice in the service of expressing personality needs (externalization), the larger number of Southerners holding anti-Negro attitudes indicates that ". . . *sociocultural and social adjustment factors are considerably more important in the South and account for the sharp differences in the regions.*" [32]

This hypothesis was supported also by data from the Union of South Africa. A study of white students at the University of Natal in 1956 showed that a measure of social conformity was positively correlated with anti-African attitudes at about the same level as authoritarianism.[33] More fre-

---

[29] E. T. Prothro, "Ethnocentrism and Anti-Negro Attitudes in the Deep South," *Journal of Abnormal and Social Psychology,* XLVII, No. 1 (January, 1952), 105-8.

[30] Thomas F. Pettigrew, "Regional Differences in Anti-Negro Prejudice," *The Journal of Abnormal and Social Psychology,* LIX, No. 1 (July, 1959), 28-36.

[31] *Ibid.,* 34-35.

[32] *Ibid.,* 35.

[33] Thomas F. Pettigrew, "Personality and Sociocultural Factors in Inter-Group Attitudes: A Cross-National Comparison," *Journal of Conflict Resolution,* II, No. 1 (March, 1958), 29-42.

quent intolerance was found among those students who had been born in Africa, those who preferred the Nationalist Party, and those whose fathers were manual workers—but these categories of students were not disproportionately made up of persons with high F-scale scores. Holding F-scores constant, Afrikaaners more often than English students were prejudiced. Among the 513 English students, a tendency toward generalized outgroup prejudice was demonstrated by the positive correlation of attitude toward any one ethnic group with attitudes towards others. But, significantly, a unique factor of all-white preference was found, apart from generalized prejudice. General attitudes of social distance toward ethnic outgroups were positively associated with the measures of social conformity, authoritarianism, and anti-African prejudice.[34] Once again the findings suggest the conclusion that: "In areas with historically imbedded traditions of racial intolerance, externalizing personality factors underlying prejudice remain important but sociocultural factors are unusually crucial and account for the heightened racial hostility." [35]

The early studies of persons with high F-scale scores noted that among the cluster of attitudes associated with prejudice was a strong concern with the opinions of others, especially in the particular form of conventional judgments of social prestige (status). We now know that an important component of authoritarianism as indexed in the early studies was acquiescence or conformity.[36]

Furthermore, evidence has accumulated to document the fact that the same personality characteristic can produce very different results in different social situations. The resulting differences in social behavior often appear paradoxical to first commonsense impressions, although *psychologically* they are not paradoxical at all. Of many cases in point, a good illustration is provided by a need for affiliation, manifest in desires to be with other people, to communicate with them, to be approved or loved by them, and so on.[37] Assuming these needs to be strong in a particular individual, we might expect him to be especially likely to enter into relationships with individuals regardless of their ethnic or racial category. We might picture such an indi-

---

[34] Thomas F. Pettigrew, "Social Distance Attitudes of South African Students," *Social Forces,* XXXVIII, No. 3 (March, 1960), 246-53.

[35] Pettigrew, "Personality and Sociocultural Factors in Inter-Group Attitudes," p. 40.

[36] There are many studies. Examples: B. M. Bass, "Authoritarianism or Acquiescence," *Journal of Abnormal and Social Psychology,* LI, No. 3 (November, 1955), 616-23; S. Messick and D. N. Jackson, "Authoritarianism or Acquiescence in Bass's Data," *Journal of Abnormal and Social Psychology,* LIV, No. 3 (May, 1957), 424-26; "Reply" by Bass in the same volume, pp. 426-27; N. L. Goge *et al.,* "The Psychological Meaning of Acquiescence Set for Authoritarianism," *Journal of Abnormal and Social Psychology,* LV, No. 1 (July, 1957), 98-103.

[37] Stanley Schachter, *The Psychology of Affiliation: Experimental Studies of the Sources of Gregariousness* (Stanford, Cal.: Stanford University Press, 1959), p. 2.

vidual as warm, communicative, sensitive to the feelings of others—and hence likely to quickly form friendly relations even with persons who initially were defined as outgroup members. But it is very clear that such predictions need not be fulfilled in actual intergroup relations. For the very need for affiliation that might otherwise lead the individual to disregard categorical lines of social distinction, will strongly predispose him to conform to the wishes of members of his own ingroup. If these significant others are prejudiced and evidence disapproval of accepting or of friendly relations with persons defined as outgroup members, our outgoing, affiliative individual may show exclusionistic behavior, and may react with fear (even panic) and hostility to situations entailing intergroup relations.

It is not enough, therefore, to know the strength of a need for affiliation. It is necessary also to know the *cultural definitions* of permissible associates, and the *social boundaries* within which the expression of affiliative needs will bring approval and other rewards rather than negative sanctions.[38] The same conclusion presumably applies to any other postulated psychological need.

Another example would be the case of orientations of trust or suspicion toward other people. *The Authoritarian Personality* suggested basic mistrust as a characteristic of prejudiced people. Later work seems to have generally supported the supposition that this is true—although partly tautological. It seems likely that distrust is indeed a generalized psychological state. People who are suspicious of others expect others to be suspicious of them. Mistrust and misanthropy includes the self. The person who feels himself to be trustworthy is likely to expect other people to trust him, and he is likely to trust others. Just as it is difficult to like other people unless one likes himself, it is difficult to trust others if one actually distrusts his own feelings and impulses. Both trust and liking express a system of beliefs and values relating one person to another. There is a tendency for people to be trustworthy who are trusting of others, and for those who are suspicious of others to be themselves untrustworthy.[39]

At the same time, the extent of trust is in part a function of the actual social environment in which the individual has to live. To many low-income persons our society is *in fact* something approaching a merciless jungle. There are areas in our great cities in which too much trust will get you killed. The degree of trusting behavior that is viable in everyday life in

---

[38] Levon H. Melikian, "Authoritarianism and its Correlates in the Egyptian Culture and in the United States," *The Journal of Social Issues*, XV, No. 3 (1959), 58-68. Cf. p. 62: "In a culture that is patriarchal and authoritarian like that of the Middle East, choice of friends is in general restricted to members within the extended family."

[39] Cf. for experimental evidence: Morton Deutsch, "Trust, Trustworthiness, and the F Scale," *Journal of Abnormal and Social Psychology*, LXI, No. 1 (July, 1960), 138-40.

urban America is certainly far short of completely believing everything one is told or of accepting everyone's behavior at face value. The completely gullible person is at best the object of pity; at worst he will be destroyed by his unrealistic failure to distinguish between people who can be trusted and those who cannot.

We have said that there is every reason to accept the contention that authoritarianism, of the kind that is indexed by the F-scale, tends to enhance the likelihood of ethnic prejudice. But neither the authoritarian syndrome nor other related personality tendencies invariably constitute either a necessary or sufficient set of conditions for prejudice, much less discriminatory behavior.[40]

This is an important contention, and we have specified some of the grounds for believing it to be true.

In the first place, there is not a necessary invariant set of functional *psychological* relationships among the various components of the authoritarian syndrome. Authoritarians usually have much repressed hostility and much anxiety concerning their relations with social objects, especially with authority figures. Stereotypy concerning "bad" social objects, with projection of suppressed and repressed desires and impulses (especially sexual and aggressive), is a characteristic mode of defense. But the role of projection may be decisively reduced in certain individuals whose anxiety primarily relates to guilt and to the control of desires unacceptable to the conscience.[41]

The syndrome of personality tendencies found among persons who have high F-scores is a loosely connected cluster of attitudes rather than a precisely defined set of basic dispositions. The lack of psychological homogeneity among authoritarians could be illustrated by any of the traits found among high scorers. As interesting as any, perhaps, is the tendency of the authoritarians to see people and their behavior in terms of sharp moral dichotomies of good versus bad, of virtue versus vice. There is no reason to imagine that moral conformity in overt behavior always corresponds to a single unitary type of conscience. The rigid moralism among highly prejudiced people found in *The Authoritarian Personality* and many subsequent

---

[40] Cf. Hyman and Sheatsley, in R. Christie and M. Jahoda, eds., "The Authoritarian Personality—A Methodological Critique," *Studies in the Scope and Method of "The Authoritarian Personality,"* p. 194: "The relationship between ethnic prejudice and certain aspects of personality appears to be well established. Those persons who view the world as threatening and unpredictable tend to be less tolerant of minority groups than those who are more at ease with their social environment. From a different perspective, those individuals who are characterized by extreme passivity toward the world (depressives) appear to have little hostility toward minority groups. The relationship between personality variables and ethnic prejudice is not simple. . . ."

[41] Cf. R. Gordon, "Personality Dynamics and the Tendency toward Stereotypy," *International Social Science Bulletin,* VI, No. 3 (1954), 575.

studies may reflect one of several possible empirical clusterings of normative sentiments that go to make up distinctly different kinds of consciences.[42]
The cynicism of the fearful, other-directed conformist is very different from
the fanaticism produced by the authoritarian-integral conscience, but both
may result in high F-scores.

The effectiveness of authoritarianism as an indicator of prejudice was
early called into question by Srole's study, which showed that a measure
of psychological anomie ("normlessness," alienation) remained highly correlated with prejudice when F-scores were held constant but that the correlation of prejudice with authoritarianism was largely removed by holding
anomie constant.[43] In short, in Srole's sample it appeared that authoritarianism might be spuriously related to prejudice, through its association with
feelings of alienation, pessimism, lostness, or helplessness in a world seen
to be uncaring and unresponsive. A replication of the study by Roberts and
Rokeach,[44] however, indicated that *both* anomie and authoritarianism remain associated with prejudice when the other variable is controlled; the
correlations with prejudice are: anomie (when authoritarianism is constant)
$= +0.37$; authoritarianism (when anomie is constant) $= +0.53$. Their study
showed that anomie, authoritarianism, and ethnocentrism tend to go together. Each tends to decrease with higher levels of education and income,
but at every level of income or education, the anomic individuals were the
more likely to be ethnocentric.

In a later study, McDill administered to white gentile adults in Nashville,
Tennessee (1957) the five anomie and the five authoritarian items from
Srole's study, which had been repeated in the replication by Roberts and
Rokeach. Responses to these items were examined against responses to
seven of the ten items from the original California ethnocentrism scale. The
correlation between prejudice and anomie is almost identical with that between prejudice and authoritarianism, and the similarity remains when each
independent variable is controlled. The first- and second-order partial correlations between authoritarianism and prejudice and anomie and prejudice are
similar, suggesting a common or underlying factor. Analysis shows that one
factor accounts for 45 per cent of the variance of the items that make up
the three scales. Included in the manifest content of the items comprising
this common factor is self-to-other alienation, a sense of an overwhelming
and threatening world, obedience to authority figures, rigid acceptance of
the *status quo,* and punitiveness toward violations of convention and of

[42] William McCord and Joan McCord, "A Tentative Theory of the Structure of
Conscience," in *Decisions, Values and Groups,* Dorothy Willner, ed., pp. 108-34.

[43] Leo Srole, "Social Dysfunction, Personality, and Social Distance Attitudes,"
paper read before the American Sociological Society, Chicago, 1951.

[44] Alan H. Roberts and Milton Rokeach, "Anomie, Authoritarianism, and Prejudice: A Replication," *American Journal of Sociology,* LXI, No. 4 (January, 1956),
355-58.

obedience. This negative *Weltanschauung* obviously fails, however, to exhaust the variance associated with ethnocentrism. A second factor seems to include optimism and social belongingness—a middle-class sense of well-being, trust and optimism—and is positively associated with those prejudices toward Negroes that involve rights of fairly close physical and social contacts. What is suggested by this finding is that in this Southern population, certain types of racial prejudice are positively associated with a contented acceptance of the *status quo*. Without going into other factors extracted in this analysis, it seems likely that this study has tapped both the negative conformity of authoritarianism and the positive conformity of those who willingly accept an inherited system of racial privilege and segregation.[45]

We have reviewed only a few of the many findings that have elaborated and modified the original formulations of the connections between personality components and ethnic attitudes. We can now examine the Cornell Studies, which, as the reader already may have suspected, have been giving hidden guidance to our review.

As we have said, *the Authoritarian Personality* was published in 1950. The Cornell Studies began in 1948, and most of the surveys using personality items had been conducted by the end of 1952, prior to the later development of more penetrating research methods of scaling and analysis. Many of our data are methodologically primitive. But we have found that many of them have stood up well and even generate fresh perspectives on the problems just reviewed.

THE DATA OF THE CORNELL SURVEYS

Although we did not set out to study psychological processes, many of the interview materials are studded with evidences of connections between expressed prejudices and deeper personal concerns. These materials illustrate, rather than demonstrate, such connections.[46] The community surveys, on the other hand, give many indications that the personality-rooted prejudice arising from emotional disturbance is characteristic only of the ex-

---

[45] Edward L. McDill: "Anomie, Authoritarianism, Prejudice, and Socio-Economic Status: An Attempt at Clarification," *Social Forces*, XXXIX, No. 3 (March, 1961), 239-45.

[46] Nothing we found in the many communities observed and among the many hundreds of persons interviewed suggested that we could reject the view that powerful unconscious processes affect reactions to intergroup relations. We saw much that was rational and much that was moral in those reactions, but we were often reminded that ". . . a dynamically powerful portion of mental life is neither rational nor moral, is adjusted neither to the external world nor to the demands of the community." [Franz Alexander, *Fundamentals of Psychoanalysis* (New York: W. W. Norton and Company, Inc., 1948), p. 17.]

tremes of prejudice and is found primarily in the small minority of the population that can be considered "really bigoted" (although not all bigots are characterized by personality-rooted prejudice). In the cross-sectional community studies, we can place the authoritarian in the social structure. We find in general that he is more likely to be less well educated, in the lower economic strata, and an older person. Although these individuals are disproportionately in the less powerful segments of the community, some of them are in strategic positions to make important decisions.

Subdimensions of authoritarianism

In the Cornell Studies, questionnaires included items that were intended to index authoritarian reactions, and it was indeed possible to show that persons giving the authoritarian responses more often expressed prejudices against minority groups. (See Table 5.1.) Among youths as well as among

Table 5.1

Relationship between authoritarian responses and general prejudice score (Adults, Hometown).

	No Minority Contacts*		One or More Minority Contacts*		Difference
	Per cent on general prejudice score	Number of cases	Per cent on general prejudice score	Number of cases	
Agree with all three authoritarian items†	70	(17)	43	(21)	−27
Agree with two	32	(56)	20	(65)	−12
Agree with one	19	(72)	16	(96)	− 3
Disagree with all three	15	(71)	7	(67)	− 8

*Contact includes any contact at work, in organization, or in neighborhood with a Jew, a Negro, or an Italian-American.
†(1) "I have to struggle for everything I get in life." Agree. (It is believed that agreement with this item reflects a conception of one's personal world as threatening and constraining.)
(2) "The most important thing to teach children is to obey every order their parents give without question even if they think the parents are wrong." (This question seems to elicit the authoritarian emphasis on adherence to discipline.)
(3) "Prison is too good for sex criminals; they should be publicly whipped or worse." (This question indexes extreme punitiveness linked with anxiety about sex.)

adults, authoritarian reactions are positively correlated with prejudice. (See Table 5.2.)

Under the broad term "authoritarian personality," however, we felt there were being grouped together a number of different reactions that might represent subdimensions of authoritarianism. Analysis of the items initially taken as indexes of the authoritarian syndrome showed three subdimensions,

Table 5.2

Relationship between authoritarian responses of youths and their social-distance feelings (High School Youths, Hometown).

	Male	Female
	(Per cent high on distasteful score)	
How much do you feel that other people can be trusted?		
Almost all can be trusted	49% (334)	39% (378)
Most can be trusted	56% (675)	47% (750)
Most can<u>not</u> be trusted	68% (59)	65% (60)
How often do you feel hurt by the things other people do to you?		
Often	66% (96)	50% (207)
Sometimes	55% (475)	49% (653)
Hardly ever	51% (494)	30% (303)
Children should obey every order their parents give without question, even if they think their parents are wrong. Do you agree or disagree?		
Agree	62% (314)	52% (347)
Disagree	51% (746)	44% (812)
How often do you feel that other people pick on you unfairly?		
Often	55% (56)	60% (63)
Sometimes	49% (406)	53% (468)
Hardly ever	50% (606)	40% (635)
How often do your parents object to the kind of companions you go around with?		
Often	60% (82)	61% (76)
Sometimes	59% (293)	54% (314)
Hardly ever	51% (696)	41% (780)

within each of which the items fit the Guttman-scale model.[47] The three scales will not themselves form a single scale. Description of the separate attitudes thus identified now follows.

The jungle reaction. Some persons look upon the world as a jungle in which each person is pitted against the others in the struggle to survive. Various students of personality have commented on the "jungle outlook" of certain prejudiced, neurotic, or authoritarian types [48] to whom ". . . the

---

[47] We are indebted to Pauline Moller Mahar for this analysis of the components of authoritarianism. Fuller treatment is given in her unpublished Ph.D. thesis, "Dimensions of Personality as Related to Dimensions of Prejudice in a Survey of a Northeastern City, 1955" (Cornell University).

[48] Karen Horney, *Our Inner Conflicts* (New York: W. W. Norton & Company, Inc., 1945).

world is a hazardous place in which men are basically evil and dangerous." [49] In the community surveys, the jungle outlook was indexed by the following items:

1. *Some say you can't be too careful in your dealing with people, while others say that most people can be trusted. From your own experience, which would you agree with most?*

2. *How often do you find yourself feeling bitter about the way things turned out for you—would you say often, sometimes, or hardly ever?*

3. *I have to struggle for everything I get in life. Do you agree or disagree?*

Reactions of moralistic condemnation. Many persons display an outraged conventional moralism. They express strong convictions about their own moral code and are quick to condemn those who deviate. The moralistic condemner combines punitiveness, conventionalism, and categorical thinking. As a rigid conformist to ingroup norms he can express his underlying hostility most easily against groups he morally disapproves of.[50] In the surveys moralistic condemnation was indexed by the following agree-disagree items:

1. *Young people today are too loose morally as far as sex goes.*

2. *Children are more prejudiced than adults.*

3. *Old people demand more consideration than they have any right to expect.*

Tendencies toward withdrawal. Some persons who show distrust and suspicion of other people appear to be lonely individuals, not closely integrated into a firm social group, who have few satisfying relationships with other people. Withdrawal tendencies were indexed by the following items:

1. *I usually feel uncomfortable about meeting people I have never seen before.* (Agree-disagree.)

2. *Respondent reports that he belongs to no organizations.*

3. *Do you know anyone personally that has good contacts with the really influential people in town?* (Yes-No.)

There is evidence that social-distance feelings toward ethnic groups tend to go along with a generalized reaction of shyness, aversion, or withdrawal toward meeting other people. In Hometown the white majority-group respondents were asked to agree or disagree with the item, *I usually feel rather uncomfortable about meeting people I have never seen before.* At

---

[49] Gordon Allport and Bernard Kramer, "Some Roots of Prejudice," *Journal of Psychology,* XXII, First Half (July, 1946), 9-39.

[50] The hostility implicit in moralism has been vividly suggested in Albert Camus' aphorism: ". . . pure and unadulterated virtue is homicidal." *The Rebel: An Essay on Man in Revolt* (New York: Vintage Books, 1958), p. 297.

another point in the interviews, they were asked to agree or disagree with the statement, *I feel a bit uneasy in the company of Negroes.* No less than 71 per cent of those who felt uncomfortable about meeting strangers also testified to uneasiness in the company of Negroes, but only 35 per cent of those who felt at ease at the prospect of new acquaintance were thus discomfited by association with Negroes.[51]

Taken together with other bits of data reported at various later points in this analysis, this finding lends weight to the notion that a certain amount of intergroup prejudice does not express a specific ethnic dislike so much as a kind of generalized timidity and feeling of awkwardness in coping with unfamiliar situations and unknown people. Such uncertainty and unease is also likely to be associated with feelings of dependence on the ingroup and fear of losing acceptance in it. These suppositions are consistent with the findings in the Hometown data that the two sociological factors that differentiate between those who are uncomfortable in meeting strangers from those who are at ease are sex and socioeconomic position. Women are somewhat more likely (30 per cent) than men (20 per cent) to report feeling ill at ease. Persons of lower socioeconomic status are more likely than those of high status to feel uncomfortable about new social contacts (37 per cent and 17 per cent).

Varieties of prejudice shown by authoritarians

Persons whose authoritarianism takes different modes of reaction also tend to manifest their prejudices in different ways. Those with a jungle outlook are more likely to perceive minorities as threatening to their welfare and trying to get ahead at their expense; the minority person is pushing in where he is not wanted, and demanding more than he has the right to demand. In his jungle, the minorities threaten his welfare and survival.

Authoritarians who react with moralistic condemnation more frequently displace their hostility onto minorities by scapegoating. They are exceedingly articulate in their affirmation of stereotypic conceptions. They are the stereotypers par excellence. (See Table 5.3.)

Persons who have the more marked withdrawal tendencies react with social-distance prejudices: they find it distasteful to eat with or to dance

---

[51]

The data: Question: *Uneasy in the company of Negroes?*	Question: *Uncomfortable about meeting strangers?*	
	Yes Per cent	No Per cent
Yes	71	35
No	29	65
Total	100	100
	(n = 106)	(n = 303)

Table 5.3

Relationship between authoritarian responses and general prejudice
depending on amount of interaction (Adults, Steelville).

	No Minority Contacts		One or More Minority Contacts	
	Per cent high on general prejudice score	Number of cases	Per cent high on general prejudice score	Number of cases
Prison is too good for sex criminals. They should be publicly whipped or worse.				
Agree	78	(87)	40	(42)
Disagree	57	(88)	48	(64)
The most important thing to teach children is to obey every order their parents give without question, even if they think the parents are wrong.				
Agree	72	(92)	51	(45)
Disagree	60	(86)	39	(62)

with a member of an outgroup, or go to parties where the minority is prominent. They also have fewer available contacts with minority persons. Where
minority persons are available, they are less likely to interact with them.
Where they do interact with them they are less likely to form friendships.
(See Table 5.4.)

The different types of authoritarians also appear to show some differences
in their reactions to specific minorities. Those with a jungle outlook seem
to be more anti-Semitic; those with withdrawal tendencies are more anti-
Negro; while those with feelings of moralistic condemnation scapegoat all
the minorities without special emphasis on any one.

A caution we must heed in examining data contributed by authoritarians
is that their dogmatic reactions may not be firmly rooted in personality disturbance, but may reflect instead a glibness and a tendency to be opinion-
ated. But it is hard to explain away the data by this qualification. The recurring correlation between feeling hurt by others and scapegoating minorities seems to require some explanation in terms of the psychological dynamics of hostility. And this the authoritarian hypothesis provides for us.
The hypothesis appears to suit some of the data on the relation between
contacts with minorities and authoritarianism. On the other hand, we might
expect the prejudice of authoritarians to be less correlated with contact with
minorities than the prejudices of nonauthoritarians. But the data in Tables

Table 5.4

Relationship between authoritarian responses and social distance
depending on amount of interaction (Adults, Hometown).

	No Minority Contacts		One Minority Contact		Two or More Minority Contacts	
	Per cent high on distaste- ful scale*	Number of cases	Per cent high on distaste- ful scale*	Number of cases	Per cent high on distaste- ful scale*	Number of cases
Some say that you can't be too careful in your dealings with people, while others say that most people can be trusted. From your own experience, which would you agree with more?						
Can't be too careful	42	(107)	44	(50)	22	(59)
People can be trusted	28	(126)	19	(70)	14	(85)
The most important thing to teach children is to obey every order their parents give with- out question even if they think the parents are wrong.						
Agree	43	(82)	38	(47)	16	(51)
Disagree	29	(150)	24	(70)	18	(94)
Prison is too good for sex criminals; they should be publicly whipped or worse.						
Agree	44	(57)	43	(35)	19	(27)
Disagree	29	(165)	26	(81)	18	(112)
I have to struggle for everything I get in life.						
Agree	45	(117)	34	(67)	17	(76)
Disagree	25	(118)	21	(54)	16	(68)

*Do you think you would ever find it distasteful: (1) to eat at the same table with a Negro (Jew, Italian)? (2) to go to a party and find that most of the people were Negro (Jewish, Italian)? (3) to dance with a Negro (Jew, Italian)? (4) to have someone in your family marry a Negro (Jew, Italian)?

5.4 and 5.5 suggest the opposite. The anchoring of authoritarian responses needs further study. (See Chapter 7.)

But in all the communities studied and no matter what measures of prejudice are used, the authoritarians are more likely than other persons to have high prejudice scores—whether the index refers to social distance, dislike, public policy, or stereotypes. In most of the analysis that follows, accord-

Table 5.5

Relationship between authoritarian responses and change in attitude towards Negroes (Adults, Hometown, 1949 and 1951).

Authoritarian Questions	Responses			
Sex criminals should be whipped, etc.	Agree	Agree	Disagree	Disagree
You can't be too careful about trusting people	Agree	Disagree	Agree	Disagree
Had contact with Negroes in last month				
Attitudes to Negroes in 1951 were				
More favorable*	37%	41%	35%	22%
Unchanged	50%	35%	59%	70%
Less favorable	13%	24%	6%	8%
Number of cases	(24)	(17)	(34)	(77)
No contact with Negroes in last month				
Attitudes to Negroes in 1951 were				
More favorable	17%	24%	19%	20%
Unchanged	68%	70%	67%	64%
Less favorable	15%	6%	14%	16%
Number of cases	(41)	(37)	(43)	(109)

*Based on 1949 and 1951 responses to six questions such as "Would you find it distasteful to eat at the same table with a Negro?" "On the whole would you say you like or dislike Negro people?" and "Generally speaking, Negroes are lazy and ignorant—do you agree or disagree?"

ingly, it is possible to select a single index of prejudice for consistent use. For the most part we have found it best to work with a scale of social distance, since we have the same measure for most of the sample populations studied. Occasionally, however, we will use other indicators of prejudice to throw light on some point of special interest. We should repeat that authoritarianism appears to relate [52] most closely to acceptance of stereotypes, somewhat less closely to social-distance feelings, and least closely to attitudes concerning public rights and public policies.

Bigots, intermediates, and tolerants. For the preliminary purpose of bringing out clearly the underlying associations, we have so classified the Hometown majority-group sample as to separate an extreme group of bigots, an opposite group of tolerants, and an intermediate category. The bigots are those individuals who consistently say they would find it *personally distasteful* to associate with Jews, Negroes, and Italian-Americans, who consistently *dislike* these ethnic groupings, and who consistently indorse *negative stereo-*

[52] We say "appears to relate," rather than "relates," because the data do not have a common metric that would allow proper comparison of identical measures of correlation. Our statement represents a judgment based on inspection of a large number of cross tabulations.

types concerning foreigners, Catholics, Negroes, and Jews. The tolerants do none of these things.

Let us now construct an *ad hoc* score of authoritarian-punitive tendencies by counting agreements with these three items:

1. . . . . *The most important thing to teach children is to obey every order their parents give without question, even if they think the parents are wrong.*

2. . . . . *Prison is too good for sex criminals; they should be publicly whipped or worse.*

3. . . . . *I have to struggle for everything I get in life.*

Scores will range from 0 (no agreements) to 3. We now find the relationship between bigotry and authoritarianism, as shown below:

Authoritarianism	Bigots	Intermediate Prejudice	Tolerants
Score	Per cent	Per cent	Per cent
High—3	28	7	0
2	31	27	1
1	26	36	63
Low—0	15	30	36
Total	100%	100%	100%
Cases	(53)	(364)	(51)

Correlates of authoritarianism

Authoritarians, as just defined, are more likely than nonauthoritarians to accept negative stereotypes of ethnic groups, to express dislike, and to find personal association distasteful. They are also less likely to actually have any interaction with members of ethnic outgroups.

Socioeconomic level. Authoritarians are somewhat more frequent in the lower than in the high socioeconomic levels. For example, in Hometown the proportion of persons rated as Low SES is 67 per cent among those with the highest scores on the index of authoritarianism, but only 40 per cent among those with the lowest authoritarianism scores.

Social inactiveness. Authoritarians tend to be socially inactive or withdrawn. For example, the proportion of persons reporting membership in clubs or other formal special-interest organizations is markedly lower among those with high authoritarianism scores:

Authoritarianism	Percentage belonging to organizations
Score	
High—3	37
2	53
1	63
Low—0	63

Nor is this relative isolation confined to formal social life. The authoritarians are also less frequently members of a close group of friends—of the high-scoring authoritarians only 25 per cent have an intimate circle of friends, in contrast to 47 per cent of the nonauthoritarians (0 score).

Political leanings. Early in our analysis of the Hometown data, an intensive item-analysis [53] of the correlates of authoritarianism showed that what passed for political liberalism (as of 1948-1950) was *positively,* not negatively, associated with authoritarianism. Our first guess was that the association reflected the moderate tendency for authoritarians to be working-class persons in favor of labor unions and governmental restrictions on business. The data did show, indeed, that the authoritarians were slightly more likely to be critical of big business, definitely more likely to be opposed to the Taft-Hartley proposals for regulation of labor unions, and more likely to favor price controls. It seemed possible, however, that the authoritarians would be more likely than others to accept public measures that promise disciplined dependence upon control and authority, in partial independence of content or ideology. "Authoritarian " might *not* be the opposite of "democratic" in an ideological or political sense. For example, there is a democratic position that favors central economic and social planning for humanitarian and social-welfare ends, but not rigidly authoritative interferences with civil liberties and rights. Indexes of *psychological* authoritarianism do not refer directly to the *ideological* level of preferences and justifications for action in the public arena: an authoritarian personality may contain an ideology stressing either democratic, fascistic, or communistic principles for social planning and control.

It seemed important, therefore, to examine the data concerning a possible tendency for authoritarians to use nonethnic, as well as ethnic, targets for prejudice. Initial indications of such a tendency come from replies to two questions designed to index a sense of threat or outgroup aggressiveness:

1. *Do you think any of these groups are getting more power anywhere in the United States than is good for the country?*
2. *Do you think there are any groups or kinds of people in this country who are trying to get ahead at the expense of people like you?*

Results show a moderate tendency (10 to 15 per cent differences) for the more authoritarian respondents to attribute excessive power and threatening aggressiveness to businessmen, "the rich," or "the upper class," and to be less likely than the nonauthoritarians to attribute these tendencies to poli-

---

[53] The following paragraphs borrow freely from Alice S. Rossi's memoranda based on this analysis. Much of her interpretation foreshadowed the critiques reported in Christie and Jahoda's later work.

ticians or the government. The hypothesis that a scapegoating reaction rather than simply a class-based ideology is involved here suggests a test based on political behavior. In the 1948 presidential election, studied in Hometown, our authoritarians who tended to be antibusiness and in favor of price controls were in agreement with the perceived position of the Democratic party. What actually happened, however, was that on each socioeconomic level the authoritarians were as likely as others to vote Republican, were less likely than nonauthoritarians to vote Democratic, and were more likely simply not to vote at all. This contradictory behavior would be understandable on the assumption that the authoritarian's attitudes toward economic groupings reflect the same kind of projective distrust and hostility we detect in his ethnic attitudes.

The generalization of suspicion and aversion to outgroups is not confined to ethnic targets, but extends to such categories as labor unions and management. An example, taken from many other cases in point, is supplied by the following data for extreme types from the Hometown majority-group sample.

Table 5.6

Relationship between authoritarian personality and perception of threat from minority groups.

	Authoritarian Bigots* (N = 31)	Nonauthoritarian Bigots* (N = 22)	Nonauthoritarian Tolerant* (N = 50)
Groups regarded as threatening			
Jews	45%	36%	2%
Negroes	23%	14%	—
Foreign born	23%	23%	2%
Catholics	16%	23%	2%
Labor unions	39%	46%	24%
Business	19%	14%	4%
Some group mentioned	90%	86%	34%
No group mentioned	10%	14%	66%

*Terms explained on pp. 103-104.

Age. The characteristics of the prejudice-prone personality are suggested more specifically by relating particular authoritarian attitudes to both the prejudices and the social characteristics of the person. Using age and, later, education as examples of important status categories, let us compare the responses of bigots and tolerants to a few of the personality items (still using the Hometown majority-group samples).

The percentages who give the distrust response—*you can't be too care-ful in dealings with people*—are as follows:

	Bigots	Tolerants
Younger persons	81 (21 cases)	22 (36)
Older persons	64 (41)	14 (15)

It is the young bigot who is most likely to see the social world as a jungle. Here is how he reacts to sex and moral deviance on the part of others:

	Percentage saying *sex criminals should be publicly whipped or worse*	
	Bigots	Tolerants
Younger	45	6
Older	14	7

By now the young bigot is beginning to pique our curiosity. He sees other people as threats and he is moralistic-punitive in attitude toward sex devi-ance. What else? He also conceives of himself as having to struggle for everything he gets in life—76 per cent agree to this statement in comparison with 70 per cent of the older bigots, 34 per cent of the younger tolerants, and only 20 per cent of the older tolerants. He is less likely than persons in any of the other three categories to accept responsibility for personal difficulties. He is much more likely to feel he deserves to "do better in life" —43 per cent say this, against only 14 per cent of the older tolerants.

In these bits of data already are suggestions that a mistrustful, self-righteous, extra-punitive, and egocentric personality may be prototypical of the bigots, especially those who are young.

Note that age generally makes less difference among the tolerants than among the bigots. This fact may lead us to guess that the bigotry of the young is more often saturated with personality-derived needs and urges, whereas the bigotry of older persons is more often a conventional response to the beliefs and norms of earlier years in American history. This inter-pretation gains in plausibility from the following data:

	Percentage saying *it is most important that children are taught unquestioning obedience*	
	Bigots	Tolerants
Younger	60	25
Older	56	47

Young or old, the bigot more often than the tolerant person believes children should be taught to obey without question. On the other hand, among the tolerants there is the reversal of the association of authoritarianism with youth. The seemingly curious pattern becomes understandable if we assume that the bigots feel a psychological pressure to accept strict obedience as a counterbalance to "undersirable" needs and impulses, whereas the tolerants—whose attitude on this issue is less compulsive— reflect the going social norms of childrearing during their own younger adult years.

Education. Examination of the relations between education and personality items among bigots and tolerants essentially confirms the image of personality-related prejudice sketched previously. The bigots far more often than the tolerants are uneducated. And whether low or high in educational level, the bigot is much more likely than the tolerant to express opinions indicative of a bitter, withdrawn, authoritarian, moralistic, punitive orientation, of a feeling that life is a jungle and other people are not to be trusted. Among both bigots and tolerants, the better-educated persons are usually less likely to agree with the authoritarian attitudes.

Intensity of authoritarian feelings. Of all the questions used in attempting to index personality characteristics, the three that seem to have been most effective were those having to do with trust in people, obedience of children, and punishment of sex criminals. In one of the Hometown surveys we asked the sample of majority-group respondents not only to agree or disagree but to tell how strongly they felt about each answer to these items. The resulting data permit a detailed examination of authoritarian tendencies in relation to prejudice and intergroup contact. In Table 5.7 we have divided the population according to the number of situations in which they have personal contacts with ethnics and then subdivided them according to responses to the three personality questions, and recorded the proportion in each subclass who manifest high social-distance prejudice toward minorities. The findings are tantalizing, and help to provide a bridge to our later analysis of social interaction and intergroup attitudes.

We note in the first place that reported intensity of feeling, as well as content of the attitudes, relates to the likelihood of prejudice. If a person agrees very strongly that one cannot be too careful in dealings with others, he is more likely to be highly prejudiced than if he merely agrees. Second, the extreme positions on the personality questions represent dramatically different attitudes toward ethnic outgroups, and this is true at all levels of intergroup contact. (For instance, note among persons with no intergroup contact the 31 per cent difference in prejudice between those who agree very strongly that you can't be too careful, in contrast to those who very strongly agree that others can be trusted.) Third, with only minor deviations, the persons with the greatest number of intergroup contacts (situations) are least likely to be prejudiced, whether or not they show authoritarian tendencies. Finally, although the tendencies are not conclusive, there

Table 5.7

Prejudice among majority-group population in relation to amount of
intergroup contact and authoritarian traits (Hometown, 1951).

Authoritarian Items	Number of intergroup contact-situations recently experienced			Total number of cases
	None	One	Two or more	(504)
Careful with people				
Can't be too careful . . .				
Agree very strongly	71	82	54	(124)
Agree	61	68	46	(92)
Can trust . . .				
Agree	45	57	39	(136)
Agree very strongly	40	28	22	(152)
Children obey without question				
Agree very strongly	60	66	61	(112)
Agree	53	83	*	(68)
Disagree	59	50	36	(137)
Disagree very strongly	45	43	34	(187)
Prison too good for sex criminals				
Agree very strongly	63	74	52	(84)
Agree	*	*	*	(35)
Disagree	51	56	33	(157)
Disagree very strongly	49	44	35	(228)

*Less than 25 cases.

is a hint that intergroup contact may have different effects upon the mistrustful, punitive, authoritarian persons than upon those without these traits.
Thus, authoritarians who experience only one situation of intergroup contact are more likely to be prejudiced than those with no contact or with
more frequent contact, whereas, the strongly nonauthoritarian persons show
lesser prejudice with *any* intergroup contact. Slight and irregular as the
latter tendency is, *it suggests the possibility that intergroup interaction may
have to be intensive and varied before it reduces the prejudice of strongly
authoritarian persons.*

We have found, then, that persons who express social distance toward
ethnic, racial, or religious outgroups tend rather consistently toward a
meaningful pattern of personality characteristics—or, if one prefers, a consistent pattern of beliefs and values. The greatest likelihood of prejudice
attaches to those persons who (1) believe in *strict and unquestioning obedience* of children to parents; (2) advocate *severe punishment* of sex criminals; (3) acquiesce in statements of *moralistic condemnation* concerning
youths, old people, or people who "do not live upright lives"; (4) manifest

a *generalized distrust* of other people; (5) report feeling *uncomfortable about meeting strangers;* (6) indicate feelings of *personal frustration* and lack of secure group belongingness. Although quantitative measures of the relative importance of these several items are not feasible with the data at hand, the statistical relationships among the various attitudes and beliefs are such that they suggest that a primary dimension of the most highly prejudiced personalities is *moralistic punitiveness* toward other people, especially toward impulsive or deviant behavior.

Conclusions and Speculations

The prejudice-prone

The main findings of this chapter are consistent with those reported in the great bulk of studies by others who have investigated the relations between personality characteristics and ethnic prejudices. The Cornell Studies, by using sizable samples of adult populations in widely separated communities, reassure us that many findings of research on college students, psychiatric patients, and other special groups can be replicated in a variety of settings in our national society. It is important, of course, to emphasize that rigid, hostility-ridden bigots form only a small proportion of the population in each of the communities studied. But the personality tendencies that create receptivity to prejudice are widespread. We have no exact estimate of the proportion of majority-group Americans who could reasonably be said to be predisposed to prejudice, but the responses to such items as the sex-criminals question suggest that it would be conservative to classify at least one-half as prejudice-prone. Any figure of this kind is highly arbitrary, of course, and can be shifted easily by changing the standard of judgment.

The importance of the personality dispositions is that they make it possible for prejudices to draw upon extra energies far beyond those that would be aroused by realistic perception of immediate advantage or disadvantage. Given the personality predispositions *and* a cultural definition of ethnic or religious groups or categories—Yankees, Catholics, Southerners, Jews, Protestants, Negroes, Puerto Ricans, and WASPS (White, Anglo-Saxon Protestants—this is a good example of the derogatory terms coined by minority-group members to refer to the historically dominant American ethnic category), prejudice easily finds a place in the psychic organization of good, sober people who value obedience, propriety, social respectability and all the other traditional and ordinary virtues. And thus it can happen that one's kindly neighbor who wouldn't hurt a fly can accept the categorical derogation of millions of people, with no apparent doubts or second thoughts. It was particularly these gentle people of prejudice who posed for us a basic problem.

Causes of attitudes—basic personality or prejudice?

All the way through our interviews and field observations, and then again in the analysis of the data, we were nagged by the difficulty of deciding what items of attitudes or behavior to interpret as manifestations of basic personality processes and which to treat as prejudices to be related *to* personality characteristics. The difficulty is greater than is generally acknowledged in studies in this field. It is instructive to try to seek out its sources.

The problem is most weighty when one seeks to deal with social-distance prejudice—with feelings of withdrawal, exclusiveness, or aversion toward persons in ethnic outgroups. In some persons it is very clear that these feelings of social distance are distinct segmental reactions, as in an extroverted, jovial person who welcomes social interaction not only with members of his own ethnic category but also with persons from a wide variety of other groupings, but nevertheless manifests strong sentiments of exclusion toward a particular racial or religious group. In other cases, however, the line becomes blurred and vague between social distance as a separately organized prejudice and social distance as a manifestation of a generalized personality characteristic of reserve, shyness, or social fear.

It immediately occurs to us, of course, that one might disentangle personality from prejudice by first measuring generalized attitudes toward other people, then indexing attitudes toward particular ethnic categories, and defining prejudice as those attitudes that deviate from the individual's generalized orientation to others. The person who shuns (or seeks) social contact with everyone, or who dislikes (or likes) everybody regardless of group membership would not be regarded as prejudiced. Only if he held attitudes of special aversion or attraction to persons considered to belong to particular social categories would he be prejudiced. But where do we draw the line? One individual is willing to accept close social contact with members of all groupings—except Dorineans, Neronians, and Moabites. Still another will accept no one except persons who, like himself, are white Baptists and natives of Green County unto the sixth generation. Where does prejudice become differentiated from personality?

The general answer seems clear. *Any* attitude or action can be regarded as expressing some aspect of a personality system. All behavior, in other words, is expressive of personality to some degree. Everything a person does can tell us something about his personality: there are no neutral acts. But— and here is an essential point—many attitudes and behaviors are so widely shared in standardized forms that the mere presence of the item in a particular person tells us very little about the distinctive modes of personality functioning in that person.

Thus we would say that all prejudices are intrinsic aspects or expressions of personality. We should, therefore, always expect them to be related in definite and lawful ways to other aspects of the perceptual and motivational organization of personality. But this does not mean that prejudices are thereby made exclusively psychological. Of course they are psychological— in the same way as is any other human response that is not purely physiological. But prejudices are saturated with, and presuppose, an elaborate cultural content, and they are both learned through and expressed in social interaction.

We do not wish to leave the impression that our questions have reached into deep-level psychological dispositions or that it is only such dispositions that are highly predictive of prejudice. Actually of course, opinions on many social and political issues are closely related to prejudice, and personality concerns are not necessarily more weighty than social concerns. A good example in point is found in Kaufman's study of concern with social status. In a sample of over 200 non-Jewish undergraduates he found that a set of attitudes expressing concern with status correlated more highly (+0.66) than F-scores (+0.53) with anti-Semitism. Furthermore, status concern remained highly correlated with anti-Semitism with F-scores controlled, whereas the authoritarianism index was no longer significantly associated with anti-Semitic opinions when status concern was held constant. Thus, ". . . concern with status is more closely related to anti-Semitism than is authoritarianism, and the relationship between authoritarianism and anti-Semitism may be largely explained by their mutual relationship to concern with status." [54]

The personal meaning of an attitude expression is not synonymous with its social meaning. What is a casual response of social conventionality to one person may be a strongly affective component of the self-system for another. One person may believe that his stereotype of Negroes is a reasonably accurate social description. To another, the stereotype is a way of expressing irresistible emotional needs, and its agreement or nonagreement with reality is relatively unimportant. He may well feel, "don't confuse me with facts."

Majority-group disinterest in intergroup relations

One oft-forgotten fact is the great extent to which the members of a secure majority group are disinterested in or unconcerned with intergroup relations. In contrast to the intense concern of minority-group persons who are struggling to change the *status quo,* the majority-group member, unless actively stimulated, tends to accept the situation as given, to repeat the well-worn stereotypes, to hold his prejudices as peripheral attitudes rather

---

[54] Walter C. Kaufman, "Status, Authoritarianism, and Anti-Semitism," *American Journal of Sociology,* LXII, No. 4 (January, 1957), 382.

than focal concerns. Except for periods of massive danger and collective trouble—as in severe depressions and in times of threat of immediate war—it is usually difficult to get the American people strongly involved in public issues. A striking case in point was provided by a study made at the height of Congressional investigations of alleged disloyalty and subversion, when Senator McCarthy was at the height of his power and when accusations of Communism were being widely and often indiscriminately applied. In such a climate of apparent national turmoil, Stouffer's analysis showed that very few Americans were greatly concerned either about an alleged internal Communist threat or about any possible danger of loss of civil liberties. Stouffer says, "These issues do not even compare with issues like personal or family economic problems, personal or family health, or other family crises." [55] To most people in the urgencies of their daily rounds, only those things are made problematic that have to be.

Our data show that persons most likely to manifest authoritarian characteristics tend to be at the same time individuals who are isolated from public responsibilities or concerns and who do not participate extensively or intensively in the organized groups of the community outside of the family. We know from other studies that such persons are likely to be politically inert—under the conditions of American life at the time of these studies—and to be little concerned with public issues and problems. However embittered and hostile such individuals may be toward minority groups and the symbols thereof, their influence on others is minimized by their isolation from the mainstream of community decision-making. Under the proper conditions, of course, these inert authoritarians can be activated as an explosive political force. We can only say that at the time of our studies most of them were pocketed within their narrow social circles of family, neighborhood, and work group. We have no way of estimating the role played in the total community pattern of intergroup relations by their sullen passivity and disgruntled prejudice. They certainly support traditional prejudices and practices of group exclusion and differential privilege. They certainly tend to resist any change. But their effective force, person for person, must be considerably less than either the more active prejudice-carriers or the powerful men, whether or not authoritarian, who make calculated decisions reflecting the "cold prejudice" of exclusiveness and protection (and advancement) of the group privilege in which they share in more than ample measure.

The core of the matter, it seems to us, is that ethnic prejudices do not really refer to *personal* likings (or preferences for association) at all, but rather to the acceptance of *shared (cultural) definitions and evaluations of*

---

[55] Samuel A. Stouffer, *Communism, Conformity, and Civil Liberties* (Garden City, N. Y.: Doubleday & Company, Inc., 1955), p. 87.

social categories as such. The crux of intergroup prejudice is not the fact that an individual white person wishes to avoid social visiting with a particular Negro. Indeed, it is very likely that there are white people with whom he does not wish close social interaction, and it may well be that he enjoys informal association with some Negro person who is exempted from the racial definition. Interpersonal likings and associational preferences that are oriented only to individual personality compatibilities could never form the *structural* alignments represented by the classification of some 18,000,000 varied human beings as "Negroes" in our society today.

CHAPTER 6

PATTERNS OF SEGREGATION, DISCRIMINATION, AND CONFLICT

In the following chapters we shall give increased attention to social factors and structures. In this particular chapter we will attempt to discover whether there is a national pattern of intergroup relations, how practices of segregation and discrimination vary among regions and types of communities, and what social conditions are associated with intergroup conflict. Variations in five major factors insure that patterns of intergroup behavior will differ from one community to another. These factors are:

1. *Size of community and size of minority population in the community.*
2. *Official segregation.* Segregated schools, restrictive covenants, separate Negro and white chapters of organizations, etc., erect highly effective barriers to interaction.

Much of this chapter represents derivations and adaptations of Robert L. Eichorn's study, "Patterns of Segregation, Discrimination and Interracial Conflict: Analysis of a Nationwide Survey of Intergroup Practices" (Ph.D. Thesis, Cornell University, 1954).

3. *Discrimination.* In all communities in the United States, although in varying degrees, discriminatory practices exist that serve to limit the number of opportunities for intergroup contact. Usually such discriminatory practices exclude minority-group members from certain activities and places and produce effective unofficial segregation.

4. *Customary community practices.* Less obvious than segregation and discrimination are the many operating practices for intergroup behavior that arise in all communities. These are community patterns that define whether or not intergroup situations are appropriate and acceptable.

5. *Intergroup positive action programs.* Active promotional efforts to increase intergroup interaction affect the opportunities available to individuals for intergroup contacts.

Size of Total Community and Minority Population

Our data show that some demographic variables are highly related to a wide range of patterns of segregation, discrimination, and intergroup conflict. Group relations are markedly different not only in the North and South, but also in big cities and small towns, and in cities with a high proportion and those with a low proportion of members of particular minorities. Demographic conditions make some patterns of intergroup relations more probable than others; they circumscribe the forms these relations take. No single demographic variable, however, is consistently related to all patterns of Negro-white or other intergroup relations.

Data from our national sample of 248 cities show significant differences in intergroup practices between large cities and small towns. Obviously, the mere fact that one city has 100,000 residents and another has 50,000 does not account for these differences. Instead, the size of the city indexes other factors that are related to intergroup practices. Some of these may be:

1. *Patterns of interaction between Negroes and whites.* In the smaller towns, Negroes and whites come into contact with each other because of the limited number of employment opportunities or recreation facilities and the proximity of their homes. Isolation depends upon a large city area and a Negro population of sufficient size to be in some respects self-supporting.

2. *The tradition of the large American city.* With the exception of a few agrarian protest movements, the smaller towns in the United States have been traditionally more conservative than the larger cities. Changes, even in intergroup relations, seem more readily proposed and accepted in the larger cities than in the smaller towns. On the other hand, our data show that overt interracial conflict tends to be a big-city phenomenon.

3. *Differences in residents of big cities and small towns.* Although the migration of rural people to the urban centers continues, not everyone

migrates. Those who derive satisfactions from living in the larger cities possibly may be psychologically different from those who prefer to live in the small towns. These hypothetical differences might account in part for different outcomes of interracial contact.

4. *Regulation of personal behavior.* In the smaller towns, an individual is likely to be known to a large proportion of the residents; in the larger cities, this is impossible. The effects of being known or being somewhat anonymous may influence behavior in interracial situations.

A crucial aspect of Negro-white relations affecting the basic meaning of population size is residential segregation. A rigid pattern of residential segregation has its sources in many of the same social conditions that give rise to other forms of discrimination against Negroes. However, once established, residential segregation becomes crucial in determining other kinds of segregation and discrimination. Concentration of Negro housing can be expected to frustrate attempts to integrate the schools for years to come in many communities, even if only because of such factors as the preference of parents for sending their children to schools within walking distance of their homes.[1]

As noted in Chapter 2, one part of the Cornell Studies consisted of a nationwide survey of intergroup practices in a stratified sample of 250 cities in all parts of mainland United States. The data provide a broad outline of segregation and discrimination in urban centers. The relevance of most of the data reviewed to the questions of main concern in our total program of analysis will be evident. Thus, we shall review the distribution of Negroes and other minorities in cities of the North and South, both large and small. The sheer population distributions affect a great many aspects of intergroup relations. For example, intergroup contact opportunities are limited by both the physical size of the minority groups and the limited number of activities in which most individuals have the time and capacity to take part. In a community with only small percentages of minority groups, majority-group members are very unlikely to have many random opportunities for contact with minority-group members. This situation, of course, does not hold for minority-group members, although such opportunities often will be of a restricted type.

In both absolute numbers and relative proportions, Negroes are concentrated in the larger cities of both the North and the South. (See Table 6.1.) However, Southern cities in each size class have larger Negro communities and a higher ratio of Negroes to whites than do Northern cities. In twenty-four cities in this sample, usually either small Northern towns or suburban areas, there are no Negroes. Jews are absolutely and relatively more important in the larger cities; they are entirely absent from only six cities.

---

[1] See page 130 for a further discussion of residential segregation.

Table 6.1

Distribution of minority-group populations in the cities of the nationwide sample.

Region	North			South*		
City size	Over 100,000	25,000-100,000	Under 25,000	Over 100,000	25,000-100,000	Under 25,000
	(71)†	(82)	(36)	(28)	(21)	(10)
Proportion foreign born in the population						
under 1%	1%	4%	6%	53%	75%	80%
1-4.9%	13	25	14	21	10	10
5-9.9%	30	23	30	14	10	0
10-14.9%	28	16	28	4	0	0
15-17.9%	17	16	8	4	0	0
18% or more	11	11	6	0	0	0
no information	0	5	8	4	5	10
Negro population						
under 100	0%	16%	45%	0%	5%	0%
100-499	4	16	25	0	0	0
500-1,499	6	29	11	0	5	30
1,500-4,999	15	26	11	4	24	50
5,000-14,999	34	6	0	0	42	10
15,000 and more	41	2	0	92	24	0
no information	0	5	8	4	0	10
Proportion Negroes in the population						
less than 1%	13%	35%	44%	0%	5%	0%
1-4%	35	33	31	4	10	10
5-9%	25	17	6	11	14	20
10-19%	24	6	11	21	14	20
20% or more	3	4	0	60	57	40
no information	0	5	8	4	0	10
Jewish population						
under 100	1%	17%	45%	0%	14%	80%
100-499	0	33	36	0	47	10
500-1,499	8	27	8	14	29	0
1,500-4,999	23	13	0	39	10	0
5,000-14,999	33	5	3	36	0	0
15,000 and more	31	0	0	11	0	0
no information	4	5	8	0	0	10
Proportion Jews in the population						
under 1%	10%	47	51	18	62	90
1-1.9%	15	24	22	39	28	0
2-4.9%	39	15	11	29	10	0
5% or more	34	9	8	14	0	0
no information	2	5	8	0	0	10

*The Southern cities are in these states: Alabama, Delaware, Florida, Georgia, Kentucky, Louisiana, Maryland, Mississippi, North Carolina, Oklahoma, South Carolina, Tennessee, Texas, Virginia, West Virginia, and the District of Columbia. "North" includes all other cities.

†Number of cities. The total percentage for each column of each of the five items equals 100 per cent.

There is a higher proportion of foreign-born in the Northern cities. The foreign-born of the South are concentrated in the larger cities; in the North they are fairly evenly distributed in cities of all sizes.

Proportion of minority group in the population

Many social scientists have thought the proportion of a minority to a majority in a population important in influencing intergroup relations. In our nationwide sample, half of the Southern cities had over 20 per cent Negro populations. Half of the Northern cities had less than 5 per cent Negro populations. Of the Northern cities, only Chester, Pennsylvania; Gary, Indiana; and East St. Louis, Illinois, had as high as 20 per cent. How does the proportion of Negroes relate to discrimination, segregation, and conflict?

The likelihood that Negroes will be segregated is greater in those cities where the proportion of Negroes is higher: in schools, playgrounds, hos-

Table 6.2

Relationship of segregation of northern playgrounds and proportion of Negro population.*

| | Proportion Negro | |
	Less than 5 per cent	5 per cent or more
	(Per cent of cities with segregated institution)	
Grade schools	3% (106)	18% (65)
High schools	2% (106)	8% (65)
Playgrounds	5% (106)	25% (65)

*This relationship is unchanged when the size of the city is controlled. All Southern schools were at this time segregated by law.

pitals, and public clinics. (See Table 6.2.) This is true for cities of all sizes of both the North and the South.

Cities with a high proportion of Negroes are more likely to have discrimination in the use of barbershops, hotels, restaurants, movies, and buses. Also, occupational discrimination against both Negroes and Jews appears to be positively related to the proportion of the respective minority groups in the population.

Some kinds of overt conflict between Negroes and whites are characteristically reported by the cities, North and South and large or small, with a high proportion of Negroes: street fights between Negro and white youths and instances of police brutality toward Negroes. The relation does not hold, or is present only in modified form in the instances of burnings of crosses, vandalism, and objectionable newspaper reporting concerning Negroes.

OFFICIAL SEGREGATION

Segregation involves a process of differentiation and distinction. As a result of natural and social selection operating through free competition and conflict an individual or group in time acquires a habitat, a function in the division of labor, and a position in the social order. By such characteristics individuals or groups are distinguished and set apart. Physical separation of groups with different characteristics—whether accomplished by force, or through sanctions imposed by another group, or by the formation of a self-contained defensive aggregation for protection against unfamiliar ideas and customs, or from escape from ostracism and persecution—achieves the same purpose, that of isolation of one group from the other.[2]

When the Supreme Court ruled in 1896 in *Plessy vs. Ferguson* that provision of separate but equal facilities for Negroes in public transportation vehicles did not violate the "equal rights" amendment of the Constitution, the way was clear for segregating Negroes on playgrounds, in schools, and in hospitals.[3] Although city ordinances restricting Negroes' area of residence have been declared unconstitutional, group pressure by whites upon members of their own race, including restrictive covenants, have also limited Negroes' choice of residence. Segregation in many communities in the early 1950's extended from the hospital nursery to the cemetery.

Playgrounds and schools

As of 1954, all of the Southern states had laws requiring separate schools for Negroes and for whites; and many Northern cities had segregated schools. The Negro schools seldom had equal building and teaching facilities, budgets, or staff, and, consequently, the education was frequently inferior. Somewhat fewer than one-third of all the elementary schools, secondary schools, and playgrounds in cities in the nation-wide sample were both segregated and judged inferior to those provided for white children, according to the standards of well-informed local people.

Approximately 5 per cent of the educational and recreational facilities were segregated but locally judged to be as good as those available for white children. Sixty-six per cent of the cities permitted some Negro and

---

[2] Charles S. Johnson, *Patterns of Negro Segregation* (New York: Harper & Row, Publishers, 1943), p. xvii.

[3] Mangum, C. S., *The Legal Status of the Negro* (Chapel Hill: The University of North Carolina Press, 1940). For a discussion of race distinctions with reference to education just prior to the Supreme Court decision in the *Brown* case see R. A. Leflar and W. H. Davis, "Segregation in the Public Schools—," *Harvard Law Review*, LXVII, No. 3 (January, 1954), esp. 420.

white children to use the same playgrounds; in 67 per cent of the cities, some children of both races attended at least some of the same grade schools; and in 72 per cent of the cities, there was some integration of high schools. In most instances, only some of the schools represented any substantial intermingling of white and Negro pupils.

About one-fifth of the cities in the nation-wide sample mentioned education as their most controversial intergroup relations problem. In only 1 per cent of the Northern cities, but in 48 per cent of the Southern cities education was reported as an intergroup relations issue. (The size of the city does not alter this relationship.)

The size of a city was not significantly related to the presence or absence of segregated school buildings or recreational facilities. In the Northern states there was a slight tendency for the larger cities to maintain segregated school systems—a consequence, in large part, of residential concentration of Negroes. In general, though, all schools and playgrounds in the Southern states were segregated, and there was much community concern about the problem. In the Northern states, schools and playgrounds were less often segregated, and concern among white people was low, as of the early 1950's.

Hospitals

In a great many cities, hospitals either were segregated or hospitals for Negroes were completely lacking. Like the schools, many hospitals were supported by taxes, wholly or in part, and were considered to be public service institutions. The medical profession officially espouses a code of ethics that does not seem to support racial discrimination. Yet, 28 per cent of the cities' hospitals were segregated; in 19 per cent, the segregated facilities for Negroes were judged inferior to the hospital facilities provided for whites.

Southern cities more often maintained separate medical facilities for Negroes than Northern cities: 93 per cent of the large Southern cities report segregated hospitals and clinics, whereas 13 per cent of the larger Northern cities had segregated medical facilities. Seventy-five per cent of the smaller Southern towns had segregated hospitals compared to 14 per cent in the smaller Northern towns. Undoubtedly, smaller towns have greater difficulty in bearing the costs of separate medical installations for Negroes. Without the sanctions of state legislation that enforce segregation in the schools, and without the direct "transfer" of behavior as from the schools to the playgrounds, some small Southern towns did have common hospital facilities. Almost all of the large Southern cities had segregated medical facilities. In the North, where it is the usual practice to have integrated rather than segregated hospitals, economic resources are not so important in determining the pattern of segregation.[4]

Formal organizations

Social scientists have often noted the remarkable proliferation of formal organizations in American communities. There are civic, social, business and professional clubs attracting different kinds of people in support of a wide range of goals. Our data from the nationwide sample support the observation that communities in the United States are indeed "organized." Almost every city has local chapters of all the national organizations for which we sought information. Only the YWCA is absent from as many as 10 per cent of the communities. Table 6.3 shows that some national or-

Table 6.3
Integration and segregation in national organizations.

Organizations	Inte-grated	No Provisions for Negroes	Segre-grated	No Organization	No answer/don't know
Masons	2%	12	79	0	7
Rotary	4	80	1	2	13
American Legion	19	8	64	1	8
Chamber of Commerce	27	46	9	1	17
YMCA	42	13	28	9	8
YWCA	48	10	24	10	8
Community Chest	64	18	6	4	8
Local Council of Churches	73	10	7	2	8

ganizations accept Negroes as members, some make no provisions for Negroes to belong, and others segregate them.

Like segregation in hospitals or schools, the pattern of segregation in formal organizations differed in cities of different size and in the North and South. These differences are of interest.

Separate organizations. In 79 per cent of the cities, Negroes belonged to

---

[4] Of course, in many of the officially nonsegregated Northern hospitals the actual day-to-day activities are substantially affected by ethnic factors. See for example: David N. Solomon, "Ethnic and Class Differences among Hospitals as Contingencies in Medical Careers," *American Journal of Sociology*, LXVI, No. 5 (March, 1961), 463-71. This study's main conclusion, on p. 469, is that: "The social system of medicine in Chicago—and, no doubt, in other large urban areas—is not a unified homogeneous whole but, rather, one which reflects the ethnic and class segmentation and stratification of the city. The medical community, like the community as a whole, consists of a set of social worlds which are to a degree separate and discrete."

segregated Masonic lodges. In almost all the larger Northern cities, separate Masonic lodges had been established for Negroes. The smaller the city in the North, the less the tendency to make provision for Negroes in the Masons. In the South, both the large cities and small towns reported separate Negro Masonic lodges.

The American Legion was second only to the Masons in having segregated organizations for Negroes. Seventy-eight per cent of the posts in Northern cities over 100,000 were segregated but about 20 per cent were integrated. The smaller the towns in the North, the fewer reported segregated posts. Instead, either Negroes were accepted into existing posts or no provisions were made for them. But again the Southern cities of all sizes usually maintained separate posts for Negroes. All Legion posts in the larger Southern cities were segregated. Eighty-two per cent of the Southern cities under 100,000 had separate posts. One Southern city under 100,000 reported no provisions for Negroes, and two had integrated posts.

No provisions for Negroes. In 82 per cent of all Northern cities and 75 per cent of all Southern cities, the Rotary clubs neither permitted Negroes nor had established segregated clubs. There was little difference between the practices of Rotary clubs in the larger cities and small towns of either region.

The Chambers of Commerce also tended to exclude Negroes and to make no separate provision for them. Forty-two per cent of the Northern cities over 100,000 made no provisions for Negroes to belong to the Chamber of Commerce. A slightly higher percentage of smaller Northern towns excluded Negroes or failed to set up separate organizations for them. However, those Northern cities in which Negroes are permitted in the Chamber of Commerce tend to have common organizations for Negroes and whites. In the South, the pattern was somewhat different. There, too, many cities reported no provision for Negroes to belong to the Chamber of Commerce, and a few reported integrated organizations. But most Southern cities either made no provision for Negroes or reported separate Chambers of Commerce for Negro businessmen.

Integrated organizations. Most of the local Councils of Churches were made up of both Negro and white ministers. But again regional differences were important. Most Northern cities, especially the larger ones, reported integrated Councils of Churches. But less than 4 out of 10 of the Southern councils were integrated. The larger Southern cities were more likely than the smaller towns to establish separate councils for Negro ministers; the smaller places more often reported no provisions for Negroes.

The YMCA and the YWCA represented hybrid forms of segregation, tending to be integrated in the North and to have separate organizations for Negroes in the South. The YWCA's were more often integrated than the YMCA's in both regions.

A similar pattern appears again in the case of the Community Chest or United Fund. Most Northern cities have integrated Community Chest directorates, but some smaller Northern towns have no provisions for taking Negroes into the drives to collect funds. About half of the Southern cities report integrated organizations, but 29 per cent of the Southern cities with populations over 100,000 established separate organizations and 21 per cent of the Southern towns under 100,000 made no provisions for Negro participation.

Let us summarize this picture, as of the early 1950's, of segregation in formal organizations. First, those organizations that appear to have a nationwide practice of segregation (Masons, American Legion) provide segregated chapters for Negroes in the larger cities of the North and South. The smaller towns of the South follow the regional folkway of separate but equal and provide Masonic lodges and Legion posts for Negroes. Lacking this tradition, the smaller towns of the North, with their smaller Negro communities, make no provisions for Negroes to belong to these organizations.

Second, if an organization maintains a practice of excluding Negroes and not encouraging the establishment of separate clubs, there simply is no provision for Negroes in any city of either region. If this practice is less rigidly enforced, as by the Chamber of Commerce, Negroes in the North tend to be taken into integrated organizations, and Negroes in the South establish separate chapters.

Finally, those religious and civic organizations that make a universal appeal to common motives of all people in all communities present a dilemma for some Southern cities. Northern cities report that Community Chest drives and ministerial groups are integrated, but in the South joint participation is not accepted in about half the cities. The larger Southern cities report the presence of separate organizations for Negroes, but in the smaller Southern towns no provisions are made for Negroes to participate. Except for these philanthropic organizations, there are usually separate organizations for Negroes in clubs or lodges in small Southern towns.

DISCRIMINATION

Segregation is one kind of discrimination. There are many other kinds that do not necessarily involve the provision of separate facilities. These are acts of selective and differential behavior which violate important institutional standards that usually are obligatory in certain areas of conduct.

Although discrimination against a minority group is more often the overt expression of prejudice, discrimination can exist without prejudice. Some discriminatory practices reflect a policy decision protecting the interests of the majority group. Some represent adherence, through the forces of group conformity, to fragments of the cultural heritage. A hotel manager may turn away Negro customers because other hotel managers turn them away. As we have said before, he may feel that his white customers would object, although they have no strong feelings one way or the other.

Discrimination in employment [5]

Eighty-one per cent of the cities report that there is discrimination against qualified Negroes in the form of failure to promote them to more skilled industrial jobs. Of these cities, 67 per cent report instances within the last year. This particular kind of discrimination in employment occurred much more frequently in the larger cities than in the smaller towns. While discrimination was reported more often in all Southern cities than in Northern cities, the differences were small. In about 20 per cent of the cities it is reported that Jewish doctors are denied full privileges at the local hospitals. More of these cities are in the North than in the South. They are also the larger cities of both regions. Both Jewish doctors and qualified Negro industrial workers are more often discriminated against in the larger cities. Jews, however, are singled out for discriminatory treatment in the Northern cities, whereas Negroes are penalized in the Southern cities.

Employment is considered to be the most controversial intergroup relations problem in 45 per cent of the communities, and is so ranked more often in larger cities than in the smaller towns. Concern about employing Negroes is greatest in the largest Northern cities and least in the smallest Southern towns.

Discrimination in use of public facilities

Discrimination against Negroes varies from community to community, from institution to institution within the same community, and from individual to individual in the same institutional setting. In one West Virginia city, Negroes' use of the same public rest-rooms as whites is a controversial issue. Across the river in an Ohio city, Negroes' use of public rest-rooms is accepted. But in this Ohio city Negroes cannot generally stay in white hotels. Marian Anderson was not permitted to stay at one of the better hotels there. (Yet, when a Negro social scientist from Cornell asked for a room in this same hotel, it was given to him without question.)

Table 6.4 shows the variability that exists in what is considered to be appropriate behavior for Negroes in different localities, from the high percentage of cities where it is acceptable for Negro women to try on dresses

---

[5] We are not here concerned with defining or analyzing the economic aspects of discrimination. For an impression of the complexity of these problems see Gary S. Becker, *The Economics of Discrimination* (Chicago: The University of Chicago Press, 1957).

Table 6.4

Acceptability of Negroes' using public facilities.

Can Negroes:	Taken for granted as not acceptable	Contro- versial	Taken for granted as acceptable	No answer/ don't know
Try on dresses in white department store?	2%	9%	88%	1%
Sit in the same part of buses as whites?	16	4	79	1
Use the same public rest rooms as whites?	17	6	76	1
Sit among whites in movies?	26	6	67	1
Have beds in hospitals side by side with whites?	29	18	52	1
Use same swimming pools with whites?	30	22	45	3
Be served in white res- taurants?	30	30	39	1
Belong to white Protestant churches?	38	31	30	1
Stay in white hotels?	39	34	25	2
Use white barbershops?	68	22	8	2

in white department stores to the low percentage of cities where Negro men can get haircuts in white barbershops. There is a remarkably orderly rank-ing of discrimination. Some behaviors are more often tabooed for Negroes than other. There is a single rank-order of acceptability of practices.

In some cases, Negroes' freedom of action is well defined. For instance, in 79 per cent of the cities Negroes can sit in the same part of buses as whites, and in 16 per cent this is not acceptable. Only in 4 per cent of the cities is this controversial. In other cases the situation is poorly defined. Twenty-five per cent of the cities report that Negroes can stay in white hotels; in 38 per cent of the cities this is not acceptable; and in 34 per cent this is a controversial issue. This means that Negroes are likely to encounter conflict; they cannot generalize from one hotel to another.

Despite this tremendous variability, discrimination definitely is patterned. Both Myrdal and Johnson earlier spoke of a "rank-order of discrimina-tion." [6] This means that different kinds of behaviors by Negroes can be arranged along a continuum of more acceptable and less acceptable. Table 6.4 shows this. It also shows that cities can be ranked in a clear unidimen-sional order of their acceptance of Negroes' use of public facilities and institutions.

However, the activities included in this list do not appear to be ordered on the "personal intimacy" continuum that Myrdal and many others have

---

[6] Gunnar Myrdal, *An American Dilemma* (New York: Harper & Row, Publishers, 1944), pp. 60-67, 587-88; Charles S. Johnson, *Patterns of Negro Segregation,* pp. 3-155, 173-85.

suggested. It is difficult to see why Negroes' being served in a white restaurant should be more intimate than their using the same rest-rooms as whites. No single one of several possible factors—intimacy, public character, potential economic gain to whites, recency of the institutions' establishment, importance of the service or facility (barbershops and churches) and so on —seems to explain the order of the items.

Thus we have several important and puzzling facts: there is great variability in the acceptability of the practices and in the consensus upon acceptability; there is a strikingly clear unidimensional order among the practices; but, there is no obviously plausible basis for the ordering. Could the clue lie either in size of the city or region of the country?

While acceptance of Negroes in public facilities is definitely patterned for the sample of the cities as a whole, Northern cities differ from Southern cities and large cities differ from small towns in the areas of freedom extended to Negroes.

With very few exceptions, Negroes in Northern cities of all sizes can try on dresses in department stores, sit in the same part of buses as whites, use the same public rest-rooms as whites, and sit among whites in movie houses. They are often excluded from swimming pools, restaurants, churches, hotels, and barbershops. In the smaller towns more often than in the larger cities, they are forbidden use of public facilities and institutions. However, more large Northern cities consider Negroes' use of these facilities to be controversial than do the smaller towns. Therefore, with the exception of Negroes' staying in white hotels, unqualified acceptance of Negroes is greater in the small towns of the North than the larger cities.

In the South, Negroes' use of most public facilities is clearly unacceptable, and in many cases their use of the facilities is not even controversial.[7] It is difficult to say in most cases whether Negroes are given more freedom to use public facilities in the larger cities of the South or in the small towns. More small towns report that Negroes can sit among whites on the buses and can use the same rest-room facilities. While Negroes' use of white barbershops, white hotels, and swimming pools is forbidden in almost all Southern towns, these were at least controversial issues, rather than unthinkable innovations, in the smaller towns.

The detailed breakdown of the data by region and size of city does not destroy the rank-ordering: on the whole, the same general ranking prevails in both North and South, and in both small and large cities within each region. The regional difference is overwhelmingly important, far outweighing city size.

---

[7] It must be remembered again that these data antedated the controversies over public transportation in the South that have followed the Supreme Court decisions of 1954 and 1955. It has not been very long since "Freedom Riders" was an unknown expression. But the stirrings of change were there long before the incidents in Montgomery, Little Rock, Jackson, or New Orleans.

We might suspect that the ordering of practices could merely reflect the sheer availability of facilities and service within a highly segregated residential pattern. That is, if a city contains a Negro ghetto that is large enough to have many of the facilities in question, those that are available to both groups on a neighborhood basis would be most likely to rank as "not acceptable" to the whites. This possibility, however, does not seem to constitute a good explanation. In the highly segregated large Northern cities, there are only few cases of cities having general exclusion of Negroes from restaurants and hotels, both of which are available on a neighborhood basis. It is true, however, that the facilities and services that are most likely to be available on a desegregated basis are those likely to be found in central districts of cities and to involve relatively transitory and impersonal situations —department stores, buses, rest-rooms, movies. General location and casual, transitory character, however, are rather weak factors in comparison with regional culture and city size.

The particular character of the facility or service is possibly significant in two cases. The first is that of the white Protestant church, which in the South clearly is a deviant in the rank-order. The anomaly of segregation in a religious institution having certain traditions and beliefs concerning brotherhood and the spiritual worth of individuals undoubtedly is partly responsible for the frequency of controversial situations. The other somewhat special case concerns barbershops, in which there appears to be a most complicated set of special factors including technical skills, the peculiar characteristics of proprietorship and unionization, the historical background (the processes by which Negro barbers were forced out in the South), and the quasi-recreational or social-club qualities of some neighborhood establishments.

In sum, it appears that the ordering of discriminatory and segregative practices derives to a large extent from functionally arbitrary historical circumstances. The practices are not sheerly whimsical or without cause; but the position of any one practice seems to be a function of many particular causes set in the context of a pervasive institutional pattern. In the South, for example, there is a generalized inclination to segregate and discriminate in nearly all areas of life. This institutionalized commitment tends to spread to a great variety of practices and settings—Oklahoma at one time had a state law requiring separate telephone booths for use of whites and Negroes. A variety of factors, suggested in our own discussion here, come to bear in different combinations upon various situations at different times. Variations in segregation and discrimination have not been neatly laid out on the basis of a single set of clear principles.

Although we can do no more than suggest a range of factors that help us to understand the "Negro Acceptability Scale," the fact that some discriminatory behaviors are so definitely ordered, without any obvious single base (intimacy, threat, competition, etc.), may have rather far-reaching implications. Persons who assume that discriminatory behaviors are random or capricious, all equally amenable to change if only the proper strategy is found, may find resistance to change especially great in some areas of Negro-white relations. On the other hand, the lack of any clear indication that the ordering of the discriminatory practices rests on a single set of strong interests (economic gain, or power, or status, etc.) suggests that item-by-item change may be possible without the necessity for a major transformation of all prejudices simultaneously or of the total distribution of power, wealth, and prestige.

The validity of the latter point is indicated by our data concerning many discriminatory behaviors and types of segregation in which neither a generalized culture pattern nor generalized prejudices seem to be as important in determining behavior as arbitrary circumstances such as an organization's policies regulating the admission of Negroes or the personal wishes of some strategic gatekeeper. In some cities the Chambers of Commerce were segregated whereas American Legion posts were integrated; in other cities the pattern was reversed. Where the norms of interracial behavior in some segmental environment were either unclearly stated or explicitly in conflict with prevailing community sentiments regarding appropriate interracial behavior, patterns of Negro-white relations tended to vary from community practices.

The data concern specific cities. It is evident from the North-South differences, however, that cities are part of larger systems and that states as legislative units are most important in the field of race relations. Indeed, there is a wealth of evidence, available to any alert newspaper reader, of the decisive importance of political policies, legal actions, and political and administrative leadership at the state level. All subordinate political subdivisions such as counties and cities may be affected by a statewide policy or movement. This conclusion has been verified by the experience of investigators who have sought to establish predictive correlations between demographic factors, on the one hand, and the rate of public school desegregation on the other. As Pettigrew and Cramer have summarized this experience:

> One of the first findings was that each state had to be analyzed separately. Apparently, the political leadership of the various states differs so widely in respect to race relations that county-by-county predictions across states is impossible. Further, the demographic characteristics of the southern states vary sharply.[8]

[8] Thomas F. Pettigrew and M. Richard Cramer, "The Demography of Desegregation," *Journal of Social Issues*, XV, No. 4 (1959), 65. This study found, nevertheless, that ". . . it is the poor, traditional, rural areas with large percentages of uneducated Negroes that form the core of racial conflict [concerning school desegregation]" (p. 70).

Residential segregation

The most ubiquitous condition reported in the national survey is that discrimination resulting in residential segregation of Negroes is typical of most American cities. The pattern of residential segregation tends to produce or perpetuate segregation in other areas of community life and sets the prevailing tone of Negro-white relations.

In over half of the cities (56 per cent), Negroes are living in either one or a few residential areas.

Table 6.5

Residential segregation of Negroes.*

Negroes are now allowed to establish residence in:

Only one area of the city 5%
Only a few areas 51%
Most areas 30%
All areas 11%
No answer/don't know 3%

    Total number of cities . . . .(221)

*This sample was stratified in such a way that the larger cities are over-represented. The sample is somewhat biased in favor of the large Northern cities.

In only 11 per cent of the cities are they living in all possible areas of residence. Even in these latter cities Negroes usually are not free to live where they choose. Pockets of Negro dwellings can be scattered throughout a city, yet any expansion into new residential areas might be resisted. Of the 93 cities stating that Negroes live in all or most areas, 55 reported that within the last year an attempt had been made to prevent a Negro from moving into a predominantly white district. In private housing, then, Negroes are rather rigidly segregated.[9]

The situation is similar in public housing. Negroes are completely excluded from public housing in 15 per cent of the 170 cities having projects. In nearly half (47 per cent) of those 145 cities that permit them to live in public-housing facilities, Negroes live in separate projects. Seventy-seven cities have mixed projects, but in 38 per cent of these, Negroes live in separate buildings. Thus, Negroes are given the same opportunities as whites in

---

[9] It is enough for present purposes to use these carefully checked estimates of residential segregation. The actual measurement of areal segregation in American cities (from published Census data and other official sources) is a large and difficult task in itself. For some of the difficulties, see Otis Dudley Duncan and Beverly Duncan, "A Methodological Analysis of Segregation Indexes," *American Sociological Review*, XX, No. 2 (April, 1955), 210-17.

only 33 per cent of the cities permitting Negroes in public-housing projects or 27 per cent of all those having projects.

There is evidence that residential segregation has increased in recent years in many cities. By 1950, 90 per cent of Chicago's 337,000 Negroes lived in a predominantly Negro area. This had not always been the case.

> In 1910 there were no communities in which Negroes were over 61 percent of the population. More than two-thirds of the Negroes lived in areas less than 50 percent Negro, and a third lived in areas less than 10 percent Negro. By 1920, 87 percent of the Negroes lived in areas over half Negro in composition. A decade later 90 percent were in districts of 50 percent or more Negro concentration. Almost two-thirds (63.0 percent) lived where the concentration was from 90 to 99 percent Negro.[10]

Now in about half (45 per cent) of the cities in the nationwide sample, housing is considered to be the community's most controversial intergroup relations problem. Sixty-one per cent of the cities reported that an attempt had been made to bar a Negro from a white residential area within the last year. This had occurred in an additional 22 per cent of the cities in the last ten years. Less than one-fifth of the cities (17 per cent) had avoided an interracial housing incident.

Thus, we know that segregation in private and public housing is the rule in American cities, and that housing is an explosive intergroup relations issue.

Actual *de facto* segregation of Negroes into highly constricted areas is a characteristic of the larger Northern cities, often to a degree greater than in Southern cities. Although there is no Southern city as large as Chicago, it is nevertheless impressive to note that Chicago may well be the most highly segregated city in the United States. In 1950, 84.1 per cent of the white population of the city lived in census tracts containing less than one per cent Negroes, and 52.9 per cent of the Negroes lived in census tracts in which 97.5 per cent or more of the population were Negro.[11]

Size of the Negro community. Residential segregation might be expected to increase directly with the absolute number of Negroes in a city. However, the relationship between the size of the Negro community and the extent of residential segregation is not simple. In the North, Negroes are more likely to be living in most areas of a city in those cities where they are either few or great in numbers. This may also be true for the Southern cities; however, there are too few cases to state this conclusively. Perhaps

---

[10] St. Clair Drake and Horace R. Cayton, *Black Metropolis* (New York: Harcourt, Brace & World, Inc., 1945), p. 176.

[11] See: Otis Dudley Duncan and Beverly Duncan, *The Negro Population of Chicago: A Study of Residential Succession* (Chicago: The University of Chicago Press, 1957).

the presence of a few Negroes is not perceived by whites as a threat; thus, initially, residential segregation is not rigidly enforced. With an increase in numbers, Negroes' residences are more likely to be concentrated. Beyond a certain point, however, Negroes cannot be contained. Their numbers alone make it necessary to spread out into other areas of residence.

In summary, residential segregation of Negroes within a city is related to its size, the region in which it is located, the proportion of Negroes in its population, and their absolute numbers. Although the associations are not highly predictive, the data do give some important clues as to the kinds of cities that are most likely to be segregated. There is a greater likelihood that Negroes living in large, Southern cities having a low proportion of Negroes and a Negro population of from 500 to 5,000 will live in a restricted residential area. Negroes living in small, Northern towns with a low proportion of Negroes and a small Negro population would more often be scattered throughout the residential areas.

Detailed cross tabulations show that residential segregation is closely associated with segregation in all other areas of community life.[12] Where Negroes are concentrated in a few residential areas, one is more likely to find segregated schools, public-housing projects, hospitals, and social organizations. There, also, Negroes' use of public accommodations is a more controversial intergroup relations issue. Residential segregation obviously reduces the neighbor-to-neighbor contacts between Negroes and whites, and participation of Negroes and whites in the many activities dependent upon proximity is rendered impossible. Concentration of Negroes in a few areas makes it possible to construct schools or hospitals for Negroes only. In time, whites come to expect that Negroes should have a separate community life of their own. Integration ceases to be thought of as a real possibility.

In cities with a long tradition of segregation, Negroes sometimes had come to resign themselves to segregation and tended to work to get the best segregated facilities possible for their own use. Thus, the presence of a segregated YMCA building may also index the Negroes' attempt to provide some recreational outlet for their youth.

Each race develops its own closed system of interaction, and frequently feelings of hostility develop toward the outgroup. Thus, residential segregation goes along with a high incidence of interracial conflict—contrary to what many people have argued. Although this association partly reflects the fact that segregation is greatest in the South, where conflict is also most likely for other reasons, even in the North incidents of Negro-white con-

---

[12] Cf. Don J. Hager, "Housing Discrimination, Social Conflict, and the Law," *Social Problem,* VIII, No. 1 (Summer, 1960), 80-87.

flict [13] are most likely in the cities with the tighter patterns of residential segregation.

CONFLICT AND PROTEST

Within each region, Negro-white relations are more often tense in larger cities than in the smaller towns. In larger cities, too, intergroup relations organizations are more active. Especially in larger Northern cities, protest organizations seem better able to achieve their goals. Although these generalizations stand as statistical tendencies, there are exceptions. Some kinds of conflict and discrimination are reported more often in Northern than in Southern cities or in small towns than in big cities. There are differences between cities of the same region and size. And there are marked internal variations within each city of any considerable size. The variations form regularized patterns—even in the disorder of violent intergroup conflict. For example, the incidence and type of violence varies with the characteristics of the ecological areas of the city. Little violence occurs in the Negro residential areas without business establishments. These are the middle- and upper-class residential areas, which do not offer extensive opportunity for looting and which typically have the better police protection. These areas also are far removed from those in which violence typically starts. The middle- and upper-class white residential areas also are relatively free from violence, except for raids by automobile on Negro domestics going to and from work.[14]

In the cities surveyed, although segregation, discrimination, and conflict

---

[13] For example, police brutality, vandalism, anti-Negro newspaper reporting, burning-cross incidents. We may note in this connection Grimshaw's observation in "Urban Racial Violence in the United States: Changing Ecological Considerations," *American Journal of Sociology*, LXVI, No. 2 (September, 1960), 112. "Violence in time of major race riots has been concentrated in Negro slums, which in many cities were served largely by white businesses. Casualties and fatalities occurred most often in slums or along their fringes, and destruction of property, particularly looting, was greatest there." And again: "In the riot in East St. Louis in 1917, the Negro section was invaded, Negro residences and businesses were set on fire, and Negroes were shot down in large numbers as they attempted to flee from the burning buildings."

[14] *Ibid.*, 109-19. This study notes on p. 109: "Urban racial social violence has occurred in every geographic region of the United States. It has not occurred in every city in every area. Certain similarities in its background and social context are found in the cities which have had major race riots. East St. Louis, Washington, Chicago, Tulsa, and Detroit all had sharp increases in Negro population in the years immediately prior to major interracial disturbance, and there were accompanying strains in the accommodative structure, generated in part by the Negroes' assaults on it and in part by the sheer pressure of population on facilities."

were quite common, there were signs of change. The more violent forms of conflict were less prevalent, and the more obvious forms of segregation in public facilities have largely disappeared from many Northern cities. But other forms of social and economic discrimination are still common. The data suggest strongly that Negroes react most militantly to segregation and discrimination in cities where some gains have been made in abolishing discrimination. A Negro community sensitive to discrimination, led by an aspiring Negro middle class, and realistically hopeful for more equal treatment tends to support militant organizations. Without presenting the large amount of evidence for this conclusion, we may illustrate the point by noting the large amount of protest activity in the larger Northern cities, at the time of our survey. See Table 6.6, which shows that the various organizations that fight discrimination are most often found in the large cities, especially in the North.

Table 6.6

Per cent of cities with organizations fighting local discrimination case within last ten years.

Region	North		South	
City size	100,000 and over	Under 100,000	100,000 and over	Under 100,000
Organizations				
NAACP	93%	51%	100%	65%
Urban League	56	9	57	3
B'nai B'rith or Anti-Defamation League	86	43	68	19
A State Commission Against Discrimination	54	18	0	3
Federal Fair Employment Practices Commission	56	21	25	3
Congress of Industrial Organizations (CIO)	72	23	68	23
American Federation of Labor (AFL)	43	5	36	6
Other	79	41	54	23
None or none listed	1	27	0	29
Total number of cities	(71)	(118)	(28)	(31)

The distribution of incidents of overt conflict of whites and Negroes is somewhat different from the distribution of active organizational efforts to fight discrimination. Such evidences of conflict as vandalism against Negro property, anti-Negro newspaper reporting, and police brutality toward Negroes [15] occur more frequently in the South and in the larger cities of both regions. Vandalism against Jewish property and derogatory statements against the group are also more likely to be big city phenomena, but it is the Northern cities more often than the Southern cities that report conflict incidents involving Jews. Street fights between Negroes and whites and conflict over housing also occur more often in the North, most frequently in the larger cities. Burning-cross incidents are more often reported in Southern cities and especially in large Southern cities. The fact that interracial conflict is more likely to occur in the larger cities than in the smaller towns may reflect, among other things, the greater anonymity, the weaker personalized social control, and the stronger feeling of whites that Negroes are getting "out of their place."

There is a particular historical pattern of violence in the South,[16] and there is still a marked tendency for violence of all kinds to be more prevalent in Southern states than in the Northern states. Sixty per cent of the Southern cities in our sample had a per capita aggravated assault rate of over one-tenth, whereas only 12 per cent of the Northern cities had a rate this high.[17]

We have seen that the region in which a city is located, the city's size, and the proportion of Negroes or other minorities are fairly good predictors of patterns of intergroup behavior. Other demographic variables, such as income level, mobility rate, population growth, or unemployment rate have predictive value only in rather special circumstances. Specific examples follow.

Population growth. Cities having rapid increases in population in the preceding decade were more likely than other cities to report (1) the use of public accommodations as a controversial problem of intergroup relations (North only); (2) discrimination against Negro workers in promotion practices (North only); (3) recent attempts to prevent Negroes from moving into predominantly white residential areas; (4) discrimination in restaurants, hospitals, department stores, and other semipublic facilities; and (5) police brutality toward Negroes.

However, the following are no more likely to occur in cities that have grown rapidly than in those with relatively stable populations.

1. High rating of general level of conflict and tension.
2. Negro-white relations considered to be a crucial problem.

---

[15] Seventy-one per cent of the large Southern cities reported publicly known instances of police brutality toward Negroes in the year preceding the survey inquiry.

[16] W. J. Cash, *The Mind of the South* (Garden City, N. Y.: Doubleday & Company, Inc., 1954), pp. 42-70.

[17] *Uniform Crime Reports for the United States and Its Possessions* (Washington, D.C.: Federal Bureau of Investigation, United States Department of Justice), XXIII, No. 2 (1952), Table 38, pp. 98-105.

3. Housing and education considered to be crucial problems.

4. Some kinds of conflict: anti-Negro newspaper reporting, street fights between Negro and white youths, vandalism against Negro property, burning crosses to intimidate Negroes.

5. Some kinds of discrimination: Negroes' use of barbershops patronized by whites or of the same sections of movies as whites.

Mobility of population. Cities with a large proportion of their population made up of people who have recently arrived have been thought to be more susceptible to intergroup conflict. New arrivals have not established community moorings and, therefore, are exempt in part from the informal sanctions that regulate the behavior of those with longer residence. Cities with a highly mobile population are usually either in agricultural areas requiring seasonal workers, or they are manufacturing cities with fluctuating demands for workers. For instance, over 9 per cent of the populations of Bakersfield, California; Spokane, Washington; and Battle Creek, Michigan, in 1950 lived in a different county the year before.[18] These could be characterized as "boom cities." The migrant workers attracted to them are often the less well educated drawn from the lower-class groups of the rural areas, especially of the South. Many of the rioters of Detroit and some in Los Angeles during World War II belonged to this type of migrant population.

Employment, housing, and the use of public accommodations are more often considered to be controversial intergroup relations problems in Northern cities with larger proportions of mobile people in their populations. For example, 61 per cent of the cities with less mobile populations reported an instance of a qualified Negro industrial worker being denied promotion because of his race within the preceding year, as compared to 76 per cent of the cities with more mobile populations. Negroes' use of semi-public and public facilities was also a more controversial issue or not acceptable in the highly mobile cities.

While a city's proportion of mobile residents is positively related to a wide range of discriminatory practices, it is unrelated to the incidence of overt conflict. Police brutality toward Negroes, interracial street fights, vandalism against Negro property, burning-cross incidents and attempts to bar Negroes from some residential area are as likely to occur in high-mobility as in the low-mobility cities. Negro-white relations were considered no more controversial in one kind of city than the other. There is even a suggestion that Jewish-gentile and Protestant-Catholic relations are more strained in

---

[18] Compare these cities to those with a small proportion of mobile residents. The latter includes: Bridgeport, Conn., Campbell, O., and Union City, N. J. In 1950 less than 2 per cent of their populations lived in other counties in 1949. No Southern cities had mobility rates this low.

the low-mobility cities. It cannot be assumed that cities having a highly mobile population necessarily have more intergroup conflict in all of its manifold forms.

Proportion of unemployed and level of income.[19] In periods of mass unemployment, such as the depression years of the 1930's, Negroes typically suffer more than white workers. The services they perform are often expendable. Given the widely shared prejudices against Negroes, white employers facing economic crises usually fire Negroes first and hire them last.

An increase in unemployment perhaps might be especially likely to increase discrimination and/or conflict if the general level of income were low relative to previous levels or to that of other areas. Then Negroes and whites of similar socioeconomic classes would be thrown into direct competition for the few jobs that were available. Employers have been known to capitalize on this racial competition, further increasing the antagonism between the races.

Contrary to expectations based on these considerations, in the nationwide sample a city's level of unemployment or the median income of its population tells us little about its pattern of intergroup relations. (The tables on which these conclusions are based were controlled on the region in which the city is located.) Negro workers are no more likely to be discriminated against in regard to job promotions in cities with a high level of unemployment than in those with a low level. Job discrimination is no more likely in the poor towns than the rich towns. Neither income level nor level of unemployment was related to the incidence of conflict. Like the other demographic variables that have been mentioned, a city's rate of employment or income level is inadequate when used alone as an index of its intergroup relations pattern.

Negro protest in tightly segregated cities. Another reaction to segregation is to fight to overcome it. Typically, within a given region and city-size class, there are proportionally more organizations working to improve conditions for Negroes in the rigidly segregated cities. These include labor unions and civic improvement associations as well as organizations interested primarily in intergroup relations.

The National Association for the Advancement of Colored People usually has a larger membership in the highly segregated cities. However, white

----

[19] Of the cities in the nationwide sample, those with the highest proportions of unemployed workers were generally located either in the Northeastern states or in California. National City, Cal., and Providence, R. I., are two cities with 7 per cent or more of their populations unemployed in 1950. Cities bordering the Great Lakes had the lowest level of unemployment. South Bend, Ind., and Wooster, O., had less than one per cent of their populations unemployed. Southern cities generally fell somewhere between these two extremes. However, cities with low income levels are almost always found in the South.

members are no more likely to join the NAACP in one type of city than the other. Nor are the NAACP's in the segregated cities reported to be any more active than those in the less segregated cities.

Summary. We have found that when Negroes are confined to living in one or a few areas of a city, civic and social organizations are more likely to be segregated, and discrimination and interracial conflict are more serious problems. Denied access to the facilities of the white community, Negroes develop their own professional class and community services. Also, in the rigidly segregated city Negroes are more likely to join protest organizations, and to move toward more militant action.

The more determined efforts on the part of Negroes to reduce discrimination and segregation through organized action tend to occur in the larger cities (but not always—witness Montgomery, Alabama), in the North (again, not always or at all times), and where both the proportion and the absolute size of the Negro population is large. Also, organized protest and defense is more likely in cities characterized by improving conditions, by the presence of a relatively large Negro middle class, and by recent instances of successful group action against discrimination.

The total pattern of the data suggests that militant response to segregation and discrimination are in large part dependent upon a community of Negroes who can realistically hope for better conditions, the leadership of an active Negro middle class, and the widespread conviction that conditions are not as they should be. There is a final factor that is important in determining whether Negroes react militantly to discrimination. To be an instigation for militant minority group activity, discrimination must be perceived by Negroes and resented by them. This may help to explain the lack of concern about discrimination in some cities where it might appear to an outsider as intolerable, and the high degree of concern with this problem in some cities where conditions are relatively favorable for Negroes.

Summary and Implications

Are Southerners more prejudiced than Northerners?

Finally, we return to re-examine one of the persistent themes that has run through all the earlier chapters of this work.

It is often claimed, in effect, that schools in the South are segregated because Southerners are prejudiced against Negroes and that schools in the North are generally integrated because Northerners are less prejudiced. But Floridians who move to New York may send their children to integrated public schools whereas the children of New Yorkers wintering in Florida often attend segregated schools. Their prejudices do not determine their behavior, since the former may favor and the latter object to segregated schools. What seems to be essential in accounting for discriminatory practices is the individual's acceptance or nonacceptance of the prevailing patterns of behavior toward minority group members.

But let us suppose that Southerners are more prejudiced toward Negroes than Northerners are. Would this, by itself, account for the regional differences in the extent of discrimination? The nationwide data raise serious questions. In many respects large Southern cities resemble large Northern cities more than they do small Southern towns. Almost all of the large cities of both the North and the South reported a recent instance of job discrimination, whereas this occurred in less than half of the smaller towns of the two regions. Furthermore, there are unaccountable local variations in discriminatory practices. In one small town, Negroes cannot participate in high school athletics; seven miles away in another small town, they may do so. Or, one restaurant serves Negroes, whereas across the street another restaurant excludes them. Are we to assume that these variations reflect only individual prejudices?

Individual prejudices are not the explanation

The nature of change in the patterns of intergroup behavior also conflicts with the notion that individual prejudices completely account for discriminatory practices. If discriminatory behavior is based on personal prejudices, then the only way to change behavior is to eliminate prejudice. This is a slow process. Yet some forms of discrimination are abolished in a relatively short time. In May, 1954 the schools of Washington, D. C. were segregated; in September they were desegregated. The prejudices of Washingtonians were *not* so malleable, but the institutional pattern did change.

The inadequacies of individual prejudices as a means of predicting discriminatory behavior and accounting for changes in practices call for a reorientation in our thinking about these problems. A frame of reference is needed to explain the *variations* in discriminatory behavior as well as the *patterns* and to account for the persistence of some practices as well as the instability of others.

Changing and resistant patterns of discrimination

The kinds of discrimination that occur in American cities are not merely random or capricious. Although an integrated YMCA is sometimes found in a city where social mingling of the races is not considered to be appropriate, in more crucial areas of intergroup contacts the patterned nature of discrimination persists. There is a cultural component in the patterns of discrimination that resists change. The etiquette of race relations in some rural areas of the Deep South has changed little in the last fifty years.

The forms of prejudice and the patterns of discrimination are part of the cultural heritage. A generation ago, Bogardus found that white Americans objected to some nationality groups more than others.[20] Then, more recently he readministered the test and found that, in general, the order of rejection of the various minority groups remained the same. There are parallels in Negro-white relations. Whites often report that they would find it more objectionable to eat with a Negro than to work with a Negro, and more objectionable to live next door to a Negro than to eat with him. The degree of personal intimacy has been suggested as the underlying dimension that explains the order of these items; however, this seems inadequate, since Negroes often live with whites as maids or nurses. Although the acceptance of Negroes in some situations and their rejection from others is difficult to explain, the effects are real. For instance, only 19 cities of the 248 in the nationwide sample permitted Negroes to get haircuts in white barbershops.

Cultural heritage prevails. Earlier it was suggested that individual prejudices do not solely determine whether or not a white person will participate in integrated activities with Negroes. Instead he tends to accept the prevailing practices of the situation in which he finds himself. The accepted policy regulating relations between the races in particular settings, then, becomes crucial. This policy can often be at variance with the local climate of opinion about race relations. For example, Southern ministers of both races may meet for lunch. Some institutional settings, such as a church or a union hall, regulated by policies of a strategic gate-keeper may be called segmental environments; these can either conform with or deviate from local opinion.

Deviations. Deviations from local patterns of discriminations are more likely to occur in some situations than in others. If the norms regulating interracial behavior are poorly defined in some situations, behavior in those situations is likely to be at variance with community sentiment. Where, for instance, do Negroes park their cars in drive-in theaters? The norms of some segmental environments may expressly forbid integration or insist upon it regardless of the prevailing community practices. The Masons, for instance, have a separate order for Negroes. On the other hand, Community Chest drives usually include both Negro and white workers. Finally, if there are competing sets of norms within any one organization, it may even happen that the tolerant set may prevail in intolerant communities, and the intolerant set may prevail in tolerant communities. There are integrated ministerial alliances in the Southern cities and segregated ones in the North.

---

[20] Summarized in G. E. Simpson, and J. M. Yinger, *Racial and Cultural Minorities* (New York: Harper & Row, Publishers, 1958).

The vicious circle of segregation

Without opportunities for getting to know Negroes, whites use the prevailing patterns of segregation and discrimination as a guide or model for their behavior in the few contacts they have with Negroes. Defensively, Negroes develop their own community life, which further reduces their contacts with whites, which in turn increases the possibility of misunderstanding and conflict, and so on in a familiar vicious circle.

Thus, we come full circle to the point at which we began this chapter. Restrictions and freedoms for intergroup contact and communication depend upon prevailing community definitions of what is appropriate and acceptable. These definitions emerge from shared social experience. Once interlocked into common expectations and interests, they set the boundaries for any given time, place, and situation for intergroup contact. But the experience of interaction, when it does occur, may in turn reinforce or modify the beliefs and norms that guide intergroup relations at the level where one man speaks to another.

From the national scene we focus upon our four communities. Limited in number as they are, they provide for much variation—as in the clear and striking contrast in the pattern of segregation in Southport as over against the more open situation in Valley City.[21] In a comparison of 15 community facilities, from churches to bowling alleys, Southport displayed the characteristic Southern pattern of complete segregation. On the other hand, in Valley City Negroes and whites shared access to many of the facilities that were regarded as public, for example, department stores, playgrounds, churches, schools, and movie theaters, although other facilities (which seem to be more personal or social) were generally segregated in actual practice, for example, restaurants, some recreational facilities, hotels, and barbershops. On the whole, however, there was an enormous difference between the partial and informal segregation in Valley City and the pervasive, tightly controlled segregation in Southport.

But even in New York State, where law and public policy are firmly set against public segregation and discrimination, our peaceful city of Hometown showed us one great initial fact: the marked isolation and separateness of racial and ethnic segments of the community. Communitywide sample surveys showed that members of various ethnic categories in Hometown tended to follow beaten social paths that did not often intersect with paths of other groups. These observations were confirmed by project observers. Research observers in Hometown noted that most people seemed to develop an "Indian path"—a well-beaten, often trod, social trail from home to work,

---

21 Cf. Lionel S. Lewis, "Discrimination and Insulation: An Inter-Community Comparison" (M. A. Thesis, Cornell University, Ithaca, N. Y., 1959), Chapters I and VI.

back to home, to lodge meeting, back to home, on Sundays to church and back, and then perhaps to visit relatives and friends. Once the pathways had developed, persons tended to stay on them; only once in a long while did they go into parts of the forest frequented by other tribes. For most persons, such paths were narrow walks of life that exposed them to only a few limited social environments. These environments bore down powerfully with their social pressures, their group processes, their standards of attitudes and behavior.

We see, then, that these routine patterns of daily activity have great significance for intergroup relations—that more than almost anything else they determine whom a person will get to know. In the next chapters we will examine the detailed patterns of group isolation and intergroup action in the four communities intensively studied.

CHAPTER 7

SOCIAL INTERACTION
AND INTERGROUP ATTITUDES

Having gained an overview of the prevalence and distribution of stereotyping and other manifestations of prejudice, and having looked at both the social and the personality characteristics associated with prejudices, we now turn to the actual behavior of individuals in intergroup activity. In this chapter we will analyze the relationships between (1) opportunities for intergroup contact, (2) actual intergroup interaction, and (3) prejudice. First, we want to know how contact-occasions are distributed. Among those persons who are exposed to the possibility of interethnic contacts, how many actually interact, and what are the social and psychological characteristics of those who do and those who do not interact? And given the fact of interaction, how do other conditions or variables affect one's ethnic attitudes?

A collaboration with Edward A. Suchman. Most of the material on pp. 144-184 is taken from Suchman's monograph, "Cross-Community Survey Analysis of Intergroup Contact." Manet Fowler's adaptations of that manuscript have been used extensively. Sections dealing with types of social participation and those that analyze changes in interaction and attitudes draw heavily upon research memoranda prepared by Alice S. Rossi.

The conditions that affect opportunity, interaction, and prejudice fall into three main classes. First, there are basic statuses and roles, indexed by such manifest characteristics as sex, age, education, and socioeconomic class. Second, there are personality variables, such as sociability or authoritarianism. Third, there are specific memberships in groups and communities, with all the social pressures and incentives they generate.

Within the context of a given community, different segments of the population will have varying opportunities for ethnic contact, depending upon the specific extent to which their status positions and roles permit or require ingroup contact.

OPPORTUNITY FOR INTERACTION

Contact determinants

In American society, sex, age, education, and economic status are four of the main determinants of contact opportunities, just as they are major correlates of degree of prejudice. It is obvious, but not the less significant, that men move in different circles from women, and young people are expected to behave differently from old people. The educated and the uneducated and the rich and the poor have different patterns of daily behavior that show up in their exposure to intergroup contacts. These statuses and roles are of basic importance in determining the "beaten paths," already mentioned, that are pursued by the individual. They indicate individuals' differing interests and desires in regard to their meetings with others—all the while setting up different standards of acceptable and appropriate behavior that affect the exposure. Of course, it is equally important to view these status and role memberships as social categories, which in themselves are not the basic "causal" variables. For example, it is not sex or age per se that affects contact opportunities, but rather the differing attitudes and behavior of the different sex and age groups. However, these classifications are extremely useful social categories for empirical observation and deserve careful analysis.

Sex. The most significant and consistent of the status and role factors is sex. In all communities and for all majority and minority groups, the male is more likely to be exposed to intergroup contact than the female. Looking at three regionally different communities (data not available for Steelville), we find that a higher percentage of men report opportunities for contact than do women. These differences are all statistically significant and consistent.

Men, who are much more likely than women to work outside the home and to belong to formal organizations, have a greater opportunity to meet people, including members of racial, religious, and ethnic groups other than their own. This basic fact means that patterns of intergroup contact will be much more influenced, directly, by men than by women. Table 7.1 indicates that males in both majority and minority groups report more contact opportunities than do women.

Table 7.1

Relationship between contact opportunities and sex of individual.

| | Per cent with higher opportunities | | | |
| | Male | | Female | |
	Per cent	Number of cases	Per cent	Number of cases
Majority group with minority				
Hometown, 1949 [2]*	83	(221)	48	(283)
Valley City with Mexicans [1]	66	(152)	43	(167)
Southport with Jews [2]	36	(166)	20	(187)
Southport with Negroes [1]	77	(166)	42	(187)
Minority group with majority				
Hometown				
Jews [2]	98	(84)	50	(66)
Negroes [3]	50	(68)	16	(79)
Italian-Americans [3]	61	(88)	7	(55)
Valley City				
Mexicans [2]	61	(62)	25	(69)
Negroes [2]	47	(109)	24	(118)
Southport				
Negroes [2]	42	(119)	22	(171)

*Figures in brackets indicate number of opportunities considered high for each group.

Age. Young and old people appear to be about equally exposed to intergroup contact, and most of the observed differences are not statistically significant. Even in Hometown among the majority group, where younger people have more opportunity for contacts than older people, this difference disappears if we take into account the sex and education of the individual. (There is a slight tendency, however, for the younger group to have consistently more opportunity despite the lack of statistical significance.) Table 7.2 illustrates that although individuals under forty-five years of age show a consistent tendency to have more contact opportunities than those forty-five years or older, the differences are not significant.

Education. As can be seen in Table 7.3, education, on the whole, tends to increase exposure to intergroup contact for all groups in all communities, with the single exception of intergroup contact between whites and Negroes in Southport. In Southport the less well-educated white is slightly more likely to find himself in an intergroup situation than the more educated white, although this is not the case among the Negroes, where the more

Table 7.2

Relationship between contact opportunities and age.

| | Per cent with higher opportunities | | | |
| | Under 45 years | | 45 years or older | |
	Per cent	Number of cases	Per cent	Number of cases
Majority group				
Hometown, 1949 [4]*	35	(262)	26	(242)
Valley City [1]	53	(178)	54	(132)
Southport with Jews [2]	31	(214)	24	(136)
Southport with Negroes [1]	63	(214)	53	(136)
Minority group				
Hometown				
Jews [3]	44	(69)	42	(53)
Negroes [3]	35	(84)	30	(61)
Italian-Americans [3]	41	(94)	39	(46)
Valley City				
Mexicans [2]	46	(82)	36	(47)
Negroes [2]	38	(141)	31	(85)
Southport				
Negroes [2]	30	(213)	31	(74)

*Figures in brackets indicate number of opportunities considered high for each group.

educated Negro has more opportunity for contact with whites than the less well-educated Negro.

This reversal, of course, reflects a basic proposition of this discussion: exposure to the intergroup situations available in a community depends to a large extent upon the individual's daily living patterns—which in turn are strongly influenced by his position and function (or status and role) in the community.

Yet, if we examine sex, age, and education simultaneously, we see that, in Hometown for example, among the majority group (the only group with enough cases to permit this detailed analysis) the age differences disappear, whereas the sex and educational differences increase. On the average, sex seems to have a somewhat greater effect than education, especially among the better educated group. The combined effect of sex and education is cumulative, as can be seen from the great difference in contact opportunities between the educated males (63 per cent and 62 per cent) and the uneducated females (14 per cent and 10 per cent), in Table 7.4.

Socioeconomic status. As in the case of education, higher occupational status and income among the minority group is more conducive than lower position to intergroup contact. This is also true for the majority group, except in Southport, where we once again find the less well-to-do whites more often than the higher-status whites having occasion to meet Negroes. In

Table 7.3

Relationship between contact opportunities and education.

	Education Level					
	Per cent with higher opportunities					
	Low		Medium		High	
	Per cent	Number of cases	Per cent	Number of cases	Per cent	Number of cases
Majority group						
Hometown*[4]	14	(122)	34	(297)	44	(80)
Valley City*[2]	14	(57)	9	(174)	21	(87)
Southport, with Jews*[2]	13	(84)	24	(170)	47	(99)
Southport, with Negroes*[2]	13	(84)	11	(170)	9	(99)
Minority group						
Hometown						
Jews*[3]	33	(33)	35	(46)	50	(69)
Negroes†[3]	23	(73)	—	—	35	(77)
Italians*[3]	34	(64)	40	(65)	77	(13)
Valley City						
Mexicans†[2]	40	(95)	—	—	49	(33)
Negroes†[2]	27	(178)	—	—	61	(49)
Southport						
Negroes‡[2]	28	(233)	—	—	41	(56)

*Low = grammar school or less; Medium = high school; High = college or more.
†Low = grammar school or less; High = high school or more.
‡Low = some high school or less; High = high school graduate or more.

Table 7.4

Relationship between combined effect of sex and education
and contact opportunities.

| | Per cent with four or more opportunities | | | |
| | Under 45 years | | 45 years or older | |
	Per cent	Number of cases	Per cent	Number of cases
Male				
High school graduate or more	63	(72)	62	(34)
Some high school or less	38	(47)	32	(68)
Female				
High school graduate or more	22	(94)	25	(53)
Some high school or less	14	(49)	10	(87)

Southport, however, the upper-status gentile is more likely than the lower-status gentile to be exposed to contact with Jewish individuals. These findings of course reflect the different pathways of daily social interaction of the Jewish and Negro minorities in a Southern town.

The differences associated with socioeconomic status remain independent of sex and education among the majority group in Hometown. The grouping with most opportunity consists of the upper-status, educated males (77 per cent), whereas the grouping with least opportunity is composed of the lower-status, uneducated females (9 per cent).

Class Identification. Related to, but distinct from, occupation and income, is the social class with which the individual majority or minority member identifies. In the two communities for which the data are available for the majority-group populations, these class differences are not as consistent as those of generalized socioeconomic standing. The majority-group member in Southport who identifies his class position as upper or middle is more likely than those who identify their class position as working or lower to have the opportunity for contact with Jews, whereas the opposite is true for contact with Negroes. Similarly in Hometown, the Jewish individual who identifies with the upper classes is more likely to find himself in intergroup situations; among Negroes, however, it is the individual who identifies with the lower classes who is more likely to encounter white persons.

We have now found that opportunities for intergroup contact present different patterns in different communities and among several minority groups. Among majority-group members, the availability of outgroup contacts is greater for men than women (and slightly more likely for younger than older persons), for educated than uneducated, for those of higher rather than lower socioeconomic position, and for those who identify themselves as middle or upper rather than working class (except for Negro-white

Table 7.5

Relationship between socioeconomic status and contact opportunities.

	Socio-Economic Status					
	Low		Medium		High	
			Per cent with higher opportunities			
	Per cent	Number of cases	Per cent	Number of cases	Per cent	Number of cases
Majority group						
Hometown, 1949 [4]*	25	(184)	29	(164)	40	(156)
Valley City [1]	56	(148)	—	—	53	(164)
Southport with Jews [1]	53	(148)	—	—	77	(196)
Southport with Negroes [1]	68	(148)	—	—	52	(196)
Minority group						
Hometown						
Jews [3]	27	(55)	—	—	47	(81)
Negroes [3]	21	(63)	—	—	42	(68)
Italians [3]	38	(47)	—	—	41	(86)
Valley City						
Negroes [2]	16	(61)	35	(121)	65	(40)
Southport						
Negroes [2]	13	(55)	34	(158)	39	(56)

*Figures in brackets indicate number of reported situations providing opportunity for contacts.

contacts in Southport, which involve persons of low education and socio-economic status on both sides). In the communities studied, Jewish persons as compared with other ethnic minorities tended to be better educated, of higher occupational status, less concentrated in segregated residential areas, and more active in a variety of formal organizations. Jewish-gentile contacts tend to involve middle- and upper-class persons. Both physical and functional proximity tend to throw into potential association across ethnic lines those individuals who are similar in education and class. From the standpoint of the majority group, the odds are that the typical encounter with a Jew will be with a person of the same or higher socioeconomic position; with a Negro, the contact is more likely to be with a person of lower socioeconomic position. We shall return to the implications of these facts at a later point.

Inventory frequency of contact

The frequency with which white-gentile persons will come into contact with ethnic persons depends, in the first place, upon the number of situations in which any minority-group people are physically present. In each community respondents were questioned in detail concerning the availability of possible ethnic contacts in major types of social settings: at work, in the neighborhood, in clubs or other formal organizations, and anywhere else. The resulting inventory of occasions for intergroup contact is summarized in Table 7.6. Together with Table 7.7, we have here an inventory of available opportunities for intergroup contact reported by majority- and minority-group members in four communities for three major areas of daily activity—neighborhood, work, and organizations.

Examples of inventory. Some of the questions asked of white gentiles in Hometown were:

1. *During the last month did you come in contact in your work with any (Negro, Jewish, Italian) people?* (Asked only of employed individuals)

2. *Do you consider any of the (Negroes, Jews, Italians) at your work a close friend that you can talk over confidential matters with or a good friend to whom you can say what you really think?* (Asked only of those whose work relationship was that of fellow worker, employer, or employee)

3. *How about you personally, do you find yourself feeling different at all toward these (Negroes, Jews, Italians)?* (Asked only of those whose work relationship was that of fellow worker, employer, or employee)

4. *How about you personally, would it make any difference at all to you if some of your fellow workers were (Negroes, Jews, Italians)?* (Asked only of those who had no Negro, Jewish, or Italian fellow workers)

Table 7.6

Situational opportunities inventory—majority group.*

| | Type of Situation | | |
	Neighborhood	Work†	Organization
Hometown, 1949 (N = 529)			
Italian-Americans	54%	39%	29%
Jews	29%	28%	30%
Negroes	14%	23%	10%
Hometown, 1951 (N = 423)			
Jews	30%	33%	33%
Negroes	14%	24%	11%
Valley City (N = 319)			
Mexicans	19%	39%	20%
Negroes	7%	40%	13%
Steelville ‡ (N = 288)			
Jews	44%	29%	27%
Negroes	31%	39%	9%
Southport (N = 354)			
Jews	43%	28%	29%
Negroes	26%	42%	2%

*Comparisons between different communities must be made with caution due to slightly different question wordings.

†This represents a minimum estimate, since respondent was asked whether he had "come in contact" with Ethnics at work, not whether there were any employed where he worked.

‡ Percentages are based on the question about "coming in contact" with Ethnics, not about opportunity for contact.

5. *Are there any (Negroes, Jews, Italians) in a club or organization that you belong to?* (Asked only of those belonging to some organization)

Similar questions were asked concerning ethnic contacts and attitudes in organizations, in the neighborhoods, and in informal social groups.

In the cross-section samples, ethnic group members were queried about their contacts with majority-group members. Some of the parallel questions asked of Negroes, Jews and Italian-Americans, for example, in Hometown were:

1. *What proportion of the persons that you personally come in contact with in your work are (Negroes, Jews, Italians)?* (Asked only of those who are employed)

2. *Do you consider any of those at your work that aren't (Negro, Jew, Italian) a close friend you can talk over confidential matters with or a good friend to whom you can say what you really think?* (Asked only of those who have contacts on the job)

3. *Do you suppose the (nonethnic group) feel different at all toward the (Negroes, Jews, Italians) at your work?* (Asked only of those who have contacts on the job)

Similar questions were asked concerning organizations, neighbors, and visiting. The same questions were repeated, in most instances, in the several surveys. Some changes in question wording, designed to eliminate difficulties encountered in field interviewing, mean that intercommunity comparisons of absolute proportions require caution.

In any community consisting of two or more ethnic categories in which the numerically predominant grouping is also superordinate in cultural and/or economic and/or political terms, nearly all members of the subordinate minorities will have frequent contacts with some member of the dominant majority. On the other hand, it will be quite possible for a large proportion of persons in the majority grouping to have no contact with members of any other ethnic category. Especially if there is a substantial degree of segregation, intergroup insulation tends to be a one-way affair.

This asymmetrical character of intergroup contacts is strikingly demonstrated in the four survey communities (compare Tables 7.6 and 7.7). One Negro family in a neighborhood of 50 white families has 50 opportunities for contact with whites; each white family has only one opportunity. The patterns of available contacts vary not only with population ratios but also with the extent of segregation, the specific minority group in question, the type of situation, and the pervasive institutionalized practices and social climates to be found in Northern, Southern, and Western areas.

Table 7.7

Situation opportunities inventory—minority group.*

| | | Type of Situation | |
	Neighborhood	Work†	Organization
Hometown			
Jews (150)	100%	65%	53%
Negroes (150)	95%	72%	36%
Italian-Americans (150)	93%	69%	47%
Valley City			
Negroes (227)	53%	53%	9%
Mexican-Americans (131)	79%	45%	14%
Steelville ‡			
Jews (67)	94%	67%	42%
Negroes (140)	76%	66%	34%
Southport			
Negroes (290)	47%	59%	8%

*Comparisons between different communities must be made with caution due to slightly different question wordings. Actual questions are given in Appendix A.
† Asked as "face-to-face contact at work," not whether available.
‡ Asked as "face-to-face contact," not whether available.

The findings

In the four communities for which we have roughly comparable data, the proportion of white-gentile respondents who reported any opportunity for contact with Negroes in any formal organization ranged from a high of 13 per cent in Valley City to a low of 2 per cent in Southport. For the four samples combined, the proportion of majority-group persons who had any occasion for possible communication with Negroes in three places were:

	Per cent
In the neighborhood of residence	19
In situations arising at work	35
In formal organizations	9
	(N = 1,384)

We may safely conclude that there is a tangible boundary between white and Negro collectivities in these communities at the time of the studies.

The extent of Jewish-gentile interaction may be illustrated by the data from Southport as reported by the white non-Jewish respondents. A reasonably clear picture of structure may be suggested by presenting the information concerning gentile-Jewish interaction in the form of a diagram similar to an organizational flow chart. Starting with the total population, it shows the progressively smaller numbers who have the more frequent and intimate kinds of contacts with Jewish persons.

Negro-white contacts in the South. But what of the Negro-white relations in the Deep South? Frequent contact and friendly intimacy between Negroes and whites—each of whom knows and respects the other "in his place"—is sometimes alleged to characterize the Southern pattern of race relations. Let us look at the information we have from Southport on white persons' reports of their interaction with Negroes in the so-called undisturbed period just before the 1954 decision of the Supreme Court, which declared unconstitutional forced racial segregation in public schools.

Of the 354 white persons interviewed, only 53 reported no contact with any Negro person. The 301 persons who did report data on some contact characterized the closest contact each had at the time with a Negro person as follows: 132 cases in which the Negro is a servant; 114 cases at work; 40 [1] cases of miscellaneous settings (sports events, store, public transportation, street, etc.); 11 cases in the neighborhood of residence; 4 cases in a formal organization.

Negroes as servants is not an outmoded stereotype in a city such as Southport, in which 44 per cent of the households had some Negro domestic

---

[1] Adjusted for duplicate reporting.

Chart 7.1

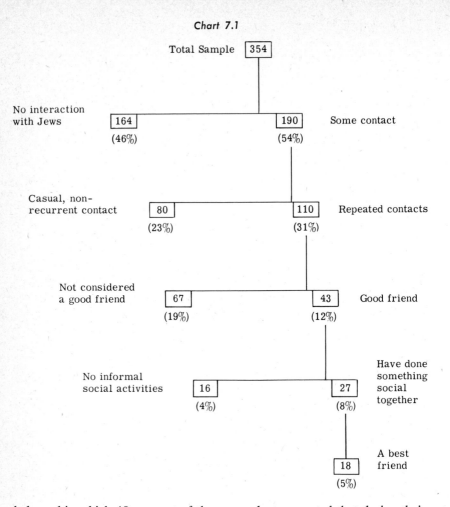

Total Sample [354]

No interaction
with Jews   [164]   [190]   Some contact
            (46%)   (54%)

Casual, non-
recurrent contact   [80]   [110]   Repeated contacts
              (23%)   (31%)

Not considered
a good friend   [67]   [43]   Good friend
             (19%)   (12%)

                                    Have done
                                    something
No informal   social
social activities   [16]   [27] together
            (4%)   (8%)

                              [18]   A best
                             (5%)   friend

help and in which 48 per cent of the respondents reported that during their own youth Negro servants worked in their homes. Is it the case, then, that the physical closeness of Negro servant and white family results in intimate sharing of experience and the growth of relations of friendship? Some white people believe that the traditional master or mistress established such relations with their devoted servants. One index of intimacy would be the sharing of confidences with the servant who has frequent access to the daily affairs of the home and family. How often does this intimacy occur? Each of the 109 respondents who reported employing a Negro person for domestic service was asked, *Do you ever talk over confidential matters with any of these Negro servants?* Just 19 persons said "Yes," and 5 said, "Yes, often." But perhaps this 5 per cent is an underestimate of the extent of actual friendships between white employers and Negro servants in this Deep South city. It is true that 40 per cent of these employers claim one or more of their servants as a good friend, but, again, just 5 per cent say they count their Negro servant among their best friends. To what extent are the other contacts intimate or friendly? Of the 301 persons reporting a closest contact, 33 characterized the Negro person as a good friend but not a best friend. Exactly 4 persons were willing to say that they considered the Negro person they knew best as *"among your best friends."* This works out to be 1.13 per cent of the white sample.

In Southport, then, white people consider themselves to have a Negro among their best friends in about 1 case out of 100. It would appear that the spontaneous formation of close friendships between white and Negro persons in the Deep South is not occurring at a rate likely to revolutionize the intergroup situation there in anything short of geologically significant periods of time.

In what situations do most contacts occur? The greatest variation in frequency of contact opportunity is to be found in regard to Negroes in the neighborhood situation, as reported by both the majority group and the Negro group itself. The proportion reporting contact opportunity ranges from 7 per cent for Valley City to 31 per cent in Steelville for majority members, and from 47 per cent in Southport to 95 per cent in Hometown for the minority's reports. (We have noted how population ratios dictate that the minority will more often report opportunity; undoubtedly also there is some underreporting due to prejudice on the part of the majority-group members.)

Organizational patterns of segregation are consistently high, especially for Negroes. Majority-group reports of mixed Negro-white organizational membership run from only 2 per cent in Southport to 13 per cent in Valley City. Among all minority groups in all communities, reports of membership in mixed organizations are almost always less than one-half of those for mixed neighborhoods. Social discrimination is most likely to be expressed in terms of such restricted organizational memberships.

Opportunities for intergroup contact at work appear to be about equal in all communities and for all minority groups. Although Negro and white, Jew and gentile are likely not to belong to the same organization, and will to varying degrees live in the same neighborhood, they apparently do work side by side in all these communities. Commerce and industry are the great mixers of peoples in our society.

Among the different minority groups, Jewish persons have the greatest opportunity for contact in their neighborhoods, while the Negroes' chances are highest where they work. Jewish patterns appear to be about the same in all communities, while Negro patterns show the greatest variations between the Northern cities as opposed to the Southern and Far Western communities.[2]

Another way to analyze intergroup contact opportunities is to tally up the intergroup situations themselves and to see what their composition is. We have also taken all the situations mentioned by majority-group members in Hometown and Valley City in which there exists an opportunity to come into contact with a minority-group member and have shown how they are distributed among the different minority groups and activities. Here the base is the number of intergroup situations that exist in a community, rather than the number of individuals who report opportunities for intergroup contact. In general, this type of analysis produces findings similar to those just reported for the previous analysis. The least frequent situations are those that involve Negroes in organizations. An interesting comparison is made in this way of the number of situations to which an individual is exposed. If the individual has only one opportunity, it is most likely to be with the minority group that has the most opportunity and in the intergroup situation that is most common. Thus in Hometown, 41 per cent of the situations, where only one situation is available, involve Italian-Americans in the neighborhood, whereas only 2 per cent involve Negroes in an organization. This variation decreases greatly when we look at those individuals who are exposed to four or more situations. This probably means that individuals who are exposed to intergroup situations that are relatively infrequent will also be exposed to those that are most common.

Also worth noting is the general heterogeneity of exposure among those who have many opportunities. There appears to be very little tendency for these situations to be concentrated around any one minority group or any one situation. For example, of the 83 individuals in Hometown each of whom had three opportunities, only one individual reports these three opportunities as being with the same minority group. The most frequent single pattern involves one each of all three minority groups. Such diversity of opportunity would raise the possibility that impersonal or social forces are more likely to determine one's contact opportunities than specific personal desires to associate with members of a particular ethnic group other than one's own.

Prejudice, personality, and contact opportunities

From the data presented we see how highly patterned intergroup contacts are—how far from being either random or free people are in their

---

[2] A comparison of this contact inventory of white gentiles with Jews and Negroes in Hometown between 1949 and 1951 shows no significant differences. This indicates both the stability of contact opportunities in a community, and the reliability of the inventory.

frequenting of situations in which such contacts might occur. The situations and individuals available for contact are selected from within rather narrowly restricted limits. Interaction is therefore a highly predetermined matter. This is especially so when such choices must be made across racial, religious, or ethnic lines.

Nevertheless, within the broad outlines of each community's social maze and primary social statuses, variations in personality dispositions and ethnic attitudes may be expected to have an influence upon contact opportunities. If we look simultaneously at the relationship of contact opportunities to ethnic prejudice and to status-role factors, we find that the greater differences are associated with the social factors. Illustrative of the findings for the survey communities is Table 7.8. The importance of the combined effect of both sets of variables can be seen from the tremendous difference between educated males who are unprejudiced (72 per cent with high opportunities) and the uneducated females who are prejudiced (only 3 per cent).

Table 7.8

Relationship between prejudice variables and contacts
and role-and-status variables and contacts.*

	Degree of Prejudice†					
	Low		Medium		High	
	Per cent reporting four or more opportunities					
	Per cent	Number of cases	Per cent	Number of cases	Per cent	Number of cases
Male						
Educated	72	(57)	60	(30)	42	(19)
Uneducated	37	(54)	35	(34)	30	(27)
Female						
Educated	28	(83)	25	(40)	5	(24)
Uneducated	21	(61)	5	(40)	3	(35)

*For Hometown majority group, 1949.
†General Prejudice Index: L = 0, 1; M = 2; H = 3.

Degree of prejudice and contact opportunities. It is evident at the same time (as Table 7.9 shows) that the more prejudiced persons are those who are less likely to find themselves in situations containing outgroup persons. This generalization holds in about the same way for several different indexes of prejudice (stereotypes, social distance, antipathy, rights of outgroups, etc.); it holds for contact opportunities with Jews, with Mexicans, and, except in Southport, with Negroes. As Table 7.9 shows, the more prejudiced members of minority groups also are less likely than the less prejudiced to have opportunities for contact with majority-group persons. (The generaliza-

Table 7.9

Relationship between degree of prejudice and contact opportunities.

	Low		Medium		High	
			Per cent with higher opportunity			
	Per cent	Number of cases	Per cent	Number of cases	Per cent	Number of cases
Hometown, 1949[1]						
General index[2]	40	(255)	29	(144)	18	(105)
Distasteful[3]	37	(198)	25	(200)	17	(106)
Antipathy[4]	40	(65)	32	(178)	28	(261)
Hometown, 1951[5]						
General index[6]	57	(93)	49	(129)	33	(201)
Distasteful[6]	58	(48)	46	(153)	37	(221)
Antipathy[7]	50	(212)	38	(167)	36	(42)
Stereotype[8]	53	(115)	49	(114)	34	(194)
Valley City						
with Negroes[9]						
Distasteful[10]	62	(42)	46	(122)	30	(155)
Rights[11]	51	(49)	43	(65)	38	(205)
with Mexicans[9]						
Distasteful[12]	68	(74)	55	(108)	46	(136)
Rights[11]	64	(94)	51	(99)	48	(126)
Southport						
with Negroes[9]						
Distasteful[13]	57	(152)	57	(103)	63	(99)
Rights[14]	59	(142)	58	(180)	59	(32)
with Jews[9]						
Distasteful[12]	72	(166)	73	(124)	45	(64)
Rights[15]	73	(263)	—	—	45	(75)
Steelville[16]						

*Appendix B describes the main scores used for indexing prejudices among the white majority-group population in Hometown.

Notes to Table 7.9, indicating scale scores considered high, medium, and low.
1. Per cent having four or more contact opportunities.
2. Low = 0,1; Medium = 2; High = 3.
3. L = 0,1,2,3; M = 4,5; H = 6.
4. L = 0; M = 1,2,3; H = 4.
5. Per cent having two or more contact opportunities.
6. L = 0; M = 1; H = 2.
7. L = 0,1; M = 2; H = 3,4.
8. L = 0; M = 1; H = 2,3.
9. Per cent having at least <u>one</u> opportunity.
10. L = 0; M = 1,2; H = 3.
11. L = 4; M = 2,3; H = 0,1.
12. L = 0; M = 1,2; H = 3,4.
13. L = 0,1,2; M = 3; H = 4.
14. L = 2,3; M = 1; H = 0.
15. Based on right to join mixed clubs only. L = yes; H = no.
16. Respondents were not asked about opportunities, but about face-to-face contacts. See interaction tables for analysis.

tions from Tables 7.8 and 7.9 also hold for samples of majority-group and Negro youths in Hometown, Steelville, and Riverton, and for Jewish youths in Hometown and Steelville.) But the differences here are less on the average than in the preceding table. The extent of exposure to intergroup contact is more closely related to majority-group prejudice toward minorities than to minority feelings toward the majority group. The only exception is the relationship found among the whites in Southport. Whether a white individual is exposed to contact with a Negro in this Southern city does not seem to be affected by the white individual's attitude toward the Negro. In this setting, intergroup contact is, so to say, more a matter of necessity and custom than of personal choice. This circumstance is also much more likely to be the case for the minority groups than for the majority group. As a general rule, the highly prejudiced person will dislike and distrust intergroup contacts and will seek to avoid them when possible and expedient. (This is a pattern of "protective selection.") Nevertheless, even highly prejudiced persons will find some occasions for contact unavoidable. Further, some of the more prejudiced will seek contact opportunities in attempts to exploit or manipulate them for personal advantage (prestige, political advantage, economic gain, etc.). Prejudice does *not* always mean avoidance.

Personality. Opportunities for contact might, also, be differentially sought and avoided by persons having different generalized personality characteristics. Analysis of a whole series of personality items shows that such characteristics do make a difference, but on the whole their apparent effects are less marked than those of the status-role and prejudice variables. Contact opportunities are most often encountered by persons who exhibit sociability; that is, who say they do not feel uncomfortable in meeting new people and who tend to meet many people rather than only a few. (See Table 7.10.) Among Negroes (only) the well-adjusted—those who do not have the more intense feelings of bitterness and frustration—are the more likely to enter into situations involving white people. For majority-group persons, authoritarianism is not related to opportunity—the authoritarians are about as likely as others to be in situations of potential contact. Among Negroes (and, in Valley City, Mexicans), the more authoritarian are less likely to report contacts with majority-group persons. Only in Hometown are there data on desires for social mobility. Among both majority and minority groups, those individuals who want to get ahead or improve themselves are the more likely to be exposed to intergroup contact.

The more opportunity the majority-group member has for intergroup contact, the more likely he is to be a person who is exposed to discussion and the printed word dealing with intergroup relations. (See Table 7.11.)

Similarly, regardless of the number of teen-age contacts, men are more likely than women, and the educated more than the uneducated, to report current opportunities for intergroup contact. The cumulative contrast be-

Table 7.10

Relationship between sociability and intergroup contact.

| | Feels uncomfortable meeting new people | | | | Meets many people | | Meets few people | |
| | Disagree | | Agree | | | | | |
	Per cent	Number of cases	Per cent	Number of cases	Per cent	Number of cases	Per cent	Number of cases
			Per cent with high opportunities					
Majority group								
Southport with Jews [1+]*	72	(262)	55	(88)	78	(183)	58	(165)
Valley City with Mexicans [1+]	—	—	—	—	59	(202)	45	(116)
Hometown [2+]	47	(303)	33	(106)	—	—	—	—
Minority group								
Southport with Negroes [2+]	36	(177)	21	(106)	41	(158)	18	(130)
Valley City with Negroes [1+]	80	(163)	66	(62)	—	—	—	—

*Figures in brackets indicate number of opportunities considered high.

Table 7.11

Relationship between exposure to discussion and print
and intergroup contact.

| | Number of available opportunities | | | |
Hometown majority, 1951	0 (126)	1 (114)	2-3 (151)	4+ (32)
Per cent read or heard anything about Negroes	30	38	46	56
Per cent read or heard anything about Jews	20	29	29	44
Per cent had conversation about Negroes	9	7	20	25
Per cent had conversation about Jews	5	9	9	16

tween the two extremes is very pronounced—80 per cent of the educated males who had 5 or more teen-age contacts now report high current exposure as compared to only 5 per cent among the uneducated females who had no teen-age contacts. (See Table 7.12.)

Other variables that affect the number of teen-age contacts are age and place of birth. The greater exposure of city-born people to teen-age contacts reflects the wider social environment open to urban as compared to rural individuals. Perhaps indicative of changing patterns of intergroup contact is the relationship of teen-age contacts to the present age of the individual. There is a great increase in the number of teen-age contacts reported as the date of birth becomes more recent. Individuals born before 1894 are less than one-third as likely as individuals born after 1934 to report teen-age contacts.

Table 7.12

Relationship between teen-age contacts and adult exposure
(in reference to sex and education).

	Number of teen-age contacts							
	None		1-2		3-4		5+	
	Per cent with four or more opportunities							
	Per cent	Number of cases	Per cent	Number of cases	Per cent	Number of cases	Per cent	Number of cases
Total group	15	(123)	31	(165)	36	(132)	50	(84)
Males								
Educated	27	(11)	62	(37)	64	(33)	80	(25)
Uneducated	25	(36)	31	(32)	38	(26)	53	(21)
Females								
Educated	3	(31)	20	(50)	25	(44)	41	(22)
Uneducated	5	(45)	13	(46)	21	(29)	12	(16)

Our image of the person exposed to opportunity for intergroup contacts, in sum, must be that of a relatively sociable, relatively non-authoritarian, attentive, and receptive person.

INTERGROUP INTERACTION

Analysis thus far suggests the social and psychological factors that influence the sheer availability of intergroup contact. But *opportunity* clearly is not *interaction*. What an individual does in a situation may be determined by factors quite different from those that placed him there in the first place. Interaction—actual communication—we hypothesized, is more likely to be the result of personal desires, more subject to control by the individual, whereas opportunity is more apt to be impersonal, due to external forces beyond the control of the individual.

Given the opportunity for intergroup contact, interaction could vary in degree of intimacy—it might remain formal and institutionalized with little personal affect, or it might result in friendships and further interaction. When, where, and how do which individuals develop interpersonal association or friendship ties? What social and psychological factors condition such interaction? At least the following factors could be expected to affect the kind of interaction that would take place: (1) the characteristics of the participants; (2) external pressures bearing upon the situation; (3) the way in which the contact comes about, and (4) the nature of the interaction itself. Thus, our attention has to turn to what takes place once the opportunity for contact exists.

But first let us note the obvious but highly important fact that the *amount of interaction* that will take place for any group in any community is strongly dependent upon the *number of opportunities* that exist for such interaction. The more opportunities the community offers an individual, the greater will be the amount of intergroup interaction. These results are given in Table 7.13. In general, minority-group members were more likely to report inter-

Table 7.13

Relationship between contact opportunities and close social interaction.

	Number of opportunities					
	Low		Medium		High	
			Per cent interacting			
	Per cent	Number of cases	Per cent	Number of cases	Per cent	Number of cases
Majority group						
Hometown, 1949[2,3]	14	(101)	30	(164)	60	(157)
Valley City[4]						
with Mexicans	12	(131)	—	—	41	(41)
with Negroes	4	(144)	—	—	25	(16)
Southport[4]						
with Jews	13	(141)	—	—	38	(97)
with Negroes	13	(168)	—	—	26	(39)
Steelville[5]						
Minority group						
Hometown						
Jews[6]	28	(35)	45	(53)	76	(62)
Negroes[6]	7	(36)	34	(64)	51	(47)
Italian-Americans[6]	44	(36)	68	(49)	80	(58)
Valley City						
Mexican-Americans[4]	35	(57)	—	—	58	(55)
Negroes[4]	22	(92)	—	—	39	(79)
Southport						
Negroes[4,7]	37	(131)	—	—	41	(88)

1. Limited to those individuals who have at least <u>some</u> opportunity for interaction.
2. Interaction means having a good or close friend with whom one does something of a social nature.
3. Low = 1; Medium = 2,3; High = 4+.
4. L = 1; H = 2+.
5. Not asked.
6. L = 1; M = 2; H = 3+.
7. Interaction = good friend; L = 1; H = 2+.

acting with majority-group individuals on all opportunity levels. This, of course, is what would be expected if interaction were simply the result of physical availability. A minority-group individual would almost have to go out of his way to *avoid* all interaction with majority-group members, whereas the majority-group member probably would have to go out of his way to *seek* interaction with a member of a minority group in the communities studied. Within the majority group there are only slight variations in interaction with the different minority groups, although the least frequent interaction was consistently with the Negro group. Within the minority groups themselves, there was greater variation, with the Negro group being much less likely than the other minority groups to report interaction. These differences become much more apparent when we look at interaction between minority groups in specific situations.

Interaction inventory

Now, let us compare the specific situations according to the degree of interaction that took place. We distinguish here between two levels of interaction depending upon whether or not the interaction also involved doing "something social together outside the home." As can be seen from Tables 7.14 and 7.15, interaction varies from situation to situation and from minority to minority. For each situation, only those indviduals who had the opportunity to interact in this situation are included. The main findings are:

1. In almost all cases, the majority group shows least interaction with the Negro minority. This difference is most pronounced on the social level.

2. Among the majority group, there is no consistent pattern of interaction according to situation. Each community has a somewhat different pattern for each minority group. In some cases interaction is more likely to occur in a work situation (that is, with Negroes in Southport), in others it may be the neighborhood (that is, Mexican-Americans in Valley City).

3. Among minority groups, both Hometown and Southport show the most interaction in the work situation, while in Valley City this tendency holds for Negroes, whereas among Mexicans more interaction occurs within organizations.

4. Among the minority groups, the Negroes in almost all cases (except at work in Hometown) report less interaction than the other minorities. Interaction for the Negroes is particularly low in Southport, except for the work situation. (See Tables 7.14 and 7.15.)

Role and status factors influencing interaction

Interaction within an available contact situation is more likely to be affected by the attitudes and personality of the participants than by their role and status memberships. This is the reverse of our finding for contact opportunities, where role and status factors were more important than personality. We interpret this to mean that the individual has a greater choice about whether or not to form friendships within a situation than whether or not to enter the situation in the first place.

Table 7.14

Interaction inventory—majority groups.

	Neighborhood			Work			Organization		
	Per cent with good or close friend	Per cent social	Number of cases	Per cent friend	Per cent social	Number of cases	Per cent friend	Per cent social	Number of cases
Hometown, 1949									
Italian-Americans	19	22	(218)	21	30	(132)*	15	36	(152)
Jews	24	8	(153)	24	19	(58)**	17	30	(157)
Negroes	15	8	(74)	30	6	(67)*	4	19	(52)
Hometown, 1951†									
Jews	17	15	(126)	21	16	(140)*	16	30	(148)
Negroes	5	7	(58)	18	8	(102)*	9	11	(45)
Valley City									
Mexicans	31	23	(62)	30	14	(125)	16	11	(64)
Negroes	9	4	(23)	9	2	(129)	18	7	(44)
Steelville‡									
Southport									
Jews	34	17	(153)	51	26	(101)	50	24	(104)

*Asked only if contact was with employee, employer, or fellow worker.
†Cannot be compared directly with Hometown, 1949 due to slightly different wording of questions.
‡Contact interaction not specified.

Table 7.15
Interaction inventory—minority groups.

	Type of Situation					
	Neighborhood		Work		Organization	
	Per cent with good or close friend					
	Per cent	Number of cases	Per cent	Number of cases	Per cent	Number of cases
Hometown						
Jews	54	(150)	67	(98)	64	(79)
Negroes	45	(142)	77	(109)	24	(54)
Italian-Americans	70	(140)	72	(103)	67	(70)
Valley City						
Negroes	43	(121)	46	(120)	50	(20)
Mexican-Americans	55	(103)	60	(59)	67	(18)
Steelville*						
Southport						
Negroes	18	(136)	44	(173)	12	(24)

*Contact interaction not specified.

In order to analyze those role and status factors influencing interaction, it is necessary to hold opportunity constant. Since we have seen that the number of opportunities has a great effect upon the number of interactions, and also that the number of opportunities is in turn strongly affected by role and status variables, in order to isolate the influence of role and status upon interaction we have to eliminate the effect of the number of opportunities. We do this by analyzing interaction according to role and status separately for different levels of available contact opportunities. The need for this controlled analysis will become clear from the following tables. The role and status factors we are considering are sex, education, age, and socioeconomic position.

Sex. In general, sex had little relationship to interaction within the different opportunity levels (Table 7.16). This means that despite the fact that men have many more opportunities for interaction than women, if women were given equal opportunity they are just as likely to interact. If we look at the difference in interaction between males and females among the majority group in Hometown regardless of opportunities, we would find that the males interact significantly more often than the females (45 per cent versus 35 per cent). This greater amount of interaction, however, is solely due to the greater amount of opportunity to interact afforded the male.

Thus we had to distinguish between two important results. In Hometown, men have more opportunity and more interaction than women. *This is a descriptive fact.* However, if we wish to analyze whether sex roles *affect* interaction, it becomes imperative to equate men and women on the number of available opportunities.

Table 7.16

Relationship between sex and interaction.

	Contact opportunities											
	Low				Medium (Per cent interacting)				High			
	Male		Female		Male		Female		Male		Female	
	Per cent	Number of cases	Per cent	Number of cases	Per cent	Number of cases	Per cent	Number of cases	Per cent	Number of cases	Per cent	Number of cases
Majority group												
Hometown*	16	(19)	13	(82)	26	(78)	34	(86)	63	(107)	62	(50)
Valley City†	10	(72)	14	(59)	—	—	—	—	50	(28)	23	(13)
Southport, with Jews‡	24	(116)	23	(122)	—	—	—	—	—	—	—	—
Southport, with Negroes‡	17	(128)	13	(79)	—	—	—	—	—	—	—	—
Majority group												
Hometown												
Jews§	—	(2)	27	(33)	41	(29)	50	(24)	43	(53)	—	(9)
Negroes‖	33	(30)	35	(34)	—	—	—	—	50	(34)	54	(13)
Italian-Americans§	—	(6)	50	(30)	61	(28)	76	(21)	80	(54)	—	(4)
Valley City												
Mexican-Americans‡	42	(57)	51	(55)	—	—	—	—	—	—	—	—
Negroes‡	29	(92)	30	(79)	—	—	—	—	—	—	—	—
Southport												
Negroes#	44	(50)	32	(81)	—	—	—	—	48	(50)	32	(38)

*Low opportunity = 1; Medium = 2, 3; High = 4+.
†L = 1; H = 2+.
‡Limited to those individuals with 1 or more opportunities.
§L = 1; M = 2; H = 3+.
‖L = 1, 2; H = 3.
#L = 1; H = 2+.

In Table 7.16 we see that men have both greater opportunity *and* inter-action among the Negro minority group in Southport. In fact, sex has a stronger relationship to interaction than the number of available opportuni-ties. Among Negroes in this Southern town, sex roles seem to determine both opportunity for interaction and interaction itself.

Education. In general, the higher-educated individuals are not only more likely to have the opportunity for contact, but also to interact, given the opportunity. This is especially true for the minority groups—with the ex-ception of the Negroes in Southport, where the less educated are more likely to interact with whites. This may well be a subcultural variation peculiar to the South. The implications for the white's stereotype of the Negro seem clear, and of basic importance for understanding the Southern situation. Among the majority groups, there is some tendency—among those with higher opportunities for contact—for *both* the lowest- and highest-educa-tional groups to interact more than the middle group. (See Table 7.17.)

Age. In general, younger people are more likely to take advantage of a contact opportunity than older people. The differences are small, however, and in the case of the Negroes they disappear among those with little op-portunity for contact, whereas among those with more opportunity, the older people are more likely to interact. Among the Jewish group also there is a tendency for the older person to interact more than the younger.

Socioeconomic status. Differences in interaction according to socio-economic status are slight, without any consistent patterns. This is also the case for social class identification. Socioeconomic level did not appear to be an important determinant of interaction for individuals with the same opportunities for interaction.

From these tables it is quite clear that variables indexing status and role have rather slight influence upon interaction *for individuals with equal ex-posure to such interaction.* This is in accord with our hypothesis about the decreased importance of these variables as determinants of interaction: their significance lies rather in their effect upon one's opportunities for contact. They are important in prescribing where we go and whom we see, but they have much less importance in influencing social interaction within these situations.

INTERACTION AND PREJUDICE

We have now examined the opportunities for ethnic contacts, and the interaction that occurs once contact exists. It is essential to examine the relation between prejudice and interaction more systematically, using the data from the several community surveys.

Out of hundreds of tabulations, there emerges the major finding that *in*

Table 7.17

Relationship between education and interaction.

	Number of opportunities					
	Per cent interacting					
	1		2-3		4+	
Majority group						
Hometown						
Grade school or less	15%	(34)	37%	(43)	71%	(17)
High school	14%	(56)	21%	(97)	57%	(102)
College	9%	(11)	50%	(24)	71%	(35)
Valley City						
Grade school or less	13%	(23)	50%	((8)		
High school	8%	(78)	27%	(15)		
College	20%	(30)	50%	(18)		
Southport, with Jews	1+					
Grade school or less	11%	(45)				
High school	23%	(112)				
College	33%	(80)				
Southport, with Negroes						
Grade school or less	13%	(53)				
High school	15%	(95)				
College	19%	(58)				
Minority groups						
Hometown Jews	1		2-3			
High school or less	24%	(25)	57%	(54)		
College or more	44%	(9)	67%	(60)		
Hometown Negroes	2		3			
Grade school or less	24%	(29)	50%	(22)		
High school	43%	(35)	54%	(24)		
Hometown Italian-Americans	1		2		3	
Grade school or less	43%	(14)	61%	(28)	68%	(22)
High school	48%	(21)	76%	(21)	86%	(36)
Valley City Mexican-Americans	1+					
Grade school or less	41%	(78)				
High school	65%	(31)				
Valley City Negroes	1+					
Grade school	19%	(81)				
High school	29%	(45)				
High school graduate	51%	(45)				
Southport Negroes	1		2			
Some grade school or less	39%	(56)	54%	(35)		
Grade school graduate or more	35%	(75)	33%	(62)		

all the surveys in all communities and for all groups, majority and minorities, the greater the frequency of interaction, the lower the prevalence of ethnic prejudice. (Note that the same correlation can be stated: the less the frequency of ethnic prejudice, the more frequent is the interaction.) This basic relationship is presented in Tables 7.18 to 7.22.

Table 7.18

Relationship between interaction and prejudice—minority groups.

		Per cent with high prejudice			
Number of Opportunities:		Low		High	
Number of Interactions:		Low	High	Low	High
Hometown					
Jews*	N =	(54)	(34)	(15)	(47)
Distasteful [1+]‡		59%	52%	60%	45%
Antipathy [2+]		64%	32%	53%	34%
Not friendly†		67%	35%	60%	30%
Negroes, 1949*	N =	(76)	(24)	(23)	(24)
Antipathy [2+]		66%	46%	61%	54%
Negroes, 1951§	N =	(21)	(17)	(50)	(62)
Distasteful		67%	47%	50%	34%
Valley City§					
Negroes	N =	(72)	(20)	(48)	(31)
Distasteful [2+]		29%	20%	21%	10%
Not friendly†		65%	45%	57%	51%
Mexican-Americans	N =	(37)	(20)	(23)	(32)
Not friendly†		76%	55%	78%	59%
Steelville‖					
Jews#	N =	(29)	(38)	—	—
Distasteful [2+]		59%	44%		
Angry**		52%	29%		
Negroes††	N =	(61)	(79)		
Distasteful [3+]		43%	19%		
Angry [3+]		68%	54%		
Anti-white [3+]		57%	44%		
Southport‡‡					
Negroes	N =	(83)	(48)	(52)	(36)
Distasteful [4+]		31%	23%	29%	33%
Angry [3+]		33%	32%	29%	28%
Not friendly†		88%	77%	92%	75%

*Opportunities: L = 1, 2; H = 3. Interaction: L = 0; H = 1.
†Based on single question—per cent replying "not very friendly."
‡Values in brackets indicate scale score values indicative of high prejudice.
§Opportunities: L = 1; H = 2+. Interactions: L = 0; H = 1.
‖Not controlled on number of opportunities (not asked).
#L = 0-2; H = 3+.
**Based on single item—per cent replying "angry" when gentile says how much he likes Jews.
††L = 0, 1. H = 2+.
‡‡Opportunities: L = 1; H = 2+. Interaction: L = 0; H = 1+.

For the majority group, the relationship exists independently of the number of available opportunities for interaction, although the differences are somewhat greater among those individuals who have few opportunities. It exists to about equal degree for majority interaction with the different minority groups and in all communities.

Table 7.19

Relationship between interaction and prejudice—majority groups.

				Per cent with high prejudice					
Number of Opportunities:	Low			Medium			High		
Number of Interactions:	Low	Medium	High	Low	Medium	High	Low	Medium	High
Hometown, 1949*									
N =	(87)	(14)	—‡	(115)	(30)	(19)	(59)	(46)	(52)
General prejudice [2.3]†	59%	42%	—	62%	44%	26%	39%	39%	37%
Antipathy [3+]	78%	58%	—	77%	63%	53%	66%	68%	65%
Distasteful [4+]	61%	64%	—	70%	66%	42%	59%	54%	44%
Hostility [3.4] (Interviewer rating)	22%	0%	—	30%	17%	0%	23%	24%	13%
Hometown, 1951*									
N =	(100)	(14)		(111)	(26)	(14)	(14)	(8)	(10)
Stereotype [2+]	60%	42%		42%	31%	14%	60%	25%	10%
Valley City**									
With Mexican-Americans									
N =	(116)	—	(15)	—	—	—	(24)	—	(17)
Likes§	70%	—	33%	—	—	—	33%	—	24%
Distasteful [1+]	81%	—	53%	—	—	—	62%	—	30%
Rights [3−]	74%	—	53%	—	—	—	54%	—	18%
With Negroes									
N =				(121)	—	(9)‖			
Likes§				72%	—	33%			
Distasteful [1+]				84%	—	33%			
Rights [3−]				85%	—	22%			

Table 7.19—(continued)

Steelville# Like [4−]	N =	—	—	(40) 30%	(95) 66%	(60) 82%	—	—

Southport**							
With Jews	N =	(37)	(60)	—	—	—	(19)	(122)
Likes§		37%	59%	—	—	—	37%	52%
Distasteful [2+]		10%	25%	—	—	—	16%	33%
Stereotype††		20%	40%	—	—	—	39%	45%
With Negroes	N =	(10)	(29)	—	—	—	(22)	(146)
Likes§		70%	79%	—	—	—	45%	72%
Distasteful [3+]		60%	61%	—	—	—	28%	63%
Rights [1−]		70%	65%	—	—	—	37%	61%
Stereotype‡‡		50%	54%	—	—	—	25%	52%

*Opportunities: L = 1; M = 2, 3,; H = 4+. Interactions: L = 0; M = 1; H = 2+.

†Values indicate scale scores considered as high prejudice.

‡Dashes will be used to indicate that this classification was not used.

§Based on single question—per cent saying they do not like or are undecided in their feelings toward Mexican-Americans.

‖When results are given for Medium column only, this indicates that no separate breakdown was made by number of interactions. All individuals however have at least one opportunity for interaction.

#This result is based on two questions asking respondent to check the minority groups with whom he has face-to-face contact and the minority groups he likes. Percentages are based on those respondents who answered either "like" or "dislike." Low interaction = 0, 1; M = 2, 3, 4; H = 5+.

**Opportunities: L = 1; H = 2+. Interactions: L = 0; H = 1+.

††Based on single question—per cent agreeing that Jews are dishonest.

‡‡Based on single question—per cent agreeing that Negroes are lazy and ignorant.

Table 7.20

Relationship between interaction and prejudice—interminority.

		Per cent with high prejudice		
		Amount of contact with other minority groups*		
		Low	Medium	High
Valley City†				
Mexican with Negro	N =	(58)	(42)	(31)
Distasteful to dance		61%	36%	10%
Distasteful to party		49%	41%	34%
Disapprove Negroes in mixed neighborhood		27%	8%	0%
Disapprove Negroes in social clubs		21%	17%	13%
Negroes with Mexican‡	N =	(121)	—	(106)
Distasteful to dance		17%		9%
Distasteful to party		22%		18%
Distasteful to eat		11%		4%
Agree Mexicans shiftless and dirty		50%		36%
Steelville†				
Italian with Jews	N =	(19)	(27)	(31)
Distasteful score [5+]		37%	15%	3%
Italian with Negro				
Distasteful score [4+]		48%	38%	8%
Southport†				
Negro with Jews	N =	(214)	(61)	(15)
Distasteful to eat		45%	23%	33%
Distasteful to party		63%	36%	47%
Agree or undecided—Jews dishonest		62%	44+%	7%

*Based upon single question asking about "face-to-face contact" with different minority groups.
† Low = 0; Medium = 1; High = 2+.
‡No medium group. L = 0; H = 1+.

The only exception is the case of white interaction with Negroes in South-port. For those individuals with low opportunity, the relationship was as high as in the other communities. However, for those whites who had high opportunity for interaction with Negroes, there is essentially no association between prejudice and interaction. Nowhere, however, can we find a real reversal in which higher rates of interaction would go together with higher rates of prejudice. (Later on we shall find examples of such "negative" associations in a few special populations, for example, white gentile women in Southport.)

In regard to the various measures of prejudice, interaction is most closely associated with feelings of like and dislike and seems to have least relation

Table 7.21

Relationship between specific interactions and degree of prejudice.

Per cent reporting feel different

	Type of Situation					
	Neighborhood		Work		Organization	
Hometown, 1949*						
Italian-American	7%	(218)	8%	(133)	2%	(152)
Jewish	11%	(153)	7%	(61)	8%	(157)
Negro	27%	(74)	16%	(67)	10%	(52)
Hometown, 1951†						
Jewish	2%	(126)	3%	(140)	2%	(148)
Negro	3%	(58)	4%	(102)	2%	(45)
Steelville*						
Jewish	6%	(127)	−4%		−4%	
Negro	36%	(88)	§		§	
Southport‡						
Jewish	3%	(153)	5%	(101)	8%	(104)
Negro	64%	(93)	17%	(147)	25%	(9)
Valley City‡						
Mexican	21%	(62)	6%	(113)	8%	(40)
Negro	39%	(23)	19%	(95)	23%	(30)

*Based on those having opportunities for contact, not necessarily interaction. Per cent
 responding "feel different."
†Based on those interacting only. Per cent responding "not so much."
‡Question asked about "dislike the idea of ethnic neighbors." Per cent responding "dislike
 the idea."
§ Attitude toward these contacts not asked.

Table 7.22

Relationship between level of interaction and prejudice.*

Per cent prejudiced toward specific ethnic group

	Level of Interaction					
	None		First name or good friend, not social		Social interaction	
Hometown majority						
Jewish neighbor	39%	(91)	22%	(50)	0%	(12)
Jewish organization	29%	(68)	28%	(41)	14%	(48)
Italian neighbor	23%	(107)	19%	(70)	2%	(41)
Italian organization	19%	(63)	12%	(34)	7%	(55)

*All minority-group members in this table have the opportunity for interaction with major-
ity members in the specific situation.

to cognitive stereotypes. The results presented in these tables are based for
the most part upon scales composed of a series of items. Many single prejudice items, not reported upon, support this general relationship between
interaction and prejudice.

Among the minority groups, the relationship held consistently for the

different indices of prejudice regardless of number of available contact opportunities, with one exception. The Negroes in Southport showed very
little relationship between interaction and prejudice. In this Southern community, once more, it appears that interaction patterns are so prescribed
by forces outside the individual's feelings that such interaction as did take
place had no effect upon level of prejudice.

Interminority prejudice was just as much related to interaction as major-
ity-minority prejudice. Anti-Semitism among the Negroes, anti-Negro feelings among the Jews, etc., are lower in the instances of interaction between
these different minority groups.

Finally, studies of majority and minority youth in three communities
showed that for this age group also, prejudice is negatively associated with
interaction.

It is at the moment an open question whether low prejudice leads to
interaction, or interaction leads to decreased prejudice, or whether both
sequences occur. Later in this chapter we shall present evidence for the
view that both do happen and probably are of roughly equivalent importance. For the moment let us simply take the basic correlation as established: high interaction, low prejudice; low prejudice, high interaction.

Before analyzing the effect of other variables related to prejudice and
interaction upon this basic relationship, let us look at the relationship between interaction and prejudice for specific situations. Does prejudice vary
according to the type of situation within which the interaction occurs?

Table 7.21 shows that, in general, interaction within the neighborhood
situation is more likely to maintain a higher level of prejudice than interaction at work or in an organization. Consistently, regardless of the situation, prejudice is more likely to exist against Negroes than against Jews.
Altogether, however, the level of prejudice against specific individuals with
whom one interacts is very low. (See Table 7.22.)

The more intimate the level of interaction, the lower the prejudice. Prejudice is almost nonexistent among the majority group with regard to those
minority individuals with whom one interacts on a close social basis. Among
the minority groups, interaction in specific situations has only a slight effect
upon the general level of prejudice. Another way to view these findings is
to ask, how much does general prejudice affect social interaction in a specific situation? The more personal the situation, for example, neighborhood
versus work, the more likely it is that prejudice will enter the picture. (See
Table 7.23.)

This finding relates to specific individuals as well as the general group:
the more intimate the interaction within a *specific situation and in relation
to specific individuals,* the less antipathy toward those specific individuals.

Perhaps more to the point as to the relation of interaction to one's attitude toward an outgroup is the relationship between interaction with a

Table 7.23

Relationship between level of intimacy and prejudice.*

	Jews in neighborhood (Hometown)		Negroes in neighborhood (Hometown, 1949)	
	First name or less	Good or best friend	First name or less	Good or best friend
Per cent high (1-4) on distasteful scale	60% (70)	48% (80)	64% (74)	60% (76)
Per cent high (1-3) on antipathy scale	59% (70)	40% (80)	85% (74)	77% (76)

*All minority-group members in this table have the opportunity for interaction with majority members in the specific situation.

Table 7.24

Relationship between intimacy of interaction with individual and degree of prejudice toward his ethnic group (Hometown majority, 1951).

Per cent who would find it distasteful to go to a party and fined that most of the people are Jewish

	Interaction with Jews		
	In neighborhood	At work	In organization
Attitude to specific individual			
Like very much	20% (35)	5% (37)	10% (41)
Do not like very much	35% (48)	30% (91)	35% (97)

	Interaction with Negroes at work		
	Per cent who would find it distasteful to eat with Negroes	Per cent who agree that Negroes are lazy and ignorant	Per cent who feel uneasy with Negroes
Like very or fairly much (61)	25%	23%	16%
Do not like very or fairly much (30)	44%	47%	50%

specific individual in a specific situation and prejudice toward the general group to which he belongs. These relationships are shown in Tables 7.24 and 7.25. They show that the more intimate the specific interaction, and the more favorable, the lower will be the level of prejudice toward the entire group.

Very little interaction takes place solely between a single majority and a single minority individual. Interaction usually takes place within a situa-

Table 7.25

Relationship between degree of liking for individual and degree
of prejudice toward his ethnic group
(Hometown majority, 1951).

Per cent who would find it distasteful to go to a
party and find that most of the people are Jewish

	Interaction with Jews	
	In neighborhood	At work
Level of interaction		
Good or close friend		
Social	7% (15)	13% (15)
Not social	16% (25)	19% (36)
Just to speak to	33% (62)	28% (36)
Not to speak to	38% (24)	39% (52)

	Interaction with Negroes at work	
	Per cent who agree that Negroes are lazy and ignorant	Per cent who would find it distasteful to eat with Negroes
Level of interaction		
Good or close friend	13% (25)	20% (25)
Not good or close friend	39% (61)	33% (61)

tional context and between groups of individuals. This situational and group definition thus becomes important in determining the individual's reaction to the situation. This is especially the case for the majority-group member. Whereas a single minority individual may find himself alone in an inter-group situation, the majority-group individual will usually have other members of his group present, and the chances are that the definition of the minority individual's status will be set by the majority group as a whole and not by the single individual.

Interaction and prejudice in relation to role and status

It is not to be expected that interaction will have exactly the same effect upon all role and status groups. Can we detect any meaningful patterns in such differential effects? Space requirements dictate that we minimize the number of tabular presentations of data. From this point on in the present chapter, we shall rely primarily on textual summaries.

Sex. Interaction is associated with low prevalence of prejudice among both men and women. (Table 7.26.) Among majority-group persons, the differences between those with and those without ethnic interaction are, on the whole, somewhat greater among the men than among the women. The differential is conspicuous in Southport, where the white women who interact with Negroes are only slightly less likely than those who do not interact to be prejudiced, and where those who interact with Jews are, if anything, more prejudiced.

Sex differences among the majority-group populations are essentially zero for those who do not have ethnic contacts, but among those who do interact, men are much less likely than women to show prejudiced attitudes.

Among the minority groups, interaction is associated with low prejudice in all groupings and in all communities, with the exception of Negro women in Hometown (based on only 19 cases). There is an irregular but possibly meaningful tendency for women more than men in the Negro and Jewish groupings to have prejudice reduced by interaction. On the whole, the seeming effects of interaction are less in the minorities than in the majority-group population.

Analyzing majority interaction with a specific minority group in specific situations, we find that lower prejudice accompanying interaction is more likely among females than males. This was especially true in regard to Italians at work and Jews in organizations.

Education. The relationship between interaction and prejudice for different levels of education shows little consistency. Among the minority groupings, there is some tendency for the association of interaction with low prejudice to be more marked among the less well educated than among the well educated. This apparent effect is particularly noticeable among the Negroes in Hometown, where the interactors showed greater prejudice than the non-interactors in the better-educated group.

For the majority group, the better educated, regardless of interaction, are less prejudiced than the less well educated. Even without interaction, a better-educated individual would be less prejudiced than a less well-educated individual who did interact. Among minority groups, sometimes the better educated are least prejudiced, whereas in other cases it is the less well-educated.

In regard to interaction with a specific minority in a specific situation, it is the less well educated who show a greater difference associated with interaction with Jewish individuals, whereas the better educated showed a greater difference in situations involving Italian-Americans.

Age. Both young and old seem to be about equally likely (17 per cent average difference for young and 18 per cent for old) to be less prejudiced with more interaction.

In general, the older individuals appear somewhat more prejudiced than the younger for the majority group, whereas among the minority groups, it is the younger who are the more prejudiced. This is true whether interaction takes place or not.

Socioeconomic status. Interaction and socioeconomic status are independent in their relationship to prejudice. For both high- and low-status groups,

Table 7.26

Relationship between interaction and prejudice according to sex.

	Males				Females			
	No interaction		Interaction		No interaction		Interaction	
Majority group								
Hometown	55%	(114)	44%	(99)	56%	(147)	31%	(71)
Steelville	76%	(51)	55%	(83)	75%	(113)	68%	(41)
Valley City	77%	(79)	38%	(21)	79%	(61)	45%	(11)
Southport with Jews	56%	(88)	29%	(28)	51%	(93)	53%	(28)
Southport with Negroes	66%	(106)	32%	(22)	57%	(69)	50%	(10)
Minority group								
Negroes								
Hometown	68%	(40)	37%	(27)	63%	(59)	74%	(19)
Valley City	63%	(65)	56%	(27)	62%	(55)	42%	(24)
Steelville	41%	(17)	33%	(46)	53%	(43)	38%	(32)
Jews								
Hometown	55%	(33)	42%	(50)	64%	(36)	29%	(21)
Steelville	75%	(8)	62%	(23)	52%	(21)	21%	(14)
Mexicans								
Valley City	88%	(33)	58%	(24)	63%	(27)	57%	(28)

*The prejudice indices used in the different surveys were:

Hometown	Majority	General Prejudice	Score 2-3
Hometown	Jew	Antipathy	Score 2-4
Hometown	Negroes 1949	Antipathy	Score 2-3
Hometown	Negroes 1951	Distasteful	Score 1-3
Steelville†	Majority	Distasteful	Score 3-6
Steelville	Jews	Antipathy	Score 2-3
Steelville	Negroes	Distasteful	Score 2-5
Valley City	Majority	Distasteful	Score 1-4
Valley City	Negroes	Friendly question	Not very friendly
Valley City	Mexicans	Friendly question	Not very friendly
Southport‡	Majority to Negro	Distasteful	Score 3-4
Southport	Majority to Jews	Distasteful	Score 1-4

†Respondents in Steelville were asked only one general question about face-to-face contacts. For purposes of this analysis, those individuals with fewer contacts will be classified as "noninteractors" while those with the higher number of contacts will be classified as "interactors."

‡Data for Southport Negroes not presented; no relationship was found between interaction and prejudice.

interaction is associated with lower prejudice; on the average, the higher SES group shows a greater decrease with interaction than the lower group.

Whether the higher or the lower SES groups are more prejudiced depends upon the majority or minority group being studied. This was true whether or not interaction took place. The point may be illustrated by the striking case of Southport, where, among white gentiles, the following situation was found.

	Socioeconomic Status			
	Low			High
Ethnic Outgroup	No Interaction	Interaction	No Interaction	Interaction
		Per cent Prejudiced		
Jew	33	29	62	44
Negroes	72	58	50	26

High SES goes with high prejudice toward Jews and low prejudice toward Negroes. Interaction is associated with lower prejudice, but the difference is negligible for low SES persons in relation to Jews.

Attitudinal and personality factors

We now know that high interaction goes with low prejudice. We have seen that certain personality variables are correlated both with interaction and with prejudice. What happens when all are involved simultaneously? To what extent, if at all, is interaction associated with lower prevalence of prejudice when general personal orientations are held constant?

Here we single out the authoritarian items, previously shown to be especially highly related to prejudice, to show the relationship of personality, interaction, and prejudice.

Authoritarianism. Among the majority group, both authoritarianism and interaction are independently related to prejudice. The more authoritarian the individual and the fewer interactions, the higher his level of prejudice. The two factors cumulate to create wide differences in prejudice between the authoritarian individual who had no interaction and the nonauthoritarian individual who did interact. These differences appeared among the majority groups in all four communities, as can be seen from Table 7.27. Furthermore, both factors appeared to be about equally important so that about the same percentage of prejudiced individuals were found among those authoritarians who did interact and the nonauthoritarians who did not interact. Interaction was equally "effective" among authoritarians and nonauthoritarians.

Among the minority groups, also, interaction is in all cases independently related to prejudice regardless of authoritarianism. However, for some groups, the individual who gives the authoritarian response is more likely to be prejudiced, whereas for other groups it is the nonauthoritarian who has the greater prejudice. Evidently, authoritarianism means something different for the majority and minority groups.

Each of the other attitudinal and personality variables that were found to be related to interaction were similarly tested. In every instance, the relationship between interaction and prejudice continued to exist regardless of

Table 7.27

Relationship between interaction and prejudice according to
authoritarianism.

| | Per cent prejudiced | | | |
| | "Authoritarian" Response | | "Nonauthoritarian" Response | |
	No Interaction	Interaction	No Interaction	Interaction
Hometown				
Score	73% (81)	60% (50)	45% (159)	27% (101)
Steelville				
Sex criminals whipped	82% (33)	63% (46)	71% (77)	57% (75)
Trust people	94% (31)	75% (20)	72% (130)	56% (103)
Valley City with Mexicans				
Score	66% (68)	41% (39)	54% (44)	24% (21)
Southport with Negroes				
Sex criminals whipped	78% (59)	64% (11)	50% (103)	26% (19)
Trust people	75% (64)	50% (8)	53% (106)	33% (24)
Children should obey	73% (94)	47% (17)	47% (73)	27% (15)
People punished	74% (94)	44% (18)	49% (61)	20% (10)

attitude or personality characteristics. Those individuals who interacted with
a member of an outgroup were less prejudiced than those individuals who
did not interact. In most cases the relationship between interaction, personality, and prejudice was independent, with both factors contributing about
equally to a prejudiced attitude.

Group pressures. The relationship between interaction and prejudice continues to exist even when controlled on a series of items indicative of group
consciousness, preference, or identification. In general, feelings of group
membership independently determine exposure, interaction, and prejudice.
The only set of variables, however, showing differences large and consistent
enough to warrant presentation concerns attitudes of Negroes toward participation with whites: those Negroes who have favorable attitudes toward
mixing with whites are less likely to be prejudiced regardless of interaction.
Similarly those Negroes who do interact with whites are less prejudiced
whether they favor such interaction or not. The two factors seem to be of
about equal importance.

Whether one's ingroup associates and reference-figures approve, tolerate,
or disapprove of outgroup contacts is a factor of great potential importance.
Direct evidence is illustrated in Table 7.28.

The two factors (interaction and social approval) seem to have about
equal weight, with the greatest prejudice existing among those majority-
group members whose friends and family disapprove and who themselves
have little interaction, whereas the least prejudice is found among those

Table 7.28

Relationship between interaction and prejudice according to
referent group approval.

	Per cent prejudiced			
	Low interaction		High interaction	
Attitude of Reference-Persons to Marrying a Jew				
Family				
Disapproves	91	(77)	77	(43)
Approves, or makes no difference	63	(81)	51	(75)
Friends				
Disapprove	93	(46)	68	(25)
Approve, or makes no difference	71	(103)	57	(96)

individuals with both approving friends and family and high personal interaction.

A suggestive differential effect is found in relation to friends' approval.
The attitude of one's friends appears to be more important among those individuals who have low interaction, whereas interaction itself appears to
make a greater difference if one's friends disapprove of mixing. Thus each
factor seems to have its greatest effect in the negative aspect of the other.

Friendship formation

Personality. There is no point in using common sense when we have un-
common knowledge that is better. But it is foolish to fail to state truths because they are a part of ordinary knowledge and therefore sound banal. Let
us say, accordingly, that whether a given individual will interact with another within a given social situation will depend, to some extent, upon his
general personality make-up. This applies to social interaction in general
as well as to that which takes place across ethnic group lines. If an individual distrusts other people or is uncomfortable meeting people, he is less
likely to seek friends than one with different personality characteristics.
Rigid, distrustful personality traits are not conducive to the formation of
intergroup friendships. We have shown already that those people who feel
that sex criminals should be publicly whipped and that people cannot be
trusted are generally less likely to interact with members of ethnic minorities than those who do not agree with these statements, when the number
of contact opportunities is held constant. The same association is present
with trust and distrust of other people in general. Furthermore, all indices
of general sociability show that attitudes of gregariousness are positively
associated with actual interaction with ethnic persons when the number of
contact-opportunities is held constant.

Personality characteristics of these kinds should be particularly relevant

Table 7.29

Relationship between interaction with ethnic persons and sociability.

	One		Two		Three	
			Number of opportunities			
			Per cent interacting			
Hometown						
Uncomfortable meeting people						
Disagree	13%	(78)	30%	(118)	62%	(24)
Agree	10%	(30)	15%	(27)	37%	(8)
Valley City			Two or more			
Make many friends	11%	(55)	53%	(21)		
Make few friends	12%	(76)	30%	(20)		
Southport with Jews	One or more					
Make many friends	30%	(105)				
Make few friends	19%	(131)				
Uncomfortable meeting people						
Disagree	28%	(189)				
Agree	8%	(48)				
Southport with Negroes						
Feel uneasy with Negroes						
Disagree	18%	(141)				
Agree	8%	(64)				

to social interaction that must take place across racial, religious, or ethnic lines. Racial, religious, and ethnic groups in American society have a long history of tension and conflict. Members of these different groups are apt to be suspicious of each other and uncomfortable in each other's presence. Many of the situations that bring them together are unfamiliar and require a period of adjustment to each other's presence. Thus personality characteristics that reflect an ability to adapt oneself to new and strange situations should be of particular importance for intergroup friendship formation. The following remarks summarize several points on personality characteristics and intergroup friendship formation.

1. *Authoritarianism*. Rigid, nonadaptive, distrustful personality traits appear to be detrimental to the formation of intergroup friendships. This is about equally true for majority and minority individuals in all cities. Although the differences observed are not large they are all consistently in the same direction. These differences exist independently of the number of opportunities available for interaction. Thus authoritarianism affects both exposure to contact situations *and* interaction within the situation.

2. *Adjustment*. Feelings of satisfaction with life show significant and consistent relationships to intergroup interaction only among members of the minority groups. Whether or not a majority member interacts with a minority member is independent of his personal adjustment, as indexed by the questions used here. It is likely that majority group members are not re-

quired to make as active an adjustment to an intergroup situation as the minority member, and thus, are subject to less than total involvement of personality. For the minority member, the presence of majority-group individuals is much more likely to make him aware of his minority status and to require some ability to adjust if he is to interact with the majority member. It is also probable that frustrated, bitter minority members would blame their unhappy condition to some extent upon the majority group, and thus find it harder to interact with them socially.

An interesting reversal of the relationship between adjustment and interaction is found among the Negro group in Southport. Here, the Negro who is dissatisfied with life is more likely to report interaction in a mixed situation than the Negro who is relatively satisfied. In this Southern city the Negro who withdraws from interracial interaction is more likely to be adjusted than the Negro who interacts. It is also likely that interracial interaction for the Southern Negro might sharpen his awareness of his position and intensify feelings of frustration and bitterness.

3. *Sociability*. While adjustment is more important for interaction among the minority groups, sociability is more important for the majority group. The minority member has to know how to *adapt* himself to a mixed situation; for a majority member it is enough to be able to make new friends easily.

4. *Mobility*. The minority individual who wishes to get ahead is not only more likely to seek the opportunity for contact with members of the majority group, but also to form friendships within these intergroup situations once he found them. For some of these minority individuals, it would appear, intergroup interaction represents a step upward in their striving for status.

Group influences. Intergroup interaction is highly subject to the individual's evaluation of how other people in his own group think and feel and his anticipation of how the members of the outgroup will act. These influences appear to be more significant for the minority than for the majority group. It seems likely that this might be due to the greater consciousness of the minority individual of membership in a particular racial, religious, or ethnic group, and to the greater salience that intergroup attitudes and behavior has for him (indexed by evidences of special ingroup attachment and concern, for example, NAACP membership, reading Negro newspapers, following customs of Jewish Orthodoxy). Significant factors bearing on group influence are:

1. *Ingroup attachment*. In general, those minority individuals who are less ethnocentric are more likely to interact with majority individuals. This is not true for Negroes in Valley City where active concern with minority-

group activities was related to a higher degree of interaction. Since we have previously found that ethnocentrism is not conducive to exposure to intergroup situations, this result is puzzling. It would seem that there is a tendency for Negroes who were active in Negro affairs to also come into greater contact with whites, but once in a contact situation, it is the less actively concerned Negro who is more likely to interact with the white. In Chapter 10 we shall return to this puzzle.[3]

2. *Teen-age contacts.* In a previous section, we saw how intergroup contact during one's youth was strongly related to exposure to intergroup contact as an adult. For all groups in all communities, teen-age contacts are related not only to the availability of contact opportunities as an adult, but also to the amount of interaction that takes place once the opportunity exists. The two factors appear to be of about equal importance—the number of contacts an individual had as a youth, and the number of opportunities he had as an adult contribute about equally to his adult interaction with members of groups other than his own. The cumulative effect of the two factors creates such wide differences as *zero per cent* with intergroup interaction among those Hometown majority-group members who had no contacts in their teens and had only one opportunity currently, as compared to *76 per cent* among those who had five or more contacts in their teens and had four or more opportunities currently.

The above association is found also for adult and teen-age close contacts. The more close friendships one had during one's youth, the more such friendships would one have as an adult.

Friendship and prejudice: the case of Hometown.[4] Those majority-group respondents in our samples in Hometown who had opportunity for contact with Negroes and Jews in the work situation, in neighborhoods, and in social organizations will be utilized for further analysis here. All respondents who reported that they came into contact with Negroes and Jews in the three situations were asked whether they had a good friend or a close friend among these groups and whether they ever did "something social together outside the home." If the hypothesis is true that the more intimate the interaction the greater the likelihood that prejudice will be reduced, we should find that those individuals who have good or close friends in the three situations will be less prejudiced than those who do not. Further, those who engage in social interaction outside the home should be less prejudiced than those who do not. Still further, low prejudice should characterize a larger proportion of those who do something outside the home with minority mem-

---

[3] This inconsistency, which appears in a single city, is a good illustration of the need to view cross-community studies as meaningful variations of the social climate, rather than simply as replications for the testing of reliability.

[4] Hometown was selected for more intensive analysis here because the data collected in this city make such analysis possible. Comparable data are not always available for Steelville, Valley City, and Southport.

bers than of those who report good or close friends among minorities but who do not interact outside the home.

There is a consistent tendency for those who report that they have either a good friend or a close friend in one of the three situations—work, organization, or neighborhood—to be less prejudiced than those who report no such interaction. (See Table 7.30.) This holds for both prejudice toward Negroes and toward Jews. The one exception to this general trend appears in the instance of interaction with Jews at work: in Hometown there is no difference in prejudice between those who have occupational contact with Jews and those who do not have such contact.

With this one exception, those individuals who report having Jews and Negroes as close or good friends in any of the three situations tend to be less prejudiced than those who respond negatively to these questions. Similarly, those who report doing "something social" with Negroes and Jews tend to be less prejudiced than those who come into contact but who do not interact in this manner. There is also a tendency for those who report doing something social together to be lower on prejudice than those who report only that they consider some Negro or Jewish associates to be close or good friends.

These results bring us finally to the pay-off of a long road of analysis, that is, to the point at which friendships form across ethnic lines. It has been clear for a long time to students of intergroup relations that the effects of contact depend upon the specific character of the interaction that develops. It is not the sheer fact that interaction occurs, but rather the type of interaction most commonly experienced between the members of two groupings that are culturally identified as different, which will change stereotypes and reduce prejudice. If the interaction occurs only rarely and in highly formalized and restricted roles, no important changes are to be expected. If contact is frequent but occurs only in restricted roles that necessarily elicit traits similar to those already incorporated in stereotypes (for example, as in the case of domestic servants or money lenders), interaction will reinforce stereotypes and will contribute to simplicity and definiteness of the stereotyped conceptions. If contact is frequent, occurs in widely differing situations, and involves many diverse roles, old stereotypes may tend to be modified in the direction of greater complexity and flexibility.[5]

Before we ask what *effects* friendships have, however, it is necessary to look more intently into their nature. It will be recalled that all respondents, white and Negro, were asked identical questions concerning opportunities for face-to-face contact with persons of the other racial category in four types of recurrent situations: (1) at work; (2) in the neighborhood; (3) in their organizations; or (4) anywhere else (for example, shopping, public

---

[5] Joel V. Berreman, "Filipino Stereotypes of Racial and National Minorities," *The Pacific Sociological Review*, I, No. 1 (Spring, 1958), 10-11.

Table 7.30

Relationship between intimacy of contact and tolerance among those
who have contacts with minorities.

Interaction with Jews in Hometown

	Close/good friend at work*		Do something social*	
	Yes (40)	No (21)	Yes (11)	No (29)
Prejudice toward Jews				
High	55%	52%	73%	48%
Low	45%	48%	27%	52%

	Close/good friend in organization		Do something social	
	Yes (89)	No (68)	Yes (48)	No (41)
Prejudice toward Jews				
High	53%	62%	44%	63%
Low	47%	38%	56%	37%

	Close/good friend in neighborhood		Do something social	
	Yes (62)	No (91)	Yes (12)	No (50)
Prejudice toward Jews				
High	58%	70%	42%	62%
Low	42%	30%	58%	38%

Interaction with Negroes in Hometown

	Close/good friend at work*		Do something social*	
	Yes (27)	No (40)	Yes (4)	No (23)
Prejudice toward Negroes				
High	67%	75%	—	72%
Low	33%	25%	100%	28%

	Close/good friend in organization		Do something social	
	Yes (16)	No (37)	Yes (10)	No (6)
Prejudice toward Negroes				
High	50%	54%	30%	83%
Low	50%	46%	70%	17%

	Close/good friend in neighborhood		Do something social	
	Yes (28)	No (46)	Yes (6)	No (22)
Prejudice toward Negroes				
High	64%	70%	33%	73%
Low	36%	30%	67%	27%

*Asked only of those individuals who report that they have had work contact as fellow work-
ers, employers, or employees.

transportation, church, taverns, or restaurants). In Southport, whites were
also asked directly about relations with any Negro servants working in their
homes. For each situation, the respondent was then asked:

*How many of these Negroes (whites) do you consider
among your best friends? _____ (number)
good friends, but not among your best friends? _____
(number)*

Interracial friendship was considered present if a respondent reported one
or more good or best friends in one or more of the four types of situations.
In those instances in which there was a reported friendship with a Negro
(or white), the respondent was asked whether he had ever done something
social together with his friend(s). "Something social" was interpreted by
respondents, as we intended, as an informal recreational or convivial association. Our first interest is in the reported friendships *in relation to* respondent's expressed attitudes toward close interracial social contacts in
general.

White persons who reported that they had a Negro acquaintance whom
they considered a good or best friend were much less likely than other
whites to express generalized distaste for close social contacts with Negroes.
This finding may appear to be obvious, if not indeed entirely tautological.

But (as we shall see in Chapter 10) Negroes who reported a good or
best white friend did not differ significantly from other Negroes in expressed
distaste for close social interaction with whites. This finding, in its turn, may
appear as surprising. The failure of friendly association to go along with
generalized social acceptance in this instance suggests that the opposite
finding for whites may not be "obvious."

How may we understand the striking difference between the white and
the Negro populations in the attitudes correlated with presence or absence
of interracial friendship? A first intuitive notion is that the difference may be
connected with different meanings attributed to interracial "friendship" in
the two populations. Let us examine this idea more closely.

Our data have clearly shown that in communities in which whites commonly manifest both prejudice and discrimination toward Negroes, there
develops a pervasive expectation among Negroes that white people will react negatively in interracial contacts, that they will demand deference, or
be indifferent, impersonal, cold, brusque, or hostile. Against this background, one might expect that any exceptions would stand out clearly. Evidences of consideration, interest, respect, or other aspects of friendliness,
which might seem very slight and inconsequential in relations between two
white persons, might take on much greater weight and value in the perceptions of a Negro of his white acquaintance's behavior. On the basis of these
considerations, we would expect Negroes to overestimate consistently the
degree of friendship being manifested by specific items of behavior on the
part of the white person.

But there is another contradictory possibility. Many Negroes have acquired by precept, or from personal experience, or both, a deep wariness and distrust of the sincerity of seemingly friendly behavior by whites.[6] To the extent that such mistrust prevails, there will be a generalized discounting of friendly behavior on the part of whites: any given increment of friendship will be devalued relative to its normal significance within one's own racial category. This process is in sharp contrast to the overestimation described in the preceding paragraph.

Another factor must be considered also. As Robert Johnson has shown, there are great differences among Negroes in the degree of desire for social acceptance by whites—from those who are obsessively "whitewardly mobile" to those who reject all contacts.[7] It seems plausible to expect that the Negroes most eager for acceptance would be likely to overestimate the friendliness of those whites with whom they interact. To the extent that this tendency exists, it would result in a spurious correlation between reported friendship and low scores on measures of social-distance attitudes.

From the standpoint of the white person reporting on his relationships with Negroes, both similar complexities and different emphases are present. First against a prevailing background of discrimination, even a mildly accepting relation may seem to the white person to warrant giving the label of "good" or "best" friend to the Negro partner. Much paternalistic or tolerant friendship of low intensity and limited scope would be expectable in a situation of this kind. In such instances, we would predict a high likelihood of exemption, leaving most generalized attitudes and stereotypic beliefs intact.

On the other hand—in a manner parallel to the mistrust by Negroes of the white person's apparent friendliness—the white may discount the Negro person's friendliness because he suspects it to be mere self-serving compliance or ingratiating expediency. To the extent that this reaction is important, the white man will tend to underestimate the genuine interpersonal liking that may have been extended to him.

Third, there does not seem to be a strict parallel from the standpoint of the white person of the "desire for acceptance by whites" on the part of Negroes. This fact reflects the asymmetrical nature of relationships between Negroes and whites as members of ascribed collectivities. Only in rare cases

---

[6] The high frequency of ambiguity and complexity in the application of diverse moral norms to issues arising out of Negro-white relations in the South has been documented in several studies. Cf. Ernest Q. Campbell, "Moral Discomfort and Racial Segregation—An Examination of the Myrdal Hypothesis," *Social Forces,* XXXIX, No. 3 (March, 1961), 228-34; Ernest Q. Campbell and Thomas F. Pettigrew, "Racial and Moral Crisis: The Role of Little Rock Ministers," *American Journal of Sociology,* LXIV, No. 5 (March, 1959), 509-16.

[7] Robert B. Johnson, "The Nature of the Minority Community" (Unpublished Ph.D. thesis, Cornell University, 1955). For the data on whiteward mobility see also Robert B. Johnson, "Negro Reactions to Minority Group Status," in Milton L. Barron (ed.), *American Minorities* (New York: Alfred A. Knopf, 1957), pp. 204-5.

and under unusual circumstances will the white stand to gain, materially or socially, from acceptance by Negroes to the same extent that some Negroes can hope to gain from acceptance by whites. The possibility does exist, however, that among a small minority of white persons an especially strong desire for social affiliation and approval may result in a tendency to overestimate friendliness of relations with particular Negro persons. Perhaps more important in such overestimation is the possibility that the white partner may accept at face value the complaint or ingratiating conduct that many Negroes have learned to produce almost automatically in treating with the potentially hazardous relations with whites. The white person might then report that he has a Negro friend, although the Negro regards the relationship as one of expedient conformity only.

Finally, many white people feel that it is wrong to be prejudiced—either because of their own internalized values or because they recognize that gross racial prejudice is often condemned by persons of prestige and authority in our society. The consequence sometimes is a sense of obligation to be tolerant, decent, and friendly toward Negro persons, and (occasionally) the consequence is a tentative guilt. Persons having these values and feelings may be expected to be predisposed to report friendship with a Negro even on a very slight basis.

Are there any data, then, that will help us to appraise the complex attitudes already mentioned? As noted previously, all Negro respondents were asked whether they had ever done anything social with white people in any of four main situations or areas of life. Over one-fourth of the Negroes responded affirmatively for at least one of the four types of situations. In sharp contrast, the number of whites who reported informal social activity with a Negro friend was so small as to preclude further analysis.

We interpret these findings to mean, first, that the white person's report of a friendship with a Negro refers to the feeling tone of a relationship in a particular, accepted social context. He apparently thinks of an individual with whom there is a relatively easy and cordial (often joking) relation on the job; or he refers to a Negro person with whom daily greetings are exchanged in passing in the neighborhood; and so on. The extension of these situational associations into diffuse multicontextual relationships is very rarely indicated in the reported friendships. Secondly, Negroes' reports of white friends are most likely to refer to diffuse relationship that spills over into informal activities outside of the primary situation in which the acquaintanceship was anchored.

Recall that Negroes who reported white friends were no less likely than those who had no white friends to find it distasteful to have close association with whites (eating, dancing, partying). When we now examine those Negroes reporting interracial friendships who *also* have done something social with the white friend, those who have had such relatively intimate association are much less likely to express social-distance prejudice than those who have not had this type of contact. The difference is highly significant (0.001 level). In contrast, Negroes who reported a white friend but no social activities with him are no more likely to be low in social-distance prejudice than Negroes who have no interracial contact at all.

Any further inferences from these data involve speculative assumptions, but two primary interpretations seem to warrant testing in future studies. The first is that Negroes tend to overestimate the friendliness of their closest white associates—or, to put it differently, that it takes comparatively little friendliness to be called friendly. This interpretation is supported by the finding that most whites describe their relationships with good or best Negro friends in terms which strongly suggest a limited and superficial association —casual amiability rather than friendship might be the appropriate description. An alternative interpretation is that the alienation from and distrust by whites on the part of Negroes are so great that only very intimate and diffuse friendships are powerful enough to reduce generalized social-distance aversions. Our own belief is that both interpretations have some validity, but the available data do not permit a more precise appraisal of their respective weights. What seems most likely is that Negroes, reacting with a certain skeptical realism, tend to report only the more intimate and diffuse contact with white persons as friendships. Certainly there is some realistic basis for caution on the part of Negro persons in moving from the experience of a given friendly relation with a white person to an attitude of generalized acceptance of close social relations with whites. Whites are much more likely to be reporting relatively superficial and situationally specific friendships. If this is the case, it is likely that a relatively few white persons are the objects of many friendship choices by Negroes; furthermore, many of the whites who report Negro friends would not be named as a friend by any Negro.

Friendship and prejudice in mixed neighborhoods. Several detailed studies were made in Hometown of neighborhoods in which one or two Negro families had moved into a previously all-white residential area, as well as of neighborhoods containing several Negro families. The findings bring out clearly the complex admixture of elements that enters into acceptance or rejection of the integrated situation. Persons least likely to accept Negro neighbors were (1) homeowners who feared effects on property values (the feared unfavorable effects most often did *not* appear), (2) middle-class families who feared loss of social status through association with low-status people, (3) long-time residents who feared neighborhood deterioration in cleanliness, morals, etc. The antipathies and fears did not, contrary to our first guess, prevent the formation of personal friendships of whites with Negro neighbors. It seemed likely that the perceived threat of an influx of Negro families was the key to nonacceptance. Whites in well-mixed neighborhoods were more likely to exhibit accepting attitudes than those living near a single Negro family. Acceptance was negatively related to social-distance feelings, but not at all to indorsement of negative stereotypes. In neighborhoods containing several Negro families, mutual aid between white and Negro neighbors was as frequent among whites with generally negative as among those with positive reactions. Although both initial prejudice and generalized authoritarian personality dispositions were found to be positively associated with rejection of Negro neighbors, the specific behavior and characteristics of the Negro families strongly influenced actual interactions of neighboring whites with them.

A summary. Our data have suggested, and to some extent supported, the hypothesis that the greater the frequency of interaction with members of another social category who are of approximately equal status in respects other than membership in this category (education, occupation, etc.), the less the tendency to accept derogatory stereotypes, to feel sentiments of social distance, or to favor public discrimination. Further examination of the pattern of interaction in relation to prejudices now suggests that the wider the variety of social categories represented by persons with whom the individual establishes any important degree of communication, the less likely that individual will be to adhere to dogmatic or categorical rejection of other individuals and the more likely he will be to accept and/or support universalistic norms in public life.

Further, we suspect, although we have no analyses bearing directly on the point from our data, that categorical prejudice is generally less among persons who have experienced a variety of social roles in their own life courses—relatively independently of the variety of ethnic contacts involved—provided that their history has not been such as to impose excessive insecurity and frustration of kinds which inevitably are felt to be arbitrary.

Types of participation: ingroup and outgroup

The findings to this point inevitably suggest that intergroup interaction may reflect the total amount of social activity or participation typical of various kinds of social persons. We have seen that despite much *de facto* segregation, insulation, and withdrawal, many people do meet ethnic outsiders—and even come to accept them as insiders. Considerable interest attaches to the individuals who leave the beaten paths of ethnically homogeneous environments, in contrast to those who do not.

In the Hometown studies, the repeated interviews with the same panel of majority-group respondents permitted the accumulation in a short period of time of much detailed information concerning each person. From these rich data, Alice S. Rossi was able to develop an elaborate analysis of total patterns of participation and nonparticipation in relation to ethnic interaction. Here we will have to discard, select, and summarize, leaving only some of the more outstanding findings. (The complete analyses are retained on file in the Department of Sociology, Cornell University.)

Rossi's analysis rests on a basic classification of respondents according to indexes of participation in community life outside the family. Table 7.31 indicates the main demographic characteristics of the participation types. To suggest something further about the people so classified, we present brief illustrative sketches, one of a housewife classed as an isolate and one of a businessman who is an active participant. As the table shows, a pattern of restricted extrafamilial participation is most likely to characterize those who are female, over 45 years of age, of low education, of low socioeconomic status, and Catholic. Examination of combinations of SES and religious affiliation indicate that in a predominantly Protestant community such as Hometown, a Catholic of high socioeconomic status is subject to some limitations of participation. Among persons of low economic level, religious background makes no difference, but among those of high socioeconomic position, the proportion of participants is 24 per cent among Protestants but only 8 per cent among Catholics. It may be that organizations geared to the interests of a higher-income group are so overwhelmingly Protestant in membership that Catholics tend not to be members, thus contributing to the higher proportion of isolates among the Catholics than among the Protestants of the same high SES.

From this beginning we seek to show the ways in which isolates and participants are differentiated from each other in terms of a variety of demographic, social-psychological, and sociological characteristics.

First, they differ in their generalized attitudes toward social interaction itself. As an index of anticipatory feelings about making new social contacts with people, we used the following item: [8] *I usually feel rather uncomfortable about meeting people I have never seen before.* Agreement with this statement was taken as indicating some degree of anticipatory social discomfort or lack of social poise. As an index of attitudes toward actual on-going social relationships, we used the following item: *I am very much concerned with how I get along with other people.* Agreement with this statement was construed to indicate a high degree of concern for one's social self, a sensitivity to the impressions one makes upon the people with whom

(*Text continued on page 195*)

---

[8] There is a high positive correlation between the "uncomfortable with strangers" item noted in the text, and another that reads "I feel a bit uneasy in the company of Negroes":

	Uncomfortable about meeting strangers	
"Uneasy in company	Agree	Disagree
of Negroes" Agree	71%	35%
Disagree	29	65
100% equals	(106)	(303)

Table 7.31

Demographic characteristics of isolates and participants.*

	Isolates	Semi-isolates	Semiparticipants	Participants
Age				
Per cent under 45	48%	51%	54%	66%
Sex†				
Per cent male	15%	38%	51%	69%
Education				
Per cent high school Graduate or better	34%	46%	57%	64%
Socio-economic status‡				
Per cent high SES (5+)	21%	27%	36%	40%
Religion				
Per cent Protestant	63%	74%	72%	84%
For each of the variables above, 100% equals	(91)	(172)	(179)	(87)

*Definitions of the participation types were: (1) participants: work for pay outside the home; belong to one or more formal organizations other than church; are members of a close, intervisiting group of friends; (2) semi-participants: have two of the three characteristics; (3) semi-isolates: have one of the three characteristics; (4) isolates: have none of the three characteristics.

†An examination of the marital status of female and male isolates and participants reveals a difference between men and women only among participants: of sixty male participants, 92% are married, 8% single. none widowed, separated or divorced; among twenty-seven female participants. however, only 44% are married, 37% are single, and 19% are either widowed, separated or divorced. Even dropping the "employment" criterion of participation and confining the definition of participation to membership in clubs and organizations and having a social clique only slightly increases the proportion of female participants who are married: the unattached woman is apparently subject to much greater pressure to "go out" and mix socially, than the male.

‡This socioeconomic status score, to be used throughout the analysis of participation, is based on: interviewer rating, self-rating of class by respondent, occupation, and source of income. It was scored as follows:

Number of points

	2 points	1 point	0 points
Interviewer Rating:	A, B	C	D
Self-Rating	Upper Middle	None, don't know, refuse to answer	Working Lower
Occupation:	Professional or semi-professional (self-employed) Professional or semi-professional (works for someone else) Managerial & executive	Self-employed (farmer) White collar Skilled labor Housewife Nonascertainable	Semi-skilled or unskilled labor Service
Source of Income:	Profits or fees Self-employed Rents Interest on savings or investments Commissions	Fixed Salaries Savings DK or NA	Wages (hourly or piece work) Private or public help (supported by family)

This yields an 0-8 point score on socioeconomic status: the higher the point score, the higher the socioeconomic status. Two groupings used in the analysis, unless otherwise noted, will consist of scores 0-3 and 4-8; three-way divisions consist of scores 0-2, 3-4, 5-8.

An Isolate — Mrs. Anna Stone

A widow, fifty, living with two sons, twenty-five and twenty-eight, together with a daughter-in-law, wife of the older son. She had lived all her life in Hometown, yet she had never belonged to any club or organization in the community, nor did she have any small group of persons with whom she had any steady social contacts. Since she married and left her job at a card manufacturing firm when she was nineteen, her life had revolved around her home and children. It had been said that she probably knew Betty Crocker soap-opera heroines better than anyone in her own neighborhood, though she had lived in the same house for twenty years. Neighbors knew her only as a small, graying woman with a pinched expression, rocking rhythmically in the corner of the porch, partially hidden by two old wisteria vines. It was on this porch that she first consented to be interviewed in connection with the 1948 vote study: One interviewer commented that she seemed to have "no interest in anything outside her little orbit"; another that she "seemed quite an unhappy person."

Nor had Mrs. Stone been a very happy person earlier in her life. She reported that she had a considerable amount of unhappiness in her childhood, completed only one year of high school, and then went to work until she married. In her teens she had no "bunch" of friends, but only one close girlfriend whom she continued to know well, until she moved to another city after her marriage; contact with this friend became confined then to exchanges of birthday and Christmas cards.

As an adult, Anna Stone was an embittered woman. She viewed the social world as a place of unhappiness and hostility. She reported that she frequently felt bitter about how things had turned out for her, often felt so frustrated she could "smash things," and that she deserved to have done better in life. She refused to accept any responsibility herself when things went wrong. Other people were viewed with suspicion, and she was very apprehensive about meeting people she had not known in the past.

When her sons suggested that she join some local civic or church club, her stock answer was that she was "too busy in the house," and "I'm not interested in those busybodies."

Though she had attended services at a local Methodist Church fairly regularly for many years, she had little but nodding acquaintances among the congregation; religion to her was a private matter, and she had no part in any of the social activities associated with the church.

When her sons brought friends or work associates to the house, she was quiet and apt to go off to her room to sew or listen to the radio. Once she knew them better, however, she was casual, made no attempt to take part in their conversations, but seemed to feel that while the world and the people in it owed something to her, she had no reciprocal obligations.

Her participation in the life going on around her was vicarious. For herself, she professed the most important things in life were "living an upright life," "doing all one can for the children," and "spending time to oneself at home." Yet, when the Hometown Gazette came bouncing onto the porch at dusk, she was an avid reader of the local gossip and personal news columns.

Lonely and embittered, she appeared to be a woman for whom life had held and still held no rich promise, since she sought none, nor would seek it where it might be found, in association with people of her Hometown.

A Participant — Mr. Ralph Hart

Married, thirty-two, and father of two children, four and seven, he lived on a quiet side street not far from the center of town, where he could be seen at dusk working in his garden, talking with his neighbors, or catching ball with his young son. From five in the afternoon till eight, these were precious hours, the quiet time spent with his family, which marked a transition between hours of intense absorption on his job, and evenings given to a variety of activities from a bowling team in the winter or softball team in spring, to meetings of the Young Men's Republican Club or gatherings of the five or six couples with whom he and his wife were intimate.

Life seemed to have been always full and interesting to Ralph Hart. As a young person he had many friends, was active in numerous teenager cliques — skating, ball, highjinks of various sorts reflecting adolescent ingenuity and spirit. He was active in the high school athletic program in Binghamton, where he grew up and attended two years of college, and since coming to Hometown where he has a promising job in a plumbing supplies firm, he had continued these interests in bowling and softball teams. He was presently interested in scouting, since his son had recently become a full-fledged Cub Scout, and although he had been approached to be a Scoutmaster, he was still mulling this over, since he had numerous other claims upon his time.

As an adult Mr. Hart was an outgoing, warm person. He viewed the world as an interesting place peopled with persons worth going out of your way to meet and know. He was eager to meet new people, made a point of visiting newcomers in his neighborhood, and was always pleasantly surprised when he found present at gatherings at friend's homes someone whom he had not known before. Yet he was also quite anxious about doing the "right thing" in his contacts with people: eager to make the right impression, to fulfill his social obligations, eager to know people who might be helpful in his getting ahead on his job.

When asked directly, he said the things that were most important to him in life were "getting ahead" on his job, "participating in community affairs," and "doing things for his children." He seldom felt embittered about how things had turned out for him in life — "everything is great." Observing him at lunch downtown, one could see how he managed to be aware of the things which were happening in town—directly, in personal contacts rather than unconsciously. In his favorite eatery he was often seen moving from table to table exchanging a few words with people he knew, while also learning the latest news concerning local industry, political activity, personal gossip. Kindly, eager, optimistic, he appeared to be a man with many relationships with the people in his community. Some of these relationships were enriching, some were merely instrumental to the fulfillment of his own needs, but in any case they came through his participation—in Hometown.

one associates. Not surprising (but comforting), is the finding that persons with a more narrowly circumscribed daily life pattern, the isolates, were more apt to express the feeling that they were uncomfortable about meeting new people (45 per cent), than the participants (17 per cent).[9] But concern for getting along with other people is most frequent among the participants (85 per cent, versus 65 per cent among isolates). Apparently the first item tends to index anxiety or withdrawal; the second, an interest in successful social functioning and making a good impression on others. The latter attitude is an ordinary accompaniment of active life in modern urban America.

A current pattern of isolation or participation seems possibly to derive from a similar childhood pattern: adult isolates were more apt than adult participants to report that in their childhood they tended to spend their time with only one or two others, or primarily by themselves. In contrast to 18 per cent of the participants, 32 per cent of the isolates were primarily lone wolves in their childhood sociability pattern. Although we do not put too much confidence in the validity of such retrospective reports, we are inclined to believe that the relationship does exist. This impression is supported by the fact that reported childhood sociability relates more strongly to having an adult social clique than to adult organization membership.

| | Childhood Sociability Pattern | | |
| | "Spent most of my time with": | | |
Adult participation	"a bunch of other kids"	"just one or two others"	"by myself"
per cent have social clique or group of friends	58% (303)	52% (63)	40% (47)
per cent belong to one or more clubs or organizations	66% (309)	60% (65)	56% (48)

[9] Women rather than men and persons of lower SES as opposed to those of higher SES are most likely to express feelings of anticipated social discomfort. There are no age differences.

We note also that the isolates were more likely than participants to have been lacking in childhood social self-sufficiency. In contrast to 10 per cent of the participants, 38 per cent of the isolates reported that as children they were "fairly much" afraid of being left alone. So, too, the proportion who felt ill at ease as adults is just 21 per cent among those who as children claimed they were "not at all" afraid of being left alone, but is 35 per cent among those who were "fairly much" afraid of being left alone.

An additional suggestion that adult isolation may be rooted at least in part in childhood sociability patterns comes when we introduce the authoritarian score into the relationship between childhood sociability and the adult participation typology: authoritarians were more likely than nonauthoritarians to have had relatively little childhood comradeship; but whether authoritarian or nonauthoritarian, the adult isolates are more likely than participants to have had a limited social life as children. The proportion of childhood isolates varies from 43 per cent among authoritarian isolates to only 12 per cent among nonauthoritarian participants.

At any rate, the behaviorally defined isolates are much more likely than the participants to manifest signs of an authoritarian orientation: 49 per cent of the isolates in contrast to 24 per cent of the participants are high scorers on the three-item authoritarianism index.[10] Older persons and those of low education and SES are more likely to be authoritarians, but with these factors controlled, participation is still strongly associated with nonauthoritarian attitudes. (Among the highly educated, however, there is a uniformly low proportion of authoritarians).

Other analyses establish the facts that: (1) being ill at ease socially is more characteristic of persons of low socioeconomic status than of high socioeconomic status; (2) lack of social ease is more characteristic of isolates than of participants, a relationship which held within each SES level; and (3) both adult social poise and the participation typology related strongly to childhood sociability; those who as youngsters were gregarious are more likely to be socially poised as adults and to be participants. In its turn an attitude of social confidence and ease is positively associated with frequency of ethnic contacts.

Social poise is associated with ethnic contacts within the isolate-participant types, most strongly among isolates (Table 7.32). Presumably there was less chance of unavoidable social contacts among isolates than among participants, which meant among other things that a social-psychological

---

[10] The following three items are used to distinguish between high and low scorers on authoritarianism:

1. *The most important thing to teach children is to obey every order their parents give without question, even if they think the parents are wrong.*

2. *I have to struggle for everything I get in life.*

3. *Prison is too good for sex criminals; they should be publicly whipped or worse.*

Table 7.32

Effect of social poise upon extensiveness of ethnic contacts
among isolates and participants.

	Per cent with two or more available ethnic contacts			
	Ill at Ease Socially		Socially Poised	
Total	52%	(97)	71%	(289)
Isolates	27%	(56)	47%	(128)
Participants	84%	(41)	91%	(161)

characteristic like social poise about anticipated contacts with hitherto unknown persons would play a more important part for isolates than for participants. When we turn to the prevalence of ethnic associates known on a
first-name basis or considered good or close friends, there is an independent
and cumulative relation between ethnic friendship formation, on the one
side, and social poise and general participation type, on the other.

Table 7.33

Relation of social poise to friendships with ethnic contacts
among isolates and participants.

	Per cent of available ethnic contacts which are first-name acquaintances or good or close friends			
	Ill at Ease		Socially Poised	
Total	42%	(125)	59%	(466)
Isolates	19%	(16)	31%	(29)
Semi-isolates	33%	(34)	48%	(112)
Semiparticipants	43%	(36)	64%	(181)
Participants	57%	(39)	71%	(144)

Table 7.33 indicates the extent to which ethnic contacts are available to
isolates and participants in Hometown. Approximately half of the participants have from five to nine ethnic contacts; that is to say, some 53 per
cent of the participants are involved in five or more situations in which at
least one ethnic individual was present.[11]

Controlling availability of ethnic contacts, we find that among participants, the higher incidence of actual interaction is among men and younger
persons, whereas there are no differences among SES levels. None of these

---

[11] It would be exceedingly cumbersome to speak of these contact scores in a very
literal fashion, such as "seventy-five per cent are involved in four or more situations
in which at least one ethnic individual is present." In point of fact, even this clumsy
statement is not quite accurate: since only three situational contexts are involved,
a score of "four or more" means that persons of more than one ethnic group are
present in at least one of the situational contexts. Except in cases in which particular stress is desired, we shall therefore adopt the language convenience of speaking
in terms of "four or more available contacts," or "four or more actual contacts,"
as the case may be, without the lengthy and clumsy, though more accurate, statements used at this point in the text above.

demographic factors are related to ethnic interaction on the part of isolates. (See Table 7.34.)

Table 7.34

Available ethnic contacts among isolates and participants.

	Isolates	Semi-isolates	Semiparticipants	Participants	Total Community
Available Contacts					
None	46%	17%	9%	1%	16%
1	40%	32%	8%	1%	20%
2–3	14%	37%	41%	23%	32%
4	—	10%	22%	22%	15%
5–9	—	4%	20%	53%	17%
100% equals	(85)	(165)	(172)	(82)	(504)

The sex differences are large, and controlling for them largely wipes out the apparent influence of age. Even when the level of exposure is controlled to some extent, by the participation typology, men are still more likely than women to have extensive ethnic contacts. The differences are very large among the participants, whether young or old. (See Table 7.35.)

Table 7.35

Available ethnic contacts among isolates and participants
(controlled by age and sex).

	(Per cent high contact)*	
	Isolates	Participants
Under 45		
Men	12% (32)	69% (87)
Women	8% (86)	37% (57)
Over 45		
Men	20% (46)	66% (56)
Women	7% (86)	30% (54)

*High = score 4–9.

Even among those women who are employed, belong to one or more social organizations or clubs, and have a social clique, there is less tendency for an extensive pattern of intergroup contacts to occur than among men with a similar pattern of general participation. Obviously exposure is still not equivalent even among the participants. Men tend to belong to organizations of a more heterogeneous social composition, and the same characteristic of greater social heterogeneity probably holds for job associates. There is the further likelihood that even if women belonged to organizations as diversified as those of men, and even if they held down jobs that placed them in daily contact with as varied groups of people, they would still tend to show less extensive patterns of contact. They have grown up in a society that does not fully approve of extensive social pathways for women.[12] These reflections suggested that status differences might militate against the development of closer social bonds between majority- and minority-group individuals, whereas status similarity would be a factor facilitating the development of intergroup friendships. The data lend some support to this argument. Among both isolates and participants, Jewish neighbors are reported as friends to a greater extent by high SES persons than by low SES persons, whereas Negro and Italian neighbors are regarded as friends more often by low SES persons than by high SES persons (Table 7.36). Note also that participants are more likely than isolates to develop friendships with their ethnic neighbors: of the six relevant comparisons there was not a single exception to the conclusion; whether SES is high or low, whether the ethnic neighbor is Jewish, Negro, or Italian, there is greater ethnic contact cultivation among participants than among isolates.

Table 7.36

Active friendships with ethnic neighbors among isolates and participants.

	Per cent who consider their ethnic neighbors good or close friends and have done something social with them			
	Isolates		Participants	
Ethnic Group of Neighbor	Low SES	High SES	Low SES	High SES
Jew	28% (29)*	38% (37)	41% (31)	46% (56)
Negro	23% (14)	19% (21)	52% (16)	28% (23)
Italian	48% (48)	35% (48)	84% (54)	52% (68)

*Case base consists of those who report having a neighbor from the ethnic group indicated.

Passing over many technical details, let us simply say that a variety of indices and methods of analysis were used to check on the possibility that any of the findings thus far reported might be distorted by artifacts of measurement. The strong association between general participation and ethnic contact was retained in each of several alternative ways of measuring

---

[12] Rossi has observed that although the limitations hold most strongly for cross-sex contacts with strangers, similar restrictions may also hold for same-sex contacts among women. Men have many contact centers where they can meet other men and engage in various activities with them, from checker-playing to basketball to pool. It is hard to think of any equivalent female contact centers that are operated on a comparable commercial basis. Such participation, even with female strangers, tends to take place under the auspices of some approved institution such as the church or charity organizations (church auctions, bazaars, bingo, etc.).

interaction. In fact, the only place at which the index used made an important difference is in the comparison of men and women. Here it occurs that when we look at *the proportion of available ethnic contacts that are developed into friendships, there are no important differences between men and women.* Thus, *if* women have equal opportunity for close acquaintance, it appears that they are as likely as the men to form interethnic friendships.

Using the same measure—proportion of "available contacts" reported as friends—it is possible to show one further relationship of some interest. In Table 7.37 the index is simultaneously related to participation, social poise, and socioeconomic status. The pattern now becomes clearer. Here, as in all preceding tables, participants retain the lead over isolates in the extent to which they cultivated their ethnic contacts—whether or not the individual is socially poised or on the high or low socioeconomic status level.

Table 7.37

Relation of social poise, participation, and socioeconomic status
to friendship formation among ethnic contacts.

	Per cent of total number of available ethnic contacts reported as friends			
	Isolates		Participants	
Social Poise	High SES	Low SES	High SES	Low SES
Poised	45% (79)	44% (62)	65% (203)	64% (122)
Ill at ease	23% (17)	43% (33)	41% (29)	49% (46)

Among those who are socially at ease, socioeconomic position no longer makes any difference; SES relates to friendship formation only among those who are ill at ease socially. Among the latter, both isolates and participants on the low SES level were more likely than their counterparts on the high SES level to develop friendships with an ethnic individual. Those least likely to cultivate their ethnic contacts were the high SES isolates lacking social poise (23 per cent); those most likely to form friendships with ethnic persons were the socially poised participants (64 per cent). The findings are consistent with interpretations already suggested: both status differences and personal orientations work in the same directions.

We suggest as a general point of perspective: much of the apparent ethnic prejudice in our community life is compounded by isolation, timidity, and social fear.

This conclusion is supported by a mass of further evidence from the Hometown surveys which shows that participants are far more likely than isolates to be aware of happenings outside their personal social circles, to vote and to be interested in political affairs, to read widely, and to show other manifestations of an active, cosmopolitan attitude toward the world.

Changes in interaction and attitudes: the chicken and the egg

Out of all the intricate relationships reviewed in this chapter three facts stand out above the others:

1. The frequency and kinds of contacts across ethnic lines vary greatly according to situational context, minority group, and status characteristics of participants.

2. Persons who are relatively unprejudiced are most likely to have ethnic contacts.

3. Persons who interact across ethnic lines are most likely to be relatively unprejudiced and to form ethnic friendships.

From the patterns of correlations among the variables we have made some tentative causal inferences. It seems safe, if not surprising, to conclude that when ethnic contacts do occur, it will be the less prejudiced persons, on the average, who are most likely to develop those close associations and friendships that will, on the whole, contribute to further reduction of stereotyping, categorical hostility, and feelings of social distance. The converse proposition is less secure, but still plausible in the light of the data: interaction with ethnic outgroup persons, under the conditions in the communities studied, will tend to reduce prejudice.

We have tried to be very cautious indeed in interpreting our findings concerning the relationship between prejudice and intergroup contact, and we have stressed the fact that even close and long-continued interaction does not necessarily lead to understanding or solidarity. We have suggested that there are conditions under which unfriendly feelings and overt conflict may be intensified by an increase in interaction, including greater exchange of information about the characteristics and intentions of the interacting parties. We believe that these points are valid, and that it is salutary to emphasize them, in the interests of clear thinking.

But no matter how careful and astringent we may try to be in dealing with the question of the effects of intergroup communication, we will not wish to overlook the fact that *absence* of communication cannot increase knowledge or understanding of the members of another group or social system. The likelihood of projective reactions, progressively diverging from veridical perception, is enhanced by blockage of communication with another system or grouping, which, at the same time, is an important object of concern to us because its members may act in ways that are highly consequential for us. An especially high likelihood of increased prejudice is created when two segments of the same community are thus mutually objects of concern, under conditions of conflict or tension and threat. The likelihood is heightened by incomplete, partial, and erratic communication, either directly or through third parties (including mass media). Under these conditions, both the concrete visibility of the others and the predictability of their responses are rendered low and problematic.

If these circumstances, which are inherently frustrating, are conjoined with chronic unresolved tension (for example, threatened school desegregation), distortions of group images are inevitable, and the possibilities of negotiation, compromise, or acceptance of new approaches to the issues are sharply reduced. The result will be the kind of situation prevailing in some American communities in which pressure is felt for desegregation of the public schools and communication has broken down between Negroes and whites and among prosegregationists, moderates, and integrationists.[13]

There are sound theoretical reasons for expecting some kinds of ethnic interaction to reduce prejudice. But there are equally cogent theoretical bases for expecting other kinds of interaction to lead to increased prejudice.[14] Which outcome is most likely, when, and why?

The relation of prejudice and interaction, considered *a priori,* is a particular kind of chicken and egg problem. Which came first? The answer? First one and then the other. Both sequences are plausible; indeed, both are known to occur.[15] Let us see whether the panel data from Hometown will help.

Change in reported attitudes and ethnic contacts. Between 1949 and 1951, a gain or a loss of one or more ethnic contacts was experienced by 38 per cent of the Hometown white gentile respondents; of those reporting a change, 73 per cent had gained a contact. More striking is the fact that a noticeable change in degree of prejudice is reported by four out of five persons (78 per cent); of those who changed their ethnic attitudes, 70 per cent indicate a lessening of negative images or feelings. It is plain that we are recording a period of increased interethnic contact and of decreased prejudice.

---

[13] A frequent outcome, then, is that ". . . the antagonists are seen as victims of blind forces of biological, psychological or social origin, or as tools in a deliberate plot initiated by people far away. They would not be seen as independent individuals, responsible for their own opinions, as real to them as one's own opinions are to oneself. Lack of contact prevents the kind of understanding based on real empathy necessary to grant antagonists autonomy, and the general feeling that the causes are exogenous to the system, combined with the perception of the antagonist as an agent of frustration, will lead to the theory of the antagonist as *directed* by something or somebody." [Johan Galtung, "A Model for Studying Images of Participants in a Conflict: Southville," *The Journal of Social Issues,* XV, No. 4 (1959), 41.]

[14] Among other examples, there is the case of increased prejudice against the Maori in New Zealand subsequent to increased contact in the later post-conquest phases when the Maori began to emerge again from reservation-like areas. As depicted by David P. Ausubel, the renewed contact had the initial effects of arousing ". . . anti-Maori racial prejudice and extra-legal discriminatory practices in employment, housing, hotel accommodation, bars, credit, etc., not unlike those directed against Negroes in northern areas of the United States." ["The Maori: A Study in Resistive Acculturation," *Social Forces,* XXXIX, No. 3 (March, 1961), 224.]

[15] Daniel Glaser: "Dynamics of Ethnic Identification," *American Sociological Review,* XXIII, No. 1 (February, 1958), 31-40.

What are the characteristics of those persons who changed either their pattern of contact, of prejudice, or of both? We first note that neither the frequency nor kind of change in either contact pattern or prejudice is closely associated with general attitudinal or personality indices. A few examples of these findings follow.

Persons who say they feel bitter about the way things have turned out for them are only slightly less likely than those who say they do not feel bitter to report a change in ethnic contacts (32 per cent versus 41 per cent). And the two groupings are equally likely to have gained or lost contacts and to have become more prejudiced or less prejudiced.

Persons who testify to feeling ill at ease in meeting strangers are only slightly less likely than the socially poised to change their ethnic contacts and to gain rather than lose such contacts. Social ease or unease is not at all related to either frequency or direction of attitude change.

Attitudes of occupational or social striving are essentially uncorrelated with any type of change in contact or prejudice.

Respondents who say they change their minds frequently are slightly more likely than other persons to report a change in ethnic contacts (42 per cent versus 34 per cent), and slightly more likely to gain rather than lose a contact. Flexibility or instability of general set is not correlated with change in prejudice, although there is an indication that if a change in attitude does occur it is somewhat *less* likely to be in a favorable direction among the more instable people.

People who testify to being concerned as to whether they are liked by others are slightly more likely to exhibit change in both contacts and attitudes—to gain contacts and to lessen in prejudice. Assuming the nonsignificant increases to be actual, we would suspect that they derive from social sensitivity rather than from a high level of anxiety.

Even the old reliable item concerning trust in people fails to differentiate between changers and nonchangers. None of the differences are significant at the 0.05 level. What does happen, however, is that those gaining new contacts tend to be the persons who at the time of the initial survey were less prejudiced. Classifying respondents by a score of generalized prejudice (in 1949), we find the following:

1949 score of general prejudice	Percentage who had gained new contacts by 1951:	
	With Jews	With Negroes
Lowest—0 (72) *	33	9
Inter- [1 (110)	20	4
mediate [2 (132)	16	5
Highest 3 (109)	10	3

* Numbers in parentheses are number of cases.

It had been thought that a higher proportion of the contacts gained by the more prejudiced would be involuntary—for example, work contacts rather than the inclusion of an outgroup person in the individual's informal social group. The hypothesis was not confirmed. There was only a slight and statistically nonsignificant tendency in the predicted direction.

These findings suggested looking for the combined influence of initial level of prejudice and initial presence or absence of ethnic contacts. We therefore hypothesized that the likelihood of gain in contacts would increase in this order: (1) no prior ethnic contact; high initial prejudice; (2) some initial contact, but high prejudice; (3) no ethnic contact, but low prejudice; (4) both initial contact and low prejudice. The actual finding is that there is not a step-by-step increase, but rather a sharp difference between those in category 1 and all others. The persons who in 1949 were both highly prejudiced and lacking in ethnic contacts were, by far, the least likely to acquire new contacts. Differences among the other three groupings are slight. It is important, however, to call attention to the fact that group 2 is just as likely as group 1 to accept new ethnic contacts: people who were initially high in prejudice but who had established some ethnic interaction went on to gain additional contact. The general finding may be stated positively: having had one or more ethnic contacts *and/or* a low initial level of prejudice predisposed a person to gain ethnic contacts.

Table 7.38

Initial prejudice and ethnic contacts in relation to increase
in ethnic contacts (1949–1951).

| | Per cent reporting gain of new ethnic contact | |
Ethnic contact, 1949	High prejudice	Low prejudice*
None	20% (137)	36% (126)
One or more	42% (45)	40% (50)

*Low = less than 3 "distasteful" responses.

The general pattern of social participation is strongly related to changes in ethnic contacts: participants are far more likely than the less active persons to report a change (Table 7.39). If the more isolated persons do change, however, they are somewhat more likely (but not significantly) than active participants to gain rather than lose ethnic contacts. The participants, surprisingly, are slightly less likely than the isolates to change their prejudicial attitudes, but favorable or unfavorable changes are not consistently related to the extensiveness of general participation.

There is a great and significant tendency for men (55 per cent) more often than women (25 per cent) to report a change in ethnic contacts, and when a change had occurred, men were slightly more likely than women

Table 7.39

General pattern of participation in relation to changes in
ethnic contacts and prejudice.

	Isolate	Semi-isolate	Semiparticipant	Participant
Ethnic contacts				
Per cent changers	12% (66)	34% (140)	40% (142)	61% (75)
Per cent gain contacts among changers	100% (8)	77% (48)	76% (57)	62% (46)
Prejudice				
Per cent changers	87% (66)	76% (140)	77% (142)	72% (75)
Per cent more favorable	70% (57)	64% (108)	72% (110)	78% (54)

to gain instead of losing ethnic contacts. However, there were no differences between men and women either in the proportion changing their attitudes or, among those whose ethnic attitude changed, in the proportion who developed a more favorable orientation. The greater prevalence of ethnic contacts on the part of the majority-group men appears to be primarily a consequence of their more extensive pattern of interactions outside the contexts of family and neighborhood.

Changes in ethnic contacts tend to be most frequent among persons in the highly active years 35-44, but there are no important age-associated differences in the proportion gaining contacts, nor are there any significant differences by age in the reported changes in ethnic prejudices.

Persons of low socioeconomic status are very slightly more likely than those of high SES to report changes in ethnic contacts, especially gains, and to become more favorable in attitude.

Most differences associated with educational levels are small. There is a statistically significant difference (0.05 level) between college educated and others in the percentage who have gained or lost ethnic contacts, but the proportion of those who experienced a change who *gained* a contact is actually somewhat larger among the small group of persons with only a grade-school education. Differences in prejudice change are not associated with educational levels. On the whole, education does not seem to be an outstanding factor in influencing changes in interethnic association or attitudes.

Analysis of a more detailed kind brings out several relationships concealed in the associations reviewed thus far.

The data in Table 7.40 shows no large differences by educational level in proportions changing their attitudes toward Negroes or Jews. But among the better-educated respondents there tends to be a decrease in prejudice among those who acquire new ethnic contacts. Four out of every five of the better educated who gain contacts show more favorable attitudes toward Negroes, whereas less than half of the small number who lost contacts show decreased prejudice. On the other hand, among the less well

Table 7.40

Proportion of respondents showing lessened social-distance prejudice
toward Negroes and Jews (Hometown, 1949–1951).

| | Education of Respondent | |
Change in ethnic contacts, 1949-1951	Less than high school graduate	High school graduate or more
	Attitude toward Negroes	
Lost contact	67% (12)	46% (17)
No change	73% (78)	71% (84)
Gained contact	61% (31)	84% (45)
	Attitude toward Jews	
Lost contact	61% (13)	50% (16)
No change	72% (78)	64% (80)
Gained contact	68% (34)	71% (38)

educated, there is no relationship between change in contact and change in
attitude. The better educated may be more receptive to the new experience
of ethnic contact, or they may have a different kind of contact (for example,
a noncompetitive relation with a well-educated ethnic person), or both.

It would seem very reasonable to suppose that it might be the highly
prejudiced persons who feel intensely about their attitudes who would resist
change in attitude even if they gain new ethnic contacts. In the 1949 study,
each respondent rated the strength of his own social-distance feelings toward Negroes and toward Jews. Using both social-distance and intensity
scores, we derive Table 7.41. The hypothesis is not confirmed. In every
comparison save one (decrease in prejudice toward Negroes), the highest
frequency of change and of decrease in prejudice comes among those with
the more intense attitudes. The most striking transformation occurs among

Table 7.41

Attitude change among respondents who gained contacts (1949–1951).

| | Low Prejudice | | High Prejudice | |
	High intensity	Low intensity	High intensity	Low intensity
Per cent who change attitude toward				
Jews	74% (23)	60% (35)	96% (24)	33% (30)
Negroes	70% (23)	68% (35)	71% (24)	63% (30)
Per cent of changers who decrease in prejudice toward				
Jews	83% (17)	53% (21)	83% (23)	70% (10)
Negroes	69% (16)	79% (24)	70% (17)	62% (19)

the intense anti-Jewish grouping—where 96 per cent change in attitude, and 83 per cent of these shift toward a less prejudiced attitude. Apparently something like a conversion occurred in these cases; at any rate they contrast sharply with the frozen prejudice of the low-intensity anti-Semitic persons, where only 33 per cent change their orientation.

Possible reasons for change in attitude. The possibility is raised by these data that many highly prejudiced persons—precisely because they are involved, concerned, and sensitive to a problem—may be more open to change through realistic experience than other prejudiced persons who feel less concern and probably less attitudinal dissonance. Extreme closure against new experience may result in a low-temperature prejudice blocked off from the individual's vital concerns and highly inaccessible to modification through personal contacts.

An effort was made to check upon some of these possibilities of interpretation. It was hypothesized that the persons least likely to change their attitudes would be those with intense attitudes supported by a harmonious contact pattern (either prejudice-no contact or unprejudiced, with contact). These respondents were compared with those with an inconsistent contact-prejudice profile and low intensity of attitudes. No differences in percentages changing attitudes toward Negroes or Jews were found.

Another possibility is that the extreme types of prejudiced persons—the bigots and tolerants of Chapter 5—will be those least likely to change. But this is not so. In fact it is just those of intermediate prejudice who are least likely to change their attitudes. In the case of attitudes toward Negroes, the initially tolerant are most likely to change; for attitudes toward Jews, the bigots are most likely to shift under the condition of new ethnic contact. The bigots (who agreed with nearly every prejudiced statement we could present to them) are not so rigid as to be immune to new ethnic experience; two-thirds of them show a decrease in prejudice toward Jews, a third in their attitude toward Negroes.

Other findings. Consistent with these results is the additional finding that neither the frequency of over-all change in attitudes nor the frequency of decreases in prejudice is consistently related to authoritarianism, as indexed by our three-item score. Authoritarians are as likely as nonauthoritarians to experience a change in ethnic contacts. The authoritarians are less likely than others to change attitudes toward Negroes—but more likely to decrease in prejudice towards Jews. Authoritarians who have gained ethnic contacts between 1949 and 1951 are just as likely as nonauthoritarians to acquire more favorable attitudes towards Jews and almost as likely to become more favorable toward Negroes. (See Table 7.42.) *If* contacts can be established, even quite marked prejudices—within the range found in Hometown (we do remember that this is not Johannesburg, South Africa, or Jackson, Mississippi)—are not sufficient to nullify the tendency of interaction

Table 7.42

Authoritarianism and attitude change among persons gaining
ethnic contacts (1949–1951).

	Personality Index	
	Authoritarian and semiauthoritarian	Nonauthoritarian
Attitude toward Negroes		
Per cent who change	60% (57)	75% (51)
Per cent of changers who decrease in prejudice	74% (34)	72% (38)
Attitude toward Jews		
Per cent who change	63% (57)	65% (51)
Per cent of changers who decrease in prejudice	62% (36)	67% (22)

to reduce prejudice. Some self-selection is still at work; as is shown on p. 203, the proportion gaining new contacts decreases with the level of general prejudice. But even the highly prejudiced authoritarians, when they come into continuing contact with a minority group, apparently tend to become less negative in their orientations.

Other data show that most of the effect of contact on the more highly prejudiced persons comes from gaining two or more new ethnic contacts. Gain in contacts with Jews tends to accompany reduced prejudice toward both Jews and Negroes. Gain in contacts with Negroes accompanies more favorable attitudes toward Negroes, but there is no clear carryover into attitudes toward Jews. On the whole, although there are some suggestions in the data of a generalized reduction in outgroup prejudice, the main weight of the findings is on the side of specificity of effects—that attitudes toward each minority are best viewed separately in analysis of effects of contacts.

It will not do, of course, to assume, because ethnic contacts are associated with reduced prejudice, that it was *only* the relationship with the ethnic person(s) that is involved. Intergroup relations always involve, in addition to the two parties in a particular relation, the reference groups of the participants. The most relevant groups of reference in outgroup contacts are made up of individuals who are known or believed to have attitudes toward what is happening that could be of important consequence to oneself. We thought originally of comparing persons without reference groups with those whose family and close friends shared or did not share the respondent's own attitudes. However, there were too few cases in which the individual reported that he had no relevant referents. The contrast finally developed was between persons who mentioned family and/or close friends (spouse, siblings, parents, close friends, etc.) as referents versus those who mentioned nonfamily individuals or groupings (doctor, minister, business acquaintance, etc.). The supposition was that those mentioning a family reference group would less often show changes in attitudes. In fact, the data show a slight, although consistent, tendency in the expected direction, even in those instances in which a family member or close friend disagrees with the respondent's position. The group of cases most likely to change, and then in a positive, less prejudiced direction, consists of persons who admit to prejudiced feelings but have nonfamily referents not sharing these feelings. Thus, the data reflect to a limited degree the tendency of a tolerant ingroup environment to induce changes in attitudes toward outgroups.

Let us be quite explicit in the recognition that none of the data just reviewed can be said to prove that personal interaction alone *causes* a change in prejudice. It could be, for example, that persons most likely to interact with an outgroup person are on the average more ambivalent, conflicted, or dissonant in their attitudes, and that the internal processes thus set up would result in the observed changes whether or not ethnic interaction had taken place.[16] Future research into interethnic interaction and attitude change will find it useful to concentrate in considerable detail upon the actual character of the specific person-to-person relationships and the conditions under which interaction is initiated, increased, decreased, or terminated. The significance of particular variables or factors varies with the *combinations* of them found in the context of these relationships. For example, in the Hometown studies it was found that zero per cent of the older, educated men having contacts with Negroes on the job form friendships with these Negroes —as compared to 62 per cent of the young, uneducated men. This contrast is related, of course, to the fact that all the job contacts of the young, uneducated whites with Negroes are between fellow workers, whereas half of the contacts of the older, educated men are employer-employee contacts. Or, again, in the reports of majority-group respondents on their relations with Jewish or Italian-American persons, friendships occur more often when the Jewish or Italian-Americans are on a higher income level than the reporting member of the majority group, whereas for Negroes, more friendships are reported when income levels are the same. For all three ethnic groups, however, visiting in each other's homes is more likely to take place when the associating persons are of equal income status. Visiting is least likely when the majority-group member is of higher income status than the ethnic group member.

An analysis of who approached whom to begin a close contact (still using the Hometown data) shows lower-status individuals more often approached

---

[16] See the data and discussion in Chapter I of Patricia Kendall, *Conflict and Mood: Factors Affecting Stability of Response* (New York: The Free Press of Glencoe, Inc., 1954).

higher-status persons. Thus, where the ethnic group was of higher income than the majority group, 77 per cent of the majority-group members report themselves as initiating the contact, as compared to 60 per cent where the two groups were the same, and only 29 per cent where the ethnic group was lower. In the microsociology of ethnic relations the trading of individual and group marks of status rankings is an important process deserving further intensive study.[17]

In 1949 and again in 1951 each of the white non-Jewish respondents was asked to characterize each contact with a Negro or Jewish person as to the closeness of the relationship, ranging from sheer proximity (available) to a close friend with whom informal social interaction occurs. Of all the maintained contacts with Jewish persons reported in 1949 and in 1951, one-half in 1949 had not progressed to a first-name basis and only 20 per cent were instances in which there was shared informal social activity. Of contacts with Negroes, 58 per cent were merely available and only 8 per cent entailed doing something social together. Tables 7.43 and 7.44 show

Table 7.43

Shifts in closeness of maintained Jewish contacts (1951).

		Available	First name	Good friend	Close friend	Do something social together	Total*
	Available	29%	11%	2%	4%	3%	49%
	First name	2%	4%	1%	–	2%	9%
1949	Good friend	3%	3%	6%	–	4%	16%
	Close friend	–	–	1%	1%	4%	6%
	Do something social together	1%	2%	5%	4%	8%	20%
	Total	35%	20%	15%	9%	21%	100%

*Based on 225 contact-units.

Summary
No change.......................... 48%
Decrease in Closeness........ 21%
Increase in Closeness......... 31%

all the changes occurring between 1949 and 1951.[18] Approximately half of the Jewish contacts and two-thirds of the Negro contacts remain in 1951 at the same level of closeness as in 1949. The difference between the proportion of "no-change" cases for Jewish and Negro contacts suggests that

---

[17] Cf. much of the analysis by George C. Homans in *Social Behavior: Its Elementary Forms* (New York: Harcourt, Brace & World, Inc., 1961), pp. 196-204. Note particularly (p. 204): ". . . in any pair, the man lower in esteem is apt to originate more interaction than the man higher."

[18] Note that numbers in the tables refer to contacts, not persons. The present interest is in the relationships to ethnic persons.

Table 7.44

Shifts in closeness of maintained Negro contacts (1951).

		Available	First name	Good friend	Close friend	Do something social together	Total*
	Available	43%	11%	3%	1%	—	58%
	First name	1%	3%	1%	—	—	5%
1949	Good friend	3%	1%	6%	1%	2%	13%
	Close friend	3%	4%	—	7%	2%	16%
	Do something social together	—	2%	2%	1%	3%	8%
	Total	50%	21%	12%	10%	7%	100%

*Based on 225 contact-units.

Summary

No change......................... 62%
Decrease in Closeness........ 17%
Increase in Closeness......... 21%

since prejudice toward Negroes is greater than towards Jews, there is a greater tendency for Negro contacts to remain at the same level of closeness than for the Jewish contacts: 62 per cent of the Negro contacts in contrast to 48 per cent of Jewish contacts have undergone no change in the closeness of the social tie between the white gentile respondents and the ethnic individuals.

But where change does take place, does it tend to be in the positive direction of a more intimate social relationship with the ethnic individuals? The evidence indicates to us the fact that only a slight movement in that direction occurs: 31 per cent of the Jewish contacts are characterized by an increase in the closeness of the contact, but 21 per cent have undergone a decrease in closeness. And in Negro contacts there is about as large a proportion of decreased closeness cases (17 per cent) as there is of increased closeness (21 per cent). However, we shall see that when the situational context of the contact is taken into account a more optimistic result will appear.

Lost contacts—dropped during the two-year period—were predominantly those that never involved any genuine personal interaction: the proportion that never even reached first-name basis is 82 per cent for Negroes and 60 per cent for Jews. The tendency for the lost contacts to be less intimate than those maintained or gained is found in each of the contexts of neighborhood, organizations, and work.

Table 7.45 presents several important comparisons of closeness of contacts in the three contexts. Comparing the total proportion of stable contacts—those which have remained at the same level of closeness between the two panel surveys—among the three contexts, we note that there is a very sharp tendency for neighborhood contacts to remain at the same level

Table 7.45

Stability and change in degree of closeness of contacts maintained by
situational context and ethnic group.

		No Change		Change		
	Available	First name or closer	Total no change	Increased closeness	Decreased closeness	Total
Negro maintained contacts (91 cases)						
Neighborhood	57%	19% =	76%	9%	15%	= 100% (32)
Organization	42%	17% =	59%	20%	21%	= 100% (24)
Work	27%	14% =	41%	37%	22%	= 100% (37)
Jew maintained contacts (224 cases)						
Neighborhood	49%	19% =	68%	16%	16%	= 100% (86)
Organization	20%	19% =	39%	38%	23%	= 100% (97)
Work	10%	21% =	31%	41%	28%	= 100% (41)

of closeness, organization contacts much less so, and work contacts, least
likely to remain at a stable level of closeness. For example, 7 out of 10 maintained Jewish contacts in a neighborhood do not change in the level of closeness, in contrast to 3 out of 10 among contacts at work. For each context,
Negro contacts are more likely than Jewish to remain stable, but the relative
differences among situational contexts still hold.

Why does this pattern emerge? Why are neighborhood contacts so unlikely to change over time? For one thing, there are probably subtle differences in the general social definitions of contacts made in these three situational contexts.

In the neighborhood context, for example, we have witnessed a change
in the nature of "neighboring" with the increase of urbanization itself: the
specific geographic area of a city in which people live often does not involve a strong sense of belonging to either the area itself or the people in
it. The area may serve as some sort of status symbol, but only because of
the type of persons with a certain level of income or kind of background
who live there, not because of persons as individuals known and closely
associated with. The role of neighbor has therefore increasingly come to
connote merely someone who is known to live in close geographic proximity.
It may be partly for this reason that we find the least change in closeness
to be characteristic of contacts with ethnic individuals in the neighborhood.

Indeed, this may well be as true of nonethnic contacts as of those between ethnic and nonethnic.[19]

Participating in an organization, on the other hand, is likely to involve an individual's putting forward his social self: one of the purposes of attending meetings of organizations, for ethnic as for nonethnic individuals, is obviously that of meeting and getting to know other people who share some common interest in the goals and activities of the organization. People are, in short, more willingly exposing themselves to the cultivation of contacts in the organizational context than in either of the other two.

Work contacts call for still another social definition. Frequently there is little real choice of one's associates on the job. Whatever the initial impressions of co-workers may be, we are required to interact with them rather closely on the work task. (Frequently even lunching together is not completely a voluntary thing, but a matter of going along with a group.) Many pressures for talking, gossiping, and sharing the day's activities during the many hours spent on the job can readily have the effect of considerable change in the degree of closeness of relationships developed at work.

Of course, such partially unavoidable contact on the job does not necessarily mean the formation of closer friendship ties. Apparently, however, some change is more likely to occur in the work context than in either the organizational or neighborhood contexts. Thus, as Table 7.45 shows, for the Negro contacts that have persisted from 1949 to 1951, only the work context shows any large proportion of change in a positive direction: 38 per cent of the maintained Negro contacts on the job have changed to a more intimate nature, 22 per cent of them have receded to a less close relationship. For organization and neighborhood contexts, contacts with Negroes are just as likely to retreat to a *less* intimate basis as to a *more* intimate basis. For the Jewish contacts, on the other hand, both organizational and work contexts appear more conducive to change in the direction of a more intimate basis.

Our statistical findings and the qualitative analysis of other studies point to a similar model of change. For instance, Jeanne Watson's detailed study of a small number of persons who reported experiencing an important change in their attitudes toward Negroes or Jews suggested that there are four main stages in such changes in attitude. First, there is a predisposing experience of change in socio-cultural setting—a new job, entering military service, moving to a different community, going to college, being promoted, getting married, joining an organization. Second, there is a change in general social attitudes as a response to the new situation as a whole. Within this

---

[19] It is easy in the study of specific subgroups in our population to lose sight of the general social characteristics which apply to ethnic groups or interethnic contacts in much the same way as they do to the larger American social scene.

pattern of change, there is, third, a precipitating experience that calls into question the person's orientation to Negroes or Jews, for example, he himself is the object of discrimination analogous to racial discrimination, or he unexpectedly finds himself working with a Negro person. Fourth, after the initial changes, there may be reinforcement of the altered attitudes through further experiences.[20]

A clear segmental change in attitude and behavior toward a specific minority group is especially likely when a person moves as an unsupported individual into a new community or group in which the norms differ from those previously found. The person can shift his overt behavior and redefine his attitude in terms of appropriateness to a particular social context.[21] With minimal involvement or defensiveness he can alter the isolated attitude to fit the need to behave in Rome as the Romans do. Such changes, however, probably tend to be isolated—not tied up with a basic structural reorganization of attitudes—and primarily have their effects on cognitive beliefs of a relatively superficial kind. The more important changes are structural; they affect the pattern and mode of organization of many specific attitudes. Structural changes usually require strong influences operating repeatedly upon central regions of the personality.

We now have seen that many status factors and personality indicators seem less closely related to attitude change than the initial level of prejudice in combination with the general pattern of social participation of given individuals. Is there any way of deriving a clearer view of the relative contributions to changed attitudes of (1) the initial prejudice as over against (2) effects attributable to ethnic contacts themselves? Short of controlled experiments in the field, the best approach is to inspect the full pattern of change in the Hometown panel data.

Analysis of a sixteen-fold table relating changes between 1949 and 1951 in contacts with Jews and Negroes to changes in social-distance prejudice shows the following:

1. 60 per cent of respondents did not change at all in prejudice or in contacts.

2. 15 per cent remained stable in contact pattern but changed in prejudice (a slight net *decrease*).

3. 18 per cent did not change in prejudice but did in contacts—overwhelmingly in the direction of *increased* interaction.

So far, therefore, we see that *in 93 per cent of the cases there is no clear directional effect between prejudice and outgroup contact.* Of the remaining

---

[20] "Some Social and Psychological Situations Related to Change in Attitude," *Human Relations,* III, No. 1 (1950), 22.

[21] *Ibid.,* p. 29.

7 per cent, exactly one-half either increase in prejudice as their ethnic contacts decrease or lose prejudice as their outgroup interaction increases—in short, they fit the hypothesis that contact decreases feelings of social distance. The residual one-half of the cases who reported change in both contacts and prejudice are the contrary ones: they either lose outgroup contacts while becoming more accepting in attitude toward Negroes or Jews, or they gain contacts while becoming more prejudiced.

Computation of an index of mutual effects indicates that there is no significant difference between effects attributable to contact and those that may be assigned to prejudice. Essentially, therefore, these data suggest that over a two-year period our Hometown respondents probably were about equally divided between those who were led by new ethnic contacts to change their attitudes and those who by their initial attitudes were effectively predisposed to change their pattern of intergroup contacts. The movement was clearly toward increased ethnic contact (78 persons gained, only 28 lost contacts), with only a slight net reduction in prejudice (52 persons less versus 43 persons more prejudiced). (See Table 7.46.)

Table 7.46

Ethnic contacts and social-distance prejudices toward Negroes and Jews
(White gentiles, Hometown, 1949 and 1951).

| 1949 Contact and prejudice | 1951 | | | | |
| | Contact | | No Contact | | |
	Low prejudice*	High prejudice*	Low prejudice	High prejudice	Total cases
Some ethnic contact†					
Low prejudice	50	9	6	5	70
High prejudice	12	40	4	13	69
No ethnic contact					
Low prejudice	35	11	62	18	126
High prejudice	10	22	27	99	158
Total cases	107	82	99	135	423

*"High" means that respondent found "distasteful" 3 to 6 of six situations involving close social contact with Negroes or Jews. "Low" means that 2 or less of the situations were reported as distasteful.
†Any actual contact with a Negro or Jew in previous month.

The most numerous category, of course, is the unaltered majority-group core, which, in so short a period of time, goes its way without perturbation of opinion or without change in its beaten paths of interaction.

Interpretation and implications

We have seen that close interethnic contacts in the communities studied are relatively rare and that they tend to attract the less prejudiced on both sides. Within each ethnic grouping, there is associational inbreeding, both by reason of positive preferences and by reason of defensive withdrawal against feared outgroup relationships. But when there is repeated interethnic associations, the statistically dominant outcomes are relatively friendly interaction and reduced prejudice, at least in the context in which the interactions occur. We did find some important exceptions, but the dominant uniformity is surely quite impressive and not at all to be taken for granted.

At first glance our major findings may seem to be highly unlikely.[22] It seems evident that if there already exists a set of widely shared stereotypes and strong feelings of social distance, any sudden confrontation with a diffuse, radically new, unstructured situation is likely to be highly threatening and to arouse fear and consequent resentment. If these reactions are intense, and if the situation is avoidable, it will be avoided. If the situation is unavoidable, but the initial fear-hostility reaction is strong, it may lead to the crystallization of a constricted relationship of subordination-superordination, closing off the possibilities of value change and the establishment of friendships.

On the other hand, stereotypes and attitudes of social distance are unlikely to be basically altered except through intensive communication that reveals commonality of beliefs and values. Consequently, the contacts easiest to initiate are just those least likely to produce change. For it is precisely the intimate and diffuse relationships that are often regarded as most inappropriate and threatening. Frazier has suggested, for example, that: ". . . it is easier to integrate the Negro or any other outgroup into a secular institution characterized by casual and impersonal contacts than into a sacred institution based upon families and the peculiar cultural traditions of the group." [23] And we find that Michael Banton believes that: "British behaviour towards coloured people is characterized not by aggressiveness but by avoidance of them in relationships which might get out of hand." [24]

It makes an important difference whether any two social groups are linked together by interaction of their leaders or upper strata or by the interaction of the less privileged or low-ranking members. In our studies, the

---

22 "We know how easily interpersonal enmity arises, how great are the secondary gains from socially legitimated hostility, how pervasive and tenaciously held are those stereotypes which stand in the service of needs, and we are acquainted with the ubiquity of 'vicious cycles' in human relations. Is it, then, totally inexplicable that, more often than not, in these studies, increased interaction leads to increased liking, even transcending those strong initial prejudices which are reinforced by and anchored in vested interests and group consensus?" [Robin M. Williams, Jr., "Continuity and Change in Sociological Study," *American Sociological Review*, XXIII, No. 6 (December, 1958), 625.]

23 E. Franklin Frazier, "Race Contacts and the Social Structure," *American Sociological Review*, XIV, No. 1 (February, 1949), 8.

24 *White and Coloured* (New Brunswick, N. J.: Rutgers University Press, 1960), p. 111.

most striking and important case of linkage at the lower socio-economic levels is in our Deep South community. In Southport, segregation is so complete that almost all Negro-white contacts are connected with work. This means that a higher proportion of Negroes with only one opportunity for contact actually interact with whites than of those whose more plentiful nominal opportunities interpose greater barriers to communication. The net effect of the highly constricted system of race relations is that the Negroes of lower economic status and lower education are precisely the ones most likely, through their work, to interact with whites. Here are the data:

Education of Negro respondents	Percentage of Negroes who interact with whites
Grade school graduate or higher	34 (137)
Less than grade school graduate	45 (91)

The general educational level of Negroes here is very low, so that our cutting point between low and high education is at the completion of elementary school. But even at this low level, the less well-educated Negroes are still the more likely to be thrown into interaction with white persons (who on the average will have more education).

The consequences of this pattern of interaction are likely to include the perpetuation of stereotypes or antipathies or both. For the poorly educated and economically poor Negro will either be working for a high-status white, who interprets the relationship in terms of traditional super-subordination, or with a poorly educated white who interprets the situation in the same terms, often with the added elements of status threat and economic competition. In neither case are the experiences calculated to reduce prejudice. Indeed, other published research includes instances in which there is a negative association between favorable attitudes and interpersonal contact with outgroup members—when the contact was involuntary and competitive.[25]

In intergroup affairs, the characteristics of a situation that invite entrance or participation thus may be exactly the opposite of those that will be effective in sustaining long-term relationships or in altering initial evaluations. A white person who believes that Negroes are inferior and/or dangerous, confronting a situation that will involve interaction with one or more Negro persons will be most receptive to the interaction when the situation is one in which he himself or other trusted white persons are in complete control, when the situation is not emotionally involving, when the interaction is con-

---

[25] Frank E. Jones and Wallace E. Lambert, "Attitudes toward Immigrants in a Canadian Community," *Public Opinion Quarterly,* XXIII, No. 4 (Winter, 1959-1960), 537-46.

ventionalized, functionally specific, clearly defined, strictly limited in content and in implications for other situations or future relationships, or when the situation is regarded as rare, exotic, or wholly unique, isolated, non-repeatable. On the other hand, the situations that are effective in altering preconceived beliefs and values are those that strongly engage the participants' emotions (sentiments, feelings) as well as their self-conceptions and their conceptions of the other persons present; the interactions are those that are relatively unbounded in content and implications and diffuse in the rights and obligations that may be invoked or created and developed; the situation itself and/or the relationships established within it are expected to be recurrent; and the individual who is our point of reference is not fully in control of the situation either in his own person or through agents or surrogates.

Let us state a crucial tautology: *a person changes his deeply held beliefs and evaluations only when confronted with compelling stimuli when in a condition of receptivity.* What is it that will make stimuli compelling and the person receptive? One of the prime factors disposing to receptivity is that the individual's vital interests—above all, his self-regard—are (1) somehow at stake, and (2) can be sustained or enhanced by the act of changing a belief or evaluation (or by the state of holding the belief or subscribing to the evaluation after the act of change). The individual must be vulnerable in his interests, for example, his self-regard, and he must be able to profit in the situation. In other words he must be significantly involved in the interaction but not too greatly threatened; he cares for the outcome, and the outcome can be good if he will only make it so, and he is able to make it so if he will (that is, if he tries).

For a long while, most findings concerning the effects of interracial contacts in the United States were based upon studies of the relatively permissive subcultures of the North and West. Also, nearly all of the studies that had suggested that equal-status contacts were associated with lesser prejudice had been carried out on situations in which there was an important degree of authoritative control by recognized legal and administrative bodies. An advantage of the data of the Cornell Studies is that they bear on the validity of hypotheses concerning interracial contact in the South and border North as well as in the West and North. They also concern not just authoritative situations such as military service but also the realm of everyday interaction in community contexts. These contacts also differ from those of earlier research in that they tend to be relatively long term as opposed to the episodic or short-term contacts of the laboratory experiment or the summer-camp studies. Our data seem to have been productive of new knowledge, and they certainly are suggestive of important hypotheses. The questions we are now able to raise point to the great value that can be derived from further study of natural interracial contacts, especially in Southern areas, with more precise specification of the qualitative and temporal aspects of the contacts.

Furthermore, existing studies most commonly have dealt with relatively impersonal, formalized, and functionally specific sets of relationships in military organizations, labor unions, factory work groups, or educational organizations. Future research should not only specify more exactly the characteristics of the interaction in any given type of situation but also should involve comparative studies of the effects of interracial contacts in several different kinds of situations.

In studying human behavior, we often gain new perspectives and insights by deliberately altering (or even reversing) the question that provoked our original inquiry. For example, we began with the question, "Under what conditions is intergroup contact likely to lead to reduced stereotyping, social distance, and dislike?" We may gain a new perspective by asking, first, "Under what conditions may we expect intergroup contact to perpetuate patterns of prejudice and discrimination?" And, we may ask, second, "Under what conditions will intergroup contact probably lead to increased prejudice and/or to accentuated discrimination and/or to overt conflict?"

Some reasonably specific hypotheses can be advanced in answer to these questions. The perpetuation of prejudice and discrimination is facilitated by the familiar vicious circle of intergroup relations: the members of a minority group are placed into recurring situations that elicit stereotyped characteristics which reinforce prejudice. Thus, the Negro appears in low-status occupations; the Jew is forced into urban trade. A firmly enforced system of discrimination and segregation can practically insure that the intergroup interaction that does occur will conform with traditional rules of subordination and social distance. There is no opportunity for anyone to observe and react to out-of-status behavior, new status-role combinations, or other forms of innovative behavior. The consequence is an incessant verification or reinforcement of traditional stereotypes, norms, and evolutions.

The general hypothesis here would simply be that *intergroup contacts in which behavior follows traditional norms of super-subordination and/or social distance will, on the whole, perpetuate and reinforce patterns of prejudice and discrimination.* This does *not* mean, of course, that such relationships necessarily instigate or maintain antipathy or that they necessarily preclude personal liking, friendship, intimacy, even love, on the part of at least one party in each relationship. Benevolent master and devoted servant; British colonial and African mistress; the Southern gentleman's son and the Negro mammy—the historical examples are legion in which warm interpersonal relationships cross the lines of group cleavage. But relationships of this kind need have no *structural* consequences for a system of *group* dominance and subordination.[26] Indeed, in a variety of ways, some of the close interpersonal relations not only conform to pre-existing norms of group position, but reinforce, often in a dramatic and highly influential mode, the relations of superordination and subordination. This would seem to be notably true of the familiar pattern in which males of the dominant grouping establish sexual relations (which may be long continued and even responsible) with women of the subordinate group, but in which males of the subordinate group are denied relationships with women of the dominant group, and in which intermarriage, and hence legitimate descent, is forbidden. Again, the devoted servant by his very loyalty gives public support to the system.

Our conclusion is that *change in intergroup relations as a consequence of friendly interpersonal relations that conform to traditional norms is very unlikely to be extensive or important in the short run.* Whether there will be extensive and important consequences in the *long run* depends primarily, it would seem, upon whether the traditional norms permit enough latitude for the acceptance into the dominant group of substantial numbers of the outgroup persons. And, it is noteworthy that such permissiveness already indicates relatively little prejudice in other regards.

Society in large measure is defined by consensus. For an orderly system of interaction to be maintained, there must be:

> . . . some degree of common orientation toward the common environment (both human and other). . . . Social reality, including the rules for communicative behavior itself, is a group property (it is meaningless to regard it as a merely individual property), but it can exist only through the participation of individuals. . . . Individuals' communicative acts are thus determined by private versions of consensus, which at the same time tend to be "corrected" by the consequences of those same communicative acts. In such ways as these are consensus and communicative behavior interdependent.[27]

Given an acceptable level and kind of consensus, intergroup relations of a cooperative and/or friendly kind will be facilitated by objective interdependence.

Real social groups are characterized by actual interdependence rather

---

[26] Cf. L. Proudfoot and H. S. Wilson, "The Clubs in Crisis: Race Relations in the New West Africa," *American Journal of Sociology,* LXVI, No. 4 (January, 1961), 317-24. Members of the Railway Club, as compared with those in other exclusive European clubs in the capital city of Sierra Leone, more often had intimate and friendly relations with Africans. This club was the last to admit (with great reluctance) any African members; and once such members were admitted, strenuous efforts were made to limit numbers and circumscribe participation.

[27] Theodore M. Newcomb, "Sociology and Psychology," in John L. Gillin, ed., *For a Science of Social Man* (New York: The Macmillan Company, 1954), p. 253.

than merely by similarity of phenotypical characteristics (appearances) of the interacting individuals whose interaction is constitutive of such groups.[28] From interdependence can grow the recognition of common fate. From joint activity can come the creation of new group ties.

Given consensus and interdependence, threat disappears and individuals can form their attachments and antipathies on the basis of personality and strictly situational factors.

The materials are now here for a miniature theory. We will speak only of situations in which external social constraints are not placed upon individuals to prevent them from initial interaction—circumstances that are somehow of minimal common interest to all present. Unless active external interference occurs, then, we predict the following:

1. When individuals interact, when neither is a *threat* to the other, either directly or indirectly, and when their cultural backgrounds are merely similar enough to *permit* personally meaningful (intimate) communication, then: (*a*) initial interaction will be *on the average* more rewarding than not; hence, (*b*) these interactions will tend to be repeated.

2. If proposition 1 is true, the statistically modal outcome of interaction will be the formation of continuing relationships of harmony or interpersonal liking. This outcome is favored by (*a*) similarity of beliefs and values and (*b*) compatibility of interests.

3. Most of the relationships thus formed (proposition 2) will stabilize at a level of acceptance, casual association, friendly acquaintance, or friendship. Some small proportion will develop into relations of great intimacy of communication, of mutual trust, diffuse sharing of values, mutual identification, and strong and complex affectivity. These are the relationships we usually call comradeship or love.

4. For relationships of the latter kind (proposition 3), the crucial factors in the maintenance of positive affection and mutually gratifying behavior become more heavily weighted by (*a*) idiosyncratic beliefs, values, and expressive patterns and (*b*) basic psychodynamic tendencies of the individual personality.

At the level of the strongest and most complete interpersonal relationships, additional sociopsychological laws come into prominence. The personality mechanisms are more freely expressed. Sensitivity to nuances of attitudes typically is increased.

The positive affection or love in intimate human relationships (whether or not sexual, although of course pre-eminently there) is not the same as

---

[28] A point often and effectively made by Kurt Lewin. Cf. his contribution in *Field Theory in Social Science,* Dorwin Cartwright, ed. (New York: Harper & Row, Publishers, 1951).

harmony or liking. We like many people we could never love. We can love a person without liking him. People who love one another often experience occasional mutual hatred as well.

We have come to believe that, as a statistical tendency, the more any individuals know of the inner life and personal histories of other individuals, the more likely they are to like the others. We do not mean a sweet and sentimental liking, nor do we think that the positive feeling will be all of one piece or without an admixture of negative feelings. Nor is it *always* true that such increases in interpersonal knowledge lead immediately or directly to friendship, agreement, or desire to associate with the other. Increased knowledge and understanding will sometimes simply reveal that the other person is a threat. Even in these instances, however, if we can comprehend why he is a threat, we will be better able to deal with him with minimal likelihood of panic, rage, and other demonstrative reactions. The result may well be realistic action coupled with compassion, rather than merely hostile rejection or attack.

CHAPTER 8

THE WORLDS
OF MINORITIES

INTRODUCTION

Many white majority-group Americans go about their daily activities with little awareness of minority worlds. Majority-group persons assume that they themselves can go where they wish, have access to any public service or facility, receive normal courtesy, and in general count upon being treated as a person. They have not reflected upon the difference it would make to be a member of a minority group that is the object of prejudice and discrimination. Few majority-group persons have ever imagined how members of racial and ethnic minorities react to hearing derogatory comments, being turned away from restaurants and hotels, and being refused employment.

In our early days in Hometown, we were repeatedly assured by white people with whom we talked that "we have no racial problem here." There is no reason to doubt that these people sincerely believed what they said.

To them "no racial problem" meant: no riots, no obvious conflict, no evidence of strong dissatisfaction with the *status quo*. But there is ample evidence that these well-meaning white people knew almost nothing of the thoughts and feelings of the small Negro minority within their city. If they wished to know more, they might well have started by reading an account of initial impressions of Hometown's Negro community from the notebook of the social scientist, himself a Negro, who later lived in the community and studied it intensively.

> Standing on the deserted corner of 9th and Caldwell Street, one can look up the block and see busy Front Street, the procession of automobiles passing, stores, a street light brightening up the area. And here, nestling against the side of the busy world of Hometown, are the ramshackle frame houses that hold the Negro community, an appendage, an afterthought.
>
> Here, Hometown's Negro people go to and fro in a closed sub-world. . . . Here, the people all know each other, recognize each newcomer by his unfamiliar face, keep tab on each other's activities, gossip, disagree, follow many little well-trodden pathways of life . . .
>
> Here, despite the diversity, is a community held together in a single isolated world, bound and irrevocably linked together by that one paramount fact of being Negro in a white world. Here the brown minority has gathered . . . [away from] the subtle exclusion, the insults, the inevitable "slips," the "sorry, we're all filled up," the overcharging, the brusque impatience, the blank, pasty-white fixed smile—until the soul rises in rebellion—while there is nothing to rebel against but the pat on the back, the monotonous singsong "You're as good as I am."
>
> So here they are, practicing a pattern of avoidance. The actual blow is forgotten; only the sting and the readiness to duck remain. A man says "What's the use?"; a man flares up in violence; a child looks at the community's flashiest man—the one with most money, longest car, smoothest big-city slang, and says—"that's what I want to be when I grow up" . . .

This chapter concentrates upon the Negro minority, for in it most of the characteristics of minority position in our society are shown in sharpest outline.[1] The data concerning the Negro minority come (1) from sample surveys conducted in six cities; (2) from the observations of Robert B.

---

[1] Among the large number of recent studies of other situations and of other minorities we found the following useful for comparative purposes: Charles Wagley and Marvin Harris, *Minorities in the New World: Six Case Studies* (New York: Columbia University Press, 1958); Hilda Kuper, *Indian People in Natal* (Pietermaritzburg: University of Natal Press, 1960); Ng Bickleen Fong, *The Chinese in New Zealand* (New York: Oxford University Press, 1960); Radhakamal Mukerjee, "Social Structure and Stratification of the Indian Nation," *Transactions of the Second World Congress of Sociology,* II, International Sociological Association, London (1954), 16-25; Benjamin N. Colby and Pierre Van Den Berghe, "Ethnic Relations in South Eastern Mexico," *American Anthropologist,* LXIII, No. 4 (August, 1961), 772-92; Anthony H. Richmond, *Colour Prejudice in Britain* (London: Routledge & Kegan Paul, Ltd., 1954); John B. Edlefsen, "Enclavement among Southwest Idaho Basques," *Social Forces,* XXIX, No. 2 (1950), 155-58.

Johnson during one and one-half years' experience as a participant-observer in Hometown (plus visits and informal discussions in the community over a three-year span); [2] (3) from participant-observation and interviews conducted by Johnson (and to some extent by Lois Remmers Dean and John P. Dean) in ten other Negro subcommunities in cities in all major regions of the United States.

The life of American Negroes in urban communities has been documented in many monographs, beginning with W. E. B. DuBois's *The Philadelphia Negro,* published in 1899. Because the Cornell studies dealt primarily with working- and lower-class Negro communities in smaller towns, much of the data concern small-town life rather than urban complexity, intergroup apathy rather than tension, with the lower-status, relatively inarticulate and uneducated Negroes rather than with the higher-status, articulate spokesmen for Negro people. In the communities studied, educated, middle-class Negro leadership is relatively rare, and white community members have limited contact with Negroes and only slight awareness of the actual intergroup relations in their own local community.

Most studies that have to do with intergroup relations actually are largely concerned with the attitudes and behavior of a dominant (majority-group) population toward one or more minorities. The two-sided or inherently reciprocal character of *relations* is often passed over or dealt with only casually. Of course, a subordinate minority is never entirely passive. Even the most deprived and oppressed population will be able to exert *some* influence upon its rulers. Even the most firmly subdued and acquiescent groupings in an ancient, traditionalized system of caste will resent and resist some aspects of their position.[3] And the reactions of a minority sometimes do strongly affect the policies and tactics followed by the majority in dealing with it— as the British found in India prior to 1949 and as Negroes are demonstrating in the United States today.

Fundamental changes in the distribution of Negro population are occurring as accompaniments of industrial and urban growth in conjunction with the pre-existing system of race relations. Between 1950 and 1960 the total Negro population of the United States increased from 15.0 to 18.9

---

[2] Major findings of this chapter are adapted from analyses made in Johnson's doctoral dissertation "The Nature of the Minority Community," Cornell University (1955), and also from Donald Leroy Noel's dissertation "Correlates of Anti-White Prejudice: Attitudes of Negroes in Four American Cities," Cornell University (1961).

[3] "A comparison of the realities of caste attitudes and interaction in India and the United States suggests that no group of people is content to be low in a caste hierarchy—to live a life of inherited deprivation and subjection—regardless of the rationalizations offered to them by their superiors or constructed by themselves." Gerald D. Berreman, "Caste in India and the United States," *The American Journal of Sociology,* LXVI, No. 2 (September, 1960), 127.

million. Because of internal migration, especially large increases occurred in California and in the industrial cities of the Northeast and Middle West. In the South, except for Florida and Texas (both having rapid metropolitan growth), increases of Negro population were small—and three states actually had substantial losses of Negro population: West Virginia (22 per cent loss), Mississippi (7 per cent), and Arkansas (9 per cent). By 1960 only 60 per cent of American Negroes still lived in the South.[4]

The movement of Negro population into metropolitan areas has been primarily into the central cities, which at the same time have been losing white population to the suburbs. Residential segregation has barred Negroes from moving out of the central areas. As a consequence of these three factors, the central cities have experienced rapid increases in the proportion of the population that is nonwhite. Already in 1960, Washington, D.C., was 54 per cent nonwhite, and 20 other major central cities were more than 20 per cent nonwhite.[5] The emerging situation is not one likely to encourage Negroes in a passive acceptance of the *status quo ante.*

In this chapter, after an overview of four Negro communities, we seek to enter into the segmental world of one such segregated, minority community in an effort to understand more fully what is involved in being simultaneously "on the inside looking out, and on the outside looking in." Next, we will try to analyze the attitudes of minorities toward the majority group, focusing upon Negroes' stereotypes and feelings of social distance toward white people. Third, we examine the patterns of Negro-white interaction in relation to prejudice. Finally, we put together our data on other minorities in an approach to understanding the main types of orientations of minority peoples in the communities studied.[6]

WHERE THE RESPONSIBILITY LIES

Valley City [7]

The urbanized area of Valley City has a population of approximately 100,000, of which 8 per cent are Negro and 8 per cent Mexican, with Japanese-Americans, Chinese-Americans, Jews, and Filipinos constituting

---

[4] See Henry S. Shryock, Jr., "Some Results of the 1960 Census of the United States," *Rural Sociology,* XXVII, No. 4 (December, 1962), 468.

[5] Donald J. Bogue and Calvin L. Beale, "Recent U. S. Population Trends: Causes and Consequences," paper presented to the Rural Sociological Society, Ames, Iowa, August 1961, pp. 18-20a.

[6] See Donald L. Noel: *op. cit.,* pp. 1-34. Our pages 227 to 235 are adapted from this work.

[7] John P. and Lois Dean, "Inventory of Intergroup Relations" (Unpublished, 1952), p. 1. Our description of Valley City and the situation of the Negro there is largely derived from the field notes recorded in this inventory.

an additional 3 per cent of the population. There are also small populations of Italian and Portuguese extraction. Valley City grew rapidly between 1940-1950, primarily because of the rise of factory-in-the-field agriculture in the environs and the growth of the oil and cotton industries. Industrial growth led to the in-migration of many white Southern workers. At the time of our study, the city appears to be dominated economically and politically by a relatively small group of entrepreneurs.

Employment situation. The members of the Negro community are largely Southern-born, working class, and subjected to a great deal of discrimination. Social disorganization is said by local informants to be extensive and the vicious circle created by discrimination is readily discernible. For example, the increase of the small Negro middle class, which is needed for resourceful leadership, is hampered by economic discrimination. There are very few Negro professionals and governmental employees. The oil industry is almost completely closed to Negroes; in the cotton industry Negroes are restricted to jobs that are unsteady, poorly paid, and operated on a work-gang basis. Negroes are found in about half of the AFL unions, where they are generally confined to the least desirable jobs. (Eighty per cent of the bricklayers' helpers are Negro, but there are no Negro journeymen or apprentice bricklayers.) There is only one important CIO union, which is in the oil industry, where Negroes are not employed in any capacity. The great bulk of Negroes are confined to the cotton industry, where they constitute about one-third of the labor force. Only a few Negroes have supervisory jobs (over predominantly Negro crews) in this industry. Some growers refuse to hire Negroes. Instead, on the ground of unavailability of native labor, they appeal successfully to the State Department of Employment for Mexican nationals, who will work for considerably less than native labor.

Housing. Much of the housing in the area of heaviest Negro concentration is substandard, and the area has been designated for slum clearance by the City Planning Commission. There is one federally aided low-rent housing project in this area. Negroes also live in a few areas that are mixed (white, Mexican, and Negro, or just Mexican and Negro) and high-status Negroes live in recently desegregated sections. Finally, a very few Negro families live in otherwise all-white neighborhoods. Housing is felt by Negroes to be a serious problem here, as it generally is in other communities.[8]

Public facilities. Hospitals, buses, rest rooms, and theaters are integrated, but Negroes generally are denied access to white hotels, churches, restaurants, taverns, beauty parlors, and barbershops. The YMCA is segregated

---

[8] Housing as the chief problem in various cities is attested by the following research: E. and G. Grier, *Negroes in Five New York Cities* (New York State Commission Against Discrimination, 1959, reissue), especially pp. 11-13 and 67-85; and E. Barth and B. Abu-Laban, "Power Structure and the Negro Sub-Community," *American Sociological Review,* XXIV (1959), 74.

but there is an integrated youth coordinating council and occasional joint activities. Personal reports of incidents of discrimination in places of public accommodation are numerous. Although nominally integrated (so far as the pattern of housing segregation permits), the school system has been the source of considerable tension.

Positive action. In the face of extensive discrimination, the several organizations to which minorities may turn are regarded by most local informants as largely ineffective. There is an Intergroup Council, many of whose leaders are teachers, which recently combined forces with the local NAACP chapter to achieve the most prominent success yet—the placement of the first Negro as a teacher (in an all-Negro school). The Council has participated in no other major successful action, and the NAACP's lack of prestige and following has hampered its efforts. Together with the integrated County Voter's League, the NAACP did successfully resolve a recent housing incident. Other organizations such as B'nai B'rith and high school and college interracial councils have largely confined themselves to intraorganization discussion.

Hometown [9]

Recall that Hometown is a predominantly industrial community with approximately 60,000 residents. It has about 75 independent industries that vary in size from a few employees to more than 5,000. Approximately 85 per cent of the eligible workers are unionized, but the unions are generally settled and nonmilitant. The community has experienced moderate economic and population growth throughout its 170 year history with the exception of a slight decline in the 1930-1940 decade.

Negroes and Jews each constitute about 2 to 3 per cent of the population, and Italian-Americans constitute another 5 to 6 per cent. There are also smaller numbers of Irish, German, Polish, and Russian-Ukrainian families. The total foreign born from all these nationality groups was approximately 7 per cent in 1940. A Committee on Human Relations, allowed to lapse at the end of World War II, was reactivated in 1950 and has served as a channel of communication among the various ethnic groups. In addition, the Committee has joined with an active NAACP branch in sponsoring a considerable amount of successful action—for example, placing Negroes in previously all-white occupations or community service agencies. The local YWCA, Ministerial Alliance, B'nai B'rith, UNESCO, United Council of

---

[9] This discussion draws upon Johnson's previously mentioned work, "The Nature of the Minority Community," especially pp. 2-3, 36-38, and 112-24, and upon John P. Dean and Edward A. Suchman, "Social Institutions" and "Political Institutions" in B. Berelson *et al., Voting* (Chicago: University of Chicago Press, 1954), pp. 37-53, 153-81.

Church Women, and a few other branches of national agencies have expressed some interest in intergroup relations and, on some occasions, cooperated with the NAACP and Mayor's Committee.

Employment. Nearly all Hometown Negroes are employed in semiskilled or unskilled industrial jobs or service occupations. In general, the various employment areas appear to be either nondiscriminatory (for example, government jobs, unskilled labor) or controversial (for example, the promotion policies for Negro employees in some large industries). Partly reflecting and partly creating this situation is the successful placing of "first" Negroes in each of eleven different occupations between 1947 and 1953. These occupations included policeman, fireman, nurse, social worker, dentist, school teacher, and telephone operator.

Housing. Negroes are concentrated in four residential areas with a few scattered in neighborhoods where all the other families are white. The oldest area of Negro settlement is about 90 per cent Negro, contains one-third of the Negro families, and is the site of all the major contact centers of the Negro community. An 1868 city directory indicates that Negroes were far more residentially dispersed then than they are now. The highest-status residential areas are definitely closed to Negroes. The areas on the fringes of the existing Negro districts are generally controversial, and only the least desirable areas near the railroad or industrial sites and areas vacated by other ethnic groups are clearly nondiscriminatory.

In the realm of public accommodations the Hometown Negro is subjected to a typically ambiguous pattern of discrimination.[10] For example lodges, most service clubs, the smaller hotels, and barbershops appear to be discriminatory, whereas patriotic organizations, political and artistic clubs, hospitals, theaters, and most restaurants and department stores are nondiscriminatory. The school system's student population is well integrated (including social activities and organizations, except for the fraternities and sororities), but the first Negro teacher was hired only recently. Informal social cliques in the community are largely discriminatory, whereas taverns, larger hotels, some Protestant churches, and the highest-status department stores are controversial. Johnson concludes that the resulting ambiguity and uncertainty give rise to patterns of avoidance that in turn create a *lag* in Negroes' perception of the current extensive objective changes in local and nationwide discriminatory patterns. The resulting overestimation of the amount of discrimination reinforces and generalizes the pattern of avoidance created initially by the pervasive ambiguity of the interracial situation.[11]

---

[10] Cf. Chapter 6.

[11] Both the defensiveness and the overestimation of discrimination are also noted by F. F. Lee in his study of another northeastern community. See "Social Controls in the Race Relations Pattern of a Small New England Town," *Social Forces,* XXXIII (1954), 36-40.

Southport [12]

Located on the Southport River 16 miles from the Atlantic Ocean, Southport is the second largest city in Georgia, with a population of 120,000, of which approximately 40 per cent are Negroes. It is one of the leading commercial and industrial centers of the South and is also the site of a large Air Force base. The city's industries include lumber and wood-working mills, cottonseed oil mills, paper and bag factories, a sugar refinery, a seafood cannery, and factories making fertilizers, paperboard, gypsum, chemicals, concrete, turpentine, paints, and steel products.

Employment. Negro employment is relatively varied, reflecting the city's multiple industries. There are four major employers of Negroes. A paper manufacturing company employs about 1,200 Negroes. Over 1,000 of these are in menial jobs, with slightly over 100 in production jobs and 5 in skilled work. There are no Negro supervisors. Over 500 Negroes are employed as longshoremen by the shipping companies; but foremen, straw bosses, and checkers are all white. There is a separate AFL-ILA local for the Negro longshoremen, but it is very weak. The longshoremen's wages, however, are above average for local Negroes; and as a result the shipping companies have more than enough labor available for each day's work. A sugar refinery hires about 500 Negroes with the great bulk in menial jobs and none in supervisory positions. Finally, small fertilizer plants employ about 500 Negroes. These plants are all-Negro except for supervisors. These four industries employ about 2,500 of the more than 20,000 Negroes in the Southport labor force.

In addition, Southport's Negroes are scattered in the following industries and occupations: hotels and restaurants, laundries, bakeries, lumberyards, domestic service, custodial service in stores and office buildings, municipal and federal employment, and construction trades. The general pattern is one in which Negroes are confined almost completely to menial positions. This pattern is broken primarily by a few of the AFL construction trades, such as carpenters and cement finishers, which have all-Negro locals. Other craft unions, such as the plumbers and machinists, have made no effort to organize Negro tradesmen. In general, the local AFL leaders do not appear to object to the traditional patterns of segregation in the major factories and trades; and although they endorse the principle of equal pay for equal work, they go along with the existing system that assures that Negroes rarely, if ever, attain equal work. The CIO is (that is, in 1952) extremely weak with only three small locals (one white, one Negro, one mixed).

---

[12] This discussion is based largely on an unpublished Intergroup Relations Inventory of Southport compiled by members of the Cornell Intergroup Relations Project staff. This includes a report entitled "The Negro Community of Southport," prepared by R. B. Johnson in June, 1952.

With its approximately 50,000 inhabitants, the Southport Negro community itself provides another major area of employment. The Negro community has a bank, two weekly newspapers, at least 75 churches, 5 insur-
ance company branches, several mortuaries, a hospital, 14 doctors, 6 den-
tists, 3 lawyers, over 300 teachers, and hundreds of small Negro businesses.
The sizeable group of professional and businessmen provides a source of
educated leaders, lacking in the smaller Negro communities, who can be
militant because they are not dependent on whites for their livelihood.

Housing. Although the bulk of Negro businesses and offices are located
in one segregated area, the residential pattern is considerably less segregated than in our three non-Southern communities. There are a few areas
where Negroes are barred by restrictive covenants, and others where the
high cost of property effectively bars all but a few Negroes, but generally
Negroes live scattered throughout the city. However, there are signs that
the Negro community is becoming increasingly segregated residentially.

Public facilities. Negroes are completely segregated in hotels, restaurants,
barbershops, schools, buses, and various other public facilities. On the other
hand, a few small religious groups (for example, Pentecostals and Christian
Scientists) are integrated, and (after recent successful boycotts) Negroes
can shop and try on clothes in local department stores. In addition, Negroes
can serve on juries, take legal action against whites, and increasingly count
on reasonable fairness in the courts. From the standpoint of morale and
race pride, a recent major victory has been the breaking of the 102-year-old
(white) newspaper policy of not using titles (Mr., Miss, Mrs.) for Negroes.
The use of these titles was illustrated in a release about the Cornell survey
that named the local interviewers—but the paper still saw fit to list the
Negro interviewers separately and to designate them as Negro.

Facilities in Southport are either separate and inferior—or else they do
not exist at all. The latter situation is well illustrated by recreational facilities. Although Southport is very close to the ocean, the closest swimming
area open to Negroes is in the state of Florida. Negroes do not attend the
roller rinks, bowling alleys, or drive-in theaters, and only 3 of the 14
movie theaters are for Negroes. Most of the Negro schools do not have
gymnasiums, and there is a severe shortage of playgrounds.

Of the 14 Negro schools only one was intended to be a school when it
was built. Many of the schools have deficient sanitary and recreational
facilities. There are classrooms where two students have to share a single
seat and some have to stand, and at least nine of the Negro schools (but
none of the white schools) have double sessions (that is, teachers instruct
two sets of students daily) involving some 4,600 students. There is no voca-
tional or commercial school for Negroes. However, in recent years teachers'
salaries have been equalized; the Negro community has a new modern
senior high school (which awarded diplomas to 200 in the spring of 1952);

and, there is a Negro state teachers college on the outskirts of Southport. Nevertheless, facilities are clearly unequal in the public school system as a whole; and the school system is still the greatest source of complaint and protest from Negro leaders.

Positive action. There is no active interracial organization working against discrimination on a broad front—unless one considers the NAACP (with its two white members) interracial. Although the NAACP has a large membership, it is not a powerful force in the Negro community. Southport had already seen concerted political activity among Negroes prior to the 1950's. As early as 1946 the Citizens' Democratic Club had achieved some success in intensive block-by-block methods of getting out the vote among Negroes.[13] The Hub, a local Negro civic club, has a membership largely made up of business and professional men and enjoys considerable respect in both the Negro and the white communities. Its major projects have included raising funds for scholarships, equalization of school and recreational facilities, slum clearance, and registration of Negro voters. A few other groups reinforce the Hub and the NAACP in specific instances, but these two are dominant. Together they provide a good illustration of a negotiating and a militant group working toward a common goal.

Steelville

Steelville, located on the Ohio River approximately forty miles west of Pittsburgh, is an industrial community of about 40,000 persons. Historically the town was very prominent in the glass and pottery industries, and pottery is still an important part of the area's industry. All other industries are by now greatly overshadowed by the huge steel plants which give Steelville (and adjacent Weirton and Follansbee, West Virginia) an important part in the nation's heavy industry.

The Negro community of about 4,000 constitutes the largest minority. Persons of Jewish background compose about 3 per cent of the population; there are sizable numbers of Germans, Irish, Polish, and Italian-Americans. The latter groupings constitute a large part of the city's Catholic population, which numbers approximately 12,000. The Jewish population is relatively well integrated into the community. Catholic-Protestant and Negro-white relationships provide the focal points of intergroup tension.

The city has an Intergroup Goodwill Council, organized in 1947, which is chiefly composed of social agency executives, school teachers, and clergymen. There is also a local chapter of B'nai B'rith and of the NAACP. The NAACP is largely inactive, but it has a few militant, persistent members, one of whom is also prominent in the exceptionally active and influential

---

[13] Cf. the comments of Alexander Heard, *A Two-Party South?* (Chapel Hill: University of North Carolina Press, 1952), pp. 203-4; and the sequel, pp. 213-14.

United Steelworkers of America (C.I.O.) local. Together these four groups were able to secure the passage, almost in spite of themselves, of a local Fair Employment Practices Act in the fall of 1951. Each group has been beset by apathy or internal difficulties, however, and intergroup relations do not seem to be greatly affected by these organizations.

Employment. In the Negro community, the largest number of workers are employed in the local industrial plants. When the union local was organized in 1937, Negroes were in menial jobs only, but as of 1952 they were well integrated in production jobs and had top skilled jobs (where seniority permitted) [14] plus some supervisory positions. Negroes participate from top to bottom in the union local, which is actively working toward total on-the-job integration—in the presently all-white clerical division as well as in production. Several small plants and one large pottery concern do not hire Negroes. The AFL unions locally are discriminatory in policy. There are no Negro carpenters, plumbers, or painters (and only one Negro electrician) in Steelville—although there are Negroes qualified for these occupations. The primary excluding device is apparently a special increase in the already high initiation fees imposed upon Negro applicants.

A few Negroes are employed by city and federal government agencies, but white-collar employment is slight among Steelville Negroes. There are three Negro policemen, seven postmen, and one librarian, plus one Negro doctor, one dentist, and two undertakers. In short, discrimination in employment does exist and the Negro middle class is small.

Housing. Housing, as elsewhere, is regarded by many Negro leaders as the most serious trouble spot in the community. Negro families are the principal occupants of several blocks in the central section of the city, a congested, segregated area. There are also scattered blocks in which the residents are mostly Negro. There is one mixed neighborhood inhabited by 30 Negro and 28 white families. In addition 46 Negro families live in predominantly white neighborhoods. There are no Negro families in the elite section of town. In contrast, the majority of Steelville's Jews are scattered throughout the general residential area.

Public facilities. Discrimination with regard to public facilities and services seems more severe in Steelville than in Hometown or Valley City. Negroes are accepted on the public golf course, as customers in local stores, and as clients by white professionals, but they are denied access to most restaurants,[15] taverns, hotels, barber and beauty shops, night clubs, and

---

[14] Prior to organization of the union, Negroes were classified as general labor and could not accumulate seniority. Thus some departments are still all-white because no Negro has sufficient seniority to qualify.

[15] The CIO scored a victory here recently when it successfully picketed several restaurants (located near the steel mills) that refused to honor union meal tickets when presented by Negroes. The restaurants capitulated within minutes of the start of picketing.

miscellaneous recreational facilities. A local hospital offers segregated semi-private rooms but integrates Negroes in the wards. Churches and theaters also belong in the controversial category: Negroes are accepted but often made to feel unwelcome. Negroes indicate that the theater management tries to maintain separate seating arrangements. The YMCA offers an inter-racial gymnasium and basketball league, but ministers are the only Negroes allowed in the dormitory or accepted as Y members, and the swimming pool is available only on a segregated basis.

The school system is another area of concern to Steelville Negroes. There are no Negro teachers, and eight of the ten grade schools and one of the two junior high schools are all white or predominantly white. The high school is integrated—approximately 10 per cent Negro—and all scheduled activities are integrated including lunchrooms, organized activities, and social events. Nevertheless, social cliques are segregated (although reportedly friendly), and mixed dancing is prohibited. In a case of reverse discrimination, there are some indications that Negroes have used threats to eliminate potential white competitors from the athletic teams. Some local white persons have complained about Negro predominance in the major sports.

Community similarities and differences

Although discrimination exists in each of the four cities, there are several important contrasts in the situation of the Negro in the communities from which our samples are drawn. First, the employment situation of the Negro is relatively good and improving in Hometown and Steelville but very bad in Valley City. The Southport situation is mitigated by the considerable employment opportunities available within the large Negro community there. Second, housing is the most serious problem for Negroes in each of the communities, except in Southport, and there are signs that segregation is increasing there. The problem is especially severe in Valley City. Third, discrimination in public accommodations is most severe in Southport and Steelville. By comparison the situation is more open in Valley City and Hometown, although discriminatory facilities (barbershops, hotels) are still numerous.

Finally, the communities vary in the extent of their organization to fight discrimination. Hometown is probably best armed, with two strong, active organizations. In Steelville most of the relevant organizations are locally described as weak, but there is a nucleus of interested leaders, and the CIO local is said to be a real force against discrimination. Valley City's organizations are not strong but have scored one or two isolated successes. Southport has no interracial organizations but does have two active and moderately successful Negro organizations. The presence or absence of educated, economically independent leaders is crucial for the all-Negro organizations.

This description of the four cities and of the situation of the Negro in each provides a background for our subsequent analysis of the attitudes of Negroes in each city. We shall note community variations as well as uniformities in these attitudes and their correlates.

THE NATURE OF THE NEGRO SUBCOMMUNITY: A CASE STUDY [16]

Minority communities are segments of larger communities, and since a certain amount of social contact, social relations, and interdependence with the larger community is almost inevitable, the minority "community" is never a completely isolated unit. Rather, it should be considered as built around a core of characteristics, modified by a variety of peripheries. The core elements are a history, a territorial base, a clustering of primary institutions, a set of functional relationships with a dominant or majority community, and a special frequency of social interaction within the minority community.

The extent to which a minority-core community exists will be related to the amount of prejudice, discrimination, and reactions to contact on the part of the majority group. In most American communities, for example, Jews are more acceptable to the white majority-group community than are Negroes; Italian-Americans more acceptable than Jews; Irish-Americans more acceptable than Italians, etc. Hence, unless the minority is a separatist group (for example, the Amish, Mormons, Hutterites, Hopi), the greater the amount of majority acceptance, the less the likelihood that this core community will exist.

Variation in degree of integration of individual members into the minority community

The minority individual may be spatially isolated, a newcomer to the community, or a transient having little motivation to participate in minority community affairs. The individual may be nonparticipant by virtue of confining home tasks, illness, old age; or the individual may be excluded from participation because of unacceptable acts, scandal, alcoholism, etc. Further, some persons are withdrawn or apathetic.

Some persons are exemptees permitted by whites to participate in areas of the general community where minority-group members are generally prohibited. In a few extreme cases the individual may consciously reject the minority group and seek complete acceptance from the majority group. Or, the individual may be a "marginal man," uncertain of his group member-

---

[16] This section, again, is adapted freely from Johnson's "The Nature of the Minority Community."

ship or ambivalent about his desire to be classified as a minority-group member. Finally, the individual may be "bought" by the majority group, or used by the majority as a source of information and contact with the minority in a manner that would be damaging to the minority group.

In summary, the minority-core community consists of a grouping of individuals clustering spatially; sharing common activities and institutions; sharing common interests, values, beliefs, and sentiments; being to some extent isolated and excluded from participation in the life of the larger community; sharing an awareness of minority-group status, a feeling of interdependence with other group members within or without the specific community, and a sense of psychosociological group unity that forms the basis for a *potential* tendency to act in unison toward the improvement of minority-group status.

In the remainder of this section we treat Hometown's Negro community as a specimen minority community and examine the extent to which the conditions of the ideal-type minority community are realized there.

Relationship between spatial and sociopsychological community

The Negroes of Hometown are to varying extents members of both a spatial and a sociopsychological community, and there is a close correlation but *not* a one-to-one relationship between existence in the spatial community and existence in the sociopsychological community. The relationship instead takes the form of a four-fold table, with membership in the two types of community as the two variables, as follows:

1. *Membership in both spatial and sociopsychological communities.* Most of Hometown's Negroes fall into this category, and in other areas of the country the closer one approaches the Deep South communities, the greater is the proportion of Negroes in this category. These community members, on the one hand, are likely to live in predominantly Negro neighborhoods, to belong to all-Negro churches, voluntary organizations, and informal social groups, and to experience the bulk of their social interaction with other local Negroes, despite possible interracial contacts in their work, school, and shopping life. On the other hand, they also belong to the sociopsychological Negro community in that they feel a unity with other Negroes in Hometown and in other Negro communities, based on common experiences, common allegiances and sentiments, and common awareness that they are considered by the majority group to be a different, and somewhat undesirable unity.

2. *Membership in sociopsychological but not in spatial community.* A small proportion of Negroes in Hometown, probably not over 5 per cent, reside in predominantly white neighborhoods, and the fact of being extremely busy, ill, rearing children, or lacking transportation prevents their social participation in the core of the Negro community. Nevertheless they

are strongly identified with other Negroes, read the Negro press frequently, contribute as much as they can to Negro churches and other causes, and maintain close contact with Negro relatives and friends through visiting and correspondence. They are likely to be older and Southern born.

3. *Membership in spatial but not in sociopsychological community.* Another small segment of Hometown's Negro population lives in the areas of greatest Negro settlement, participates to a limited extent in the Negro institutional life, but feels almost no identification with Hometown's Negroes and strongly resents being lumped into a similar classification. In contrast to the preceding group, these members are almost always younger and Northern born.

4. *Membership in neither spatial nor sociopsychological community.* The small number in this category, who are likely to be older and Northern born, are those who have succeeded in moving out of the predominantly Negro community and have dropped membership in Negro churches and voluntary organizations for membership in white ones. In addition, they have severed most of the bonds of identification with other Negroes; they express disinterest in racial problems and minimize their exposure to Negro media of communication. They generally remain out of things unless traumatic, unpleasant racial experiences happen to them, in which case they often return, psychologically, to the Negro community for support.

The sense of sociopsychological unity felt in the Negro community of Hometown and in the other Negro communities is strengthened by still another factor characteristic of minority communities—the awareness of membership in a national or an international minority community. Thus the Hometown Negro lives in both the general community and the Negro subcommunity, and these two worlds might be further subdivided. On the one hand, Negroes are partially members of the Hometown general community, interacting with many white persons, utilizing the banks, schools, stores, public and private agencies of the general community, and listening to local radio programs and reading local newspapers; they are also exposed through these and other channels to the general American culture pattern. On the other hand, they are in many ways confined to the local Negro community, living in semi-isolation from the general community and participating in the segregated institutional life of the Negro community; they are also members of a *national Negro collectivity* with interests, relatives, membership groups, and reference groups in other regional areas.

Forces causing identification of Negroes with a national Negro community

In varying degrees, Negroes in Hometown feel a sense of common group identity with Negroes in other parts of the country because of their minority-group status. This feeling is particularly strong when disturbing instances of white prejudice and discrimination against the Negro in other parts of the country occur. In addition, pride in the success of Negroes in other communities prompts such behavior as Hometown Negroes' cheering for a visiting professional baseball team instead of the local team, because the visiting team had Negro players.

The Negro press is the main channel of communication by which news of Negroes in other parts of the country is conveyed. Ninety-one per cent of Hometown Negroes read one or more of the national weekly Negro newspapers, and half read them every week. Hence, potentially, nearly all of Hometown's Negroes are exposed to the current news about racially relevant events and about happenings in any of the major areas from which local Negroes are likely to have come, particularly from Southern towns. This information serves to relate many Hometown Negroes to the community of origin and reinforces their continued interest in the communities from which they came.

Identification with Negroes in other communities is also maintained by the frequent visits of Hometown Negroes to other communities, including Southern communities. For example, 71 per cent of Hometown Negro youths reported that they had visited another city for several days during the past two years. Generally, a Negro visiting another city will immediately seek contacts within "the colored folks' part of town."

Not only is there much visiting, but also Negroes are often more geographically mobile than are members of the larger community. Twenty per cent of Hometown Negroes and 33 per cent of Hometown's native American white Gentiles were born in Hometown; 24 per cent of the Negroes and 14 per cent of the whites had been in the community less than five years. Half of a sample of 100 Hometown Negro youths reported that they had lived in at least one other city besides Hometown. This geographical mobility, which includes occasional seasonal shuttling of individuals between Hometown and Southern communities, keeps high the Hometown Negro's awareness of activity in other Negro communities. Nearly every Negro family has relatives living in the South, and ties are maintained by correspondence, visiting, and migration of family subunits.

Finally, a large number of Hometown Negroes belong to local branches of regional or national organizations, for example, the NAACP (22 per cent of Hometown Negroes report membership); the local branch of the African Methodist Episcopal Zion Church (27 per cent attend this church), and the lodges and female lodge auxiliaries (20 per cent report membership). Since the NAACP is nearly all-Negro and the church and lodge organizations are all-Negro, national policy for these organizations, passed on to local branches, links the Hometown Negro community with a national Negro community. These facts help to explain why some Hometown Negroes have an interest in other Negro communities that often equals or exceeds interest in the Hometown community. However this phenomenon is also an effect of the Hometown Negro's awareness of his social isolation from the general community.

Just as the spatial community has in the past created the sociopsychological unity of community members, it is possible that in the future the acceptance of Negroes in previously white neighborhoods, churches, organizations, and voluntary social groups might gradually disperse the spatial Negro community, and the ensuing identification of Negroes with nonracial issues, interests, aims, and goals could reduce the sociopsychological unity of Negroes that exists today; that this latter process is already occurring may be shown by the comparison of Southern and Northern Negro communities. It may be assumed that only when these processes have taken place will the Negro community as an entity disappear.

We now turn to the internal description of the Negro subcommunity of Hometown.

Hometown's subcommunity

Over half of Hometown's Negroes are Southern born, and the Southern Negro way of life has many vestiges here. Examples are the great importance of kinship ties; strong adherence to the church as the center of social life; warm friendliness, even toward the stranger; informal welfare—taking care of the needy; a folklore and a smattering of superstitious beliefs; a great consciousness of the racial caste barrier; and a tendency to divide the white outgroup into two extreme categories—the wealthy or substantial people, and the poor trash. Allied with these traits are elements of the village mentality and its accompanying suspicion of outsiders, clannishness, curiosity about business of other community members, gossip, a belief that everybody knows everybody else's business, and a constellation of village types—the town drunk, the town gossip, the village idiot, the bad girl, the ne'er-do-well.

And finally, some of the members of Hometown's Negro community who came from larger Northern urban areas bring with them an entirely different way of life—greater aggressiveness, exploitativeness, and expectation of the exploitative motivation of others, indifference to other community walks of life besides one's own, conspicuous expenditure, nonconservative dress, and occasional emulation of patterns of deviant behavior they bring from "the big city."

Since the end of the Civil War, the Negro population of Hometown has roughly doubled; the City Directory of 1868 listed 179 Negro households, and a current census lists about 400. However, of the present Negro population, only 8 per cent reported that their fathers were born in Hometown, and only 4 per cent said their grandfathers were born there.

The family patterns of Hometown Negroes do not differ markedly from family patterns described in other studies of Negro communities. On the one hand, a large segment of the families are stable, struggling to buy their home, improve their property, and educate their children as far as possible. On the other hand, there are a large number of broken homes (regretted but not condemned by the community), a scattering of some of the larger families into different households, and a few common-law families. Only fifty-seven per cent of Negro adults reported themselves as "married— spouse present," as compared with 78 per cent of native white American gentiles, 91 per cent of Italian-Americans, and 96 per cent of Jewish informants. Of the 93 unmarried Negro youths interviewed, 22 per cent did not have their mother living in the home with them, and 42 per cent reported that their father was not living in their home. One-third of the youths did not know their father's present occupation, and two-thirds of a sample of 150 Negro adults did not know what the occupation of their father's father had been. Forty per cent of the youths said that they had brothers and sisters living in other communities; another 40 per cent reported relatives living in their home who were not parents, siblings, or grandparents.

At the time the study of Hometown's Negro community began, most Negroes were employed in semiskilled or unskilled industrial positions; service occupations, like janitor, porter, attendant, waiter, and busboy; and domestic service. Very few were in white-collar occupations. Besides a few taverns and restaurants, the few Negro businesses were limited to the small, personal-service category—barbers and beauticians, caterers, owners of rooming houses. Reference to the old City Directories shows that the occupational level of Hometown Negroes is probably lower today than in 1868. At that time, there were thirteen Negro barbers who catered to white customers; today there are four, and they cater only to Negroes. Though most Negroes in 1868 were listed as laborers, many were masons, blacksmiths, shoemakers, teamsters, etc.; today there are almost no Negroes in the skilled trades. The 1868 Directory even reported a Negro physician, though old-time residents of the Negro community described him as "some old fool who mixed up some roots and herbs and called himself a doctor."

The community's focal points of activity are located in a two-square-block area—churches, taverns, playgrounds, lodge halls, and "after-hours joints." Each of these is stratified to some degree. There is a high-status Methodist church attended by the community pillars; a somewhat lower-status but larger and more lively Baptist church, which has more Southern-born members and is less likely to frown on loud amens, handclapping, and lusty singing; and a still lower-status "sanctified" church, isolated from the rest of the Negro community, where rigid prohibitions are placed on drinking, smoking, and dancing, and where Sunday night services attain such an emotional peak that more secular people in the nearby tavern incline their heads, wink, and aver that "the sanctified people are getting the Holy Ghost tonight."

The three taverns are likewise stratified to cater to different socioeconomic levels. The highest-status tavern is clean and attractive looking, with comfortable booths, many mirrors, leather seats, shiny chromium. Around the corner is a somewhat lower-status tavern. It was once closed by the police after a series of fights and disturbances, but it has recently reopened under white management; the bartenders are both white and Negro, and the cliques composing its clientele are partly interracial and extremely harmonious. One block from the highest-status tavern is the lowest-status one; it is far noisier than the rest, particularly on Saturday night. Most higher-status Negroes avoid it and look askance at anyone who goes there; however, some of the younger ones occasionally attend, murmuring apologetic statements —"It's dirty down there, but it fascinates me," or "Why spend money for the movies when you can watch those 'gandys' and 'bean pickers' down at Sammy's?"

Finally, the after-hours places also exhibit a pattern of stratification. Five or six places serve primarily the lower-status and predominantly migratory Negroes. Other more expensively equipped establishments strive to attract white customers. These places serve liquor in coffee cups and furnish jazz music by musicians of both races who have finished their stint in the downtown nightclubs.

Though it is not often reported on questionnaires, a large number of Hometown's interracial contacts occur in these after-hours joints; and here, because of the combination of music, alcohol, and sex, some of Hometown's most intimate and also most tension-laden racial relations exist. In terms of apparent motivation, the white customers might be divided into lovers of jazz music, friends of Negroes who frequent these establishments, alcoholics or "winoes" drifting in from the bars fronting the nearby railroad yard, and white males seeking Negro females. Among the white visitors are prominent community lawyers and politicians, the younger middle-class, fast-moving set, workingmen in plaid shirts and work caps, and poverty-stricken older bums and winoes.

A summary description of community participation adds organizational membership as another life axis:

Summarizing Table 8.1, regardless of organizational membership, frequent churchgoers are less likely, as might be expected, to visit places where alcohol is sold; however, among active churchgoers, those who belong to organizations are more likely to visit taverns and after-hours places than those who do not belong to organizations. Many of the tavern goers do not drink in the taverns, but merely watch, greet, and interact with other com-

Table 8.1

Church and organizational participation by tavern and after-hours
participation (150 Negro adults, Hometown).

Organizational membership:	Belong to organizations		Do not belong to organizations	
Church attendance:	Every or most Sundays (44 cases)	Occasionally or never (23 cases)	Every or most Sundays (23 cases)	Occasionally or never (49 cases)
Per cent attending last month				
Highest status tavern	32%	48%	26%	29%
Medium status tavern	18%	27%	13%	31%
Lowest status tavern	23%	46%	22%	57%
Least notorious after-hours place	18%	18%	9%	29%
Medium notorious	11%	24%	–	22%
Most notorious	5%	12%	–	14%

munity members. Participants in Hometown's Negro community not only
represent a wide range between respectability and nonrespectability but
also form a continuum ranging from full, active, and rich participation in
all walks of subcommunity life to almost complete isolation, nonparticipation, and the abstention from interpersonal communication.

Our own observations underline the fact that the racial and cultural minorities of any area, though often assumed to be quite homogeneous, actually exhibit complex patterns of social differentiation. The intricate differentiation and stratification of the Negro subcommunity was documented
progressively by the participant-observer as his research led him to divide
the community into two residence types, five socioeconomic levels, eight
other statistical categories, sixteen clique groupings, and fifty discrete subcommunity groupings.

For all of this marked and complex internal differentiation [17]—almost
entirely unnoticed by the environing white community—it is still true that
there is a diffuse kind of racial unity. Its basis is not objective similarity
of social characteristics nor even of most beliefs and values. It lies rather in
a sensed common fate and in both the fact and the awareness of interdependence. An important measure of consensus and unity was demon-

---

[17] Still another example of diversity within ethnic categories is given by Rose Hum
Lee's analysis of the very different groupings of Chinese in the United States, that
is, the sojourners from rural Kwantung, the urban students and intellectuals (largely
from central and northern China), and the Americans of Chinese ancestry. Cf. *The
Chinese in the United States of America* (New York: Oxford University Press, and
Hong Kong: Hong Kong University Press, 1960).

strated, in the course of our observations, by the capacity of the Negro subcommunity to accomplish positive social action despite its complex internal differentiation and stratification.

The commonality of fate arises in large part from the pressure of the white society. Most Hometown whites have no important social interaction with any Negro person. But Negroes have considerably more contact with whites, as we shall see later in detail.

It has been said that the Hometown Negro community shows a core and less definite peripheries. First, there is a set of independent and segregated minority community institutions and organizations: religious institutions and their attendant social groupings, voluntary organizations such as lodges and social clubs, ethnic organizations such as the NAACP, athletic teams, and informal social cliques. In addition, the Negro community possesses a number of peripheries which consist of the isolated, disaffected, marginal, and "whitewardly mobile" persons.

NEGRO-WHITE INTERACTION, HOMETOWN: THE NEGROES' POINT OF VIEW

Frequency of contact

It became clear early in the Hometown surveys that most white majority-group persons had only very limited contacts with ethnic group members. Approximately half of the adults in the sample had no personal contact with any of the three minority groups in any of the situations that were asked about—employment, neighborhood, clubs or organizations, and informal social groups. Another 25 per cent had contact with a member of one ethnic group in one of these situations. Thus, 75 per cent had no contacts with at least two of the three ethnic groups in any of these situations. For each type of situation asked about, more majority-group members had contacts with Italian-Americans than with Jews, and more had contacts with Jews than with Negroes. Majority-group members were less likely than minorities to have a contact that was a really friendly one: only 16 per cent had a good friend who was a Negro; 33 per cent had a friend who was Italian-American; and 38 per cent had a friend who was Jewish.

Table 8.2 shows the available contact, extent of personal friendship, and socializing between whites and Negroes in places of employment, neighborhoods, clubs or organizations, and informal social groups. Table 8.3 shows the nature of the relationship with the closest local contact of the other race. Both tables are based on 529 native American white gentiles. Regardless of the attitudes and personal preferences of Hometown Negroes, a complete withdrawal from contacts with whites is almost impossible. No matter whether the available contact is in neighborhood, employment, organization, or informal social group, the small proportion of the community

Table 8.2

Nature and depth of interracial contacts reported by whites about
Negroes and by Negroes about whites (Hometown).

	Whites, with Negroes (529 cases)	Negroes, with Whites (150 cases)
Employment		
Per cent who have had an available contact	23% (67)	63% (95)
Per cent of those with available contact who have claimed member of other group as a personal friend	38% (24)	81% (77)
Per cent who have done something special together ouside the home	17% (4)	—
Per cent who have visited back and forth in each other's home	0%	—
Neighborhood		
Per cent who have had an available contact	14% (74)	95%
Per cent of those with available contact who have claimed member of other group as a close or good friend	23% (17)	48% (72)
Per cent of those claiming close or good friend who have done something social together outside the home	35% (6)	—
Per cent who have visited back and forth in each other's home	18% (3)	—
Club or organization		
Per cent who have had an available contact	10% (52)	36% (54)
Per cent of those with available contact who have claimed member of other group as a close or good friend	23% (12)	24% (36)
Per cent of those claiming close or good friend who have done something social together outside the home	83% (10)	—
Per cent who have visited back and forth in each other's home	0%	—
Social group		
Per cent who have had an available contact	2% (8)	31% (47)

Table 8.3

Closest interracial contacts (Hometown).

	Whites, with Negroes (529 cases)		Negroes, with Whites (150 cases)	
Per cent who reported <u>no</u> contact with members of the other group	67%	(355)	0%	(0)
Per cent of those reporting contact who say closest contact is:				
A business contact	66%	(113)	70%	(108)
A social contact	4%	(7)	18%	(27)
A neighborhood contact	9%	(15)	9%	(13)
Another type of contact	21%	(21)	3%	(4)
Per cent of those reporting contact who say that member of the other race is a close or good friend	20%	(28)	73%	(109)
Per cent of those reporting close or good friend who say they have done something social together outside the home with member of other race	32%	(9)	38%	(41)
Per cent of those reporting a close or good friend in other race, who have visited back and forth in each other's home	14%	(4)	28%	(31)
Per cent of those having experienced neither of the two previous activities, but who have been invited to a social occasion at the home of closest contact of other race	4%	(1)	12%	(9)

that is Negro insures that the Negro contacts with whites will greatly outnumber the reverse.

The factors of enforced contact with whites and continual near-presence of whites is more significant in smaller than in larger Negro communities. The tendency to glance about and observe whether white persons may be listening to ingroup jokes and epithets or to Negroes' comments about affairs involving race relations or shortcomings among Negroes is one indication of a greater awareness and self-consciousness about minority-group membership than would be observed in larger Negro ghettos where white faces are less often seen.

Attitudes towards interaction

When presented with items in a social-distance scale inquiring about attitudes toward certain types of interaction with members of the other race, white and Negro persons in Hometown gave the following responses:

Per cent saying they would find it a little bit distasteful to:	Hometown Whites (N-529)	Hometown Negroes (N-150)
Eat at the same table with a member of the other race	49% (262)	14% (21)
Dance with a member of the other race	82% (433)	33% (50)
Go to a party and find that most of the people there are of the other race	80% (417)	31% (46)
Have a person of the other race marry someone in their family	99% (521)	49% (74)

In situations of interracial job contacts in Hometown, most white persons reported that they did not feel different toward the Negroes they were in contact with on their jobs (83 per cent), and most Negroes stated that they thought the white workers on the job did not feel different toward them (69 per cent). However, of whites who stated that they did feel different toward Negroes contacted on their job, and of Negroes who felt that whites on the job felt different, the pattern of "prejudice reaction to prejudice" is illustrated:

Statements by whites concerning on-job contacts with Negroes:

They work well together, but there is a feeling. The white employees wouldn't eat at the same table with them or make friends outside their work.

Whites shouldn't have to work beside Negroes—I don't approve of it—all right to work in the same place, but not with them.

I'd prefer not to work with them, though some are good workers and mind their own business.

They're all right if they stay in their place. I don't go out of my way for them. Give a colored person an inch and they'll take a mile.

Statements by Negroes concerning on-job contacts with whites:

I'm not particularly fond of "paddies" myself. Some of them will speak to you in the plant, and won't speak outside.

They act as if they are better than someone else, and I'm no poorer than they are.

If I find out they don't want to be bothered with me, then I just don't want to be bothered with them.

I don't care how a white person treats you. They have a feeling in 'em that you're colored—I know my place, no matter where I am.

Defensive minority attitudes

Prejudice and stereotyped thinking of members of the white community find their counterpart in some compensatory prejudice and stereotyped thinking on the part of the Negro. Reactions of Negro persons to whites include a general bewilderment at outgroup traits that are not understood; awe, respect, and admiration drawn from the general community's assumption of superiority of whites; defensive pride; and disparagement of the white group as a whole. Casual statements of this nature are often heard: "White man's the damnedest thing I ever saw"; " 'Course a white man can do anything he want to anyway"; "White people don't know how to have fun"; "White people aren't sincere." At a meeting of a fairly well-educated group of militant Hometown Negro leaders, members of the group concluded their discussion of intergroup relations with statements like: "White people are full of deception"; "Whites are the worse people in the world"; ". . . and jealous"; ". . . and absolutely no morals . . ."

However, the most ubiquitous conception of Negroes is that the white person is prejudiced against him. This belief is partly stereotypic since there is often no differentiation between various types of white people and types of prejudice. No doubt this belief more closely approximates reality than does the prejudice of whites toward Negroes. In response to white's prejudice, the Negro often articulates a reciprocal prejudice, suspicion, and withdrawal, with accompanying rationalizations. In Hometown most Negroes felt that their *closest white contact* was different from most whites; the difference was thought to be lack of prejudice against Negroes. An open-ended question asking why the white contact was different from most whites was answered either by a statement that this white person was less prejudiced, or it was answered in more general terms such as that this person was more broadminded, liberal, or just more friendly. Among those who claimed the white person as a best friend, the responses almost unanimously referred to the white friend's lack of prejudice. Samples:

She is more broadminded—more understanding. Not prejudiced.

Broadminded about the race question—they want to be in on discussions. I knew them all my life.

He don't know no color. Everybody is the same color.

On the other hand, respondents who designated their closest white contact as just somebody they knew to speak to and somebody towards whom they felt different expressed some reservations about the nonprejudice of their white contacts:

He's not the fresh type. He talks very strongly for the Negroes. Don't know whether he'll live up to it or not.

Stated summarily, the Hometown Negro (1) is aware of the strong prejudices of Hometown whites, and (2) has a reciprocal prejudice; (3) has a stereotype of whites, similar to (but probably more accurate than) white stereotypes of the Negro. The Negro's stereotype of whites is focused on the belief that the white person is prejudiced and, hence, (4) many Negroes do not attempt more interracial contact than is absolutely necessary; and (5) the Negro's frequent feeling that his closest white contact is different from most whites is based on the belief that the white person deviates from the general tendency of whites to be prejudiced against Negroes.

Isolation: Action and Reaction

In large measure the negative aspects of relations between white and Negro persons in Hometown are directly generated by partial isolation, resulting in a reinforcement of alienation. As we have previously suggested, barriers to greater association between whites and Negroes are maintained by the lack of available interracial contacts; these barriers lead to inadequate understanding and a consequent perception of the other group as hostile. This perception, particularly in the case of the Negro, increases Negro suspicion and avoidance of whites, thus reducing communication. The reduction of communication, in turn, leads to a growth of stereotypes and negative expectations on both sides, expressed in group norms that lead to continued awareness of the outgroup's hostility, and then to a reactive hostility in the ingroup.

Barriers to communication

On the part of the Hometown Negro, the barriers to communication with members of the general community are created by three major factors: (1) the reality—the actual existence of such factors as limited interracial contact, prejudice on the part of Hometown white persons, discriminatory practices, and the language of prejudice; (2) the Negroes' reactions to this reality; and (3) the lag in the Negro's perception of recent objective changes in intergroup-relations patterns on both the national and the local level.

The reality. Two-thirds of Hometown white people have no available contact with Negroes; 5 per cent of Hometown whites report a Negro close friend or good friend; white persons report a considerable amount of social distance and antipathy against Negroes; both white and Negro persons hold to some stereotypes (roughly half of Hometown whites agreed that "generally speaking, Negroes are lazy and ignorant"), and one-fourth of the Negroes agreed that "no matter how nicely he treats a Negro, a white person doesn't really mean it." Thus, a considerable amount of racial discrimination does exist in Hometown, and Negroes are aware of it. White people use the language of prejudice, and Negroes' expectation of and anxiety and resentment about actual encounters with prejudice are fairly extensive.

Negroes' reactions. In reaction to these actual circumstances, Hometown's Negroes develop patterns of avoidance and reluctance to enter any area where prejudice or discrimination may be encountered. For example, 64 per cent of a sample of 150 Hometown Negro adults agreed with the statement: *Negroes shouldn't go into business establishments where they think they're not wanted;* and, when presented with a hypothetical situation, *Suppose you were downtown with a group of your Negro friends, and they asked you to go with them into a restaurant that you were pretty sure didn't serve Negroes—would you go?* 71 per cent of Negro respondents said they would *not* go in. One hundred Negro youths were asked several questions about avoidance and showed a similar tendency. Ten per cent of the youths agreed that *I keep away from white people as much as I can;* 29 per cent agreed that *it is best to stay away from white people; then you will avoid all embarrassing situations;* 57 per cent agreed that *Negroes shouldn't go into business establishments where they think they're not wanted;* and 77 per cent agreed that *if a business place refuses to serve me, I think I should leave without causing any trouble.*

Field observations suggested that Negroes are deterred from greater interracial contact because of the expectation that a white person will make a racial slip and insult the Negro, and because of the strain of feeling the necessity of maintaining a type of behavior that is acceptable to white middle-class standards or the fear of doing something that will "embarrass the Negro race." It appears that better educated Negroes, regardless of place of birth, acknowledge fewer deterrents to interracial contact than do less well-educated Negroes; that educated Southern-born Negroes express the greatest apprehension about the racial slip; that Northern-born Negroes express more concern than Southern-born Negroes about having to avoid controversial subjects like intermarriage. Less well-educated Negroes, regardless of place of birth, are more likely to state that they do not understand white people. Factors that do not act significantly as deterrents to greater interracial contact include fear of disapproval from one's peers, suspicion of a white person's possibly exploitative motive, and dislike of white people.

The respondents were presented with a printed card describing a set of intergroup situations; they were asked two questions, which, together with responses, are given here:

Are there any of these situations that make you feel a little bit uncomfortable?
Are there any of them that make you feel good?

Make respondent feel uncomfortable		Make respondent feel good
88%	When a group of Negroes gets noisy and boisterous around white people	1%
45%	When a white person tells you "you're just as good as I am"	23%
37%	When you are with Negroes who are trying hard to impress the white people	31%
29%	When a white person asks you how it feels to be a Negro	24%
21%	When you are the only Negro in a group of people	21%
15%	When a white person that you don't know goes out of his way to be friendly to you	55%
9%	When you see white people in the Negro business establishments	38%
—	When a white person talks to you about Jackie Robinson, Ralph Bunche, and other "credits to your race"	83%

It may be seen that negatively evaluated behavior of other Negroes in an interracial situation is particularly likely to cause discomfort to the respondent, and that certain testimonials and other attempted rapport devices also cause discomfort. On the other hand, evidence of white friendliness, seeking out of Negroes, and compliments about outstanding Negroes are more likely to produce favorable than unfavorable reactions.

Lag. Many reactive practices and avoidance techniques developed by Negroes in the South may become inappropriate or overreactive techniques in the Hometown situation. The casual and unreflective use of the language of prejudice by white persons thus may produce an unexpected and angry reaction from Negroes. The barriers to interracial communication are increased by the white person's lack of awareness about the historical background and current sensitivity of the Hometown Negro.

In addition, the avoidance patterns and the insulation of Hometown's Negroes is perpetuated by another type of lag—the lag between actual positive changes in the attitudes and behavior of Hometown whites and the Negro's perception of these changes. Thus, the avoidance and isolation of Hometown Negroes is influenced not only by objective existence of prejudice and discrimination, but also by a distorted conception of the prejudice and discrimination that remain. This conception is partially attributable to social isolation.

Evidence of the social isolation of Hometown's Negro population repeatedly appears in casual statements of community members. A statement like, "It's all over town" generally means "all over the Negro community," and even this meaning is restricted to the solid core of the Negro community. References to "the prettiest girl in town," or "the meanest man in town" usually are intended to be confined to the boundaries of the Negro subworld. The term "we" usually refers to Hometown Negroes or to Negroes throughout the country rather than to Hometown in general.

At one time, the Cornell participant-observer was reassured by a lifetime resident of the Negro community that he could feel free to discuss confidential subjects over the telephone since the only people who could possibly be listening on the party line were *white people*—obviously regarded as so completely removed from the Negro's life that it didn't matter what they heard.

Hometown Negroes perceived the social world more as part of a psychological community of 1,200 Negro members than as part of a Hometown community of 60,000 people. For example, when asked the question, *If you were asked to use one of these four names for your social group, which would you belong in: the upper class, middle class, working class, or lower class?* Hometown's Negroes were more likely than Jews, Italian-Americans, or native American white gentiles to put themselves in the *upper* class:

Native American White Gentiles (N-486)	Jews (N-150)	Italian-Americans (N-150)	Negroes (N-150)
3%	6%	3%	21%

Evidently, Negroes evaluated themselves in terms of a reference group composed of Negro community members; their standard of comparison was the working-class Negro community, rather than the general Hometown community. Cross-sectional surveys of white and Negro respondents in three other communities in different regions of the United States showed consistently that Negroes were more likely to classify themselves as members of the upper class than were majority-group members or other minorities.

A summary. Although the minority community bears a functional economic relationship to the majority community, the patterns of majority prejudice, discrimination, and employment of the language of prejudice (and the minority reactions to these phenomena) create a socially isolated subcommunity whose perceptions are bounded by the psychological limits of the minority community rather than those of the general community.

The customary and sometimes necessary practices of minority adaptation developed in extremely stressful intergroup situations, such as race relations in the South, may become inappropriate reactions in a less stressful environment.

Given some substantial basis in an original reality, if a minority-group member *defines* a situation as discriminatory, then it *is* discriminatory in its consequences. The lag between positive changes in the sanctions that govern acceptance of minorities, and the minority's perception of these changes produces situations in which the end result is one of discrimination, regardless of intent or actual circumstances.

Neither the absence of legal segregation nor the existence of nominal freedom to associate with other groups assures a free flow of interaction and communication between these groups. On the contrary, the presence of prejudice, discrimination, the language of prejudice, and the Negro's perceptions of these factors, have produced a largely socially isolated community that we have termed a "world in the shadow." We will consider later how these individual minority reactions may crystallize into an awareness of minority-group status, a constellation of minority social types, and finally, a sense of group membership and group identification.

RECURRENT PATTERNS IN NEGRO COMMUNITIES

The Hometown Negro community cannot be considered as typical of most Negro communities. Hometown is neither a large metropolis nor a rural area, and the majority of Negroes live in one or the other of these. The Hometown subcommunity exists in a state where no segregation or discrimination is legally required and where the state laws against discrimination are quite strong. The town is less than 3 per cent Negro. Nevertheless, the Hometown research experience, affected by the fact that many Hometown Negroes were from other metropolitan or rural areas, furnished several insights and hypotheses about Negro community life in general. These served as guides for investigation in other areas.

In the process of studying eleven Negro subcommunities of varying sizes in different regions,[18] certain patterns appeared in every community.

Internal community structure

Everywhere, the social isolation of the Negro subcommunities, stemming from a lack of complete integration into general community life, caused an identification with the national Negro community or with Negroes in other areas, as well as with the larger local community. Each Negro community echoed, with modifications, the stratification patterns of the general community; in each case, respondents would differentiate between a higher-status level of stable, respectable families and a lower-status level of disorganized individuals with less stable family patterns. In each community the social organization comprised a solid core of separate institutions and at least three distinct peripheries: a segment withdrawn from the Negro community and semi-integrated into the larger community; a segment newly

---

[18] The eleven were: Elmira, Auburn, and Poughkeepsie, N. Y.; Lancaster, Pa.; Steubenville, O.; Weirton, W. Va.; Savannah, Ga.; Tucson, Ariz.; and Bakersfield, Calif.

arrived, transient, and lacking in community membership and reference groups; and a segment that was nonparticipant or "on the shelf."

Reaction to prejudice and discrimination

In each community Negroes had far more contact and interaction with whites than the reverse; this contact was greatest in the occupational field and lowest in informal social mixing. Even in the northern-most areas, informal social interaction between Negroes and whites was very infrequent.

Most Negroes in each community tended to overestimate the number of business establishments in which Negroes would not be wanted. The current rapid changes in intergroup relations cause a lag in the Negro's perception of acceptable and nonacceptable areas. Negative reaction to the language of prejudice existed in every Negro community, varying only slightly from one region to another.

Each Negro community was partially interdependent with the larger community, but to some extent spatially separated, and always socially isolated from the general community. In every community, Negroes took for granted as acceptable their participation in certain aspects of community life, took other aspects for granted as unacceptable, and focused their attention on a few specific controversial areas where the right of Negroes to equal treatment was a current concern.

Reactions to minority status

In each community awareness of being Negro was high, the subject of intergroup relations was frequently discussed, and most Negroes tended to define situations involving interracial contact in racial terms. In each community the Negroes internalized the values and beliefs of the general community to the extent of feeling and expressing a certain amount of self-disparagement when viewing the Negro community as compared with the general community.

In each community for which cross-sectional data exist, feelings of hostility, insulation, and apathy tended to be higher among the older, the less well-educated, the less participant, and the Southern-born Negroes. In each community the articulate progressive sentiments about race relations were likely to be stated by the younger and better-educated community members who expressed sentiments of militancy, relative friendliness toward the outgroup, and a belief in the desirability of integration—what we have termed the New Negro Creed.

Negro leadership

All communities, even the smallest, showed a diverse Negro leadership in various walks of life, that is, church centered, organizational, political, representative, race leadership, etc. The pattern of generalized leadership by a single person was infrequent.

In each Negro community, two extreme types of intergroup leadership were clearly perceived by community members: militant, progressive *race* leadership and accommodating, ingratiating *Uncle Tom* leadership. Every Negro community showed a gradual trend of shifting allegiance from the more accommodating to the more militant type of leadership. In each community militant protest leadership came not from the poorest, most deprived victims of racial discrimination, but from the higher-status, though not necessarily highest-status, and the best-educated community members and from those who had reference groups and source of information and support outside the local community.

These recurrent patterns exist, in varying degrees, in many and probably most American Negro communities. However, lest the homogeneity of Negro community life be overemphasized, we must indicate some of the intercommunity variations discerned in the course of interviewing and participant-observation.

Variations in Negro participation in the community

In a small upstate New York community Negroes took for granted the acceptability of their using most community facilities but bitterly complained of the necessity of having to go twenty-six miles for a haircut—their symbol of race prejudice and discrimination. In a larger New York community, use of the barbershops was taken for granted as unacceptable, and the right to enter white restaurants and taverns was the main source of controversy. In a border-state steel town the possibility of entering white taverns and restaurants was never considered by Negro community members, but they were concerned over their inability to use the city's swimming pools, which were available to Negroes in the other two cities. In a border Southern town community members were claiming the right to attend motion-picture theaters, an area that had just been opened to Negroes in the border Northern town through a legal court case. In a small Deep South town, Negroes assumed the unavailability of all of these facilities, but made tentative and hesitant protests about the fact that the Negro ecological community, 40 per cent of the town's population, had no paved roads or sidewalks. And in a small Far West community, the most controversial intergroup relations problem was whether Negroes should be allowed to live in the town at all.

Nor were these the only variations.[19] Negro communities differed in the

---

[19] Field observation of such differences in patterns of acceptability led to the inclusion, in the national mail questionnaire, of questions about the acceptability, unacceptability, or controversial nature of Negro participation in ten community public institutions and facilities. These questions were the basis of the findings already reported in Chapter 6.

kinds of internal differentiation—by church-affiliation, by economic levels, by social classes, by length and stability of local residence (old settlers versus newcomers), by skin color, by Northern or Southern origin. In Northern areas the influx of Southern-born migrants often put Negro group identification to its severest test—creating stereotyping, apprehension, hostility, and divided counsels. Though similar in skin color, the old settlers and the incoming Southern Negroes are often as culturally divergent in many patterns of behavior as any two ethnic groups one would find in America today. Added to these differences is the old-settler's belief that the migrant is destroying the precarious balance of intergroup relations, and the migrant's feelings of hurt and resentment at being rebuffed by "our own people." These divergent views create potent negative conditions for the subcommunity's coordinated action or group identification. The old-settlers' perceptions of the migrants include realistic appraisals of differences based on rural residence, inadequate education, and the partial social disorganization that often accompanies mobility from rural South to urban North. However, the old-settlers' perceptions also include distortions similar to the white persons' stereotypes of the Negro. Although data to test the point are not available, it is certain that the differences between old settler and migrant in income, education, family stability, church attendance, consumption of alcohol, and crime rate are far less than supposed.

Not only is it becoming increasingly evident that the fate of all Negroes, regardless of place of origin, is to be a common fate, but also an increasing amount of militant minority action in the smaller Northern communities is being led by the recent Southern migrants of stable family, high aspiration, and fresh memory of race relations in the South. NAACP leadership in several communities was composed largely of Southern-born persons. The leading "race man" in one Northeastern city came there from Alabama when he was twelve years old and in the third grade. Smarting from memories of Southern intergroup relations, he was determined not to return. Of the most militant, bitter, and relentless "race man" encountered in this research, a respondent explained: *"That man and his family came here 28 years ago in an old broken-down Ford that struggled all the way from Georgia with a keg of molasses, a bushel of corn bread, and sixteen children —and they've all done well."*

As illustrated in Hometown, the multiplicity of intracommunity differentiation does not preclude the possibility of concerted minority community effort. In particular, the research in two Deep South communities where the pressure from the white majority group was strong revealed that despite numerous internal cleavages, Negro community members were able to define racial situations in terms sufficiently similar that concerted action was achieved to an extent that alarmed the majority group. In the smaller Deep South community, shortly after a nearby raid of the Ku Klux Klan, Negro community members boycotted the stores where Klansmen worked, until their employers actually discharged the known Klansmen. In Southport, half the town's Negroes were persuaded to vote by the united efforts of the more militant and the more accommodating leadership organizations—by the three ministerial alliances, the seven competing Greek-letter organizations, the respectable old settlers and the heads of the numbers racket—despite the fact that internal dissension among these groups was great. In Negro communities if racial conflict is imminent and if the racial issues are clear, the potential for concerted minority action often will outweigh the numerous smaller cleavages that exist.

A summary statement on variation in the most noticeable types of internal differentiation in Negro communities is that (1) the universal patterns of stratification and differentiation vary in emphasis from one specific Negro community to another, (2) the growing awareness among Negroes of the mechanisms of prejudice and discrimination cause them increasingly to modify or restrain their manifestations of intracommunity negative attitudes, and (3) the many possible types of variation are usually noncumulative and do not serve as a divisive cluster of characteristics completely separating one part of the community from another.

Sociological Correlates of Social-Distance Feelings among Negroes [20]

Most of the knowledge concerning variations in prejudice in the United States is based on studies of majority-group persons. This leaves a gap in our knowledge and is an obstacle to the development of a unified theory of intergroup prejudice. Our purpose in this section is to retest various intergroup generalizations by studying intergroup attitudes among Negroes.

We shall discuss community variations in social-distance feelings, as well as the relation of these attitudes to: socioeconomic status, age, marital status, sex, and social participation. The basic measure of prejudice is the index of social-distance used in Chapter 4, a three-item score that conforms to the Guttman-scale pattern. A respondent is considered high in social-distance feeling if he rejects social contact in even one item, except in Southport where he must reject two or three types of contact to be considered high in social distance.[21]

---

[20] This section is based on Noel, "Correlates of Anti-White Prejudice," pp. 85-135.

[21] For brevity persons high in social-distance feelings will often be designated as "prejudiced." The various sub-group differences will be tested for statistical significance by use of X^2. In all cases we shall apply a two-tailed test with correction for continuity whenever the number of degrees of freedom is one. See A. L. Edwards, *Experimental Design in Psychological Research* (New York: Holt, Rinehart & Winston, Inc., 1950), pp. 64, 82, 99 n.

Community variations in prejudice

It is not news that anti-Negro prejudice is more common in the South than in other sections of the United States,[22] but the fact has important implications. Pettigrew has reaffirmed the general finding on the basis of survey data gathered from small samples in each of four Southern and four Northeastern communities,[23] and Pinkney has shown that white residents in Southport are more likely to indorse an anti-Negro stereotype than whites in Hometown, Valley City, and Steelville.[24] Thus if we entertain the hypothesis that prejudice breeds counterprejudice, the fact that Southport Negro residents are far more often prejudiced [25] than those in the other three communities (Table 8.4) comes as no surprise, although it runs counter to the belief of many white people.

Table 8.4

Variability of prejudice by community.

| | Community | | | | |
Prejudice score*	Valley City (227)	Hometown (150)	Southport (288)	Steelville (140)	Total† (805)
3	7%	9%	33%	9%	17%
2	9%	18%	26%	15%	18%
1	19%	33%	19%	31%	24%
0	65%	39%	22%	45%	41%

*Based on response to three social-distance items involving eating with, dancing with, and having someone in the family marry a white person. A score of three indicates that the respondent finds all three situations distasteful and, therefore, indicates the highest amount of prejudice. See Appendix D.
† x^2 = 157.2, df = 9, p < .001.

The general economic situation of the Negro in Valley City and Southport, as described previously, does not seem to explain the significant variation in prejudice. Negroes appear to be economically better off in the Southern city. Likewise, education does not explain the difference. The two samples are almost identical in the proportion of highly educated respondents, and, as Table 8.5 indicates, those persons who are low in education are

[22] Arnold Rose, *Studies in Reduction of Prejudice,* American Council on Race Relations (1947), Section III, pp. 1, 2 (mimeographed).

[23] Thomas Pettigrew, "Regional Differences in Anti-Negro Prejudice," *Journal of Abnormal and Social Psychology,* LIX (1959), 28-36.

[24] Alphonso Pinkney, "The Anatomy of Prejudice" (Ph.D. thesis, Cornell University, 1961), p. 60.

[25] A statement that one group is "more prejudiced" than another is shorthand for the statement that a greater *proportion* of the one group than of the other scores high in expression of feelings of social distance; that is, aversion to intimate social interaction.

Table 8.5

Relationship of education to prejudice among Negroes.

Education†

Prejudice*	Valley City		Hometown		Southport		Steelville		Total‡	
	High (49)	Low (178)	High (30)	Low (119)	High (56)	Low (231)	High (43)	Low (97)	High (178)	Low (625)
High	33%	36%	47%	65%	32%	65%	44%	60%	38%	56%
Low	67%	64%	53%	35%	68%	35%	56%	40%	62%	44%

*Henceforth we will dichotomize the prejudice groups as High (prejudiced) and Low (unprej-
udiced) as discussed in Appendix D. A prejudice score of one or more on the three-item
social-distance scale is considered prejudiced in all cities except Southport where a score
of 0 or 1 is considered unprejudiced and 2 or 3 is prejudiced.
†Education is, throughout this study, split into High (high school graduate or more) and Low
(some high school or less). This is a rather stringent requirement for high education in a
depressed minority but the only alternatives are to consider those with some high school
as high in education or to split education into three groups. With either alternative the
clear relation to prejudice remains, but the latter alternative is rejected because of the
unnecessary complication of further analyses and the former is rejected because education must be reasonably high if it is to genuinely, not just spuriously, counter prejudice.
‡x^2 = 17.4, p < .001.

much more likely to be prejudiced in Southport than in Valley City. The
difference in social-distance feelings seems primarily to represent regional
variation in *norms* regarding the majority group. This normative variation
is undoubtedly a response to the racial attitudes and practices of the dominant group in the South as compared with the West.

Among the three non-Southern samples, the relative lack of prejudice in
Valley City is not a function of the proportion of Southern-born migrants
in each community. The proportion of respondents who are Southern born
is actually considerably greater in Valley City than in Hometown and Steelville (85 per cent as opposed to 56 and 60 per cent respectively). The lesser
antiwhite prejudice in Valley City is conceivably due to the multiplicity of
salient outgroup targets for hostility that that community provides,[26] but
this hypothesis seems farfetched for the situation there. More convincing
is the simple notion that the lower proportion prejudiced in Valley City is
a response to a more liberal normative order in the West than in the Midwest and Northeast.[27]

For the four samples combined, over 40 per cent of the respondents do

---

[26] This point is discussed with respect to minority persons by K. B. Clark, "Racial
Prejudice Among American Minorities," *International Social Science Bulletin,* II
(1950), 506-13 (especially 512); see also R. M. Williams, Jr., *The Reduction of
Intergroup Tensions,* Social Science Research Council Bulletin 57 (1947), p. 59.

[27] On the basis of a general measure of toleration of differences, S. A. Stouffer
has reported that the West appears to have the highest proportion of tolerant persons
and the South the smallest proportion, with the East and the Midwest intermediary.
[*Communism, Conformity, and Civil Liberties* (Garden City, N. Y.: Doubleday &
Company, Inc. 1955), pp. 129-30.]

not manifest any social-distance reaction toward whites, and almost two-thirds give the prejudiced response to no more than one of the three index items. In contrast, almost two-thirds of the 1,430 white respondents interviewed in the same four cities scored high on an equivalent measure of anti-Negro feelings.[28] These data suggest that Negroes are less likely to manifest self-conscious race prejudice than whites. The research literature comparing race prejudice among Negroes and whites is not unanimous but on the whole reports findings consistent with these.[29]

Socioeconomic status and prejudice

From the review in Chapter 4 of relationships between socioeconomic status and various measures of prejudice we have learned caution. It will be recalled that correlations seem to depend in part upon the particular aspects or dimensions of both status and prejudice that are indexed in any particular study. In this section we will examine four indices often considered to refer to socioeconomic status, in relation to expressions by Negroes of social-distance feelings toward whites.[30]

Education. Most studies among white people show that anti-Negro prejudice and amount of formal education are negatively correlated. Our data (Table 8.5) indicate that the relationship in the Negro community is parallel to that found in the majority group.[31] The inverse relationship clearly holds

[28] Pinkney, "The Anatomy of Prejudice," pp. 65, 85, and 258-62.

[29] E. T. Prothro and J. A. Jensen, "Comparison of Some Ethnic and Religious Attitudes of Negro and White College Students in the Deep South," *Social Forces,* XXX (1952), 426-28; Frank R. Westie and Margaret L. Westie, "The Social Distance Pyramid: Relationships Between Caste and Class," *American Journal of Sociology,* LXIII (1957), 190-96; J. B. Edlefsen, "Social Distance Attitudes of Negro College Students," *Phylon,* XVII (1956), 79-83; G. A. Steckler, "Authoritarian Ideology in Negro College Students," *Journal of Abnormal and Social Psychology,* LIV (1957), 396-99.

[30] See: Rose, *Studies in Reduction of Prejudice,* Section III, p. 6; F. Westie, "Negro-White Status Differentials and Social Distance," *American Sociological Review,* XVII (1952), 550-58; J. Harding, B. Kutner, H. Proshansky, and I. Chein, "Prejudice and Ethnic Relations," in G. Lindzey, ed., *Handbook of Social Psychology* (Reading, Mass.: Addison-Wesley Publishing Company, Inc., 1954), p. 1039; and G. W. Allport, *The Nature of Prejudice* (Reading, Mass.: Addison-Wesley Publishing Company, Inc., 1954), pp. 79-80. Allport's assessment with regard to education and prejudice is much more cautious and tentative than that of Harding *et al.,* whereas he is much more positive than they in linking economic status and prejudice.

[31] The relationship among whites has been qualified by Stember's recent reanalysis of over a score of studies (primarily based on public opinion poll data) relating education to anti-Jewish and anti-Negro prejudices. Stember finds that the better educated are less likely to endorse stereotypes and they are more willing to grant public rights (equality) to minority persons, but they are more intolerant of intimate personal relations with minority persons than are the less well educated. In other words, the relation of education to prejudice depends on the dimension of prejudice involved. C. H. Stember, *The Effect of Education on Prejudice Against Minority Groups,* American Jewish Committee, Institute of Human Relations (1960), p. 232.

in Southport, and there is a consistent (although nonsignificant) tendency in this direction in the other three communities. The educated tend to be less prejudiced than the uneducated in all four cities, and over all four combined, the difference is significant at the 0.001 level. That the relationship is far from perfect between communities is obvious from the table. Nevertheless, the relationship is sufficiently strong to suggest a definite need for controlling education when examining the relationship between prejudice and other sociological variables.

Occupation. Previous studies of Negro Americans report contradictory findings concerning the relationship between occupation and attitudes toward whites. Westie and Westie, using a modified Edwards index of occupational status, found among a sample of 92 Indianapolis Negro males that high status went along with less social-distance feeling toward whites.[32] On the other hand, Cothran studied a random sample of 174 New Orleans Negroes stratified on the basis of occupation, education, and income and found that middle-class Negroes tend to have the most favorable (or least unfavorable) stereotypic conceptions of white people, whereas lower-class Negroes are most unfavorable and upper-class Negroes intermediate.[33] Although the upper class was less prejudiced than the middle class on some of the stereotypes, and the differences between the three classes were frequently not significant, the over-all relation between status and prejudice is curvilinear.

Using occupation only as an index of status, our data (Table 8.6) conform more closely to Cothran's finding than to that of the Westies, despite the fact that both our status and prejudice indices are more similar to the Westies'.[34] Although the differences are not statistically significant, those persons in middle-status occupations are least prejudiced in both Valley City and Southport.

Cothran argued that the lower-class Negro has no one in relation to whom he can feel superior, and he has a poor chance of mobility up the class

---

[32] "The Social Distance Pyramid: Relationships between Caste and Class." This study used three status categories. A more detailed analysis of these same data using only two status categories is provided by F. Westie and D. H. Howard, "Social Status Differentials and Race Attitudes of Negroes," *American Sociological Review*, XIX (1954), 584-91.

[33] T. C. Cothran, "Negro Conceptions of White People," *American Journal of Sociology*, LVI (1951), 458-67. This study has been replicated on a sample of 100 Negroes in Rochester, N. Y., but the authors do not make explicit their general finding with regard to the relation between class and prejudice. [P. A. McDaniel and N. Babchuk, "Negro Conceptions of White People in a Northeastern City," *Phylon*, XXI (1960), 7-19.]

[34] Cothran dealt with stereotypes, whereas our data and those of the Westies are based on social-distance measures of prejudice. Relevant here, though unsubstantiated, is the suggestion by Harding, *et al.* that the contradictory findings regarding economic status and anti-Negro prejudice may be due to variations in the attitude dimension under study. ["Prejudice and Ethnic Relations," p. 1039.]

Table 8.6

Degree of Negro prejudice toward whites in relation to Negroes' status.*

Occupational status‡

Prejudice†	Valley City			Southport			Total		
	High (9)	Medium (49)	Low (60)	High (21)	Medium (73)	Low (87)	High (30)	Medium (122)	Low (147)
High	44%	31%	43%	57%	47%	60%	53%	40%	54%
Low	56%	69%	57%	43%	53%	40%	47%	60%	46%

*Data from Hometown could not be used in this table because only the breadwinner's occu-
pation was determined and not whether the respondent or someone else was the breadwinner. The Steelville data were omitted for the reason discussed in note (‡). In Valley City
and Southport all respondents who were employed were included regardless of whether they
were full or part time, or were the chief breadwinner.
†Prejudice is high in Valley City if the respondent finds one or more of the social-distance
items (eating, dancing, and marrying) distasteful; in Southport if he finds two or more distasteful.
‡High status occupations include the professions and proprietors and managers, middle
status includes white-collar and skilled and semiskilled workers, and low status includes
laborers and domestics. Steelville was omitted from this analysis because the semiskilled
were coded in the same category with unskilled laborers. (However, even on the basis of
this categorization, the same curvilinear relationship was found in Steelville although the
number of cases was very small (8 each) in the high and medium status categories.)

ladder, whereas upper-class Negroes have reached the social mobility ceil-
ing imposed on members of the Negro caste. Both of these conditions en-
gender frustrations leading to prejudice, which the better-adjusted middle-
class Negroes are able to avoid.[35] In the present study, data are available
from the respondents in Valley City and Southport that permit us to see
whether prejudice relates differentially, by occupation, to various items indexing frustration. This will provide a partial test of Cothran's interpretation.

Three questions that might be taken as crude indices of frustration common to the Valley City and Southport interviews are:

1. *Sometimes I feel so frustrated I just feel like smashing things.*
2. *How often do you get upset by the things that happen in day-to-day
living: often, sometimes, or hardly ever?*
3. *When one Negro does something wrong the whole Negro race suffers
for it.*

The first item represents a direct testimony of frustration, whereas the second item assumes that frustration is generally associated with getting upset. The third item is only indirectly related to frustration but emphasizes
the racial factor that is central to Cothran's explanation of prejudice among
upper-status Negroes. Judging from these indices, the upper-status Negro
is generally less frustrated than either of the other two status groups (Table

---

[35] Cothran, *op cit.*

8.7), although the differences are generally slight and the second item yields results largely in line with Cothran's hypothesis. More sensitive measures of frustration might reverse this generally negative finding, but these data do not clearly support the frustration explanation.

Table 8.7

Relationship between occupational status and frustration tolerance among Negroes.

| | Occupational status* | | | | | |
| | Desert City | | | Southport | | |
Frustration†	High (9)	Medium (49)	Low (60)	High (21)	Medium (73)	Low (87)
Smash things						
Agree	33%	37%	57%	10%	30%	39%
Not agree	67%	63%	43%	90%	70%	61%
Get upset						
Often or sometimes	56%	47%	57%	57%	53%	53%
Hardly ever or no answer	44%	53%	43%	43%	47%	47%
Race suffer						
Agree	56%	61%	63%	48%	55%	53%
Not agree	44%	39%	37%	52%	45%	47%

*High status occupations include the professions and proprietors and managers, middle status includes white-collar and skilled and semiskilled workers, and low status includes laborers and domestics.
†The response listed first indicates frustration.

Competition might provide an alternative explanation of our occupation-prejudice finding. The Westies suggest, for example, that the most direct competition for scarce, distributive values occurs among lower-class persons, whereas white and Negro white-collar workers, businessmen, and professionals are rarely in competition across the race line.[36] However, it is likely that many Negro businessmen and professionals feel that they lose business to their white competitors and thus are aware of competition that upper-class whites do not recognize. Pierson has suggested that it is not the competition per se but a frequently associated sense of threat to status that gives rise to out-group prejudice.[37]

We do find that high-occupational status accompanies social-distance feelings and that the curvilinear relation between occupation and prejudice is retained in both high and low educational levels (Table 8.8). Thus, Negroes in professional and managerial occupations are more likely to be

[36] Westie and Westie, "The Social Distance Pyramid."
[37] Donald Pierson, "Race Prejudice as Revealed in the Study of Racial Situations," *International Social Science Bulletin,* II (1950), 467-78.

Table 8.8

Relationship of occupation, education, and prejudice among Negroes.

	Education†						
	High				Low		
	Occupation						
Prejudice*	High (20)	Medium (37)	Low (16)		High (10)	Medium (85)	Low (131)
High	45%	27%	31%		70%	46%	56%
Low	55%	73%	69%		30%	54%	44%

*See Appendix D.
†High education means high school graduate or more while low education means some high school or less.

prejudiced than those in lower white-collar and semiskilled jobs.[38] In addition, Table 8.8 shows that education is more closely related to social-distance attitudes than occupation is.

Home ownership. Consistent with the notion that prejudice will be greater among the less advantaged is the finding that homeowners are less often prejudiced than renters and roomers in all four samples (Table 8.9). Even with educational level held roughly constant, home ownership is associated with low prevalence of social-distance feelings.

Subjective class. Subjective class designation has generally proven to be an ineffective way of assigning individuals to social classes (nearly everyone says he is either middle class or working class),[39] and this study provides no exception to the rule. Unlike our other indices of status, the status subgroups as determined by this method do not differ from each other in extent of prejudice in any consistent manner.

Thus, the subjective index of status does not effectively differentiate the prejudice groups; [40] among the three indices that do differentiate, education is more highly related than the other indices to prejudice. Moreover, educa-

---

[38] In each case the occupational subgroups (for example, professionals, managers) that are classed together into *one* status category show generally similar breakdowns in proportion prejudices. However, skilled workers are more likely to be prejudiced than any subgroup except proprietors and managers. For a discussion of some problems involved in the use of occupation as a sociological variable, see E. Gross, "The Occupational Variable as a Research Category," *American Sociological Review,* XXIV (1959), 640-49.

[39] For a general critique of "Class as Class Consciousness," see M. M. Gordon, *Social Class in American Sociology* (Durham, North Carolina: Duke University Press, 1958), pp. 193-202. See also R. M. Williams, Jr., *American Society,* rev. ed. (New York: Alfred A. Knopf, Inc., 1960), pp. 131-35.

[40] In our samples 16 per cent of the Negroes consider themselves upper class. Compare this figure with Davie's estimate that 80 per cent of Negro Americans fall in the lower class and only 5 per cent in the upper class. [M. R. Davie, *Negroes in American Society* (New York: McGraw-Hill Book Company, Inc., 1949), p. 416.]

Table 8.9

Relationship of home ownership to prejudice among Negroes.

	Home owner									
	Valley City		Hometown		Southport		Steelville		Total†	
Preju- dice*	Yes (134)	No (91)	Yes (65)	No (84)	Yes (121)	No (167)	Yes (33)	No (105)	Yes (353)	No (447)
High	33%	37%	52%	68%	49%	66%	52%	55%	44%	58%
Low	67%	63%	48%	32%	51%	34%	48%	45%	56%	42%

*See Appendix D.
†$x^2 = 16.0$, $p < .001$.

tion is generally chronologically prior to occupation and seems to be a more basic measure of social rank for the purposes of this study.[41]

Age, marital status, and sex and prejudice

Other studies of both white and Negro populations have reported inconsistent, often contradictory, findings concerning relationships between prejudice and age, sex, and marital status. This situation has led Gordon Allport to conclude that although claims relating to these variables ". . . may hold for single studies, they do not form a firm basis for generalization." [42] Obviously this is not a happy situation.

All too often the association of these variables with prejudice is simply reported without any attempt to use statistical controls or to explore characteristics of the sample(s) involved that might account for the contradictory findings. Age, sex, and marital status are basic to the organization of all societies; they deserve analysis. We shall try to explore their interrelations with each other and with other variables that might logically be expected to affect their relation to prejudice. Perhaps this procedure will help to eliminate spurious contradictions with future studies that relate these same variables to prejudice.

Age. There is a tendency for the young (below 35) to be less prejudiced than the middle aged (35 to 64), who in turn are less often prejudiced than the old (65 and over). The only exception is in Valley City (Table 8.10). The age difference is not significant in any of the communities, but the tendency for the percentage expressing high social distance to increase with

---

[41] A study of Negroes in a North Carolina city reveals that the informants view education as the chief basis of social differentiation and that the rating of a given occupation tends to be determined by the amount of education basic to the occupation. [C. E. King, "The Process of Social Stratification Among an Urban Southern Minority Population," *Social Forces*, XXXI (1953), 352-55.] On the importance of education as a determinant of status among Negroes see also Davie, *op. cit.*, pp. 416-17, 423-24.

[42] Allport, *The Nature of Prejudice*, p. 79.

Table 8.10

Relationship between social-distance feelings and age among Negroes.

						Age†					
	Valley City			Hometown			Southport			Steelville		
Prejudice*	Y (69)	M (140)	O (14)	Y (50)	M (84)	O (13)	Y (127)	M (148)	O (10)	Y (56)	M (69)	O (8)
High	33%	37%	29%	58%	61%	69%	55%	61%	90%	45%	58%	87%
Low	67%	63%	71%	42%	39%	31%	45%	39%	10%	55%	42%	13%

*See Appendix D.
†Y = 18 to 34 years; M = 35 to 64 years; O = 65 years and over.

age [43] suggests that there is probably some real difference. This finding is in accord with the evidence from the most recent studies of majority-group persons.[44]

Marital status. In his classic study of suicide, Emile Durkheim pointed out that married persons are less likely than single persons, or those whose marriages have been broken, to take their own lives. Finding the same protective tendencies in religious groupings and in other cohesive social relationships, Durkheim suggested that social cohesion protects the individual against stress.[45] If we were to assume that being married does, on the average, represent greater social cohesion than being single, divorced, separated, or widowed, we might reason that married persons would tend to be less frustrated and less vulnerable to stress. By the same token, it might be supposed that they would have less need to express prejudice and would be less threatened by the possibility of interaction with members of outgroups.

In actual fact, however, as in the case of white persons (Chapter 4), the single persons among Negroes in all four samples show the lowest prevalence of social-distance prejudice, and the divorced, separated, or widowed tend to be most likely to manifest feelings of social distance. The differences revealed by Table 8.11 are significant (0.05) in three of the four samples, and over all the samples combined the difference is significant at the 0.01 level.

---

[43] This does not mean necessarily that people become more prejudiced as they age. It simply indicates that the generations vary in the proportion prejudiced and unprejudiced. This undoubtedly reflects, in part, the changing social climate.

[44] See, for example, Stouffer, *Communism, Conformity, and Civil Liberties,* p. 89, and C. L. Hunt, "Private Integrated Housing in a Medium Size Northern City," *Social Problems,* VII (1959-60), 196-209.

[45] E. Durkheim, *Suicide,* trans. G. Simpson (New York: Free Press of Glencoe, Inc., 1947), especially Book Two. See also R. Merton, *Social Theory and Social Structure* (New York: Free Press of Glencoe, Inc., 1957), especially pp. 96-99, for a restatement and extension of Durkheim's theory.

Table 8.11

Relationship between marital status and prejudice among Negroes.

	Marital status†											
	Valley City			Hometown			Southport			Steelville		
Prejudice*	Si (15)	M (167)	O (45)	Si (18)	M (82)	O (43)	Si (50)	M (186)	O (52)	Si (20)	M (89)	O (31)
High	20%	34%	44%	44%	54%	74%	44%	61%	70%	35%	63%	45%
Low	80%	66%	56%	56%	46%	26%	56%	39%	30%	65%	37%	55%

*See Appendix D.
†Si = single; M = married; O = others (including separated, widowed, and divorced).

Actually these data are not inconsistent with Durkheim's views if we make the seemingly reasonable—but after the fact—assumption that social-distance feelings toward white people are approved (that is, are normative) in the Negro community. The married are more likely to belong to organizations than either the single or other persons (56 per cent as opposed to 47 and 51 per cent respectively), lending some support to the belief that they are best integrated into the community structure and, therefore, are more likely to be prejudiced if the norms approve prejudice. The even greater likelihood of prejudice among persons who are separated, widowed, or divorced might well be a function of frustration or personality difficulty associated with the loss of the marital partner as well as lesser social cohesion. Since the relationship between marital status and prejudice might be a dependent function of another variable, we shall consider this possibility further after examining the relationship between sex and prejudice.

Sex. Although earlier studies among majority-group persons were equally divided in revealing men or women as more likely to be prejudiced,[46] several more recent studies report that women are more often prejudiced than men.[47] In the Negro communities studied here the relationship is very clear. Females are only slightly more likely to be prejudiced than males in Valley City, but the tendency is strong in Steelville and significant (0.01) in Hometown and Southport (Table 8.12). Over the four samples combined the difference is highly significant (0.001 level).

So far we have seen that the young are consistently less likely to be prejudiced than those not young and that the single and the males are significantly less likely to be prejudiced than their counterparts. It is possible, however, that only one of these relationships is genuine—for example, the

---

[46] See Rose, *Studies of Reduction in Prejudice,* Section III, pp. 4-5.

[47] See, for example, J. G. Martin and F. R. Westie, "The Tolerant Personality," *American Sociological Review,* XXIV (1959), 521-28; Pettigrew, "Regional Differences in Anti-Negro Prejudice," and Stouffer, *Communism, Conformity, and Civil Liberties.* Edlefsen, "Social Distance Attitudes of Negro College Students," also found in his study of 174 Negro college students that females showed significantly more social-distance prejudice toward a variety of outgroups than did males.

Table 8.12

Relationship between sex and prejudice among Negroes.

	Sex							
	Valley City		Hometown†		Southport‡		Steelville	
Prejudice*	Female (118)	Male (109)	Female (82)	Male (68)	Female (169)	Male (119)	Female (75)	Male (63)
High	36%	34%	71%	49%	66%	49%	60%	48%
Low	64%	66%	29%	51%	34%	51%	40%	52%

*See Appendix D.
†x^2 = 6.8, p < .01.
‡x^2 = 8.1, p < .01.

difference in the age and marital groups may simply reflect a disproportionate number of females among the young and the single in our samples. To
test this possibility we have controlled each of these variables with respect
to the other two in three cities.[48] Table 8.13 is a summary with control on
two variables from which can be derived the three tables that control
one variable—that is, the sex-marital status, age-marital status, and sex-age
combinations. The data are not broken down by community inasmuch as
the pattern of relationship is consistent across communities and the number of cases would be very small in some individual community cells.

Table 8.13

Relationship between sex, marital status, age, and prejudice
among Negroes.

	Sex							
	Female				Male			
	Marital status†							
Prejudice*	Single		Not single		Single		Not single	
	Age‡							
	Y	NY	Y	NY	Y	NY	Y	NY
Column #:	1	2	3	4	5	6	7	8
Number of cases	(27)	(9)	(117)	(173)	(34)	(18)	(55)	(143)
High	63%	33	61%	72%	29%	39%	47%	55%
Low	37%	67	39%	28%	71%	61%	53%	45%

*High prejudice is one to three distastefuls (eat, dance, marry) in Hometown and Steelville
and two or three distastefuls in Southport. Low prejudice is zero, or zero and one (in
Southport), distastefuls.
† Not single includes divorced, separated, and widowed, as well as married.
‡ Y = young (18-34); NY = not young (35 and over).

[48] Valley City is omitted from this part of the analysis because none of the three
variables under consideration significantly differentiates the prejudice groups there.

Although Table 8.13 contains a rather complex body of information, its main message is that sex, age, and marital status are independently and cumulatively associated with social-distance prejudice in such manner that prejudice is least often found among the younger, single males and is most often present among older females who are or have been married—an extreme range from over 29 per cent in the former group to 72 per cent in the latter.

Finding so clear and marked a set of relationships in survey analysis provides a challenge to see whether other control variables can be found to remove or modify the obtained correlations.

Education, highly related to prejudice as we have seen, has been increasingly available to American Negroes in the past two generations.[49] Thus it is possible that the tendency for the young to be less prejudiced may simply reflect their greater education. This could be the case in Southport but not in Steelville (Table 8.14).

Table 8.14

Relationship between age and prejudice in two Negro communities, with education controlled.

	Southport				Steelville			
	Education†							
	High		Low		High		Low	
	Age‡							
Prejudice*	Y (32)	NY (24)	Y (95)	NY (137)	Y (24)	NY (19)	Y (32)	NY (65)
High	31%	33%	63%	67%	38%	53%	50%	65%
Low	69%	67%	37%	33%	62%	47%	50%	35%

* See Appendix D.
† High education means high school graduate or more; others are low education.
‡ Y = young (18-34); NY = not young (35 and over).

The fact that the single are significantly less likely to be prejudiced than others is not an artifact of sex or age. Perhaps it could be due to education, if we reason that those who remain single are likely to get a better education than those who marry. Table 8.15 indicates, however, that those who are single are much less likely to be prejudiced than their nonsingle counter-

---

[49] E. Ginzberg et al., The Negro Potential (New York: Columbia University Press, 1956), pp. 43-50. For example, approximately 6.2 per cent of Negro males born 1905-09 graduated from high school as opposed to approximately 20 per cent of those born 1926-30. In our total sample 22 per cent of the respondents had graduated from high school; in the one sample where data were collected only 11 per cent of the respondents' fathers (as opposed to 31 per cent of the respondents in that sample) had graduated from high school.

Table 8.15

Relationship between marital status and prejudice among Negroes, with education controlled.*

Education

	High		Low	
		Marital status‡		
	Single	Not single	Single	Not single
Prejudice†	(24)	(105)	(64)	(385)
High	17%	45%	52%	66%
Low	83%	55%	48%	34%

*Based on combined Hometown, Southport and Steelville samples.
† See Appendix D.
‡ Not single includes divorced, separated, and widowed, as well as married.

parts at either educational level. Another long-shot control on organization membership proved even less able to alter the relationship. We have, then, a genuine difference in prejudice between the marital groups.

Consecutive control on a variety of relevant variables demonstrates that sex bears a strong and tenacious relation to social-distance prejudice in the Negro community. Not only do age and marital status fail to eliminate the relationship, but education, interracial contact, and organization membership also fail to alter it markedly. The uncontrolled sex difference may be magnified or reduced for one or the other level of education, contact, or social participation; but it remains sizable at both levels or values of each of these variables.

In addition, females remain much more often prejudiced than males when militance and authoritarianism [50] are held constant. We conclude that the sex difference in anti-white social-distance prejudice is a genuine, not a spurious, difference. This reaffirms and elaborates the earlier finding reported by Edlefsen from his study of social-distance prejudice among Negro college students.[51]

One possible explanation of this marked sex difference in prejudice lies in the double burden of race *and* sex placed upon Negro females.[52] Thus Simpson states that "Negro women suffer from the same discrimination that

[50] Smith and Prothro have indicated that Negro females are more authoritarian than males [C. U. Smith and J. W. Prothro, "Ethnic Differences in Authoritarian Personality," *Social Forces,* XXXV (1957), 334-38]. Both militance and authoritarianism are important correlates of prejudice among Negroes.

[51] Edlefsen, "Social Distance Attitudes of Negro College Students." This part of Edlefsen's study was based on a modified seven-item Bogardus scale.

[52] For a comparison of the status of white women with that of Negroes see C. Kirkpatrick, *The Family* (New York: The Ronald Press Company, 1955), pp. 158-60, and G. Myrdal, *An American Dilemma* (New York: Harper & Row, Publishers, 1944), pp. 1073-78.

afflicts Negro men, and in addition, being women, they have not the opportunities for uninhibited social life which serve as outlets for the frustrations of men." [53] Prejudice may be one form of aggression or expression of aggression, and this application of the frustration-aggression-displacement hypothesis would then seem reasonable in the light of the double-standard prevailing in American society.

Two available pieces of evidence bear on this explanation. First, white women also should be consistently more prejudiced than white men; but as we have indicated, there is considerable fluctuation from study to study in regard to the relation between sex and prejudice.[54] Second, our data lend only slight support to the idea that women are more likely to be frustrated than men. For example, in our total sample 43 per cent of the males and only 4 per cent *more* of the females agreed with the item: *Sometimes I feel so frustrated, I just feel like smashing things.*

Pettigrew has offered some evidence in support of a cultural interpretation of the sex difference in prejudice.[55] He argues that in the white population women are especially regarded as the "carriers of culture," and therefore they reflect the cultural norm *vis-à-vis* Negroes (that is, anti-Negro prejudice) more directly than males. Relating our data to this interpretation, we have already seen (Table 8.4) that there is considerable anti-white prejudice in the Negro community. In addition, Negro females are significantly more likely to attend church frequently than are Negro males. However, females who attend church are less likely to be prejudiced than those who do not attend. This contradicts the "carriers of culture" explanation, which is further undermined by a reversal in the relation between sex and prejudice when a different index of prejudice is used.[56]

However, there is no difference between males and females in regard to acceptance of the stereotype that: *No matter how nicely he treats a colored person, a white man doesn't really mean it.*[57] These variations are in accordance with an early study of majority-group persons that indicated that the relation of sex and prejudice varied with the type of prejudice involved.[58]

---

[53] R. L. Simpson, "Factors in the Attitudes of Two Minority Groups Toward Each Other" (M. A. Thesis, Cornell University, 1952), p. 104.

[54] We also indicated, however, that the more recent studies do consistently report that women are more apt to be prejudiced than men. A recent study reports no over-all difference in anti-Negro prejudice but finds that women are slightly more likely to be anti-Semitic. Pinkney, "The Anatomy of Prejudice," p. 85.

[55] Pettigrew, "Regional Differences in Anti-Negro Prejudice."

[56] This fluctuation also undercuts an alternative explanation to the effect that Negro females are less vulnerable to discrimination and are, therefore, more likely to express their prejudice.

[57] On four stereotype items involving various other minority outgroups, there were no significant differences by sex, and each sex was slightly more likely to endorse two of the four stereotypes.

[58] E. S. Bogardus, "Sex Differences in Race Attitudes," *Sociology and Social Research,* XII (1928), 279-85.

The sex difference in social-distance prejudice emphasized here is apparently a function of the intimate social situations used as indicators in our basic measure of prejudice.

In this analysis of age, sex, and marital status the data seem to eliminate a number of possible explanations for the relation of both sex and marital status to prejudice, although the information does not allow testing the explanations offered for these relationships. We must leave it to future studies to verify or reject these explanations.

Social participation and prejudice

Many studies have shown that socioeconomic status and social participation are generally positively related; [59] we have found earlier in this chapter, that SES is inversely related to social-distance prejudice. Thus we expect prejudice and social participation to be inversely related. Several indices of social participation are available to provide tests of this hypothesis among Negroes.

Church attendance. As with other forms of social participation, people who attend church may do so for different reasons; and several studies have suggested that those who are merely conventionally or externally religious are likely to be high in prejudice.[60] Thus, insofar as frequence of church attendance is an index of conventional religiosity, its predicted relation to prejudice is the opposite of that predicted in terms of social participation.[61]

We, nevertheless, predicted a positive relation between church attendance and prejudice, on the basis of previous studies of these two variables.[62] The data show no consistent relationship between these variables among Negroes in the communities studied. This finding may suggest that future studies will do well to devise ways of disentangling the influences of social participation, conventional religiosity, and intrinsic religious beliefs.

Voting. Political participation has been all but completely denied to the

---

[59] See, for example, J. C. Scott, Jr., "Membership and Participation in Voluntary Associations," *American Sociological Review,* XXII (1957), 315-26. Scott footnotes ten studies supporting the status-participation relationship, p. 325. This relationship has been documented by E. H. Mizruchi, "Social Structure and Anomia in a Small City," *American Sociological Review,* XXV (1960), 645-54.

[60] See, for example, Allport, *The Nature of Prejudice,* pp. 451-53; and T. W. Adorno, E. Frenkel-Brunswik, D. J. Levinson, and R. N. Sanford, *The Authoritarian Personality* (New York: Harper & Row, Publishers, 1950), especially Chapters 6 and 18.

[61] Cf. the discussion of extrinsic and intrinsic religiosity in relation to prejudice by G. W. Allport, *Personality and Social Encounter* (Boston: Beacon Press Inc., 1960), Chapter 16.

[62] We were especially influenced by the fact that Richard L. Simpson, using the data obtained from the present sample of Hometown Negroes, found a significant positive relationship between the frequence of church attendance and anti-Jewish prejudice. "Factors in the Attitudes of Two Minority Groups Toward Each Other," p. 77.

Southern Negro from the late nineteenth century until very recently,[63] and the incidence of voting among Northern Negroes has been very little studied. It is thus very interesting in itself to note that 35 per cent of the Southport Negroes and 63 to 74 per cent of those in the Northern and Western samples reported voting in the 1948 presidential election.[64]

We find that Negroes who vote are less likely than nonvoters to express social-distance aversions toward whites. Inasmuch as voting is positively related to socioeconomic status, the voting-prejudice relationship may be a spurious reflection of the status-prejudice relationship. We test this possibility by holding education constant.

Table 8.16

Relationship between voting, education, and prejudice among Negroes.

	Education ‡			
	High		Low	
	Voted §			
Prejudice†	Yes (88)	No (41)	Yes (201)	No (246)
High	41%	37%	56%	70%
Low	59%	63%	44%	30%

*Based on the combined samples for three cities. Valley City was omitted because neither education nor voting differentiated the prejudice groups in that sample.
†See Appendix D.
‡High education means high school graduate or more and low education means some high school or less.
§Based on reported voting in the 1948 presidential election.

As Table 8.16 indicates, voting does not differentiate the prejudice groups among the educated, but, among persons low in education, those who do vote are clearly less likely to be prejudiced than those who do not vote. The trend is clear and consistent across samples; for the combined samples, 70 per cent of the little-educated nonvoters but only 56 per cent of the little-educated voters are high in prejudice (significant at the 0.01 level). Thus voting is related to prejudice only among persons low in education.

Organization membership. Organization membership is a more inclusive

---

[63] On the history of the Negro and the vote see, for example, V. O. Key, Jr., *Politics, Parties, and Press Groups* (New York: Thomas Y. Crowell Company, 1952), pp. 604-16. See C. Van Woodward, *The Strange Career of Jim Crow* (New York: Oxford University Press, Inc., 1957) concerning Negro political activity in the South from 1865-1900.

[64] Inasmuch as only 50 per cent of the total electorate voted in the 1948 election (*The New York Times,* November 20, 1960, sec. 5, p. 50), these figures seem suspiciously high. There is, however, no effective way of assessing the validity of our data on this point, and we shall have to assume that any error is random with respect to our analyses.

index of social participation than either church attendance or voting. As with voting, however, there is a large cross-community variation in the index's relation to prejudice. The tendency for organization members to be less prejudiced than nonmembers is not present in Valley City and only slight to moderate in Hometown and Steelville, but it is significant (0.01) in Southport. Excluding Valley City, the relationship of prejudice and organization membership is significant at the 0.001 level for the other three samples combined.

However, the relationship is only partially independent of the effect of education. Among the low-education group the effect is consistent and siz-

Table 8.17

Relationship between organization membership and prejudice among Negroes.

	Organization member†							
	Valley City		Hometown		Southport‡		Steelville	
	Yes	No	Yes	No	Yes	No	Yes	No
Prejudice*	(90)	(131)	(85)	(65)	(126)	(155)	(96)	(44)
High	36%	36%	58%	65%	49%	66%	51%	61%
Low	64%	64%	42%	35%	51%	34%	49%	39%

*See Appendix D.
†Based on membership in one or more social, religious, business, fraternal, or service clubs or organizations.
‡$x^2 = 7.8$, $p < .01$.

able in all three samples, and for the combined samples persons low in education who belong to organizations are significantly less likely (0.001) to be prejudiced than persons who do not belong to organizations. Thus, like voting, organization membership is consistently negatively related to prejudice, independent of education, only among persons low in education.

Social clique membership. A final available index of social participation is participation in an informal social group—that is, "a certain bunch of close friends" who visit back and forth in each other's homes or get together fairly often. It seemed likely that the social isolate would be more prejudiced than the participants, but the actual differences are slight and not always consistent with this expectation. However, if the norms of the Negro community approve of social-distance attitudes, this lack of a difference may reflect a conflict between group reinforcement of the norm and the general tendency for participation to be associated with low prejudice.

Thus, the relation of social participation to prejudice is greatly dependent upon the index used and the particular community sampled. Church attendance does not relate differentially at all, but voting and organization membership are fairly strong indicators of low prejudice in Hometown and Steelville and are excellent indicators in Southport. However, these relationships are maintained only among persons of low education. Social clique membership per se is an ineffective differentiator; but when combined with an analysis of the respondent's perception of the outgroup attitudes of other clique members, it yields results sufficiently promising to warrant further investigation.[65]

Summary

The nature of our samples warrants a twofold summary of the findings presented in this section stressing: (1) the similarities and divergences in the sociological correlates of anti-Negro and antiwhite prejudice and (2) the most significant sociological correlates of social-distance prejudice against whites.

Several generalizations based on varying amounts of evidence from studies of majority-group persons are confirmed in this study. These generalizations include the following: (1) the more highly educated are less likely to be prejudiced than the relatively uneducated; (2) regardless of age, education, or sex the single are much less likely to be prejudiced than any other marital group; and (3) social participators (especially organization members) are less likely to be prejudiced than nonparticipants. Each of these basic findings, it will be recalled, was confirmed in the data obtained from majority-group persons.

However, the most outstanding cross-racial uniformity is that of regional differences in prejudice. Southport Negroes are far more likely to be prejudiced than those in any of the three non-Southern cities, whereas Valley City Negroes are least likely to be prejudiced. Such explanatory variables as education and the general economic situation of the Negro do not appear to account for these differences. We attribute these differences to regional variations in outgroup norms.

There are also some significant divergences in the role-and-status correlates of social-distance feelings among Negroes as compared with whites. Thus there is a clear tendency for Negroes of high occupational status more often to manifest social-distance feelings than middle-status Negroes, whereas among whites higher occupational status generally goes along with less social-distance prejudice. Another major racial difference is that among the Negroes studied females are much more likely to be prejudiced than are males. In addition, the finding remains intact despite consecutive

---

[65] In Hometown among both Negro and Jewish persons, prejudice against the *other* minority is greater among those who tend to be social isolates (not a member of organizations or a close group of friends). [See Richard L. Simpson, "Negro-Jewish Prejudice: Authoritarianism and Social Correlates," *Social Problems,* VII, No. 2 (Fall, 1959), 144.]

control on age, marital status, interracial contact, organization membership, education, authoritarianism, and militance.

A major variation between samples—in addition to the community variations in extent of prejudice—concerns the failure of *any* of the sociological
variables to significantly relate to prejudice in Valley City. In contrast, no
less than seven variables are significantly related to prejudice in Southport.
This striking difference may reflect the relative lack of a stable social structure in the Valley City Negro community. Over four-fifths of the Negroes
in our sample have migrated to the city from other regions. There was also
a heavy in-migration of whites between 1930 and 1950, and the rapid
growth has not been conducive to social cohesion or the development of
community leadership and concern for the general welfare. Pinkney has
suggested that this looseness of social structure is associated with the relative lack of ethnic prejudice in Valley City [66] although it may be indifference
rather than tolerance that is the characteristic attitude. Southport in contrast is a highly structured community.[67] Thus both the degree of rigidity
in the social structure and the existence of a strong normative system help
explain community differences in prejudice.

Although the Valley City case prevents the generalization from being
statistically significant in each of the four samples, the finding that the
single are less likely to be prejudiced than either of the other marital categories is otherwise clear. The curvilinear relation between occupational
status and prejudice is consistently supported by the data. In addition, organization membership, voting, sex, and education are either significantly
related to prejudice or approach significance in all samples except Valley
City.

Finally, the findings with regard to socioeconomic status and prejudice
raise several crucial questions concerning the competition theory of prejudice. Conflicting evidence and interpretations suggest the need for more
precise testing of the competition theory, with data that would permit simultaneous analysis of (1) mobility aspirations, (2) frustration, (3) perception of whites as on-the-job competitors and as competitors who deny Negroes jobs in discrimination, (4) various indices of status, and (5) various
dimensions of prejudice.

---

[66] Pinkney, "The Anatomy of Prejudice," p. 21. However, the relation of the
basic sociological variables to anti-Negro prejudice in Valley City suggests that the
Valley City white community is more highly structured than the Negro community.

[67] Those comments pertain to the *general* community social structure. However,
a considerable part of the community differences in prejudice may be due to a
marked bias in the correlation between interracial relations and our index of prejudice. Thus in a social structure where rigid segregation is the strongly sanctioned
norm, a high score on our prejudice index may represent adjustment to reality and
not genuine prejudice. For example, Southern Negroes and whites might consider
it distasteful to eat together because to do so would risk social disapproval or even
physical danger.

We turn now to an examination of the psychological correlates of prejudice.

PSYCHOLOGICAL CORRELATES OF SOCIAL-DISTANCE PREJUDICE
TOWARD WHITES AMONG NEGROES

Many students of intergroup relations have come to feel a need for comparative studies of personality characteristics as related to prejudice in
different social groupings and environments. Our data from samples of
Negroes in each of the four cities in which white people were studied provide an opportunity to study personality-prejudice relationships in different
social climates and for a minority ethnic population.

In the four cities, Negroes are, on the whole, more likely than whites to
agree to authoritarian statements (Table 8.18).[68] It might be expected that
because of racial discrimination and segregation, Negroes in the Deep South
would be more often authoritarian, but the data fail to support this inter-

Table 8.18

Comparison of responses by Negroes and by whites to so-called
authoritarian items.

Items and respondents:	Valley City	Hometown	Steelville	Southport
	Per cent agreeing with items in:			
Children obey*				
White respondents	34%	36%	48%	54%
Negro respondents	57%	62%	54%	56%
Sex criminals severely punished*				
Whites	not	24%	45%	38%
Negroes	asked	37%	31%	34%
People can't be trusted†				
Whites	32%	43%	not	34%
Negroes	68%	not	asked	52%
		asked		
Total cases				
White	(319)	(529)	(288)	(294)
Negro	(227)	(150)	(140)	(288)

*Data from Noel, "Correlates of Anti-White Prejudice," p. 143.
†Data from Lionel S. Lewis, Discrimination and Insulation: An Intercommunity Comparison,
M. A. thesis, Cornell University, 1959, p. 53, and unpublished tabulations.

---

[68] Several other studies have reported that Negroes tend to score higher than
whites on the F-scale, for example: C. U. Smith and J. W. Prothro, "Ethnic Differences in Authoritarian Personality," pp. 334-38; W. J. MacKinnon and R. Centers,
"Authoritarianism and Urban Stratification," *American Journal of Sociology*, LXI, No.
6 (May, 1956), 610-20; H. Greenberg, A. L. Chase, and T. M. Cannon, Jr., "Attitudes
of White and Negro High School Students in a West Texas Town toward School Integration, *Journal of Applied Psychology*, XLI, No. 1 (February, 1957), 27-31.

pretation. Could the differences be due to a higher proportion of low-income, low-status persons in the Negro population? It has been shown by Hyman and Sheatsley [69] and by Christie [70] that F-scale scores are likely to vary inversely with educational level and occupational rank. Lipset has assembled much evidence suggesting that certain kinds of authoritarian attitudes tend to be especially frequent among working-class persons.[71] Our own data (Table 8.19) clearly show that lower-status persons in the Negro samples

Table 8.19

Relationship of authoritarianism to occupational status among Negroes.

Authoritarianism*	Education†		Occupational status‡		
	High (178)	Low (627)	High (30)	Medium (122)	Low (150)
High	30%	55%	23%	40%	59%
Low	70%	45%	77%	60%	41%
	$X^2 = 35.1$, p = < .001		$X^2 = 12.4$, df = 2, p < .01		

*Respondent is rated high in authoritarianism if he gives the authoritarian response to two or all three items indexing authoritarianism.
†Respondent is rated high in education if he is a high school graduate or more. The relationship remains equally strong if we split education into three groups with the middle group having some high school or being a high school graduate. This part of the table is based upon the combined data from all four samples. The difference between education groups is at least ten per cent in every sample.
‡High status occupations include the professions and proprietors and managers, middle status includes white collar and skilled and semiskilled workers, and low status includes laborers and domestics. This part of the table is based upon data collected from employed respondents in Valley City and Southport.

are significantly more likely to be authoritarian than those in higher statuses, either by educational or occupational criteria.

The suggestion that the greater frequency of authoritarian responses among Negroes as compared with whites is derived from predominantly lower educational and occupational status can be given a further test. A single item concerning the importance of teaching children to obey was asked in both the Negro and white samples in all four cities. When occupational status is held constant, the racial difference in authoritarianism—as indexed by this item—is largely eliminated. Negroes of medium occupational status remain somewhat more authoritarian than their white counterparts, and low-education Negroes are much more likely than low-education whites to give the authoritarian response, but there is no difference in au-

[69] H. H. Hyman and P. B. Sheatsley in Christie and Jahoda, " 'The Authoritarian Personality'—A Methodological Critique," pp. 112-17.
[70] R. Christie, "Authoritarianism Re-examined," pp. 172-82.
[71] S. M. Lipset, "Democracy and Working-Class Authoritarianism," *American Sociological Review*, XXIV, No. 4 (August, 1959), 482-501.

thoritarianism among the other subgroups. Replies to the question concerning childrearing are thus more nearly a function of class than of race. This finding suggests that class may account for an important part of the ethnic variance in (general) authoritarianism.[72]

Clearly authoritarianism is inversely related to education and occupational status among both whites and Negroes, but several authors have suggested that we must be very cautious in interpreting even this relationship. Thus, Christie states that although the acceptance of a given F-scale item may reflect paranoid tendencies among middle-class persons, it may represent reality for lower-class respondents.[73] Nevertheless, and for whatever reason, lower-status persons are more likely to endorse authoritarian items than are persons of higher status. Class therefore remains a very plausible explanation for racial differences in authoritarianism.

The nature of authoritarianism among Negroes is further revealed by the finding (in Hometown) that those who show manifest concern for status (trying to get ahead, or to get into a better class) tend *less* often to be authoritarian *or* to show social-distance reactions to whites. Those who counsel striving apparently are the less withdrawn, the not-yet-defeated believers in upward mobility, and it is these more hopeful people who are most accepting of contact with white people.

For our four samples combined, authoritarianism is significantly (0.01 level) associated with high social-distance prejudice against whites. (Table 8.20.) However, there is much variation from one community to another, and the relationship of prejudice and authoritarianism is weaker than might have been expected on the basis of the findings from studies of white people. It may, indeed, be the case that the overriding impact of the behavior of whites shapes social-distance attitudes of Negroes relatively independent of authoritarian attitudes.

In addition to the general index of authoritarian attitudes just used, other specific items bearing on other facets were asked in one or more of the communities. Data from Southport show that it is those Negroes who advocate severe punishment for moral transgressors and who condemn young people for sexual laxity who are most likely to express distaste for social contacts with whites. Similarly items expressive of distrust toward other people, of bitterness, of feelings of having to struggle for everything are positively associated with social-distance feelings toward white people.

Other items indicative of generalized feelings of frustration, aggression,

---

[72] For the three items used as the index of authoritarianism in Hometown the per cent indorsement by Negroes ranges from 37 to 82 (average, 60), that of 150 Italians from 23 to 52 (average, 40), that of 529 majority-group whites from 24 to 43 (average, 34), and that of 150 Jews from 12 to 32 (average, 25).

[73] Christie, "Authoritarianism Re-examined," in R. Christie and M. Jahoda, *op. cit.,* p. 175.

Table 8.20

Relationship between authoritarianism and prejudice among Negroes.

Authoritarianism†

	Valley City		Hometown		Southport		Steelville		Total	
Prejudice*	High (115)	Low (112)	High (104)	Low (46)	High (132)	Low (156)	High (49)	Low (91)	High (400)	Low (405)
High	42%	29%	64%	52%	67%	52%	55%	55%	58%	46%
Low	58%	71%	36%	48%	33%	48%	45%	45%	42%	54%
	X^2 = 3.78, p < .06		X^2 = 1.51, p < .25		X^2 = 5.84, p < .02		No difference		X^2 = 10.3, p < .01	

*See Appendix D.

†Respondent is rated high in authoritarianism if he gives the indicated response to two or all three of the following items: 1) "Children should obey every order their parents give without question even if they think the parents are wrong" (agree); 2) "Some say that you can't be too careful in your dealings with people while others say that most people can be trusted. From your experience which would you agree with more" (can't be too careful); and 3) "Prison is too good for sex criminals. They should be publicly whipped or worse" (agree). The second item was worded somewhat differently in Steelville; and the third item was not asked in Valley City, so the following was substituted: "When things go wrong for me, I usually find it's my own fault" (disagree). This item was not asked in Southport but approximately the same per cent gave the authoritarian response to it as the third item, above, in Steelville and Hometown.

and disturbance are only slightly and inconsistently related to antiwhite responses. However, those persons who feel that, "when one Negro does something wrong the whole race suffers for it," are significantly more likely than those who reject this view to express a desire to "get even with whites for some of the things they have done to Negroes."

Several questions were asked Negro respondents concerning their feelings about personal relations with others. As in the case of white persons, it was expected that persons who report general feelings of insecurity or uneasiness in social relations would be those who would most often manifest social-distance prejudice against the racial outgroup. Table 8.21 shows that this hypothesis is supported.

This relation between sociability and prejudice cannot be explained by the available indices of frustration because their relations to prejudice are too weak (in Southport) to account for these significant differences. However, among those who are high in authoritarianism neither asociability nor feeling withdrawn are related to prejudice, but the relationships remain significant among those low in authoritarianism. This finding lends considerable support to Mahar's contention that withdrawal, as opposed to gregariousness, is an important component of so-called authoritarianism.[74]

[74] P. M. Mahar, "Dimensions of Personality as Related to Dimensions of Prejudice in a Survey of a Northeastern City" (Ph.D. Thesis, Cornell University, 1955), pp. 48ff. Mahar notes that this component was neglected in the California study where the samples were heavily biased in favor of organization members. She indicates that difficulty in establishing warm interpersonal relationships is closely related to (other) components of authoritarianism.

Table 8.21

Relationship between sociability and prejudice among Negroes.

	A-sociability†		Feel withdrawn‡	
	High	Low	Yes	No
Prejudice*	(93)	(195)	(114)	(401)
High	71%	53%	60%	46%
Low	29%	47%	40%	54%
	$X^2 = 6.98$,		$X^2 = 6.71$,	
	$p < .01$		$p < .01$	

---

*See Appendix D.

†Respondent is rated high in a-sociability if he gives the underlined response to two or all three of the following items: (1) "I usually feel uncomfortable about meeting people I have never seen before" (agree); (2) Respondent classifies himself as making few close friends; and (3) "From your experience would you say that most people are easy to get along with or hard to get along with?" These items are available only for the Southport sample.

‡Respondent is classified as feeling withdrawn if he gives either of the underlined responses to the following item: "How often do you get the feeling that you just don't belong anywhere—would you say often, sometimes, or hardly ever?" These data are based on the combined Valley City and Southport samples.

Prejudice and quasi-psychological characteristics associated with minority status

Based upon the study of the Hometown Negro Community, R. B. Johnson concluded that the Negro is highly aware of his minority status and reacts to it primarily in terms of five main aspects or continua: (1) hostility-friendliness (toward whites), (2) self-hatred–race pride, (3) lassitude-militance, (4) avoidance-"whiteward mobility," and (5) insulation-integration. In terms of these continua Johnson distinguishes between an Old Negro Creed based upon insulation or avoidance, lassitude, self-hatred, and hostility toward whites and a New Negro Creed stressing militance, integration, friendliness, and a lack of prejudice toward whites.[75] This dual characterization is the primary basis for the hypotheses now to be examined.

Arnold Rose reports that ". . . a leading Negro social scientist admitted in private conversation that he believed *all* Negroes hated whites."[76] This would hardly be too surprising if it *were* true, but our data indicate that only 28 per cent of the 665 adult Negroes interviewed in Valley City, South-

---

[75] Our indices of several of these variables differ somewhat from Johnson's, and we do not distinguish between the avoidance and insulation continua. This distinction seems to be primarily based on a judgment as to whether the individual desires to leave his group as an individual (whitewardly mobile) or desires to have his group as a whole integrated into the broader American social structure. Our data do not permit us to make this subtle distinction with confidence.

[76] A. Rose, *The Negro's Morale* (Minneapolis: University of Minnesota Press, 1949), p. 113.

port, and Hometown agree with the statement *Sometimes I hate white people.*" [77] This may appear to be one of the more remarkable findings of this study, the more so because the item says "sometimes," and the responses were given, without exception, to Negro interviewers. It may also seem surprising to find that Negroes who say they hate whites are not significantly more likely to score high in social-distance feelings toward whites (see Table 8.22). Although the two attitudes thus appear to be largely

Table 8.22

Relationship between hostility toward whites and social-distance prejudice among Negroes.

Prejudice*	Hate†		Friendliness‡		
	Agree (137)	Not agree (378)	High (202)	Medium (548)	Low (55)
High	53%	47%	46%	53%	65%
Low	47%	53%	54%	47%	35%
	$X^2 = 1.44,$		$x^2 = 6.94,$ df = 2,		
	$p < .25$		$p < .05$		

*See Appendix D.
†Based on response to the item: "Sometimes I hate white people" (agree or disagree) which was asked only of the Valley City and Southport respondents.
‡Based on response to the following item: "In general how friendly or unfriendly are your feelings toward whites? Would you say very friendly, fairly friendly, rather unfriendly, or not friendly at all?" The last two categories are considered low in friendliness. This item was asked of respondents in all four samples.

independent of each other, the issue is confused by the fact that the degree of expressed friendliness toward whites is significantly related to social-distance prejudice. Less than half of those who are very friendly toward whites are high in prejudice, whereas almost two-thirds of those who are not friendly are high in prejudice.[78] Nevertheless, even this relationship is much weaker than was expected.

Self-hatred also showed a much weaker relationship to social-distance attitudes than was anticipated. In contrast, *militance* is inversely related to social-distance responses: *high* militance and *low* prejudice go together. Militance, as opposed to lassitude or defeatism, centers around protest aimed at the elimination of discrimination or, positively, the achievement of equal status. Common sense might suggest that those who protest are likely to be negatively prejudiced toward persons associated with the protest target

---

[77] This item was not included in the Steelville interview schedule.

[78] Note that only 7 per cent of the four samples combined say that they feel *less* than fairly friendly toward whites. This nicely complements the fact that only 28 per cent of the Negroes agree that they sometimes hate whites.

or condition, but the opposite effect is observed: *the militant are significantly less likely to be prejudiced than the nonmilitant.*

Avoidance, as manifested by defensive insulation and suspicion of whites, shows the predicted positive relation to feelings of social distance. Indeed, the proportion of the samples showing prejudice is only one-third of those low in defensive insulation but is three-fourths of those high in defensive insulation. Suspicion of whites is much less sharply related to prejudice but still reaches significance at the 0.05 level.

In general, then, among Negroes the relations between psychological characteristics and prejudice are mainly similar to those found in studies of prejudice among majority-group persons. There is, however, a series of quasi-psychological characteristics unique to minority persons—and probably largely a product of the minority experience—that show some relationships to prejudice that may be thought very surprising. Thus, expressed hatred of whites is quite rare in each of the communities surveyed and is only weakly related to social-distance prejudice. Conversely, moderate friendliness toward whites is the norm, and degree of friendliness is associated with slight social-distance feelings. Group self-hatred, like hatred of whites, has only a weak positive relationship to prejudice, but *militant advocacy of Negro rights is clearly associated with low prejudice.* Finally, Negroes who are suspicious of whites and those who try to avoid whites are significantly more likely to express social-distance feelings toward whites than the nonsuspicious and noninsulated.

In the next section *generalized* prejudice among Negroes is studied in relation to minority-group identification in an effort to further specify the character of prejudice among Negroes.

GENERALIZED PREJUDICE AND INTERMINORITY
AND INTRAMINORITY ATTITUDES

Numerous studies among the white majority-group populations show that prejudice against any one ethnic group tends to accompany prejudice toward other ethnic groups. Will the tendency of prejudices to form a generalized pattern of outgroup rejection be replicated among Negroes? The Cornell Studies found that prejudiced whites tended to have negative attitudes toward some categories of ingroup (white) persons. Will the same tendency appear among Negroes, that is, if they have negative attitudes toward white people will they at the same time reject the Negro group (self-hate)?

On the first point, the findings are clear: among Negroes, as among whites, prejudice toward one outgroup is associated with prejudice toward other outgroups. The best data for illustrative purposes came from Valley City, where the same social-distance question was asked concerning whites,

Jews, Indians, Mexicans, Chinese-Americans, and Japanese-Americans. As Table 8.23 shows, over four-fifths of those who would not find it distaste-

Table 8.23

Generalization of prejudice among Negroes.

Prejudice score*	Number of minorities respondent would find it distasteful to be at a party with†		
	0 (152)	1-3 (36)	4-5 (39)
3	1%	11%	23%
High 2	3%	17%	26%
1	13%	33%	28%
Low 0	83%	39%	18%

*See Appendix D.
†Based on whether respondent would find it distasteful to attend a party where most of the people were Jewish, Japanese, Chinese, Indian, or Mexican.

ful to attend a party dominantly attended by any one of the five other minorities also do not manifest prejudice against whites. If a Negro person finds most of the minorities distasteful, the odds are very high that he also rejects whites. Or, among Negroes who accept whites on all three counts, only 14 per cent reject any minority; among those who show any social-distance reactions to whites, fully 67 per cent object to one or more of the other ethnic groups. The finding is strongly supported by data from the other communities, based on various indices of prejudice.[79]

So Negroes, too, manifest generalized prejudice.[80] But, again as with whites, prejudice also contains specific components. In the case of Negroes in Southport, of 178 persons classified as high in social-distance prejudice against whites, there were 86 who were low in antiminority prejudices. Nearly one-third of all Southport Negroes show prejudice *only* against white people. The corresponding figure in Valley City was only 15 per cent. The tendency for social-distance feelings to be reciprocal seems clear in Southport.

As we have already stated in Chapter 3, attitudes toward outgroups constitute only one side of ethnocentrism; the other consists of attitudes toward the ingroup—identification, loyalty and pride, or self-deprecation and inward-turned hostility. It is possible that minority persons who reject outgroups may manifest both positive and negative group identification. Alternatively, it might be that group self-hatred among minority persons represents an extension—or a sociological ultimate, as it were—of generalized

[79] See Noel, "Correlates of Anti-White Prejudice," p. 177. (Association between antiwhite and antiminority prejudice is significant beyond the 0.001 level in each sample.)
[80] Richard L. Simpson, "Negro-Jewish Prejudice: Authoritarianism and Social Variables as Correlates," *Social Problems*, VII, No. 2 (Fall, 1959), 141-43.

prejudice. This generalization of rejection has been shown by at least one previous study, which found a significant positive relationship between generalized prejudice and anti-Semitism among a sample of Jewish college students.[81] Evidently our analysis must allow for the possibility of widespread ingroup ambivalence among Negroes. For this purpose we require independent indices of positive and negative ingroup attitudes.

Table 8.24

Acceptance of stereotypes among Negroes, by educational level.

	Valley City		Southport	
Stereotypes*	Elementary school	Some high school or more	Elementary school	Some high school or more
"Generally speaking, Mexicans are shiftless and dirty."	63%	49%	52%	39%
"Although some Jews are honest, in general Jews are dishonest in their business dealings."	54%	45%	50%	46%
"This country would be better off if there were not so many foreigners here."	50%	35%	43%	39%
Total cases	(117)	(109)	(154)	(135)

*Adapted from Lionel S. Lewis, Discrimination and Insulation: An Intercommunity Comparison, M. A. thesis, Cornell University, 1959, p. 12.

The following three items provide an index of negative group identification:

1. *Negroes blame white people for their position, but it's really their own fault.*

2. *Negroes are always shouting about their rights but have nothing to offer.*

3. *Generally speaking, Negroes are lazy and ignorant.*

Construction of an index of positive group identification or group pride is complicated by the existence of several different types of pride [82] and by

[81] J. Himelhoch, "Tolerance and Personality Needs," *American Sociological Review,* XV (1950), 77-88.

[82] This is not to imply that there is only one type of self-hatred. However, the different types of self-hatred seem to be intrinsically related, perhaps scalable, whereas the four types of minority-group pride (nondefensive, militant, nationalistic, and ethnocentric) revealed by a survey of the literature appear to be more nearly independent among themselves.

the problem of distinguishing those persons who lack group pride from those who are militant critics of *existing* group efforts. However, militancy itself is a kind of group pride, and we selected the following three items as a working index of positive group identification:

1. *I don't worry much about the race problem because I know I can't do anything about it.* (*Agree*—Disagree)

2. *Do you ever get the feeling that it is just not worth fighting for equal treatment for Negroes in this town?* (*Yes*—No)

3. *Negroes shouldn't go in business establishments where they think they're not wanted.* (*Agree*—Disagree)

Persons who gave an affirmative response to two or all three of the former set of items are considered high in self-hatred, whereas those who gave an affirmative (italicized) response to two or all three of the latter set are considered low in militant group pride. Combining the two indices allows us to isolate three types of group identification: *identifiers* (that is, persons high in group pride and low in self-hatred), *ambivalents,* and *disparagers.* A similar combination based on the indices of anti-white and antiminority prejudice provides us with a fourfold classification of respondents with respect to prejudice. The *ethnocentrics* are high in prejudice on both indices, the *deviants* are high in antiminority prejudice but low in antiwhite prejudice, the *antiwhites* are high in antiwhite prejudice but low in antiminority prejudice, and the *liberals* are low in prejudice on both indices. (This analysis was conducted by Donald Noel.)

We now can examine the supposition that among minority persons general rejection of outgroups is associated with rejection of the ingroup. The data presented in Table 8.25 support this hypothesis. Comparing the extremes we find that three-fifths of the liberals but only one-third of the ethnocentrics are identifiers, while another one-third of the ethnocentrics but only one-eighth of the liberals are disparagers. Ethnocentrics are significantly high in group disparagement and significantly low in group pride. Table 8.25 also reveals that the liberals and antiwhites each separately constitutes a distinct population, whereas deviants and ethnocentrics compose a common third population. Herein lies a clue to an explanation of the basic finding.

An authoritarian concern to identify with the strong and to reject the weak might well be heightened in minority authoritarians because of the dependent position that their group occupies *vis-a-vis* the powerful majority —those who reject other minority outgroups because they are weak might be expected to reject the ingroup as well. By the same token that authoritarians in the majority group who reject outgroups tend to glorify the all-powerful ingroup, minority authoritarians would tend to disparage or reject the weak ingroup as well as outgroups.

Several bits of evidence support this interpretation. First, deviants who

Table 8.25

Relationship between rejection of outgroup and rejection of ingroup
among Negroes.

	Antiminority prejudice			
	High	Low		
	Antiwhite prejudice			
Group Identification	High (Ethnocentrics) (131)	Low (Deviants) (53)	High (Antiwhites) (119)	Low (Liberals) (212)
Positive	32%	32%	39%	59%
Ambivalent	34%	38%	46%	29%
Negative	34%	30%	15%	13%

$$X^2 = 47.5, p < .001, C^* = .29$$

*C is the coefficient of contingency, expressing the association between two sets of categories. Its upper limit depends on the number of categories: for a four-category table this limit is .866.

manifest prejudice toward the weak minority outgroups but not toward the majority form a common population with the ethnocentrics in terms of both group identification and authoritarianism, suggesting that prejudice toward weak outgroups is the crucial determinant of attitude toward the ingroup. Second, although authoritarianism is significantly related to both antiwhite prejudice and antiminority prejudice, it is slightly more closely related to the latter ($C = 0.21$ versus $C = 0.14$). Third, there is independent evidence that group pride is enhanced by effective organization to combat discrimination—that is, organization oriented toward improving the group's power position.[83] Finally, authoritarianism is negatively and significantly related to group identification in each of the three prejudice types. Moreover, the degree of relationship between the type of outgroup prejudice and group identification is markedly lower among non-authoritarians than among authoritarians.[84]

We conclude that *in the samples studied, Negroes who reject a variety of outgroups also reject the ingroup more often than do Negroes who do not reject outgroups.* This contrasting relationship between ingroup and outgroup attitudes is interpreted as a function of the ingroup's position in the power structure of the total society. The findings re-emphasize the impor-

[83] The relevant data are given in Noel, "Correlates of Anti-White Prejudice," pp. 218-21.

[84] Several previous studies have indicated that authoritarianism is associated with negative group identification. These studies include Himelhoch, "Tolerance and Personality Needs;" M. Radke Yarrow and B. Lande, "Personality Correlates of Differential Reaction to Minority Group Belonging," *Journal of Social Psychology,* XXXVIII (1953), 253-72; and an unpublished study reported in M. M. Grossack, "Group Belongingness Among Negroes," *Journal of Social Psychology,* XLIII (1956), 167-80.

tance of the minority group as an object of study. Intergroup generalizations cannot be automatically transferred from the majority to the minority group.

Finally, we must note that contrary to some impressions there is no necessary opposition between pride in membership in a deprived and subordinate group and the desire to escape from the burdens and penalties of that group membership. The ambivalence of many Negroes in the United States about being a Negro does represent both genuine pride and race loyalty, on the one hand, and a realistic sense of the personal disadvantages and difficulties occasioned by racial prejudice and discrimination, on the other. It is not too farfetched to suggest that white Americans who have served in combat in the Armed Services should find it especially easy to understand this combination of grim pride with a recognition of the drawbacks of membership.

Interaction and Prejudice

What will be the effects of Negro-white interaction upon the attitudes of Negroes? Do we expect high rates of interaction to go along with low prejudice? Or will frequent interaction only multiply and accentuate the sources of friction, intensify competition, and multiply the occasions for frustration, leading to high levels of prejudice?

A strong case could be made for the expectation that white-Negro interaction will be associated with high prejudice. Certainly we already know that the greatest prevalence and greatest intensity of prejudices among whites are found in those parts of the nation in which Negroes constitute a large proportion of the population and in which Negro-white contacts are more frequent. Furthermore, there are impressive theoretical grounds for doubting that interaction will reduce prejudice on either side or increase friendliness or intergroup harmony. For example, it seems plausible to suppose that the circumstances most likely to produce interaction are also those most likely to throw Negroes and whites into economic competition, as in industrial employment, or into relations of great inequality and super-subordination, as in master-servant relationships. In either case, the possible sources of threat and hostility are fairly obvious. Besides all this, we know, quite apart from race or ethnic relations, how easy it is for personal dislikes to arise among close associates, how ubiquitous are the internal promptings to hostility, how avidly men seem to search for scapegoats.

There is a still further possible source of the exacerbation of dislike and of the strengthening of stereotypes through the interaction of members of a dominant racial group and the less privileged members of a subordinate grouping. Given the historical facts—the existence of distinctive categories, differential treatment, unequal education, segregated environments, and so on, it is likely that each of the two segments of the population will not only believe the other to be different but that each will, in fact, differ in many attitudes, behaviors, customs, beliefs, and values. To throw together people who so differ—is this not to court the possibility of confusion, low-ered predictability, frustration of expectations, clashes of beliefs, and dis-agreement on values and social norms?

Under a system of forced segregation, furthermore, the subordinate group develops strong avoidance tendencies, illustrated in our studies by the differ-ences between Valley City and Southport shown in Table 8.26.

Table 8.26

Avoidance tendencies of Negroes (Valley City and Southport).

	Valley City	Southport
Would prefer joining social club which was all-Negro rather than mixed.	30%	71%
Believe it is not right for a colored person to marry a white person.	33%	70%
Believe it is best to stay away from whites to avoid all embarrassing situations.†	21%	35%

*Adapted from L.S. Lewis, op. cit., p. 16.
†Among these same respondents, 83 per cent in each of the two cities reported opportunities for contact.

It is not that the custom of racial separateness has been gladly accepted by Southport Negroes. Their avoidance reactions do not increase with length of residence in the community (actually there is a slightly greater prevalence of distasteful responses among the shorter-term residents).[85] Furthermore, in Valley City with its high proportion of Southern-born Negroes [86] there is markedly greater acceptance of interaction with whites. Nor does ex-pressed hostility toward whites seem to account for the avoidance pattern in Southport. Both manifest friendliness and hatred are about as frequent in Valley City as in Southport. Avoidance is not merely the mirror-image of whites' dislike of association; in both communities, the great majority of whites prefer separation in those contexts in which it already exists and accept contact where it traditionally has been accepted. Whites' expressed hostility toward Negroes is higher in Valley City than in Southport.

Southport Negroes are aware of racial segregation and discrimination, and they are in touch with the outside world. Yet there is much resigna-

[85] Lewis, "Discrimination and Insulation: An Intercommunity Comparison" (M. A. Thesis, Cornell University), 1959, p. 25.
[86] Fully 85 per cent were born in the South Atlantic and South Central states.

tion and apathy. In the face of whites' dominant economic and political power in the city and state and of the rigid attitudes concerning segregation, a social pattern of withdrawal and insulation has been evolved. Experience has taught that contacts with whites are often unpleasant and sometimes dangerous. Comfort and safety lie in minimizing the occasions for involvement with whites. But this protective insulation in no sense constitutes an endorsement of enforced segregation.

For most Negroes in American society, exposure to contacts with white persons is not ordinarily a matter of free choice. Especially at work, interaction with whites is frequently unavoidable, and the numerical preponder-

Table 8.27

Relationship between opportunity for interracial contact and prejudice among Negroes.

	Opportunity†											
	Percentages											
	Valley City			Hometown			Southport			Steelville‡			Totals		
Prejudice*	H (32)	L (51)	N§ (41)	H (19)	L (11)	N (2)	H (44)	L (71)	N (58)	H (18)	L (21)	N (3)	H (113)	L (154)	N (104)
High	34%	49%	34%	79%	91%	(2)	57%	55%	69%	56%	81%	(2)	54%	59%	56%
Low	66%	51%	66%	21%	9%	—	43%	45%	31%	44%	19%	(1)	46%	41%	44%

*See Appendix D.

†Opportunity for equal status interracial contact means that 1) There are some whites in at least one organization the respondent belongs to; 2) There are some whites living within a block or two of the respondent; or 3) The respondent has some face-to-face contact with whites in his work (see note ‡). High means the individual has opportunity in two or all three of these situations, low means opportunity in only one situation, and none indicates no opportunity. Persons who have friendship and/or social contact with whites are omitted from this table.

‡In Steelville respondents were asked only if they came in contact with whites in their neighborhood, organizations, or at work. Such contacts are interepreted here merely as opportunities for equal status contact.

§H = High; L = Low; N = None.

ance of the white population in most communities makes frequent contact with whites a matter of very high statistical likelihood. Consistent with these conditions, in the four cities studied (Table 8.27), there is no relation between exposure of Negroes to contact with whites (opportunity for contact) and generalized social-distance prejudice. Negroes who say they find it distasteful to have close contacts with whites are just as likely as the less prejudiced Negroes to report exposure to contacts with white people. In none of the four samples is there a significant difference in prevalence of prejudice as between persons having high and low exposure or between persons having any opportunity and those having no exposure at all.

There are striking differences among the four cities, located in three different major regions of the county, in the distribution of opportunities for contacts. In Hometown and Steelville virtually everyone in the Negro samples reports exposure to interracial contact in at least one area of life activities, but in Southport and Valley City one-fifth of the respondents report no contact opportunity in any situation. The interregional differences derive primarily from the neighborhood and organizational sectors, rather than from the area of work.

As compared with the combined Valley City-Hometown sample—taken to illustrate general non-Southern situations—the Southport sample reported a far smaller proportion of friendships developing from contacts. The differences were: 28 per cent for the neighborhood, 10 per cent for organizations, and 31 per cent for work. These differences reflect the massive impact of Southern culture and social organization. But within each of the communities, the variations in friendship formation among the three types of situations are very impressive. The differences as between neighborhood and work in the proportions of cases in which contact opportunities were converted into friendships are roughly equivalent to the differences between North and South. The enormous cumulative effect of both regional and situational variables may be illustrated by the extreme comparison between Hometown's work situation and Southport's organizations. Of every 100 Negroes at work in Hometown, 97 have contact opportunity and 80 report friendships. Of every 100 Negroes who participate in organizations in Southport, only 19 have opportunity for contact with whites, and fewer than 5 have any white friends in that situation.

If competitive threats to differential rewards and prestige status are not too acute, work situations are especially likely to provide conditions conducive to the formation of intergroup friendships, namely: (1) opportunity occurs regularly and frequently; (2) the situation has a firm social structure and clear boundaries, a fact which probably reduces psychological insecurity and threat; (3) common interests and shared activities tend to produce similarities of beliefs, values, and norms. We believe that this characterization probably fits the situations in our survey communities. As Table 8.28 shows, in every instance the greatest likelihood of reported friendships with white persons attaches to work situations. Thus, for the Negroes in our samples both opportunities for interracial contact and actual friendly relationships with white persons are maximized in the situation of work.

Once more, however, we must confront the reported friendships with the same respondents' testimony concerning their informal social relationships with white persons. The data are in Table 8.29. Southport respondents with only rare exceptions did not engage in diffuse recreational or convivial activities with whites, even with those regarded as good or best friends. *In a society with rigidly institutionalized segregation and discrimination, the situationally developed friendships that cross group lines generally remain bound to the limited social contexts in which they arise and are not extended*

Table 8.28

Situational inventory of friendship contact with whites when opportunity
for contact is given.

	Situation†					
	Neighborhood		Organization		Work	
			Percentages reporting friendship contact‡			
Community*	Per cent	Number of cases	Per cent	Number of cases	Per cent	Number of cases
Valley City	45	121	48	23	58	108
Hometown	48	142	24	54	79	106
Southport	18	136	21	24	39	165
Totals	37	399	29	101	56	379

*Steelville had to be omitted because the friendship data there refer only to the one closest
contact rather than to all contacts, situation by situation.
†The number of cases for each sample in each situation is the number who report an opportunity for contact in that situation. Thus opportunity for contact is constant across situations here.
‡Respondent is considered to have friendship contact in a given situation if he reports that he
considers at least one white in that situation among his good or best friends. If a given
respondent reports that two whites are best friends and three others are good friends, this
is still only one respondent reporting friendship contact.

Table 8.29

Situational inventory of social contact with whites when opportunity
for contact is given.

	Situation†					
	Neighborhood		Organization		Work	
			Percentages reporting social contact‡			
Community*	Per cent	Number of cases	Per cent	Number of cases	Per cent	Number of cases
Valley City	24	121	26	23	28	108
Hometown	30	142	22	54	47	106
Southport	1	136	0	24	5	165
Totals	18	399	18	101	23	379

*Steelville is omitted because the data on social contact refer only to the closest contact rather
than to all contacts, situation by situation.
†The number of cases for each sample in each situation is the number who report an opportunity for contact in that situation.
‡Respondent is considered to have social contact with whites if he does something of a social
nature (for example, going to a sports event or visiting in each other's home) with any of the
whites he contacts in his neighborhood, work, or organization.

to a wider range of activities or situations. In much less extreme form, the non-Southern communities show a constriction of socializing in comparison with friendship.

With the exception of the work situation in Hometown, there is little variation from one social context to another in the proportion reporting that they have done something social with a white person known in that context. Interaction that might be regarded as strictly social can occur as an intrinsic part of interaction in the neighborhood or in organizations; but in the case of work it is more likely that "something social" involves a separate contact away from the place of work. Relatively cordial interpersonal relationships with white co-workers are *comparatively* easy to develop within the highly structured, functionally specific activities connected with the job, but further informal social interaction is much more difficult.

We now know that among both Negroes and whites the greatest incidence of authoritarian moralism, punitiveness, and suspicion is found among uneducated persons of low income and occupational status. Most (although not all) types of racial prejudice are most frequent at the lower levels of education and economic position, and especially among the socially isolated segments of working-class strata. Diffuse hostility and generalized ethnocentrism are prevalent at these levels, and are complicated by ingroup deprecation. These, it may be granted, are unpromising conditions for intergroup contact. They are made even more unpromising by partial forced segregation, which throws the mutually fearful or hostile parties together only in extremely casual and/or overtly competitive settings.

Even so, if there is repeated, continuing Negro-white interaction, some friendly relationships will emerge, partly through self-selection, partly through exemption of individuals, but also through the reorganization of attitudes to allow lessened generalized social distance.[87]

The great reservoir of social-distance prejudice against whites is found among the uneducated Negroes who have no close social contacts with white persons. Such persons typically have been restricted to low-paid, low-prestige occupations. As a usual thing they have been brought up in segregated environments. Their main contacts with whites have been casual or work-connected interactions—primarily with lower-class persons. Their experiences with white people have included instances of severe frustration, deprivation, insult, and hurt. They have been compelled to suppress or repress their aggressive reactions. They are often both fearful and resentful. In any event, they do not feel adequate to cope with hypothetical situations of close informal associations with whites. Bitter and withdrawn, they often look upon the prevailing prejudice and discrimination manifest among whites

---

[87] Cf. Ernest Works, "The Prejudice-Interaction Hypothesis from the Point of View of the Negro Minority Group," *American Journal of Sociology,* LXVII, No. 1 (July, 1961), 47-52.

with an attitude of hopeless resentment. They lack the self-confidence and race pride of the well-educated and economically secure Negroes.

Nevertheless such effects of the social experiences associated with low education *are* importantly counteracted by diffuse informal association with white persons. Informal social contact with whites is significantly associated with low social-distance prejudice, in fact, only among Negro persons with less than a high school education. Social contact has no discernible effect among the relatively well educated, but among the less well educated there is a large difference (24 per cent) in the proportions high in prejudice (significant at the 0.001 level).[88] If we reverse the tabulation to hold contact constant, educational level is not appreciably correlated with prejudice among those who associate socially with whites. Thus both education and social contact are negatively related to prejudice, but if a person has *either* high education *or* a close social relation with a white person or persons, the other factor has a negligible further association with prejudice.

All respondents in both the white majority group and the Negro samples were asked whether there were any white people (or Negroes) in their neighborhood, in their organizations, at their place of work, or in any other area of face-to-face contact whom they considered as good or best friends. As we saw in Chapter 7, whites who had interracial contact of this nature were much less likely to be high in prejudice than those who did not have such contact. *On the other hand, Negroes who had friendly, equal-status contact with whites were not significantly less likely to be prejudiced*: the difference, although in the expected direction, could have occurred by chance seventeen times in one hundred. This slight association of contact with low prejudice has such important possible theoretical and practical implications that further analysis, using a more sensitive index of contact, seems desirable.

All the respondents in both samples had been asked if they had ever done anything social with white people (or Negroes) in any of the four areas previously mentioned. Over one-fourth of the Negroes responded affirmatively for at least one of the four areas, but the number of whites having such social contact was insufficient to permit further analysis. The major finding was that *Negroes who have had this intimate social contact with whites are much less likely to be prejudiced than those who have not had this type of contact.* This difference is significant at the 0.001 level.

Who are the Negroes actually most likely to have informal social relations with white persons? In terms of the gross factors of age, sex, education, marital status, and pattern of social participation, the answer is clear. Negroes who report interracial social contact tend to be: male; relatively well educated; active in organizations; persons with a history of interracial con-

---

[88] Noel, "Correlates of Anti-White Prejudice," p. 299.

tacts in earlier years; and middle aged (35 to 64 years) rather than very young or elderly. (Marital status is the one social factor not related to contact.)

Overriding these indices of individual status is the highly significant (0.001) regional difference in the proportion of Negroes having social contacts with whites. Only 6 per cent of the Southport respondents have this contact as opposed to 27 per cent in Valley City, 41 per cent in Steelville, and 56 per cent in Hometown. This undoubtedly reflects not only the regional differences in racial climate, but also the marked differences in the size of the Negro community in each of the four cities. It seems very clear, then, that in the Negro community sociological factors are highly related to the likelihood of interracial social contact.

When we examine the relation between contact and a series of five attitudineal variables, a drastically different picture emerges. Only status striving relates significantly to contact. Two-thirds of the strivers but less than half of the nonstrivers report social contact with whites. Of the other psychological variables, not even the "feeling that you just don't belong anywhere," bears any significant relation to contact.

Unless counteracted by other forces, we would expect the rigid, non-adaptive, distrustful personality traits characteristic of the authoritarian syndrome to be detrimental to the formation of intergroup friendships

Table 8.30

Psychological correlates of social contact with whites.

Correlate*	Per cent reporting social contact		Based on samples†	Level of significance
	Per cent	Number of cases		
Authoritarianism				
High	26	(400)	1-4	No difference
Low	29	(405)		
Status striving				
High	68	(72)	2	.01
Low	45	(78)		
Get even				
Agree	20	(167)	1,3,4	No difference
Not agree	21	(488)		
Race suffer				
Agree	22	(400)	1,3,4	.40
Not agree	18	(255)		
Don't belong				
Often, sometimes	11	(114)	1,3	.20
Hardly ever	16	(401)		

*See Noel, "Correlates of Anti-White Prejudice."
†Valley City is sample #1, Hometown is #2, Southport is #3, and Steelville is #4.

among both majority- and minority-group persons. In our data authoritarianism is not related to friendships when all cities are considered together; if we omit the Southport data, the authoritarians are significantly (0.05) less likely to have social contact than the nonauthoritarians. Aggression toward whites, as manifested by the desire to "get even," does not relate to contact at all, and race-associated frustration slightly reverses the expected relation between contact and prejudice. Clearly, these data do not support the hypothesis that attitudinal variables are more important than role and status variables as determinants of actual interracial contact. Rather, it appears that, among the Negroes studied, the reverse is true.

On the other hand, the attitudes we have regarded as stemming rather directly from the minority experience do relate to intergroup contact in a manner similar to the sociological variables. Respondents who manifest a militant group pride are significantly more likely to have interracial social contact than nonmilitants and, conversely, those who score high in group self-hatred clearly tend to have less contact than those who are relatively lacking in self-hatred. *In other words, it is the individual who identifies*

Table 8.31

Variables rooted in the minority experience as correlates of social contact with whites.

Correlate	Per cent reporting social contact		Based on samples*	Level of significance
	Per cent	Number of cases		
Militance				
High	24	(376)	1,3,4	.02
Low	16	(279)		
Self-hatred				
High	11	(172)	1,3	.15
Low	17	(343)		
Friendliness toward whites				
High	37	(202)		
Medium	30	(448)	1-4	.001
Low	15	(55)		
Defensive insulation				
High	5	(194)	1,3	.001
Low	21	(321)		
Suspicion of whites				
High	8	(168)	1,3	.01
Low	18	(347)		

*Valley City is sample #1, Hometown is #2, Southport is #3, and Steelville is #4.

positively with his racial group who is likely to have interracial contact.[89]
Interracial contact, we suggest, increases the salience of race and, therefore, the contact is acceptable or repugnant depending upon the basic attitude of the minority individual toward his own racial membership.

This brief survey of the relation of basic social and psychological characteristics to the occurrence of equal-status intergroup contacts indicates that
many of these factors do affect the likelihood of contact. Nevertheless, relatively sizable proportions of virtually all the social and psychological subgroups do enter into social contact with whites (Table 8.31). Thus, if the
data obtained from members of these samples of Negroes can be generalized,
we still need to know a great deal more about the determinants of intergroup contact. This has been a neglected area of research despite its important implications for the contact theory of prejudice.

Summary

This analysis of Negro-white contacts shows that the mere fact of opportunity for equal-status contact is not related to prejudice at all. As a
determinant of actual contact, opportunity retains its importance, of course;
and it is found to vary by region and by situation, being most common in
Hometown and Steelville and in the work situation. Ignoring the marked
regional variations, fully one-eighth of the respondents in the combined
samples do not report even one situational opportunity for contact, and
one-third of the respondents have one opportunity or less. Just over one-
fourth of those interviewed report actual informal social contact with whites
in intimate settings (home, social clique, etc.); one-half indicate that they
have white friends. These figures are clear indicators of the segregated
nature of the social structure. However, the contact that does exist provides
a basis for increasing integration, which we shall discuss further in Chapter.
10.

We find a tendency for those Negroes having white friends to be less
prejudiced toward contact with white people than those without any white
friends, but the difference is definitely not significant. The low degree of
association is not due to the operation of the exemption mechanism, and
thus it is suggested that the respondents are using different standards of
friendship for whites as compared to other Negroes. This interpretation is
strengthened by the fact that friendship is not correlated at all with prejudice except among those persons who also have close social contact with
whites.

Social contact, on the other hand, is significantly related to differences

---

[89] Whitewardly mobile individuals, characterized by status striving and self-hatred,
are likely to constitute a prominent exception here.

in social-distance prejudice, and this relationship remains when we hold constant such basic social and psychological variables as education, sex, social participation, authoritarianism, aggression, and frustration.[90] Thus it appears that the association of contact with low prejudice is genuine and, therefore, the hypothesis that equal status contact reduces prejudice is valid among Negroes as well as among majority-group persons.

The findings concerning three of the variables used as controls in analyzing the contact-prejudice relationship deserve specific mention. First, interracial social contact is associated with low prejudice among Negroes regardless of their degree of suspicion of whites. This finding undercuts the possibility that friendship does not relate to antiwhite prejudice because the suspiciousness of Negroes toward whites means that a more intimate level of contact is required to secure an equivalent reduction in prejudice. Second, although defensive insulation appears to account for the contact-prejudice relationship, defensive insulation and contact belong to the same causal complex; hence, controlling any part of this complex would naturally weaken the original relationship. Third, social contact seems to have an even greater effect on the prejudice of authoritarians than on that of non-authoritarians. In common with a similar finding, reported in Chapter 7, for white people, this datum conflicts with the findings of the one other pertinent study in the literature and suggests a need for further research on this point.

The similarity of the pairs of participants who interact across group lines and the degree to which each diverges from the other's stereotyped conception of members of his group are believed to be highly important determinants of the effect of contact on prejudice. Various subgroups of the population were studied in terms of the likelihood of their members having social contact with whites. In brief, the data indicate that the Negro who reports interracial social contact is most likely to be an educated, male, organization member, residing outside the South, who is a nonauthoritarian, sociable striver, and who strongly identifies with his race while remaining friendly, nonsuspicious, and noninsulated *vis-à-vis* members of the majority group.

The main findings from the analysis of Negroes' reports of interaction with whites may be summarized as follows:

1. Opportunities for Negro-white interaction are most frequent at work, least in organizations and informal social life.

2. Friendship formation, as viewed by Negroes, is most likely in the work situation.

---

[90] In several cases, the basic relationship was eliminated in one partial, but if we reversed contact and the control variable we found that contact also eliminated the relation of the (original) control variable and prejudice in at least one partial.

3. Both opportunities for contact and reported interracial friendships are *least* common in the Southern city. Even equating frequency of contact, the Southern environment is least conducive to friendly relations, from the standpoint of the Negro.

4. Negro persons who report one or more best friends who are white are less likely to express social-distance feelings toward whites in three of four communities, but in Southport prejudice is unrelated to having or not having a white friend.

5. But Negroes who have a relationship with a white person that has involved informal visiting or recreational activity are consistently and significantly more acceptant in generalized attitude toward close social relationships with white persons.

6. Informal social contact is significantly associated with low social-distance prejudice among both men and women—the interaction-prejudice relation is independent, in this sense, of sex roles.

7. Informal social interaction is associated with low prejudice among Negroes who are, and those who are not, members of formal organizations, but the correlation is significantly large only among nonmembers.

8. Authoritarians are no less likely than nonauthoritarians to have informal social interaction with white persons.

9. The association between informal social interaction with whites and low social-distance prejudice is just as marked among authoritarians as among nonauthoritarians.

10. Attitudes of generalized avoidance of whites—"defensive insulation" —are highly related to social-distance prejudice among Negroes who do not have informal social relationships with whites. The effect of defensive insulation is so great that only a negligible number of insulates have such informal social interaction.

11. Informal social contact with whites also is significantly associated with low social-distance prejudice among Negroes who report feelings of race frustration, and the correlation is maintained even among those who express vengefulness toward whites.

12. Joint Negro-white social activity remains associated with low social-distance prejudice among Negroes who express generalized suspicion of white persons as well as among those who do not.

Thus, although Negroes often are avoidant in attitudes toward whites, and although fear, suspicion, and antipathy are frequent, when interaction *does* develop into a diffuse, personalized relationship, not only the specific attitude toward a particular white person but also the generalized orientation toward close association tends to be favorable.

OTHER REACTIONS TO MINORITY STATUS

Students of Negro-white relations in the United States who have come to know particular Negro individuals well have noted the accuracy and acuteness of Negroes' knowledge and understanding of the behavior of white people.[91] Close interdependence has often made such knowledge a prerequisite for survival. At the same time Negroes have necessarily learned the attitudes of whites toward Negroes. Frequent ambivalence toward white people on the part of Negroes is an expectable consequence.

One of the great handicaps of American Negroes until very recent times was the lack of a positive ethnocentrism that could unite the various segments of the Negro population in collective efforts to improve their position. As a consequence of slavery and later systematic discrimination, Negroes' acceptance of the majority group's culture entailed initial acceptance of white values, including ambivalent deprecation of their own physical traits and social characteristics.[92] One of the clearest indications of the pervasiveness and depth of Negroes' acceptance of the evaluations of the white culture comes from studies of Negro children.[93] Negro children sometimes manifest tendencies "to show a preference for and to emulate white children . . . [these tendencies] . . . express a measure of the acceptance of cultural stereotypes about their own race, and their fear of the image of the aggressive Negro." [94] Other studies have shown that Negro children attending segregated or semisegregated schools tend to be more favorable in attitude toward white children than white children are toward them.[95] It is the

[91] This was true even before World War II and even in the Deep South. See, for example, John Dollard's discussion of accommodation: "Even though their personalities seem well accommodated to the caste system, it should not be thought that the Negroes are too stupid to realize the nature of the situation. They understand it quite well, in fact much better than do members of the white caste. . . ." [*Caste and Class in a Southern Town* (New York: Doubleday & Company, Inc., 1957), p. 252.]

[92] "Without a common rallying point, except their color (about which they have tended to have mixed feelings if not open regret), they have found it difficult to unite their members against exploitation by the larger society." (Wagley and Harris, *Minorities in the New World*, p. 270).

[93] K. B. Clark and M. K. Clark, "Skin Color as a Factor in Racial Identification of Negro Pre-School Children," *Journal of Social Psychology*, XI, First Half (February, 1940), 159-69; K. B. Clark and M. K. Clark, "Emotional Factors in Racial Identification and Preference in Negro Children," *Journal of Negro Education*, XIX, No. 3 (Summer, 1950), 341-50; R. M. Goff, "Problems and Emotional Difficulties of Negro Children Due to Race," *Journal of Negro Education*, XIX, No. 2 (Spring, 1950), 152-58.

[94] John D. Campbell and Marian Radke Yarrow, "Personal and Situational Variables in Adaptation to Change," *The Journal of Social Issues*, XIV, No. 1 (1958), 33.

[95] D. H. Russell and I. V. Robertson, "Influencing Attitudes toward Minority Groups in a Junior High School," *School Review*, LV, No. 4 (April, 1947), 205-13; E. Helgerson: "The Relative Significance of Race and Facial Expression in Choice of Playmate by the Pre-School Child," *Journal of Negro Education*, XII, No. 4 (Fall, 1943), 617-22.

"capture" of Negroes by white standards of judgment that makes possible this rather remarkable phenomenon.

It is indeed remarkable that Negroes in the United States have so rarely been attracted by separatist, racist, or nationalistic programs and have remained on the whole so firmly attached to characteristically American democratic ideology and assimilationist and integrationist sentiments, even in the face of a century of rebuffs since the attainment of emancipation. There are a number of causes that lie behind these facts, but the overwhelming preference of Negroes, *so far,* for peaceable, legal, and educational means in the struggle for equality of political and civil rights and liberties is not automatic or to be taken for granted.

Yet, *distrust of white people is nearly universal among Negroes who have experienced severe discrimination.* In the communities we studied, it was impossible to find a Negro person who had not at some time been hurt, rebuffed, insulted, or deprived by a white person in a manner clearly based on a categorical racial distinction. It would be strange indeed if such experiences did not produce at least an initial wariness and reserve in dealing with whites, even with those who appear to be unprejudiced and friendly. The defensive insulation so produced is not merely a kind of rational prudence. It is also a *potential* basis for a fundamental moral and political alienation from white society altogether. In the characteristics we have found among lower-class Negroes lie the conditions for Negro racism of the kind manifested, since the time of our surveys, by the Black Muslims, initially drawn predominantly from lower-class urban males.[96] In their racial nationalism, rejection of Christian religion, advocacy of segregation of whites from Negroes, and their doctrines of Negro racial superiority, the so-called Muslims express the deep frustration and hostility of segments of the Negro population and reflect a reverse image of the white racism that has so aroused their bitterness. The impact of African nationalism upon the American Negroes' sense of identity has not yet been fully revealed or charted.

Chauvinistic reactions are especially to be expected when a new sense of group identity converges with the objective possibility of collective action in an urban setting. The underlying frustration and hostility typically have been built up reactively out of a Southern background. These facts are noteworthy:

1. Negroes are less likely to express feelings of social distance or dislike toward whites than whites are to express these feelings concerning Negroes. The differences are statistically significant and large and are consistently found in diverse communities.

---

[96] C. Eric Lincoln: *The Black Muslims in America* (Boston: Beacon Press, Inc., 1961).

2. Prejudice of whites against Negroes is much more frequent in the South than in other parts of the nation.

3. Prejudice against whites on the part of Negroes is likewise higher in the South than in other parts of the country.

4. Prejudice of Negroes toward white people is greater with reference to Southern than to Northern whites.[97]

5. Hostile and disparaging attitudes and behavior of white people toward Negroes generate hostile alienated and defensive attitudes of Negro people toward whites. In general, communication of information concerning the attitudes of Group A toward Group B will be most effective in producing favorable change in attitudes of Group B toward Group A when it can truthfully be communicated that most A's are *not hostile* to most B's and are *ready to be friendly* but that they *do reject as unjustified any hostile attitudes of B's toward A's.*

What we are reviewing here is a specific empirical example corresponding to what Radcliffe-Brown has called a "universal principle of just retribution": that good should be repaid with good, evil with evil; that unfriendly as well as friendly orientations and actions are to be reciprocated.[98] What is perhaps surprising is only the extent to which many American Negroes have renounced the concept of retribution.

In general it seems safe to say that in our society individuals who are low in socioeconomic level, for example, in income, occupational prestige, and education are disproportionately exposed to *external constraint.*[99] Low and uncertain income, for example, limits what a person can have and what he can do—limits him to a greater extent than he would choose, were he free to choose. It restricts his range of adaptive responses to his world. It exposes him to high risks, to physical and psychological hazards and indignities. (The experience of an injury or disease known to be preventable is after all a deep insult to the integrity of the person.) Furthermore, the experience of external restraint is increased to the extent that the reference groups and reference individuals of the person are perceived to be in better circumstances; this is experience of relative deprivation, which appears to be so important in many of the situations produced by discrimination against members of minority groups. The sense of "cramp"—of being unjustly restricted, hemmed in, trapped—is still further accentuated to the extent

---

[97] Cf. Samuel A. Stouffer *et al., The American Soldier,* II, Chapter 10, 556-66 and 580-82; also, for example, J. B. Edlefson, "Social Distance Attitudes of Negro College Students," *Phylon,* XVII (1956), 79-83.

[98] A. R. Radcliffe-Brown, *A Natural Science of Society* (New York: The Free Press of Glencoe, Inc., 1947), pp. 132-34.

[99] See Bruce P. Dohrenwend, "The Social Psychological Nature of Stress: A Framework for Causal Inquiry," *Journal of Abnormal and Social Psychology,* LXII, No. 2 (1961), 296-98.

that the relational system of the individual fails to give him reliable emotional support and needed cognitive guidance in coping with the difficult circumstances in which he finds himself. And there is abundant evidence that such partial failure of the interpersonal support system is very common among deprived minority groups at lower socioeconomic levels.

There are other reasons for expecting that individuals of a subordinate minority group in American society will be unlikely to fully accept their position. Among other things, dissatisfaction is generated by the idea of personal rights and personal dignity in a democratic society. It is quickly realized by anyone that personal dignity is an empty phrase unless it refers to *actual* rights in the ordinary affairs of life: to be able to safeguard one's home, children, women, family, property; to vote; to hold a job for which one is qualified; to receive minimal social courtesy; to be free of coerced obligations to give deference, and so on. In the case of most American Negroes, the nominally universal rights enjoyed by white people are daily flouted in their own cases. The *inevitable* result is a sense of systematic and unjust frustration and deprivation.

Exactly *what* a man will regard as a frustration, deprivation, or humiliation will be affected by his cultural background, his group membership, and his particular social position. But no matter where the lines are drawn, they are drawn somewhere, and no men will easily and willingly accept that which they define as deprivational and humiliating. They may have to put up with it, but they do not have to like it.

Middle- and upper-class Negro families are able to translate a measure of economic independence into selective insulation from those contacts with whites that are most likely to be threatening to self-respect. By the same token they are able to instill in their children a sense of dignity and rectitude that leads to strong resistance to any claims by whites to servility in interracial behavior. Where interaction with whites is unavoidable, the relatively well-educated and skilled Negro person is, indeed, also able to command a degree of mannered restraint from many white persons, which gives at least some consensual validation to his implicit claim to treatment consistent with his self-image. This does not mean that white persons will necessarily *like* the behavior of the middle-class Negro. On the contrary, they often will resent his claims. But they will not be able to consistently avoid recognizing the legitimacy of these claims, which are based on values widely acknowledged within the majority group.

Finally, we must add a brief note on the case of ethnic minorities lacking the peculiar historical status of the Negro. Knowing the great prevalence and strength among minorities in the United States of desires for assimilation and integration, it is easy to minimize unwittingly the common tendency for culturally distinctive groupings here and elsewhere to tenaciously defend their separateness and distinctiveness. Such religioethnic islands as the Old Order Amish of Pennsylvania lie close at hand. Numerous examples are found elsewhere.[100] Even in the United States efforts to preserve distinctive ethnic characteristics have been as genuine a part of the American saga of intergroup relations as efforts to assimilate. Ethnic identity has been defended in the name of creative diversity, safeguarding a universally valuable heritage, giving children security of belonging, preventing delinquency, and so on.

It seems likely that there is a curvilinear relationship between social assimilation into the host community and the degree of integration and stability of the ethnic community. The most highly integrated community is likely to resist assimilation and to provide many satisfactions to hold its members. The highly disintegrated ethnic population is likely to be rejected by the host community and forced into a marginal position. In between lies the maximum likelihood of successful assimilation. A case in point appears to be that of American Jews. Because of the well-known concentration of American Jews in the larger cities, a certain imbalance, perhaps, has crept into the social science literature. Most Jews live in great metropolitan centers, and the numbers in cities under 100,000 and in smaller towns and villages are comparatively very small. But it is overlooked, in this view, that most of the non-Jewish persons whose behavior and attitudes toward Jews we should try to understand are *not* in New York, Chicago, Los Angeles, Boston, Detroit, Minneapolis, or San Francisco.

Our own studies suggest that cultural assimilation of Jews in smaller cities is relatively quite advanced.[101] The studies of Jewish life in the survey communities were later supplemented (1958) by Peter I. Rose's investigation of small-town Jews in New York State.[102] The latter study was limited to communities with populations below 10,000, having 10 or fewer Jewish families and outside of metropolitan counties. The isolated or semi-isolated Jews in these communities proved to be "bi-cultural" rather than marginal. Rather than being on the periphery of two cultures and psychologically torn between them, the small-town Jews actively participate in both. They strongly identify with fellow Jews, want their children to remain Jews, are opposed to interfaith marriage. At the same time, they identify with the local community, participate actively in a variety of community organizations, and

---

[100] Cf. Wagley and Harris, *Minorities in the New World,* pp. 46-47 for a description of the striking case of the Fulnio of Aguas Belas in Pernambuco in Brazil, a people that has insisted upon a closed society and has retained its tribal identity, language, and much of the original culture.

[101] For a summary of one set of data from Hometown, see Bernard C. Rosen, "Minority Group in Transition: A Study of Adolescent Religious Conviction and Conduct," in *The Jews: Social Patterns of an American Group,* Marshall Sklare, ed. (New York: The Free Press of Glencoe, Inc., 1958), pp. 336-47.

[102] "Small-Town Jews and their Neighbours in the United States," *The Jewish Journal of Sociology,* III, No. 2 (December, 1961), 174-91.

are active in many informal social activities. Overwhelmingly, they feel themselves accepted without discrimination, even while many become conscious of themselves as "ambassadors to the gentiles."

The picture of bi-culturality with satisfactory acceptance by gentiles reported by the small-town Jews is not fully in accord with the conceptions held by gentile leaders in the same communities. About 80 per cent of these leaders subscribe to prejudicial stereotypes concerning Jews ("money-minded," "more aggressive than most people"), and the prevalence of acceptance is not related to presence or absence of direct contact with Jewish persons. Yet, gentile persons who had experienced continuing and relatively intimate contact with local Jews view their close Jewish acquaintances favorably and regard them as "different," "not the Brooklyn type," and so on. These exemptions when followed by repeated and intensive contact and personal association often led to an alteration in the image and evaluation of Jews more generally.[103]

CONCLUSION

It bears repeating that the notion of a minority group does not refer to all deprived, disadvantaged, or disesteemed groupings or social categories; these may be class groupings, occupational categories, political parties, and many others. Minorities rather are any culturally or physically distinctive and self-conscious social aggregates, with hereditary membership and a high degree of endogamy, which are subject to political, or economic, or social discrimination by a dominant segment of an environing political society.[104]

A simple sequence of facts is crucial in this connection: if other people act toward any aggregate of individuals as if the aggregate were a collectivity with an identified and definite membership, then all members of the aggregate will be treated alike in certain ways. To the extent that they are treated alike, the members of the, now emergent, collectivity will come to

---

[103] "Repeated personal and informal contact in the home and around town can serve as a significant factor leading towards the ultimate reduction of prejudice against Jews." (*Ibid.,* p. 190).

[104] This description incorporates and specifies the characteristics mentioned by Wagley and Harris: "In résumé, we have mentioned five characteristics by which the distinctive nature of minorities may be defined: (1) minorities are subordinate segments of complex state societies; (2) minorities have special physical or cultural traits which are held in low esteem by the dominant segments of the society; (3) minorities are self-conscious units bound together by the special traits which their members share and by the special disabilities which these bring; (4) membership in a minority is transmitted by a rule of descent which is capable of affiliating succeeding generations even in the absence of readily apparent special cultural or physical traits; (5) minority peoples, by choice or necessity, tend to marry within the group." (Charles Wagley and Marvin Harris, *Minorities in the New World,* p. 10.)

be alike in at least some of their interests and values. To the extent that they come to share common interests and values, the likelihood is increased that awareness of common interests will grow. To the extent that this awareness becomes general, the likelihood of concerted action is increased. It is exactly this kind of development that is reflected in recent political activity and social movements among American Negroes.[105] We found the point well illustrated even in the small, weak, and much-divided Negro community in Hometown. Under great difficulties there had developed a common awareness of minority-group status and of the white outgroup's definition of Negroes as separate and inferior. This awareness gradually coalesced among leaders around sensitive symbols of discrimination and led to organized concerted action (through both Negro and white leaders), which in the five years during which we were able to observe developments resulted in the following new patterns in the Hometown community:

1. Hometown's first Negro fireman, social worker, hospital nurse, visiting nurse, dentist, professional baseball players, school teachers, policeman, telephone operator, laboratory technician, and highway state trooper.

2. Hometown's first Negroes on the Board of Directors of the interracial settlement house, YWCA, and Community Chest.

3. Hometown's first Negroes in the local college and in the public housing project.

Segregation creates systematic uniformities of environments for Negroes —environments that differ from those of whites. The same holds for discrimination. Every systematic social differentiation results in one segment of a delimited population having common experiences that differ from those of some other portion or portions of the internally differentiated population. Both the uniformity of experience within a segment and the difference between one segment and another are important in the relations that may exist between and among segments. In general, the more uniform the environment, the greater the similarity of experiences, hence, the greater the commonality or homogeneity of culture. On the whole, also, the more uniform the environment and the more homogeneous the culture within one differentiated segment of a society, the greater are likely to be its differences from some other segment of the society.

Segregation and discrimination generally are found together. Segregation almost always involves discrimination, although this is not a matter of absolute necessity. Discrimination, on the other hand, can be extensive and elaborate even with a minimum of segregation. Indeed, there obviously has to be *some* interaction for discrimination to occur at all.

---

[105] Alexander Heard, *A Two-Party South?* (Chapel Hill: University of North Carolina Press, 1952), p. 210.

Even though discrimination and segregation tend to be associated, they are different social patterns, and have different consequences. In complete segregation the differences of social norms that develop in the two segregated populations are noncomplementary. There is, by definition, no interpersonal contact, hence no reciprocity (except for the possible limiting case of norms of avoidance). Differentiation thus means divergence through entirely separate worlds of experience. In the case of discriminatory patterns of interaction, by contrast, the differences that develop between segments (social categories) include *complementary* differences. As between groupings A and B under a system of discrimination that involves widespread and frequent interpersonal contact of A's and B's, the experiences of each will consist of three parts: (1) entirely within the ingrouping; (2) unilateral action of A toward B or vice versa with no awareness or minimal awareness (on the part of one or both) of the other's experience (beliefs, values, feelings); (3) reciprocal action, with awareness and/or mutual role-taking.

Actions of A toward B and of B toward A under a discriminatory system will tend to be conventionalized and formalized (for example, racial etiquette). The categorical definition of the other party encourages unilateral action with minimal awareness on the part of members of the dominant grouping (type 2 above). Yet even in very rigid and restricted interaction, it is difficult, over any considerable period, to prevent type 2 actions from being transformed into type 3. Interpersonal understandings will emerge; attachments and antipathies toward particular persons will grow up; rewards and frustrations will come to be associated with specific individuals; idiosyncrasies and exceptions will point up individual differences. And, above all, a certain amount of "taking the role of the other" will develop, just to the degree that interaction involves the same concrete persons in relatively stabilized interpersonal relations over a relatively extended period of time. At worst, this development may only match the masochism of the slave against the sadism of the master. At best, it may lead to the disappearance of *categorical* discrimination, through the emergence of equalitarian mutuality from shared experience.

When a person whose initial attitudes are adverse to associating with the members of a certain social category is brought into repeated contact with a person of that category, he will be placed under strain. Being in a state of strain is an uncomfortable condition, and the person will attempt to reduce the strain. It seems likely that the most favored way of first coping with the strain will be to seek to minimize any interaction that does not provide information congruent with the prejudiced individual's initial definition of the situation. Complete withdrawal from the situation is one obvious possibility, but escape is often costly (for example, giving up a desired job, defying Army regulations, selling one's home, losing business to a competitor). Driving out the outgroup member is a possibility, often actualized, but it, too, often is costly. Failing these extreme solutions, the restive participant may try to deal with the given situation without changing his beliefs or evaluations. For example, he, a white man, will seek to routinize relations with a Negro co-worker in terms of a highly restricted "superior-inferior" relationship on the job. For this attempt to be at all successful in reducing strain requires that the allegedly subordinate member acquiesce to some important degree in this relationship. Failing such acquiescence and attempted routinization, if ego continues in the situation, *some* minimal alteration in his orientations is inevitable. Somehow he must come to terms.

Minimal change may be achieved by two types of restrictions, one social, one psychological. At the social level, interaction may be held to a small quantity of highly conventional, routine exchanges. At the psychological level, change may be limited to an isolated or compartmentalized response, for example, defining the instance at hand as an exception, leaving the main body of ethnic attitudes not only intact but still firmly embedded in a system of basic existential orientations toward people. In many intergroup interactions, the most frequent outcome is just this kind of limited friendly acceptance of outgroup persons on the job, in the union, as near-dwellers in a housing project, as fellow members of a military group, in school or college.

Such relationships fall short of intervisiting relations of friendship and far short of giving and receiving in marriage. There is no inherent necessity that will press such relationships in the direction of greater and greater mutuality, intensity, diffuseness, or intimacy. They may—and usually do—become stabilized at the level of mutual acceptance, more-or-less cordial, at a level of relatively low involvement.

Two important additional things should be said about these limited, low-intensity relations of mutual tolerance and acceptance that remain embedded in a context of functional specificity. First, limited as they are, such relationships nevertheless represent a situation drastically different from the hostility of forced subordination or of overt group conflict. Their importance is not downgraded by the fact that they do not involve the actual and total disappearance of categorical distinctions. Second, the level of casually amiable coexistence we have tried to suggest is, after all, about as far as most so-called ingroup friendships go in many areas of present-day American life. Social peace and a relatively satisfying community life in a pluralistic society do not require either total consensus [106] or intense brotherly love. A lot is accomplished if mutual toleration permits the growth of

---

[106] Under the conditions of a particular field experiment, Newcomb shows that ". . . the stronger an individual's attraction to another person, the greater the likelihood that he will perceive agreement with that other person concerning objects important and relevant to him." [Theodore M. Newcomb, *The Acquaintance Process* (New York: Holt, Rinehart & Winston, Inc., 1961), p. 70.]

interdependence and, then, of understanding, sufficient unto the orderly functioning of viable communities.

We must remember, however, that as *personal* interaction (which nevertheless occurs on terms of categorical discrimination) diminishes in the highly segregated urban environment, the processes of reciprocal social control, even such unequal control as existed on the old-style Southern plantation, tend to break down. Fewer and fewer interactions of a Negro person with a white person involve repeated contact with the same concrete individuals over a long period and in many areas of life. Shared experiences decrease; mutuality of role-taking diminishes; interdependence of *particular* persons across the color line becomes less prevalent and less crucial. Withdrawal of reciprocity on the part of a specific person becomes less effective as a sanction.

To the extent that person-to-person reciprocal social control breaks down, the regulation of intergroup interaction either fails altogether or is shifted into the area of collective and formalized controls—above all, administrative and legal action. Hence, the greater the diminution of informal control, the greater the likelihood that intergroup relations will come to have an important political aspect.

Lack of continuous, fine-grained communication among the subgroupings of a social system exposed to rapid changes, especially from outside, means that when changes finally *are* communicated the new information is likely to be unexpected and massive and correspondingly difficult to accept and cope with rapidly. If members of each segment of a community are in touch almost exclusively with a communication net confined to that segment, even changes arising from local sources will become known belatedly and fitfully in other portions of the social structure. If the changes are of a character to pose problems of adaptation, the more erratic and delayed the communication, the more difficult the subsequent coping behavior is likely to be.[107]

It seems likely that in the long run the greater the extent to which a subordinated ethnic grouping is permitted and helped to acquire the *cultural and social characteristics that are highly valued in the dominant grouping,* the less likely it is that enforced segregation and systematic discrimination can be maintained.[108]

Historically, the Negro minority in America has tried each of the alterna-

---

[107] For a specific illustration see: Johan Galtung, "A Model for Studying Images of Participants in a Conflict: Southville," *The Journal of Social Issues,* XV, No. 4 (1959), 38-39; also, Robin M. Williams, Jr. and Margaret Ryan, eds.: *Schools in Transition* (Chapel Hill: University of North Carolina Press, 1954), pp. 80-110 and 233-41.

[108] Cf. Eugene P. Dvorin, *Racial Separation in South Africa* (Chicago: The University of Chicago Press, 1952), pp. 191-92.

tives that Wirth has mentioned in his delineation of four types of minorities: (1) militant outbursts (as expressed, for example, by the hundreds of ante-bellum slave insurrections [109] or by the leadership of Harriet Tubman and Fredrick Douglass); (2) pluralism, as advocated by Booker Washington and his followers; (3) secession, as illustrated by the huge popular support given by Negroes to Marcus Garvey and his Back to Africa movement, or by the post-Civil War migration to Kansas by "Pap" Singleton and his followers; and (4) assimilation.

Each of these movements has, in the past, fallen short of successful con-clusion. Militant outbursts failed because of the superior power of the domi-nant group and the lack of full Negro support. Pluralism has not endured because the economic interdependence of whites and Negroes was too com-plex to insure any permanent separation of the races and because the close relationship of pluralism to differential treatment and inferior resources of Negroes became increasingly clear. Secession proved impractical since the bonds linking the American Negro to Africa were not culturally realistic and because the cultural linkage and socioeconomic interdependence of the Negro with American life proved stronger than anticipated. Assimilation has hitherto failed because of the extent of anti-Negro prejudice and discrimina-tory practices that are embedded in the American culture and because the ultimate legislative authority has failed to remove completely the legal struc-ture supporting segregation or to implement fully the laws protecting the civil rights of American minorities.

Our current observations of action in Negro subcommunities leads us to believe that American Negro leaders have largely abandoned the first three of these alternatives and have currently selected as their area for purposive action the removal of current statutes and practices perpetuating segrega-tion and discrimination, holding as the ultimate goal, integration into all walks of American community life. The value premise underlying the efforts of most Negro leaders observed in this study certainly was the desirability of integration. This was articulately stated more often in the North than in the South; however, the words and actions of leaders in both regions of the country indicated a belief in the eventual end of segregation and the neces-sity of positing integration as their goal. The strongest group solidarity in smaller Negro communities exists among the persons most dedicated to militant action toward integration, and their actions are couched with care-ful reference to democratic ideals. Though this orientation encourages strong

---

[109] Louis Wirth, "The Problem of Minority Groups," in Ralph Linton, ed., *The Science of Man* (New York: Columbia University Press, 1945), p. 354. The myth of the universal contentment of slaves hardly deserves further refutation. Cf. *The Southerner as American,* Charles Grier Sellers, Jr., ed. (Chapel Hill: The University of North Carolina Press, 1960), 16: ". . . during the Civil War the loyalty of slaves to their masters was the exception rather than the rule." It may be recalled that about 200,000 Negroes served in the Union armies.

pride in racial membership, it also reiterates the desirability of integration into democratic American society. Many affirmations of this approach to social action were expressed by militant Negro leaders in the communities we studied. Even the most militantly hostile race men indicate that if America actually lived up to its democratic ideals, they would be satisfied, or they state that they look forward eventually to a National Association for the Advancement of *all* People.

The simultaneous emphasis of Negro leaders on group solidarity and desire for integration has come about partly because they believe that integration is opposed by such a large segment of the white population that it can be achieved only by concerted, cooperative endeavor. In general, the strong emphasis on Negro solidarity and race pride are compatible with the desire for integration because the Negro is so inextricably a part of the American culture and society that the values and sentiments used to stimulate race pride and promote group unity are very similar to nominally dominant values and sentiments that are held in the general community toward which the Negro aims.

Thus, this group solidarity of Negroes in America is directed toward goals directly compatible with the manifest ideals of the national culture, despite the social isolation of most Negro communities. Whether hope too long deferred may eventually drive the awakened and aspiring Negro population into movements of nationalistic separatism now depends upon the white citizens and their leaders and government.

CHAPTER 9

SITUATIONAL VARIATION,
EXEMPTION, AND SOCIAL CHANGE

PATTERN AND VARIABILITY

Throughout the preceding chapters we have concentrated upon the search for patterns, for regularities, correlations, sequences. We found much regularity. Yet all social behavior occurs here and now, in a particular place, at a particular time, with a particular combination of people and circumstances. The stability of recurrent social patterns is the outcome of numerous interrelated processes; it is dynamic, not static. Recurrence is the persistence of constancies through endless variations, like the subtle identity of a man's signature, so indefinitely varied and so unmistakably similar from one time to the next. We use a signature as an identifying sign of a continuing entity, a person. Yet we can detect forgery by finding that two signatures purporting to have been made by the same person are *literally* identical.

Our research never allowed us to forget the facts of variability and change. In attitudes and behavior relating to ethnic relations we found marked variations and differences: among communities; between North and South; among different racial and ethnic minorities; in different settings of interaction (work, neighborhood, etc.); in different specific situations within these settings; among different participants in the same concrete situation; and within the behavior of the same participant over a period of time. All studies showed much variation in intergroup relations in different communities and different situations.[1] Nor is such variation confined to our own society. Research on intergroup relations in Britain documents the fact of "remarkable regional variations" [2] in relations between the host population and colored immigrants as well as in the character of the immigrant communities themselves. Within the United States, studies of racial desegregation repeatedly call attention to ". . . the crucial role of the situation in which the individual is required to function." [3]

Situational variations in the responses of the same person seem to be great enough to raise important problems for general behavior theory.[4] One such problem, for example, is whether we can get better predictions from a certain amount of information about the situation or from a certain amount of information about the individual's attitudes or about his past behavior in other concrete situations. There is no simple answer or set of answers to this problem. Different individuals vary in responsiveness or resistance to differences in situations. Different types of situations exert more or less pressure upon personality-determined dispositions to act. The kind of information required for prediction varies with the permutations of individual and situational variables, from instance to instance.

It seems clear, however, that we will rarely be safe in taking a nominalistic view of either psychological person or sociological situation. Both are entity constructions, to be treated with the same care and methodological respect.

> Is there variance among a population of responses collected at various times from various persons which is associated with the individual? This turns out empirically to be equivalent to the reliability coefficient of a psychological measure. These are often high, but occasionally get as low as zero, and uniformly tend to be lower as the persons under study are more homogeneous sociologically. . . . Often enough one can predict re-

---

[1] Compare the conclusions of the several articles in *The Journal of Social Issues,* VIII, No. 1, and IX, No. 1.

[2] Sydney Collins, *Coloured Minorities in Britain* (London: Lutterworth Press, 1957), p. 17.

[3] John D. Campbell and Marian Radke Yarrow, "Personal and Situational Variables in Adaptation to Change," *The Journal of Social Issues,* XIV, No. 1 (1958), 29.

[4] Isidor Chein, "The Problems of Inconsistency: A Restatement," *The Journal of Social Issues,* V, No. 3 (1949), 52-61.

sponses better from knowing a person's social locus and immediate setting than one can from a knowledge of this biological person's responses in past situations." [5]

When we wish to predict collective or group behaviors, all of the possible differences between individual attitude and individual action remain, but additional sources of divergence between attitudes and subsequent behavior come into play.[6]

A concern with consistency in intergroup relations initially developed in large part independently of related work in other topical areas of sociology, anthropology, and psychology. In the field of intergroup relations the concern was to understand discrepancies between creed and practice, on the one hand, and between different situations or contexts, on the other. Meanwhile psychologists concerned with social perception and cognitive processes were developing the ideas of balance, congruity, and dissonance. These concepts all involved ". . . the notion that thoughts, beliefs, attitudes and behavior tend to organize themselves in meaningful and sensible ways. . . . The concept of consistency . . . assumes that inconsistency is a noxious state setting up pressures to eliminate it or reduce it." [7]

As a consequence of the work of experimental psychology, especially as illustrated in the publications of Heider,[8] Festinger,[9] Newcomb,[10] F. Allport,[11] and others,[12] we have been made sharply aware of problems of balance and imbalance in perceptions and of consonance and dissonance in cognitive processes. Important findings from research on these problems lend further depth to the abundant sociological and anthropological studies of situational variability.[13] Available evidence leaves no doubt that knowl-

---

[5] Donald T. Campbell, "Common Fate, Similarity and Other Indices of the Status of Aggregates of Persons as Social Entities," *Behavioral Science,* III (1958), 14-25. Reprinted in *Decisions, Values and Groups,* Dorothy Willner, ed. (New York: Pergamon Press, 1960), p. 200.

[6] Herbert Hyman, "Inconsistencies as a Problem in Attitude Measurement," *The Journal of Social Issues,* V, No. 3 (1949), 40.

[7] Robert B. Zajonc, "The Concepts of Balance, Congruity, and Dissonance," *Public Opinion Quarterly,* XXIV, No. 2 (Summer, 1960), 280.

[8] F. Heider, "Attitudes and Cognitive Organization," *Journal of Psychology,* XXI, First Half (January, 1946), 107-12.

[9] Leon Festinger, *A Theory of Cognitive Dissonance* (New York: Harper & Row, Publishers, 1957).

[10] Theodore M. Newcomb, "An Approach to the Study of Communicative Acts," *Psychological Review,* LX, No. 6 (November, 1953), 393-404; and "The Prediction of Interpersonal Attraction," *American Psychologist,* XI, No. 11 (November, 1956), 575-86.

[11] Floyd H. Allport, *Theories of Perception and the Concept of Structure* (New York: John Wiley & Sons, Inc., 1955).

[12] For example, C. E. Osgood and P. H. Tannenbaum, "The Principle of Congruity in the Prediction of Attitude Change," *Psychological Review,* LXII, No. 1 (January, 1955), 42-55.

[13] L. Proudfoot and H. S. Wilson, "The Clubs in Crisis: Race Relations in the New West Africa," *American Journal of Sociology,* LXVI, No. 4 (January 1961), 317-24.

edge of generalized prejudice alone would have been an exceedingly poor basis for understanding the outcomes of intergroup interaction.

Illustrations

The Cornell Studies accumulated a considerable body of systematic observations in community contexts, showing instances of seemingly inconsistent behavior. For example, a restaurant proprietor testifies in vigorous terms that he does not and will not accept Negro patrons. On the following day a Negro member of the field staff enters the establishment and is served with promptness and cordiality. And the opposite pattern is abundantly documented: individuals testifying to interracial goodwill and acting in an equalitarian, nondiscriminatory manner are later observed in other situations to express strong prejudice and to act accordingly.

Illustrations of the variability of behavior were found in many different settings. For example, we initiated several situations in a mixed Polish-Ukrainian-Italian neighborhood in which about 40 Negroes lived in three old houses. They were the only Negroes who lived in this section—southerners who originally had come north as migratory bean pickers in the fields nearby. Prejudice against them was outspoken not only on the part of the whites in the neighborhood, but also on the part of northern Negroes living in other sections of the city. We were told again and again that establishments in the area discriminated against them. The field staff mapped the area carefully, and designated some thirty-odd establishments as an initial panel. Then the staff members patronized each of these establishments, and in the course of conversation tried to ascertain each proprietor's policy on handling Negro trade. Finally, at the most promising of these establishments, test cases were set up. These illustrations are illuminating:

1. At the S Tavern, the bartender told white fieldworkers that he tells Negro customers he is out of what they want. If they want to use the phone, he tells them it is out of order. This was surprising, because a Negro fieldworker had already used the phone and had been served. When four Negroes visited a few days later, they were served without incident.

2. Five Negro researchers stopped at another tavern; the reception was extremely friendly. A few hours later, white researchers asked him if Negroes ever came to his place. He denied that they did. Another fieldworker put the same question to his wife a few days later. She also denied it.

Consider the following: the setting was a rather run-down tavern patronized by a close-knit group of laborers—a very informal social center for a group who professed strong dislike of Negroes. There was evidence that Negroes were not served there. A white researcher visited the place several times, to get to know the bartender and his operating practices. Then he arranged to have a Negro fieldworker meet him there one afternoon at 5:30 P.M. At 5:25 the white fieldworker informed the bartender:

> *Say, Frank, I want to ask you something. I'm working with a colored fellow on this survey. I told him to meet me here at 5:30. Okay with you?*
>
> Bartender: *D'you say* colored? *Oh, jeez—what'd you do that for? I don't serve colored here. You shouldn'ta done that. I don't want to have any trouble. As soon as I got one in here they'd all start coming in. Can't you meet him someplace else?*
>
> Fieldworker: *I told him to meet me here at 5:30.*

The next several minutes witnessed an energetic attempt on the part of the bartender to convince the researcher that he could not serve the Negro because there would be violent objections from the white patrons. The researcher countered this argument by naming all the places nearby where Negroes are served without incident. Finally, a compromise:

> Fieldworker: *Look, Frank, I'll make a deal with you. You serve us one drink and we'll get out. I can't head him off at the door. He knows what the score is. He'd know it would be because you wouldn't serve him. I don't want to embarrass the guy. He's a nice kid. You serve us one drink—then we'll go someplace else—okay?*
>
> Bartender: *Well, okay, but drink it fast, will ya, and then beat it. I don't want to have any trouble. And don't introduce me to him. I don't want the people here to think I know him.*

The Negro was served. There were stares all around, but nothing more. When the white fieldworker returned two days later, the bartender was unusually friendly.

In some situations there were no appropriate behavioral cues to guide the confused participant. A white woman who taught a theatrical make-up class was thrown into a flurry of aimless confusion when a Negro girl who unexpectedly attended the practice session of her class asked her for an appropriate shade of powder. She knew which shade would be best, but she had no idea of how to react to a Negro girl attending the class. With no other adult present from whom she might get cues, she persisted in her aimless confusion.

Actual versus hypothetical definitions of intergroup situations

Although the research difficulties are tremendous, some progress has been made in studying the relation between attitudes expressed in one situation and attitude expression or other behavior in other situations. The basic problem here has traditionally been formulated as the problem of attitudes versus actions, or of the predictive value of attitudes (elicited in a research situation by interview, test, or other techniques) for behavior in real-life situations. It has long been recognized that there is an extremely wide variation in the degree to which attitudes and actions are or are not consistent or stable. Our first approach was to compare white majority-group persons' responses to hypothetical situations with their reports of their feelings and actions in *actual* situations.

A random sample of majority-group persons in Hometown reported whether or not they had contact with Negroes or Jews in any of three social contexts: in the neighborhood, in clubs or organizations, or on the job. For each social context in which they had contact with a minority-group person they were asked, *Do you feel different about these (Negroes, Jews)* [*than about persons like yourself*]? For each social context in which they did not have contact, they were asked if they thought they would feel different if they were to have contact. The responses of those people who do have contact with a member of a minority group in any of these social contexts can then be compared with the responses of similar people who do *not* have contact. The latter are responding to imaginary, hypothetical situations; the former are reporting their attitudes within a known and defined social context. Consequently the comparison is in reality a comparison of general orientations to a particular range of situations, rather than a more precise comparison of the definitions of strictly comparable individual situations. With all its limitations, this method of comparison yields highly interesting results. Responses to hypothetical situations show a regular pattern, similar to the pattern we have come to expect of a series of attitude items that constitute a single attitude dimension. But responses to actual situations are much less inclined toward unidimensionality: they are far more responsive to the particular idiosyncrasies of the individual situation.

The proportion of people who think they would feel different toward Negroes in a *hypothetical* situation is significantly greater than the proportion of people who think they would feel different toward Jews, in all three social contexts. Table 9.1 summarizes these differences between actual and hypothetical situations by comparing the proportion of people who feel different (or think they would feel different) toward Jews and toward Negroes in each social setting.

The respondents were classified into more homogeneous subgroups on the basis of their social and psychological characteristics. Nineteen separate characteristics and combinations of characteristics were used in this way— some of them indexing background characteristics (such as sex, age, education, and occupation), others the respondents' aspirations, and still others

Table 9.1

Comparison of the definitions of actual and hypothetical situations
involving Negroes and Jews

	Percentage difference between the proportion of people who feel different toward Jews and the proportion who feel different toward Negroes	
	Actual Situations	Hypothetical Situations
Social Context		
Neighborhood	+16%	+52%
Organization	+ 3%	+32%
On the job	+ 9%	+17%

their general psychological orientations. In many of these subgroups, *for actual situations* there is either no difference in the proportions of people who feel different toward Negroes and toward Jews, or the proportion of people who feel different toward Jews is actually greater than the proportion who feel different toward Negroes. This is never found to be true with respect to hypothetical situations. There is almost no relationship between any of these social and psychological factors and the definition of *hypothetical* situations. The proportion of people who think that they would feel different toward Negroes or Jews in any particular hypothetical situation does not seem to depend on the particular characteristics of that group of persons—only on the intimacy of the situation and whether it is Jews or Negroes who are involved. But this is far from the case for *actual* situations. *These definitions are far more dependent on the particular social relations that minority- and majority-group persons develop within the contexts of particular situations.* These social relations are dependent not only on the stereotyped beliefs that each group has of the other, but also—and far more importantly—upon the social and psychological characteristics of the individuals who interact in these situations. It would seem that individuals' hypothetical expectations of how they would act in the situation are significantly modified by their actual experiences with particular Negroes and particular Jews in particular situations.

Many other pieces of evidence pointed in the same direction. Thus five studies of the racial attitudes of white high school students consistently showed also that the individual: (1) reacted more favorably to actual than to hypothetical situations, and (2) was less likely to state that he or she would object to the presence of Negroes as social contacts than to state that other white students would personally object.

Situational Patterning in Intergroup Relations [14]

One major conclusion of this analysis is that the technique of asking people how they would behave in hypothetical situations has only limited usefulness for research on the *situational* components of behavior. It is apparent that the crucial variables that enter into the definition of actual situations play a much smaller role in the definition of hypothetical situations. Thus the problem we have posed—to understand the conditions under which attitudes and action are or are not consistent or stable—requires a more direct even if less refined research technique than asking about hypothetical situations in a structured questionnaire. In ensuing research, we relied primarily on participant-observation, combined with interviews of major participants in the observed situations.

In using the concept, situation, we were faced with a complex notion, previously used to cover many different social phenomena. Like the terms "society" and "culture," it has served to call attention to relationships. By so doing, it has prevented us from overlooking factors that must be taken into account for scientific analysis to do full justice to the empirical phenomena of behavior. And it has pointed up similarities among types of behavior that on the surface appear to be quite different.

Nevertheless, the concept must be more carefully delineated. We came to define a situation as a series of interactions, located in space and time, and perceived by the participants as an event: in this usage "situation" is a delimiting term, cutting out from the flow of experience a particular series of interpersonal actions that are seen by the participants as a describable event, separable from preceding and succeeding events, constraining the participants to act in particular ways, and having its own unique consequences.

As we have mentioned previously, the most easily accessible intergroup situations were the least fruitful for our purposes: many of these were so highly patterned [15] that we could only describe an existing state of affairs, but could not study the processes by which this particular state of affairs had come into being. It was only in those few situations where the par-

---

[14] A considerable part of this section appears in condensed and somewhat different form in Melvin L. Kohn and Robin M. Williams, Jr., "Situational Patterning in Intergroup Relations," *American Sociological Review,* XXI, No. 2 (April, 1956), 164-74.

[15] "Although situations are in their very nature dynamic and unique, as soon as they become socialized—that is to say, built into the framework of society—they tend to become standardized to a certain extent. Thus we must distinguish between what is called patterned and unpatterned situations." Karl Mannheim, *Man and Society In An Age of Reconstruction* (London: Routledge & Kegan Paul, Ltd., 1940), p. 301.

ticipants' behavior was not already highly patterned by past experience in similar situations that we were able to study the processes by which people develop their definitions of a situation.

Since hypothetical situations were not adequate, and actual unpatterned situations occurred but rarely, the research worker was left with little choice but to initiate new situations. The procedure had to be covert, for if the participants knew that the situations were created for research purposes their definitions would be radically altered. Thus were many problems necessarily created, on both ethical and practical levels: The procedure involved a degree of manipulation; it posed a degree of danger to the participant-observers and perhaps to other participants as well; it created barriers to observation and interviewing. Lacking preferable alternatives, however, we felt justified in initiating the series of 43 situations in which we could observe and interview in a reasonably systematic fashion.

In their social contexts that were neither so intimate as automatically to exclude Negro participation, nor so functionally specific as to make acceptance of Negroes unproblematic, these situations were initiated. Such episodes were most likely to be found in service establishments such as restaurants and taverns. Within this restricted area—public service establishments, voluntary organizations, and the like—in which it was possible to initiate situations, we attempted to vary the situational conditions to the maximum degree possible.

Our conclusions are based necessarily on studies in a very limited range of social institutions: we could not initiate new situations in industrial organizations or in schools. Thus we cannot assert that the present findings are directly applicable to institutions outside of the range studied. It seems probable, however, that though the processes by which unpatterned situations arose in these institutions were certainly different from those of some other areas of our research, the processes by which they came to be defined by participants were similar.

In service establishments with little previous occasion to confront Negro patrons we staked out our participant research program. We studied many such establishments. In each instance we attempted, by informal interviews with key persons, to canvass the state of affairs before initiating action. Then we brought in Negro patrons. Observers located at strategic points recorded all overt behavior. Later, whenever possible, we returned to reappraise the situation and interview as many of the key participants as possible. All participant-observers later recorded chronologically the events that had transpired and filled out recording forms that had been designed to elicit their interpretations of these events. (See Appendix E for samples of recording form.)

As an example of the procedure followed, let us consider one of these situations in some detail. A Negro couple (members of the research staff) entered a working-class tavern that was known to discriminate. White observers, some of whom had patronized the establishment frequently enough to be able to ask questions without arousing undue suspicion, were seated at strategic spots throughout the tavern. The following is the chronological accounts written by the Negro researcher, a stimulus participant:

Researcher: Entered at 10:15. People looked around, but we strode dauntlessly to table near fire. Most people seemed to look around, notice us, and comment. I needed a match and went to the couple in the first booth. The fellow had a lighter. I asked for a light. He replied eagerly, *Yes, sir,* and flicked his lighter for me. Testing the afternoon hunch on restrooms, I went to the men's room. As I passed the ladies' room, the bartender blocked my way.

Bartender: *What did you say?*

Researcher: *How do you do. I didn't say anything. I'm looking for the men's room.*

Bartender: *I'll show you.* He leads me to the men's room, stands at the next urinal in a grand rapport gesture, and says confidentially, *Now, mind you, I don't have anything against you people. I went to school with you folks and I've got a lot of friends among you. But some of my customers don't like to see you in here. Five or six of them have already complained to me and left. Now I can't have that. I hope you'll understand if I ask you to leave.*

Researcher: *It's pretty hard to understand. I went to war for these people.*

Bartender: *Yeah, I went to war too. But some of our people are funny. They don't like to see you in here. So I'll have to ask you to go.*

Researcher: He leaves, and another young Caucasian enters. I am pretty damn upset. I say to him, *I suppose you're one of these fine people who wants me to leave.*

Man: *No, no, everybody's all right with me. What's the matter, you have some trouble?*

Researcher: *You're damned tootin'.* I go back to the table. Several people are entering and leaving for no apparent connected reason. No one comes to wait on us. Ten minutes later I go to the cigarette machine. Bartender stops me again.

Bartender: *Say, are you going to leave or are we going to have some trouble? Some of the boys are pretty hot. Now I suggest that you get out of here before something happens. We don't want your kind. Remember, I've told you.*

Researcher: I go back to the table. L (the Negro girl) is enthusiastic. The waitress comes near to clean off a table, and L calls her three times. Waitress tosses her head and leaves. Band returns (from intermission) and begins to play. After about five danceless numbers, three couples move out on floor. We go to dance. Here comes bartender again.

Bartender: *Now look, I've told you three times. War or no war, now you get out of here. We don't want you. I've got my customers to think of. Come on, get off the floor and get out of here before you have trouble.*

Researcher: I ask him to call the cops if there's trouble, but he demurs and shoves us off dance floor. We leave. Must have been a great sideshow to the white customers and observers, but I'm boiling so much I could kill every white face. Decide I'm through with this damn stunt. As we left, a fellow standing in front of the cigarette machine said, *Hell, we're all Americans. I'm all for you.* Bartender was just behind us, shepherding us out, and he stopped and asked, *What did you say?* I didn't hear the rest, but the fellow was evidently championing us in a weak but determined way. Maybe there is some hope for some white folks.

This is the chronological report of the same incident by one of the white observers:

Observer: I arrived to find the bar crowded. D and J (observers) arrived, went through barroom to dance hall just as I was climbing on a recently-vacated stool at the bar. Proprietor was serving a tray of drinks to blonde waitress. The bartender was standing akimbo at north end of the bar, waiting for electric mixer to finish stirring a drink for him. Door opened, Negro researchers walked in, going through barroom and into hallway to dance floor. Blonde looked around at them, staring, then looked back at proprietor with her mouth open.

Proprietor (amazed): *Well, how do you like that!*

Bartender (turning): *What?*

Proprietor (simultaneously with blonde): *Those two jigs that just walked through here.*

Blonde: *Two colored people just went in.*

Bartender (in surprise): *Where'd they go?*

Blonde: *Into the dance hall.*

Observer: Enter Jane, a second waitress, from kitchen.

Jane: *I'm not going in there. What can we do? This never hap-pened before.* (to proprietor) *What'll we do?* (anguished) *Do I HAVE to serve them?*

Proprietor (peering through service peephole from bar to dance floor): *Let 'em sit.*

Bartender: *Yes, stay away from them. I didn't see them. Where'd they go?*

Blonde: *They're at the table for six. What are we going to do?*

Jane: *I'm not going in there. This is awful.*

Observer: Proprietor ducks under the lift-up gate at the end of the bar, takes a quick look into dance hall, then back under the gate board to his station behind the bar.

Proprietor: *Just let them sit.*

Observer: For the next several minutes, the proprietor inquired anxiously, from time to time, *What are they doing now? Did they go?* Each time he looked more amazed. Said to me, *Never in my time here did we have any of them at the bar.* After a wait of perhaps 15 to 18 minutes:

Proprietor: *Well, I'm going to see that they leave.*

Observer: He took off apron, started to duck under the bar gate again, then said to bartender: *You better go in and get them out of there. I don't think I should go, because my name's on the license . . . if there's any trouble.*

Schoolteacher (sitting with husband at the bar): *How can you get them to leave?* (then to observer) *She was an attractive little thing, wasn't she?*

Proprietor (again): *I wish they'd go.* (then to blonde waitress) *Are any of your customers leaving?*

Blonde: *A couple, but I think they were leaving anyway. They'd asked for their check. Others are looking around at them, and they're all talking about it . . . it gives me the creeps to have to walk in there, and know they're staring at me, expecting me to come over and wait on them.*

Jane (to observer): *We never had colored people here. This is the first couple that ever went in there.* (shrugging) *I'm just not going in. What a time they picked to come! Saturday night—our busiest time! Why didn't they make it some weeknight?—there aren't so many people here.*

Observer: By this time the bartender had taken off his apron, left the barroom, and a few minutes later returned and went directly into the men's room, followed by B (the Negro researcher).

Proprietor (after a minute or so): *Where did the bartender go?*

Jane: *In the men's room.*

Teacher: *They've been in there quite a while.*

Proprietor (ducking under gate, apron and all): *I'd better see what's going on. He may have a knife.* (Goes and peers through four inch opening, as he holds the door ajar. Returns.) *They're okay.*

Observer: Bartender returned to bar, researcher to the dance hall.

Bartender: *He wanted to give me an argument. Said he was a veteran.*

Proprietor: *They all have something like that to say, I guess. I want them to get out. What did he say?*

Bartender: *He said yes.*

Observer (turning to man on stool next to him): *This is some situation, isn't it?*

Man (venomously): *It stinks!*

Blonde (watching Negroes through doorway): *He's sitting down. It's a good thing the orchestra is having intermission.*

Proprietor: *Yes, I suppose they'd be dancing.*

Bartender: *That looks like that Robeson stuff.*

Blonde: *I can't think of any time I've seen colored people in here.*

Bartender: *Stay away from them. Don't look at them. Don't let them catch your eye.* (Waitress departs for dance hall again.)

Youth at bar (to proprietor): *Maybe you can get a date.* (Proprietor snorts, ready to blow his top.)

Teacher: *He's getting cigarettes.*

Bartender: *Where is he?*

Jane: *At the cigarette machine.*

Bartender (apron and all, under the bar gate again): *I'll tell him to get going.* (Goes and speaks to researcher, then back to bar.) *They'll leave, I think. I told him there were a couple of fellows were going to see about it, if they didn't.* (Just about this time the orchestra's intermission is over; they return to the bandstand.)

Proprietor: *There goes the band. I suppose they'll start to dance now. I wish I'd thought to hold up the orchestra until they got out of here.* (to blonde) *Watch them now.* (to Jane) *Jane, get me a sandwich, will you?*

Teacher: *You're in a tough spot, aren't you? Are you going to serve them?*

Proprietor: *No.*

Bartender: *We'll have to put them out for causing a disturbance.*

Blonde: *Four of my couples have left.*

Proprietor: *That does it! Go in and get them out of there, NOW!*

Observer: Bartender went into dance hall, one man followed him, and three or four other men gathered around. The Negro researchers walked out through the bar. Bartender went back behind the bar and the man resumed his seat.

Proprietor (who had followed, with his eyes, the Negro girl as she left): *Did you see the cute little smile she had on?*

Bartender: *Well, that buck thinks he's tough, I guess. Robeson stuff.*

Customer: *You could have served them. They got rights!*

Bartender: *You want to make something of it? Are you with them?*

Customer: *No, I'm not with them. They got a right to have a drink. You all stink.*

Bartender (threateningly): *Pick up your change and drift. You want to drink with them? Go on down to the C.D. Bar. Lots of them there.*

Observer: Man picked up his change and stalked to door, mumbling.

Proprietor: *What the hell do you suppose is the matter with him? He's not drunk.*

Teacher: *Maybe he's one of those people who has Negro friends.*

Another customer: *In Germany those black bastards got everything they wanted. Excuse me, Ma'am.* (to teacher) *Two or three of them would come along and take a white soldier's girl right away from him. I hate their guts. They want to stay away from me. I just wish you'd told me, I could have thrown them out . . .*

Proprietor: *You can if they come back. You can throw out their whole gang. They've probably gone to get the bunch. I don't think they came in just to get a drink.*

Teacher's husband: *No, I think they came here deliberately to get served or make trouble. If they dropped in for a drink, they would have left when the bartender talked to him. I think this must be planned somehow.*

Bartender: *Yeah, Robeson stuff. Spooks! Little Peekskill, they wanted to make out of this place.*

Teacher: *I feel sorry for them.* (to me) *She looked like a real nice girl. I have to teach my children tolerance and things like that . . .*

From reports such as these, documenting 43 situations, we were able to amass a considerable body of data on behavior in relatively unpatterned situations. These data not only provide a basis for demonstrating variability of behavior in intergroup situations, but also for developing hypotheses about the ways in which relatively unpatterned intergroup situations are defined by the participants.

Very concretely, the unpatterned situations uniformly served to show these characteristics:

1. In public places of business, the owner or manager or representative frequently does not know whether or not he will act in a discriminatory way. We observed that in such situations, he actively seeks cues from his white customers that may indicate whether or not these customers would object to his serving Negro patrons.

2. Consequently, the first overt acts by any white customer are likely

to be disproportionately important in determining whether or not the owner decides that his customers object, and hence, whether or not the Negro would-be patrons are served.

3. At least in the particular situations observed, direct intervention by a white customer on behalf of a Negro customer almost always brought service for the Negro person; we have described the one exception we found.

4. Inquisitive white interviewers who ask whether a restaurant serves Negroes generally receive a negative reply, partly because of the businessman's assumption that anyone interested enough to ask the question is likely to be strongly prejudiced against Negroes.

5. Typically discrimination is not simply a matter of serving or not serving, admitting or not admitting. A whole battery of behavioral devices are used: delayed service, brusqueness, spilled soup, cold coffee, heavily salted food, watered beer, overcharges, and the classic case of ostentatious breaking of glasses used by Negro patrons to demonstrate to them and to the white patrons that whites will not be served from the same glasses.

The situations observed, it must be stressed, were all selected precisely because they were relatively unpatterned. Behavior was not predetermined by the participants' past experiences in similar situations. Obviously, most situations in which Negroes interact with whites are not of this variety— it is the atypical situation that is defined on the spot, on the basis of idiosyncratic factors operating in this situation. To put these unpatterned situations in perspective, it is helpful to view them in the context of intergroup situations generally.

1. In stable, recurring, intergroup situations, well-defined and mutually-understood patterns of behavior have become institutionalized into patterns of appropriate conduct.

2. Frequently, as in many aspects of intergroup relations in the Deep South, the appropriate conduct will be different for Negro and for white. But it also is frequently the case, as in casual, functionally specific situations in the North, that appropriate conduct for whites and Negroes will be the same.

3. However, especially in small northern cities, most majority-group persons had extremely limited contact with members of minority groups. Even in the on-the-job situations their contact was likely to be almost entirely with other majority-group persons.

4. In those situations where the acceptance of minority-group persons on a nondiscriminatory basis is well patterned, majority-group persons generally consider the established pattern to be appropriate.

5. But in situations in which there is *not* a pattern of acceptance of minority-group persons, such behavior is likely to be thought of as inappro-

priate or even shocking or outrageous. (Thus, when the majority-group person is asked how he would act in a hypothetical situation, he will frequently say that he would discriminate.) [16]

6. Situations in which neither discriminatory nor nondiscriminatory behavior is patterned may be called *unpatterned* or partially patterned situations. In these, the forms of interaction may be unpatterned for a variety of reasons. For example, the situation may be so foreign to the past experiences of participants that they find themselves in a quandary. Or any individual participant may feel constrained to act in two or more different and incompatible ways. Or several participants may hold entirely different definitions of the situation.

7. These unpatterned situations are focal points for change in intergroup relations. New patterns of nondiscriminatory behavior *may* emerge from these situations. New patterns of discriminatory behavior *may* emerge too. Because the unpatterned situation is shot through with ambiguity and clashes of interest, apparently minor and idiosyncratic factors may decisively affect the outcome of the situation. In situations observed in this research, such factors as pressure of time, spatial arrangements, initial conduct and self-confidence of the minority-group persons, emotional states of the participants, and expectations as to the precedent-setting character of the situation, have all at one time or another been of great importance.

8. When an unpatterned situation does become defined, it tends to lose its affective charge, to be taken for granted—to become built into the framework of society. Where the new patterns that are developed in the unpatterned situation are carried over to subsequent situations, this process constitutes an important avenue of social change. Of course, not all unpatterned situations generate new patterns of behavior; and only a small proportion of the patterns that are developed are ever carried over to subsequent situations.[17] Nevertheless, any unpatterned situation is *potentially* the generator of social change.

---

[16] In the analysis of the empirical materials, we distinguish between actual and hypothetical situations on the basis of whether or not the individual has periodic contact with members of the minority social category in that particular type of situation. This operational distinction may obscure the fact that situations may be more or less actual, more or less hypothetical. An individual's orientation may be different for a hypothetical situation that he considers quite improbable (such as the prospect of having Negroes in his social clique) from what it would be for a hypothetical situation that he considers likely to occur. Similarly, there may be important differences between his orientation to an actual situation in which he is only segmentally involved and one that he considers to be very important. It is possible to think of situations as more or less real for the participants—the principal difference between actual and hypothetical situations being that the former are more real by virtue of the fact that the participants have experience in them.

[17] An important problem with which the present research did not attempt to cope is to determine the conditions under which definitions *are* carried over to subsequent situations.

Defining unpatterned situations [18]

In these situations it appeared that the participants attempted to achieve cognitive clarity by striving to assimilate the situation to their past actual or vicarious experience, that is, to categorize it as one instance of a type of situation with which they knew how to cope. The process, of course, was rarely as rational or as purposive as this formulation would imply. Yet behavior in these situations could be interpreted as an attempt to see a socially unstructured situation in terms of one or possibly even of several alternative socially acceptable structures. For example, in the foregoing illustration, the bartender and waitresses perceived the situation as one that could be categorized in either of two ways: (1) here were two Negro out-of-towners who did not realize they were not welcome here; (2) here were a couple of troublemakers who were trying to create trouble here.

The importance of being able to categorize the situation was suggested by their dilemma. If the situation were the first type, they could expect the Negroes to leave when asked politely. If the situation were the second type, they could expect resistance to such a request—the Negroes might cause an immediate disturbance, "come back with their gang," or file suit for violation of the New York State law. Thus the way that the bartender and the waitresses categorized the situation had important implications for their expectations of the Negroes' behavior and for their own feelings of how to act in the situation.

In this example two relatively clear-cut definitions of the situation were possible. At the extreme, even this degree of structure was lacking. In such instances participants reacted by confusion: either the situation was so totally outside the range of their experience or it partook of so wide a variety of possible definitions that these participants were initially unable to see any usable pathway for action at all.

It seemed useful to distinguish between these two possible reactions in an unpatterned situation: to see, first, that the individual could be almost totally unclear about what behavior to expect from others and what would be appropriate action on his own part; to identify, second, cases in which he could have reasonably definite, but contradictory, expectations of how others would act and how he himself should act. We saw that these two reactions differed in degree only, and it was difficult to distinguish between them in some concrete situations. Nevertheless, the distinction was useful because the probable future actions of the person whose orientation was primarily marked by *confusion* were evidently different from the probable

---

[18] Analysis based on Melvin Kohn, *Analysis of Situational Patterning in Intergroup Relations* (Ph.D. thesis, Cornell University, 1952).

future actions of the person whose orientation was primarily marked by *contradiction.*[19]

In the situations studied, the participants who were primarily *confused* actively sought cues from others' behavior that could be useful in clarifying their own definitions of the situation. Where formal leadership roles existed, other participants turned to the presumed leaders for clarification.

The unfamiliar situation is, by definition, initially one of uncertainty, which is another way of saying that it induces some degree of insecurity. Past experience does not suffice as a guide, and old norms may not lead to the usual results. New situations are likely, therefore, to instigate heightened alertness—including a generalized vigilance toward cues that may indicate what action will lead to what consequences. Under the circumstances of uncertainty and sharpened attentiveness, the individual who first acts with an appearance of decisiveness and confidence is likely to have marked influence. It can and does often happen that the people in leadership positions are themselves confused; for them the situation is not even structured enough to suggest where to turn for clarification. We saw that, in consequence, action on the part of *any* other participant became disproportionately important in determining their definitions. Confused participants sought indices of how others defined the situation. Since the crucial question in many of these situations was whether or not membership in a particular racial category (Negro) precluded membership in other groups or categories, the first action to be taken by a white was often interpreted by all as an index of acceptance or rejection.

Initial behavioral cues, of course, could be variously interpreted. The cues themselves were often ambiguous, allowing of several alternative interpretations even to similarly-situated persons. Furthermore, some persons seemed to be more sensitive to nuances of behavior than were others, for reasons that did not seem related to their roles in the situation. However, the most important factor in how participants interpreted behavioral cues was their status in the situation. The behavior of individuals playing certain crucial roles in the situation was more likely than was others' behavior to be taken as an index of the group's orientation. Also, in formal organizations the members frequently took their cues from the behavior of their elected officials. If the club president greeted the Negro lecturer warmly, confused club members were likely to listen attentively. But there were

---

[19] We are at the moment concerned only with situations where the individual participants are initially unable to achieve consistent workable definitions of the situation. Situations where two or more participants have different definitions of the situations will be considered later. In this latter case each participant has a consistent definition, and the problem is that of how definitions are modified, rather than how unstructured situations become defined.

other situations we observed at length in which confusion was never resolved—a permanent state of immobilized chaos was our last report.

The situations just mentioned were instances in which one participant
(or one group of participants) felt that two or more possible orientations
were applicable to the situations. In other situations, two or more *different*
participants held *incompatible* orientations. A case in point was the situation in which the Negro researcher was ejected from the tavern. Both the
researcher and the bartender presented arguments that seemed to make his
own orientation the more logical of the two, but neither seemed to act as if
he really thought he could convince the other. Rather, each seemed to be
reinforcing his own values. Each comprehended the other's orientation well
enough to be able to offer counterarguments, but neither sympathized with
the other's position. Each seemed to become more and more emotionally
involved as the other staunchly defended his own position and suggested
the implausibility of his opponent's.

In other words, in these situations in which the conflict of orientation
centers on values that are highly important to the participants, overt conflict serves only to strengthen initial orientations and to increase the emotional involvement of the participants in the situation.

In some situations, conflict of orientation between participants led to one
of the participants acceding to the other's demands. But, in none of the
observed situations did direct and overt interpersonal conflict seem to
change the initial orientations of the protagonists, though it often forced
one of the protagonists to accede to the other's demands.

The redefinition of a situation on the basis of minimal initial cues from
key participants tended to be the typical event only in those situations
dominantly characterized by confusion or ambiguity. Where two alternative
definitions were applicable to the situation (that is, where the problem was
one of contradiction or conflict rather than of confusion), different behavioral consequences ensued. Usually, in such situations, it was possible
to resolve the conflict by exempting the particular situation from one of the
two definitions—in effect, by assigning one definition of the situation a
higher priority than that accorded the other one. Two forms of exemption
were apparent in the observed situation:

1. A particular *type of event* could be exempted from a more general
definition, as when a restaurant owner who in other contexts did not discriminate against Negroes did discriminate against them in his restaurant
because he felt that business took precedence over other values.

2. A particular *individual* could be exempted in a range of situations—
as when a white treated a particular Negro as different from other Negroes
and therefore acceptable in contexts where other Negroes would be unwel-

come. One bar owner, for example, served former high school classmates, though he refused to serve other Negroes.[20]

On occasion, however, neither of the alternative definitions can be avoided; the situation constrains the participants to act on the basis of both definitions simultaneously. For example, at a dinner meeting tendered to party workers of a major political party, many of the white participants wished to avoid eating with the Negro party workers but at the same time did not wish to rebuff them and risk losing Negro votes. Their common mode of behavior was to act in a friendly fashion toward these Negroes but not to sit at the same tables with them. When all other tables were fully occupied, some of the whites waited for new tables to be set up so that they would not have to sit at tables already partly occupied by Negroes. This seemed to be an instance of a common mode of behavior by which the whites attempted to act in partial conformity to both definitions of the situation, the definition that this was a solidary group of party members and the definition that this was an interracial situation. Though they had to eat at tables adjoining the tables at which Negroes were seated, they did not have to eat with Negroes. Though they rebuffed these Negroes, they did not entirely alienate them.

It appeared that when an individual was constrained to act on the basis of two or more mutually incompatible definitions of the situation, he would seek a compromise solution by which he deviated as little as possible from the action appropriate to each of these definitions.

Processes of modification of orientations

In addition to studying behavior that occurred *during* an unpatterned situation, we also studied the sequential development of new attitudes *after* the initial situation. One of the first rewarding approaches came in the form of a highly intensive study in the Hometown Negro community of the progressive modification of Negroes' attitudes toward the white (Jewish) research observer who was the close associate of a trusted Negro sociologist living in the community. It was found that different social types of people modified their orientations to the white researcher in decidedly different ways. The race men reoriented themselves to the white researcher by exempting him from their expectations of a white person. Other people

---

[20] Calling this behavior exemption does not necessarily mean that the bar owner perceived his action as making an exception of these particular Negroes; he might have seen it simply as serving friends. Nevertheless the effect of his action is exemption, whether he consciously perceives it that way or not, because from the observer's point of view he is acting differently from the way he would act toward other Negroes.

modified their expectations of this particular white more gradually; in some instances he eventually was redefined in terms of new social categories that recognized his being white but stressed similarities of his position to that of particular Negroes—for example, categories like "we northerners" and "Negroes and Jews like us." The principal difference between the modifications of orientation made by race men and those made by others seemed to be that the race men had such rigid expectations of whites' behavior that they could cope with an unusual white only by treating him as if he were not white. Other members of the community, having less rigid expectations, were able to modify their expectations of this particular individual while still treating him as a white.

Encouraged by what was felt to be a successful exploration, we sought for an opportunity to observe a group of people engaged in a continuing series of situations. Since we had been participating in the social lives of the minority communities for many months, we could reasonably expect that we would be aware of the formation of any such group. As it happened, when a group that met these criteria did form, its leading members were close personal friends of the researchers. Thus there were few problems of rapport, for these participants explained the purposes of our research and the legitimacy of our aims to the others.

Example of change in attitude. The following description of a specific civil rights court case illustrates the way in which attitudes of two minority-group individuals changed through a series of events.[21] One night in August, two Negro couples attempted to escape the summer heat of the city by driving off into the countryside. Twelve miles out of the city, the men decided to stop at a tavern to purchase cigarettes and get a drink. Their wives decided to wait in the car until the men saw how well dressed the crowd was; the women were wearing slacks, and were reluctant to enter the tavern if other women were more formally dressed. One of the couples had previously been served there, so no one expected to encounter discrimination. They encountered what they regarded as a brusque refusal to serve them. They left immediately, quietly if angrily, in spite of the fact that the refusal occurred in the presence of Negro waiters, one of whom quit his job on the spot in protest.

Two days later the wife of one of the men telephoned the president of the local chapter of the NAACP, who in turn suggested that the men revisit

---

[21] All names, except those of the researchers, are pseudonyms. This chronological account is not an attempt to report all the events of the case. Rather, it is an attempt to follow a small group of the leaders of the local chapter of the NAACP and the plaintiffs in the case through a series of situations beginning with the discriminatory incident and ending with the victory celebration after the settlement. We shall not attempt to follow the defendant and his lawyer through a comparable series of situations.

the tavern in the company of the executive committee of the NAACP chapter.[22] A first visit was, from their point of view, ineffectual: the proprietor was absent, and his son equivocated. A second trip found the proprietor prepared. After protesting his own lack of prejudice, he argued that he could not risk a boycott by white customers. When this argument fell on unresponsive ears (the NAACP president waved a copy of the State Anti-Discrimination Statute in his face), he argued that he didn't care what the law said, he simply was not going to serve Negroes. Then ensued a long debate, ending in an impasse, on whether or not minority groups should insist on service where they were not wanted.

The NAACP leaders attempted, without success, to interest the local district attorney in taking court action. Then, with tacit approval by the prospective plaintiffs, they established contact with the state NAACP legal department. Initial plans for court action were made, followed by a delay of several months before the case was tried. The period of quiescence was marked by the plaintiffs' loss of interest in the case.

The weekend preceding the case brought feverish activity on the part of the NAACP lawyer and two members of the executive committee, first in questioning witnesses and later in detailed cross examination of one waiter who reported that he would testify for the defense. Other members of the executive committee, the second waiter, and another participant-observer were brought in during the last stages of this examination—at a time of open conflict, with the lawyer and NAACP president accusing the dissident waiter of selling out the race. The incident ended in excited denunciation of the turncoat by the waiter who had quit his job in protest against discrimination.

Up to this point the plaintiffs had not participated. They and their wives joined the group at a meeting called to plan strategy for the trial. The first order of business was a dramatic account of events in the case up to that time. Then the lawyer interrupted abruptly to ask for his clients' minimum demands. He added that cash settlements generally weren't very high in this type of case. The plaintiffs said nothing. But the president jumped in to aver that "these men aren't in this for cash. They're in it for the principle of the thing!" He paid tribute to "men who have the guts to stick it out." A member of the executive committee spoke about the effects that this case would have on the Negro community generally. Others spoke *for* the plaintiffs. One asked that the men be given a chance to speak for themselves— but he too congratulated them "for having the courage to go through with the case *for the principle of it!*"

---

[22] Robert B. Johnson attended these conferences in his role as a member of the NAACP executive committee. Johnson, and others of the research staff who were involved in later situations, filled out detailed research reports after each period of observation.

The lawyer asked the plaintiffs directly: "How do you feel about this?" A long silence followed. Then one plaintiff said that he and his friend were fighting for the good of the race. He said that he hoped this action would benefit the Negro community as a whole. He said that he believed in *action* to improve the position of Negroes. He added that he was a poor man.

At once the president exclaimed that he too was a poor man but that even if it meant losing his job, he would stick it through. There was no further ambiguity about money. The lawyer congratulated the plaintiffs for not seeking monetary retribution and then asked the group as a whole for a statement of minimal demands. Almost all members of the group spoke up now, including the heretofore-silent plaintiffs and their wives. All agreed to a policy enunciated by the president: the demands were to be a full public apology, together with a statement by the proprietor that he would not discriminate in the future.

Succeeding events need not be described in detail here. The defendant, upon pressure from the judge, settled the case in court on the plaintiffs' terms.

For present purposes, the most striking aspect of this series of events was the radical change in the behavior of the plaintiffs. Their behavior in the discriminatory situation had been passive; upon their return to the community they did nothing to institute action against the bar owner. Personality studies of the two men, based on detailed life history data, indicate that this passive acceptance of the intergroup relations *status quo* was entirely in keeping with their behavior in other situations. In fact, they had but a few weeks before this incident predicted (in response to a questionnaire-interview administered to a cross section of the Negro community) that in such a situation they would leave the establishment without saying anything and take no further action. Yet in the course of these situations the positive or negative evaluation of their behavior by a militant group of Negro leaders became important to their own evaluations of their behavior; their self-conceptions changed to those of race men, or fighters for the good of the Negro community; their definitions of the discriminatory incident and of their own subsequent behavior were enlarged to include an evaluation of how these actions affected other Negroes in the city; and their passive behavior was transformed into militancy.

In broadest outline, this change can be viewed as the consequence of a long series of successive redefinitions of the situations in which they participated. The most readily apparent change in the plaintiffs' orientation was their coming to depend upon the NAACP leaders as referents. But why did the NAACP come to play this role?

It would seem that the plaintiffs must have been predisposed, at least to a limited degree, to see the NAACP definition of the situation as legitimate

—even if not the only legitimate definition. Once they were involved in the NAACP activities, several factors conspired to commit them more and more firmly to the NAACP group: the NAACP leaders could and did shame them by holding out the threat that they would be regarded by the community as quitters; at the same time, these leaders were able to argue the logic of their philosophy, and to demonstrate by their own action how their philosophy worked in practice; continued group enterprise brought the satisfactions of group *esprit de corps* and of participation in something important; finally the plaintiffs' behavior brought approbation from some other members of the Negro community.

At the same time, other pressures generated by the situations served to bring the plaintiffs' definitions into harmony with that of the NAACP leaders. Perhaps the most important event here was the cross examination of the dissident waiter. The NAACP leaders could not have asked for a more compelling demonstration that the point at issue was a moral principle, with all other considerations irrelevant. A clear dichotomy was drawn between those who sell out the race and those who fight for the race. If the dissident waiter stood as the symbol of selling out, his courageous colleague embodied the virtues of the man of principle. In the face of his sacrifice of his job, who could undertake to do less?

For the plaintiffs, acceptance of the NAACP position brought a change in self-conception: they now thought of themselves as race men. It also brought a rewriting of history, to bring all past events into line with their present definition. If you ask them now, they will tell you that their orientation has not changed. They are, and always have been, militant. From the very beginning, their one interest has been to fight discrimination. That is why they were so quick to bring the NAACP into the case.

In spite of this, their change in self-conception has not been productive of other militant action. Although they may continue to think of themselves as race men, and although they may behave like race men in any future situation in which they are directly refused service, they have given no evidence that they are likely to engage in a wider range of interracial activities on behalf of the Negro community.

Conclusions about changing attitudes. In this section we have given examples of interpretation of the processes by which participants define unpatterned intergroup situations and the processes by which definitions are in turn modified over the course of time. We recognize that the research has been conducted within a very limited range of institutional contexts, but it is likely that the present interpretations are applicable to many situations arising in other social contexts; for that reason, we present our summary in the form of the following hypotheses amenable to testing in a broad range of institutional contexts:

1. AMBIGUOUS OR CONFUSED DEFINITIONS. When an individual is constrained to act but feels that he cannot predict the consequences of his own or other participants' behavior, his response to the situation will be to seek cues from other participants' behavior. Where he can turn to persons in formal leadership roles, he will do so; but where this is not possible, the behavior of *any* other participant will be utilized as an index of how other participants define the situation. Where there are no appropriate behavioral cues available, the confused participant will tend to perseverate in his confusion until new action intervenes to structure the situation.

2. CONTRADICTION OR CONFLICT OF DEFINITIONS. When an individual is constrained to act but feels that two or more distinct definitions (each with its appropriate behavioral imperatives) are applicable to the situation, he will first attempt to resolve the conflict by exemption, that is, by assigning one definition a higher priority than that accorded to others. (This can be done either by exempting a particular type of event or a particular person from a more general definition.) Where this is not possible, he will attempt to achieve a compromise solution by which he can act in partial conformity to both (or all) definitions of the situation. When even this is not possible, he will seek to withdraw from the situation, unless otherwise constrained. If constrained, he will behave inconsistently, wavering between the two alternative definitions, until new action intervenes to structure the situation.

3. MODIFICATION OF DEFINITIONS. Direct, overt interpersonal conflict is not likely to change either party's definition of the situation; its principal effect is likely to be the reinforcement of each combatant's values. Major changes of definition are more likely to be the result of a series of minor redefinitions, each dependent upon one or more of the following:

4. CHANGED REFERENTS. When an individual's experience in a situation (or in a series of situations) leads to the reinforcement of particular reference groups, or to the internalization of new reference groups, his ideas of how he should act in the situation will be modified to conform to his modified self-conception.

5. EXPECTATIONS OF CONSEQUENCES. When an individual's experience leads to modification of his expectations of the consequences of his own behavior, his ideas of how he should act in the situation will be modified to meet his new expectations of these consequences. Similarly, when an individual's experience leads to the modification of his expectations of how other participants will behave, his ideas of how he should act in the situation will be modified to meet his new expectations of their behavior.

It must be emphasized that the situations chosen for analysis tend to occur at the peripheries of community structure or in new or changing contexts. It is precisely in marginal situations that racial and ethnic lines are least likely to be clearly drawn. Much of the relatively unstructured interethnic contact, for example, is a matter of the participation of the younger men in the recreational penumbra of community life.[23] Most of these interactions have no structural consequences; the essential pattern of ethnic relations is left as it was before. Structural change means that the norms change, for example, that there is shared acceptance of a new rule such as "regardless of race any well-behaved customer will be promptly and politely served." Changes in the discrete attitudes of separate individuals need not lead to new social norms, obligatory upon others within a group, community, or society. Between the individual's personal experience and the potential modification of a social norm often intervene the processes of exemption, to which we now turn attention.

THE EXEMPTION MECHANISM [24]

All categorical social distinctions are subject to exceptions; all stereotypes sometimes are admitted to fail to hold; all rules of intergroup behavior eventually come up against situations in which it is impossible to abide by them. Provisions tend to be made for exceptional cases and extenuating circumstances.

Exemption processes have to be taken into account in appraising the effects of intergroup interaction. Exemption mechanisms constitute one of the ways in which established systems of discrimination and supporting prejudices are maintained against the erosion of interpersonal acquaintance and friendship. Pervasive prejudices are likely to be changed *en masse* only ". . . when the basic conditions which have produced group hatreds are removed." [25] So long as these conditions are present, few intergroup friendships will be formed, and those that do arise will be subject to incessant pressure, frequently leading to exemptions. The relation of exceptions to the maintenance or change of stereotypes clearly is an important problem.

Difficulties inherent in studying stereotypes and exemptions

A promising avenue for future research would be more basic questioning about stereotypes than that employed in most studies to date. It is obvious that whenever a respondent is asked to agree or disagree with a stereotyped statement, we cannot be certain whether the respondent would have

---

[23] One illustration will suffice: in Steelville, among isolates (with no participation in work group, social clique, or formal organizations) multiple personal contacts with ethnic individuals were almost nonexistent among older women but were reported by 7 out of 10 of the men under 45 years.

[24] A more detailed treatment, used as a source here, is: Peter I. Rose, *The Exemption Mechanism: A Conceptual Analysis* (M.A. thesis, Cornell University, 1957).

[25] Donald Young, *American Minority Peoples* (New York: Harper & Row, Publishers, 1932), p. 14.

thought of the stereotype if we had not suggested it to him. He may not really believe the stereotypes with which he agrees; rather, he may be doing no more than saying "you are asking me whether I know of this generalization, and I do, and I will go along with the game you are asking me to play." Certainly it is very important if a person does thus play the game, for it means that he is likely to "go along" also in the more serious business of accepting, acquiescing in, or spreading such stereotypes outside of the interview situation. That is why it makes sense to use the techniques that we and nearly all other investigators in this field have used to elicit stereotypes that, indeed, are actually prevalent and important. But we should be clear that we are eliciting acquiescence or agreement to *formulations that the investigator presents* rather than to formulations that the respondent volunteers, or to those to which he would continue to hold under cross examination, counterpersuasion, and other modifying pressures commonly encountered in ordinary social intercourse.

Another difficulty in the study of stereotypes arises from the researcher's uncertainty about what the respondents' conceptions are of a particular minority. For example, what does the researcher mean by "Negro" and what does the respondent mean? Does the respondent include Ralph Bunche and Marion Anderson? Persons of West Indian extraction whose mother tongue is French? Nigerian students resident in the United States? Leaders of newly independent African nations? More important, perhaps, what properties are associated with his concepts of "Negro"? What cognitive dimensions are brought into play? What cues or clues are utilized in deciding that someone is or is not to be classified as a Negro?

The question might be formulated, "When is a Negro a Negro?" and the noninformative answer is, "When he is treated like one." A beard, a turban, and a foreign accent can do wonders for an American Negro traveling in the United States. The processes by which radically different social definitions are decided upon in various major types of social situations represent a largely unexplored area for basic investigation.

Kinds of exemptions [26]

Reverse-of-stereotype. One important type of exemption of persons from classification as a member of an outgroup is to regard them as lacking stereotyped characteristics attributed to all other members of the category. This is exemption by reverse-of-stereotype. When we asked respondents whether the individual they indicated as their closest acquaintance among persons of any particular ethnic group was typical of or different from most other persons in that category we were often told of the Jew who is "*not

---

[26] These types were originally suggested by Alice S. Rossi.

pushing," "more honest," "less grasping"; of the Negro who is "clean, not dirty," "brighter," "*not* lazy"; of the Italian-American who is *not* excitable, loud, or hot tempered. The individual is assessed in terms of a stereotypic image of the group or category; the stereotype is usually implicit and almost always taken for granted as unproblematic. The exempted individual is positively valued because he is thought to be not typical of the category to which he nominally is assigned.

Valued personal characteristics. A second kind of exemption is referred to valued personal characteristics of a particular person, without direct reference to any stereotypic qualities of the outgroup. We found that the incidence of reverse-of-stereotype exemptions differed considerably with reference to different ethnic groupings, but that the responses classified as references to personal characteristics (personality) were encountered with about the same frequencies in each of several ethnic categories (Negro, Jew, Italian-American). The exemptions on grounds of personality were couched in such terms as "considerate," "friendly," "good natured," "unselfish," "civic minded." These descriptions seem, in the interviews, to be essentially divorced from any connection with ethnic membership, for example, a Jewish acquaintance is simply described as "a good guy—lot of fun—easy to be around." These descriptions do not permit us to infer that the respondent has compared the individual ethnic person with the ethnic group. The relationship of respondent and ethnic acquaintance occupies a neutral ground of personalized affinities. The ways in which the ethnic acquaintance is described could equally well be applied to any member of the respondent's own ethnic ingroup.

Prestige-status characteristics. Still another mode of exemption focuses upon what we may call prestige-status characteristics: the respondent refers to his closest ethnic contact in terms of "well educated," "professional," "higher class," "high standards," and the like. Like the reverse-of-stereotype reactions, this mode of making individual exceptions involves a reference to social categories and norms, but the referents are not ethnic traits but attributes of general prestige ranking. The ethnic person is moved up, as it were, to a rank-level equal to or higher than that of the respondent, if ranked within respondent's own ingroup. This means that the attribute on which the individual is assessed is one that paves the way for greater acceptability by the respondent's ingroup. There is thus a mild form of pull in the direction of the ingroup involved in this status category.

Assimilation. Finally, exemption may be couched in terms of cultural or social assimilation. For example, white gentiles in referring to Jewish friends and acquaintances say "mixes with gentiles," "eats American food," "not orthodox," "more Americanized"; or, with reference to Italian-Americans: "no accent," "second generation," "Americanized," "doesn't just stick around other Italians." Very few references by white persons to Negroes had to do with assimilation, but some did say "associates more with white people," or "in our church—very religious." The responses suggest a conception of the individual as deviating from his ethnic group in the direction of the customs, practices, values, or beliefs of the respondent's ingroup. It comes as no surprise that this type of exemption is not the exclusive property of the white Protestant Anglo-Saxon population. The essential element in the assimilative exemptions is the pull to define the individual as almost like or *really* an ingroup person: the "honorary Jew"; "this white man seems more like our kind of colored people"; "there came a time when we would forget that they were gentiles." Acceptance of the outgroup person rests upon the degree to which he is felt to share essential parts of ingroup culture and sentiments.

In Negroes' descriptions of white acquaintances, reverse-of-stereotype and assimilation often overlapped, for the absence of expected racial prejudice can be defined in both ways: "he is more liberal—for equal rights of Negroes"; "race and color have no meaning to him"; "he doesn't stress Negroes as Negroes."

Nature of exemption

We are thinking of exemption as the partial social acceptance by a given ingroup member of some outgroup members, as associates in a situation; this acceptance refers to qualities of an individual or situation defined as different from those regarded as usual or typical of the outgroup or of the situations in which its members are found. The major types of acceptance between any ingroup and any outgroup range from the acceptance of a single outgroup member by a single ingroup member to acceptance of most members of one group by most members of the other.

Exemption may be a forestalling process by which unavoidable or positively valued ethnic contacts can be accepted and enjoyed without fundamental reorientation of attitudes or shifts in accustomed behavior or group affiliations. Under other conditions it may represent an intermediate step in a sequence of changes from stereotypy to realistic and flexible interpersonal appraisals and from discriminatory to nondiscriminatory conduct. There are instances, certainly, in which a generalized change either in personal orientations or in group norms is contingent upon the gradual accumulation of exceptions. Exemption may open up the way to further change, but it may also be a way of retaining prejudice while circumventing discriminatory patterns for some particular purpose.[27]

Exemption obviously takes its significance from the existence of categori-

---

[27] Cf. the discussion of compartmentalization, denial of differences, "mascot" attitude, and realistic acceptance in *Psychiatric Aspects of School Desegregation*, Report No. 37, Group for the Advancement of Psychiatry, New York (1957), pp. 34ff.

cal distinctions between ingroups and outgroups. Exemptions are made of 'certain exceptional individuals. Exemptions are also made of certain kinds of situations. An exempted ethnic person may be accepted in a variety of social contexts. Or some or all members of an ethnic category may be accepted in some situations but not in others. An individual Negro may be so outstanding in some highly valued accomplishments or personal qualities as to be almost completely exempted from barriers against white-Negro associations in all social settings. Or, a policy of nonsegregation and nondiscrimination within the factory may be accepted, so that all or almost all Negro workers are accepted by whites on the job, although segregation prevails in all other situations.

Processes of exemption of individuals may or may not represent a step toward either the revision of stereotypes or the alteration of discriminatory behavior. Of course we can regard the sheer fact that *any* exception to a stereotype can be admitted as evidence of a change of stereotype, but it is very clear that many exceptions often occur as isolated responses without any generalized alteration in stereotyped image or in accompanying dispositions to discriminate. This is the place of token integration, which does not basically change the main pattern but does permit individuals to salve their consciences, to feel that they are fair.

Data on exemption

Actually our data show that prejudiced people are more likely than those who are less prejudiced to regard their closest ethnic contact as different from the ethnic or racial category in which he is classified, and the frequency of exemption, in this sense, is greatest for the categories against which the most prejudice is directed. From a number of studies, we select the evidence contained in Table 9.2. Other data show that it is the individuals who express dislike toward a given ethnic group who are most likely to regard their closest acquaintance in that group as different. *To regard an individual as exceptional in relation to his ethnic or racial membership tends to be a manifestation of negative, not positive, attitudes toward the group or category as a whole.*

If exemptions tend to be made by prejudiced people, it can be reasoned that exemption will most often occur when the ethnic individual who is being singled out is of a higher economic position than the exemption. Respondents were asked to estimate whether the income level of their closest ethnic acquaintance is the same as, higher than, or lower than their own. The answers seem to reflect with some exaggeration the broad outlines of the actual economic differentials (white gentiles' estimates): the proportions ranking as same or higher were Negroes, 26 per cent; Italian-Americans, 68 per cent; Jews, nearly 100 per cent. In each ethnic category,

Table 9.2

Proportion of white majority-group respondents who exempt their closest
ethnic acquaintance (Hometown).

Number of situations in which ethnic contact is regarded as distasteful*		Closest ethnic contact among:		
		Italian-Americans	Jews	Negroes
		Per cent said to be different†		
Low	0-2	20% (55)‡	32% (47)	45% (29)
Intermediate	3-5	35% (194)	39% (163)	50% (89)
High	6+	38% (72)	51% (73)	53% (32)

*Social-distance items: respondent says he would "find it distasteful" to eat with, go to party
  with, dance with, have marry in family, etc.
†Based on replies to an open-ended question, "Would you say this person is typical or differ-
  rent from most? In what ways?"
‡Numbers of cases vary, depending upon number of respondents who reported contact with a
  person in each ethnic group.

exemptions were most frequent for the higher and least frequent for the
lower individuals. Holding relative economic status constant, exemption
when acquaintances are of higher position is most frequent for Negroes, next
for Jews, and least often for Italian-Americans—following the rank-order
of generalized prejudice. Thus high economic position facilitates a definition of an ethnic individual as an exception, and the effect is greatest for
the most disadvantaged minority.

Among the questions asked of those majority-group respondents who indicated that they had a close contact with a member of an ethnic group
was, *When and where do you see him (her)?* Answers were classified as:
place of business, in formal organizations, at social gatherings, on the street,
in the neighborhood, and various recreational and miscellaneous contexts.
It appears that it is the more informal social contacts that elicit the most
frequent exempting responses. It seems likely that these closer relationships
on the part of a prejudiced person arouse dissonance, calling for some
justificatory definition, such as exemption can be.[28]

The bases given for considering an ethnic acquaintance to be exceptional
differed systematically for the three ethnic groups that were objects of our
inquiry. Jewish contacts were most likely to be exempted on grounds of
differences from stereotyped characteristics; Negroes on grounds of attributes of high prestige status (usually education or occupation); Italian-
Americans because of assimilation to non-Italian ingroups or their culture.

If a person testifies that he feels dislike for members of an ethnic group
and nevertheless does have a close acquaintance who is from that group,
exemption tends to be in terms of how the person exempted differs from

---

[28] Rose, *The Exemption Mechanism: A Conceptual Analysis*, pp. 153-54.

Table 9.3

Types of individual exemptions for closest ethnic contacts with Jews, Negroes, and Italian-Americans (Hometown).

Closest ethnic contact among:

Type of exemption*	Jews	Negroes	Italian-Americans
Reverse of stereotype	52%	21%	9%
Personal qualities	26%	31%	29%
Prestige-status attributes	6%	32%	13%
Assimilation	16%	16%	49%
Total	100%	100%	100%
Number of cases	(113)	(77)	(108)

*Rose, The Exemption Mechanism: A Conceptual Analysis, pp. 153-54.

the negative characteristics assumed to be typical of his group. If, on the contrary, the exemptor has friendly feelings toward members of the ethnic group in general, exemption of the individual ethnic person is defined in terms of how closely he approximates characteristics that are valued as typical of the ingroup, that is, assimilation. (Hostility or friendliness is not related to personal or prestige grounds for exemption.)

There are marked differences among the various social contexts of acquaintance in the frequency of the several types of exemption. The reverse-of-stereotype strongly characterizes exemptions based on acquaintance developed at work or place of business. In informal social settings, on the other hand, exemptions tend to be in terms of assimilation. The findings are as would be expected if respondents' reports are valid descriptions of the actual properties of the situations and relationships.

The tendency, evidently, is for the grounds given for exemption to reflect, as a mirror image, the respondents' conception of the ethnic group from which his acquaintance comes. Further substantiation is found in the fact that the highest incidence of reverse-of-stereotype responses is among persons most likely to indorse negative stereotypes. The respondents who are least likely to accept stereotypes are those who exempt on grounds of assimilation.

Exemption appears to be a rather specific process in that it consists of marking off a particular individual as different from other members of his particular ethnic group, with no strong tendency to carry over the exemption process into indiscriminate friendships in other ethnic groups.

A question might be raised as to whether people for whom exemption is a more general pattern of their relationships with ethnic minorities will differ from those who exempt an individual from only *one* of the ethnic groups and from those who exempt none. (It would also be interesting to see what happens when an individual exempts two or more individuals from the *same* ethnic subcommunity, but the data do not include such responses.) However, the data do permit the construction of the following operational definitions:

1. *General exemptor.* Those who consider all three or two of the three closest Jewish, Negro, and Italian contacts different from other Jews, Negroes, or Italians.

2. *Specific exemptor.* Those who consider only *one* of the three closest ethnic contacts as different from the rest of the ethnic group to which the exempted individual belongs.

3. *General nonexemptor.* Those who have three close contacts with a Jew, a Negro, and an Italian and consider all three or two of the three as typical of their groups.

Briefly, the data show that a specific exemptor appears to establish somewhat intimate social relationships with ethnic individuals to a greater extent than does the general exemptor or the nonexemptor. Moreover, specific exemptors are less often prejudiced than general exemptors.[29]

The results of this brief inspection of processes of exemption raise more questions than they answer, but they do seem congruent with the impressions received from the preceding analyses of ethnic interaction in Chapter 7. And many of the tendencies noted in our studies of interaction have been independently observed in studies of mixed neighborhoods elsewhere.[30] Under enough situational pressure, relationships with particular ethnic individuals are tolerated or accepted even by persons hostile toward that (stereotyped) ethnic grouping represented by the exempted individual. Much of the pressure may come from coercive sanctions, for example, military discipline, or impersonal advantages, or profitable trading. Given the interpersonal contact, however, the prejudiced individual is confronted with the continued presence of another person. On the whole, we rarely encounter a more imperative or compelling stimulus than another live human being who attempts social communication with us. The cognitive richness and potential affective loading of interpersonal perception and communication make most other encounters with the environment seem rather thin by comparison.

This great apparent potential influence of elementary social behavior is constrained and reduced by stereotyping, routinized role-prescriptions, and

---

[29] Cf. Rose, *The Exemption Mechanism: A Conceptual Analysis,* pp. 166-67.

[30] Arnold M. Rose *et al.,* "Neighborhood Reactions to Isolated Negro Residents," *American Sociological Review,* XVIII, No. 5 (October, 1953), 497-507; Judith T. Shuval, "Class and Ethnic Correlates of Casual Neighboring," *American Sociological Review,* XXI, No. 4 (August, 1956), 453-58; Bulkeley Smith, Jr., "The Reshuffling Phenomenon: A Pattern of Residence of Unsegregated Negroes," *American Sociological Review,* XXIV, No. 1 (February, 1959), 77-81.

ingroup counter-influence. Conventionalized in form, reduced in affect, limited in range, and defined as an exception—thus may the new relationship be walled off from further development. Repeated interactions with the same person in a single context may result in friendship that ends each working day at five o'clock and never leads to any appreciable change in the flexibility or realism of beliefs and evaluations concerning group distinctions. The ingroup member safely exempts his friend, and there the matter ends. Retention of stereotyped orientations presumably will be increasingly put under strain both as the number of exceptions grows and as the variety of roles and social settings in which ethnic outgroup members are encountered becomes greater, provided, of course, that the individuals in question actually do differ from the stereotype.

Given repeated and varied interactions between many members of an ingroup and many members of an outgroup in many different kinds of situations, one may expect to find a point at which exemption merges imperceptibly into realistic differentiation, a point at which individuals' group memberships are taken into account but only as one set of properties along with their more particularized statuses and their unique qualities as individual persons. Should it ever happen that mutual acceptance (and rejection) thus becomes the dominant mode of interaction in a society containing different racial, ethnic, or religious collectivities, then that society will be as close to a pluralistic Utopia as the student of intergroup relations ever is likely to see in our unavoidably imperfect world.

Exemption and Change in Intergroup Relations

Change in the basic structure of intergroup relations has not been initiated in the communities studied by a spontaneous growth of person-by-person ties through the purposive acts of men of good will. This statement is true for three reasons: first, most interethnic friendships are not sought out but occur as an unintended consequence of action focused on objectives quite apart from the interpersonal relationship; second, the number of friendships is too small to alter the dominant mode of collective relations; third, the basic changes originate in forces transcending both the small group and the local community.

The nature and dimensions of interethnic friendship formation are illustrated in the 1949-1951 changes studied in Hometown. The Hometown data permit comparison of "snapshots" of ethnic interactions and attitudes taken at two points in time. These data also include respondents' own testimony concerning change or lack of change, as well as their self-diagnosis of why there was or was not change.

As Table 9.4 shows, the great majority of all new friendships with Jewish

Table 9.4

Sources of interaction leading to a new friendship with a Jewish or
Negro person between 1949 and 1951 (Hometown).

	New contacts with:	
Nature of initial contact*	Jews	Negroes
Purposive seeking-out of one person by the other	6%	3%
Joint participation in a voluntary activity or organization	23%	2%
Involuntary contact (work, neighborhood, etc.)	43%	17%
Nature of initial contact not ascertainable	9%	2%
Total	81%	24%

*Based on free answers to the question: "Could you tell me how you came to
be good friends with him (her)?"

or Negro persons developed by white gentiles over a two-year period grew
out of essentially involuntary contacts at work, in the neighborhood, or
elsewhere, or emerged as a consequence of unplanned contacts in voluntary
common activities. People usually do not cross ethnic lines in a purposive
search for interesting contacts, nor do they ordinarily seek out ethnic part-
ners as a manifestation of good will. They form friendships as they do with
ingroup persons—when their daily rounds throw them into recurrent interaction with congenial individuals. The web of friendships that forms—if it
does—across ethnic lines is a product of the unplanned interaction arising
in the ordinary joint and common activities of community life.

When asked how this new friendship had affected their opinions about
Jews or Negroes in general, there was just one person who reported a less
favorable attitude. The dominant response, however, was a clear report of
no change reported in 72 per cent of the cases of new Jewish friends and
of 50 per cent of those with new Negro friendships.

Most new ethnic contacts leading to friendly relations happened as by-
products of activities having no direct initial connection with ethnic attitudes
or relations. The same was true of the loss of ethnic friends. Persons who
in 1949 had reported a good friend who was Negro or Jewish but did not
report the same friendship in 1951 were asked what had happened. In the
majority of cases some contact was still maintained, but the relationship had
diminished owing to involuntary factors—most often, the fact that one
party to the relationship had changed jobs or place of residence for reasons
unconnected with ethnic membership. Of 58 cases of lost or attenuated

friendships, only 3 were reported to have been matters of choice on the part of either member.

In a society of close economic, political, and cultural interdependence, many large-scale organizations arise and much social change occurs as a consequence of decisions affecting the internal policies of formal organization. In this manner official racial segregation was ended in the Armed Services of the United States. In this manner much racial segregation has ended in the public schools of the nation, outside the last-ditch group of states in the Deep South. In our community studies we collected data on instances of authoritative change in organizational policies. A case of school desegregation will serve for illustration.

In Phoenix, Arizona, in 1952 in the recently desegregated Phoenix Union High School, the white students were asked a long series of questions concerning racial and ethnic minorities (including their own reactions to having Negro and Mexican students in Phoenix Union). The findings show a high degree of acceptance of desegregation, even while social-distance feelings remain frequent and while many white students retain traditional prejudices. The students were asked, *How do you think having Negro and white students together has worked out at Phoenix Union?* Replies were: "very well," 43 per cent; "fairly well," 48 per cent; "not so well," 9 per cent. (Only 2 persons out of 232 said "not well at all."). The great majority of the students who thus evaluated the results of desegregation had been in the same school rooms with Negro students (84 per cent). The favorable evaluation occurs even though half of the white pupils say they sometimes try to keep from being with Negro students at school, and just over three-fourths think the Negroes hang together rather than mixing with white students. Most of the whites are ready to have a Negro family live next door and to eat at the same table (as many did in the school cafeteria). But dancing and partying are rejected by over three-fourths, and the idea of "going steady" with a Negro boy or girl is rejected by 96 per cent.

The total pattern of responses gives a picture of acceptance of Negro students in the normal routines of the school, with little social interaction outside of classes and sports events. Of 232 boys and girls, just 9 reported any contact with Negro students in their own "crowd" or "gang." But only 12 per cent said they dislike the idea of going to school with Negroes. There is a general acknowledgment of rights of Negroes, Mexicans, and Indians to equal access to schools, jobs, and residential areas (except that a majority say Negroes should live in segregated neighborhoods). Nearly all reject some of the cruder racial stereotypes (88 per cent disagree that Negroes are lazy and ignorant). One gets an impression of a matter-of-fact acceptance of the fact of desegregation and of the Negro students in their roles as students. Informal social activity with Negroes is restrained and relatively rare.

Against a background of traditional stereotyping and recent segregation, this group atmosphere of functional acceptance is perhaps more than most local observers would have hoped for in a period of two years.[31]

Finding that prejudice is reduced after interaction with Negroes in an interracial setting does not necessarily mean that it was the interaction with Negroes that caused the reduction in prejudice. It may be, rather, that interracial settings are generally those in which there is some authoritative group norm opposed to discrimination and to the expression of prejudice. Those who continue to participate, then, may be those who come to accept (or, acquiesce in) these norms, and by virtue of that fact, to manifest reduced expression of prejudice. Nevertheless, in the case of schools, churches, governmental organizations, business corporations, labor unions, professional associations, and a host of special-interest formal organization, a change in top policy often results in massive changes in roles and operating norms affecting a large number of people. These major changes in social structure create numerous new concrete situations in which direct person-to-person communication occurs among previously separate ethnic, racial, or religious collectivities. These new interactions seem, on the whole, to eventuate in new operating practices, emerging *ad hoc* from day to day, which gradually grow into new norms of appropriate conduct. Concurrently, to varying degrees and in varying ways individuals are changing their perceptions, beliefs, and evaluations. To the degree that these changes result in greater mutual acceptance, the interpersonal relationships become less tense, less formalized, more fully communicative. As a durable web of interpersonal relationships (positive and negative) develops, it crisscrosses the older lines of ethnic cleavage. The resulting social structure is likely to be at once more complex, less rigid, and more stable than that of the *status quo ante*.

Change or stability in intergroup relations obviously depends in part upon the strength of the prejudices supporting the *status quo*. One highly important but rather neglected aspect of the force of prejudice in the maintenance of a system of group relations has to do with the interests that are linked with the prejudices. There is, for example, the prejudice that is primarily a response to the claims of other persons in one's own group to exact conformity to commonly-held opinions. Prejudice of this kind constitutes part of one's credentials of membership in the group. Clearly, the prejudice of conformity can be quite powerful, even when there is no other immediate incentive to adhere to the prejudicial orientation. Yet, it is easy to see that if everyone held prejudices only because others also held them, the force

---

[31] Results of the Phoenix study are congruent with the pattern generally found in recently desegregated schools in Border States. See Robin M. Williams, Jr. and Margaret Ryan, eds., *Schools in Transition* (Chapel Hill: University of North Carolina Press, 1954).

of adherence in the long run could not be great, and the interlocking of expectations could be relatively easily disrupted as soon as, for any reason, any considerable proportion of persons were to begin to deviate from the received opinion current in the group up to that time.

Conformity is quite another matter, however, if it derives its strength from an individual's direct interests in economic gain, political power, social prestige and ability to secure deference responses, sexual response, or other scarce values answering to strong needs and demands. If an existing set of segregative and discriminatory practices in a local community has come to be regarded by the politically and economically dominant segments of the community as an established, normal order, and if it is regarded as essential to the preservation of secure accustomed modes of interest gratification, then something more than either education or friendly personal acquaintance will be required to produce substantial reduction in prejudice or discrimination. Under circumstances of this kind the web of interpersonal expectations and demands within established groups and communities is enormously powerful. It is surcharged with affect and reinforced at every point by interdependence and by the interlocking of every set of expectancies with some other set.

From a sufficiently detached perspective, the energy with which even the smallest change in an established system of discriminatory practices or group segregation is resisted seems almost incredible and certainly difficult to explain. The proverbial visitor from outer space observing the turmoil occasioned by the attempted entrance of a few small children into public schools hitherto unaccustomed to enrollees having a particular shade of skin pigmentation might well need explanations that would tax our capacities. It is very clear that the reactions of fear, anger, and hostility often are quite disproportionate to any effects upon the realistic interests of those who manifest these reactions.

It is easy to say that the resistance to change has a symbolic character. What this appears to mean is that certain social arrangements have a significance beyond immediate utilitarian concerns—they stand for other and more remote values. Even though a change in school segregation may immediately affect no one's job, political rights and powers, income, safety, health, and the like, it may be felt to menace social prestige, racial purity, or the will of God. Persons may continue to resist changes long after they have accepted all rational reassurances having to do with identifiable effects upon their immediate practical interests.

It is well recognized in general sociological theory that vested interests have peculiar properties unlike those of interests that are not vested. Unlike a prospective gain or a fortuitous reward, a vested interest involves sentiments of legitimate claim; it is felt, in some way, to be justified, established, proper, appropriate. Any widely shared and long-continued social prerogatives come to be regarded by those who enjoy them as normal, customary, right—no matter how unjust they may be from some external ethical standpoint.

What is not so commonly recognized is that all established social arrangements are supported by multiple interests and motivations that vastly overdetermine their acceptance by those who actively participate in them and receive gratification from them.

We have been made familiar with the concept of psychological overdetermination in the motivation of specific actions by individuals. Thus, it is often said that every act is overdetermined in the sense that the motives engaged by the act are far more than would be necessary to produce the act. There is surplus energy being expended, over and above that which is directly needed to produce the act, and the act discharges psychic elements that are no part of the manifest motives or alleged reasons for the action.

We are now suggesting that an analogous (not identical) process occurs in the functioning of social groupings. Social institution and norm-regulated patterns of behavior quickly come to be overdetermined: that is, behavior carried out in conformity with (or even, just *in terms of*) the pattern will be undertaken as the outcome of numerous diverse motivations and will bring to the participants, correspondingly, numerous diverse gratifications. Almost from the beginning, therefore, the announced or manifest functions or aims of the practice or institution will be less than the actual functions, and the motives to which actors refer in accounting for their participation are only a partial reflection of the actual motives and gratifications involved. There is thus a double surplus of motivational support: both the *psychological* overdetermination of the individual's participation and the *social* overdetermination that arises from the diversity of motivations and gratifications of different actors in the same objective social pattern.

It is therefore difficult to overestimate the strength of vested interests in those institutionalized social arrangements by which the satisfaction of strong needs and desires is made legitimate and secure and by which inconvenient and uncomfortable value conflicts are evaded or rationalized.[32]

The resistance to social change, accordingly, is not just an expression of individual personality dispositions. In addition to basic personality needs, acceptance of or resistance to change in social relationships involves established interests, prospective gains (opportunity structure), social norms, ethical values, existential beliefs, interlocking expectations, and numerous diffuse sources of social conformity. These factors interact in many different patterns.

---

[32] "The master defense against accurate social perception and change is always and in every society the tremendous conviction of rightness about any behavior form which exists." [John Dollard, *Caste and Class in a Southern Town,* 2nd edition (Harper & Row, Publishers, 1949), p. 366.]

Since the outbreak of World War II, changes have occurred in intergroup relations in the United States that would have been regarded as wholly outside the realm of possibility only a few years earlier. Massive racial desegregation has been instituted in both public and private organizations involving millions of people. Discrimination in employment and in the use of publicly available facilities and services has been greatly reduced by legislative, judicial, and administrative means. Such great social changes have had, without question, widespread educative effects upon beliefs, values, and feelings of individuals and have led to new patterns of interpersonal relationships, group structures, and organizational arrangements. No corresponding changes in authoritarianism or basic character have been observed in the American population. The perhaps encouraging hypothesis thus suggested is that, to change specific patterns of segregation and discrimination in specific communities, it is not essential to substantially alter the basic personality structures of large numbers of prejudiced persons. The cognitive and evaluative orientations held by most nonpsychotic persons toward members of racial, ethnic, or religious outgroups are responsive, in important measure, to reality. Decisive alterations in these orientations can be brought about by changes in social reality—ranging from new interpersonal relations with ethnic individuals to recognition of the legitimacy of a decision by the Supreme Court or the authoritative judgment of a religious leader. Reality can be brought to us by new information, although we may reject the information.[33] It can be revealed by personal confrontation of situations that enable us to take the role of the other across categorical lines of group cleavage. Situations most conducive to the growth of new understandings and realistic adjustments will be those in which highly important outcomes are unavoidably dependent upon long-continued cooperation among individuals no one of whom has overwhelming power. If we can recognize the fact, it will be seen that such situations have become very common in our society.

---

[33] Rejections and distortions of the real situation are most marked when people feel most threatened. "Just as the threat of danger provides a major impetus to the origin of the ego, so do threatening events exert the greatest strain on the ego's perceptual function." Irving Sarnoff, "Psychoanalytic Theory and Social Attitudes," *Public Opinion Quarterly*, XXIV, No. 2 (Summer, 1960), 255.

CHAPTER 10

STRUCTURES AND PROCESSES
IN MULTIGROUP SOCIETY

We have now examined a wide sampling of recent research on ethnic relations. The primary focus has been upon Negro-white and Jewish-gentile relations within selected communities in the United States during a middle decade of the twentieth century. Occasional backward glances at history and outward glances into other societies have encouraged us to believe that many of the conclusions may have some enduring applicability to human social behavior at other places and in other times. Nevertheless, the limitations of the analysis are many. In view of the enormous range of variability of human cultures, past and present, any one of our generalizations may find its contradiction in some situation not now represented in our research-based knowledge.

However, the facts and insights yielded from our study seem to require the formulation of salient general implications. It is now time to appraise what portions of the findings stand out as of greatest general and long-range interest.

Basic Structures of Society: A Review and Commentary

A review of the term "intergroup relations"

The term intergroup relations has been lifted out of a nontechnical vocabulary and adapted to specialized usage. Accordingly, it often carries different meanings to persons of different backgrounds and experiences. If taken quite literally, "intergroup relations" presumably are relations between or among any human social groups. It seems acceptable to have the word "relations" refer to relatively stable, recurrent social interactions. The more difficult term seems to be "intergroup," for "group" can signify a great many different things, as we discussed in Chapter 3. In its most common sociological meaning, "group" refers to an aggregate of persons characterized by frequent interaction, some awareness by the constituent members of themselves as members of the collectivity, some sense of obligations and rights, both internally and *vis à vis* outsiders, and some relatively important degree of continuity through time. In this description we have included the criteria of (1) frequency of interaction, (2) awareness of corporate existence and of an ingroup-outgroup distinction, (3) a normative system, and (4) continuity. Clearly "groupness" is a matter of degree. At one extreme we simply have a population—an aggregate of individuals unconnected by any kind of interaction. At the other pole of maximum groupness, we find a definite, relatively permanent social body that commands exclusive loyalties and firmly regulates the behavior of its members. Between these extremes are many gradations.

In common usage, when we say "group" we usually mean a *small* group —one in which every individual can form some concrete impression of the other members. Although it would be misleading to specify an exact number marking the upper limit at which a group ceases to be small, the level of six or seven members usually is the point at which additions to size begin to markedly decrease the individual's capacity to fully perceive and react to every other member in a single encounter as a concrete individual.[1] By the time a group reaches the size of thirty or so, at any rate, we always will be able to observe that subgroups have formed and that members are *categorized* in various ways, rather than being apprehended as fully specific individuals in all their concreteness. Such categorizing involves perceptual and conceptual selectivity, in which there is a sharpening and accentuating of characteristics that are at the focus of attention, and an ignoring or "level-

---

[1] See Robert F. Bales, Paul A. Hare, and Edgar F. Borgatta, "Structure and Dynamics of Small Groups: A Review of Four Variables," in *Review of Sociology: Analysis of a Decade,* Joseph B. Gittler, ed. (New York: John Wiley & Sons, 1957), pp. 394-95.

ing" of other characteristics. The resulting simplified categories obviously provide a means of securing high predictability and great economy of attention and effort in social interaction. Individual persons, in all their rich uniqueness, disappear into such categories as enlisted men, union workers, Catholics, professors, Negroes, or women. Interactions based on *some* categorical distinctions probably are indispensable, especially among mobile, urban populations, but such categorical relations evidently differ from the diffuse, personalized relationships characteristic of small groups.

Main divisions of groups in the United States

In recent years the usage has grown up of speaking of intergroup relations when the reference is to those relations among individuals or collectivities that are primarily affected by racial, ethnic, and religious distinctions.[2] It might be preferable to speak of intercategory or intercollectivity relations, were it not that "intergroup" is so widely embedded in current usage. Ethnic distinctions based upon national origin or language have diminished greatly in importance in the United States today as a result of pervasive assimilation during the last four decades of drastically restricted immigration. We do have an important residue of subtle cultural diversity as a consequence of the varied national backgrounds of the population. We do retain a number of such interesting ethnico-religious islands as the Amish in Pennsylvania. But from the standpoint of national considerations the most crucial relationships are those involving the largest racial minority, American Negroes, and those involving Protestants, Jews, and Catholics as members of the three great religious categories. To understand the processes involved in these relationships we need to draw upon a few basic conclusions of modern social theory.

The complexity of studying intergroup relations

The study of intergroup relations potentially involves every major discipline within the social sciences—and indeed has important ramifications in the humanities as well. Anthropologists have long studied the contact and intermingling of peoples and have been especially interested in problems of acculturation and assimilation. Psychological investigations have contributed to our knowledge of stereotyping, of positive and negative attitudes, of the

---

[2] An alternative designation is "ethnic group": ". . . a collection of people considered both by themselves and by other people to have in common one or more of the following characteristics: (a) religion, (b) racial origin (as indicated by identifiable physical characteristics), (c) national origin, or (d) language and cultural traditions." [John Harding *et al.*, "Prejudice and Ethnic Relations," in Gardner Lindzey, ed. *Handbook of Social Psychology*, II (Reading, Mass.: Addison-Wesley Publishing Company, Inc., 1954), p. 1022.]

learning of prejudices, of personality dimensions of prejudice, and of various psychological processes involved in the changing of attitudes and behavior. Sociology has contributed in several of the areas already named, as well as in the study of group structures, social types, patterns of discrimination, leadership, and changes in group membership. Economics, for the most part, has not devoted much attention to intergroup relations, but economic considerations clearly enter into questions of discrimination and prejudice in a very important way.[3] At the present time it certainly is obvious that political science has a stake in the understanding of intergroup behavior and attitudes.[4] Finally, historical analysis stands to contribute greatly to our factual store, to our sense of perspective, and to the possibilities of solid comparative study.[5]

The fact that the study of intergroup relations lends itself to these various approaches offers real advantages, but it suggests at the same time that we have to do with a highly diverse collection of phenomena. Is there any intrinsic order among the facts having to do with intergroup relations, or is the field merely a haphazard aggregate of data, held together only by the intellectually irrelevant circumstance of a set of practical interests? It seems to us that there is an intrinsic theoretical order, which provides a framework for systematic study. This framework derives from our knowledge of common features in the structure of all social systems.

Four basic structures

All known social systems contain four basic structures that develop directly from human capacities for communication and evaluative conduct, within a population occupying a more or less restricted territory. First of all, in any society there will be a definite *kinship* system, providing for regulation of sexual relations and for the physical care, socialization, and status placement of children. Second, there will be *territorial communities,* emerging from the pressures to define rights and obligations and to maintain order within an immediate area of work and residence. Third, there will be a ranking system of invidious esteem—a system of *social stratification.* Fourth, to the extent that distinctive subcultures emerge and maintain social contact, each with the other, there will be *ethnic groupings.*[6]

---

[3] Cf. Gary S. Becker, *The Economics of Discrimination* (Chicago: The University of Chicago Press, 1957).

[4] Cf., for example: V. O. Key, Jr. (with the assistance of Alexander Heard), *Southern Politics in State and Nation* (New York: Alfred A. Knopf, 1950); H. D. Price, *The Negro and Southern Politics* (New York: New York University Press, 1957).

[5] For example, Oscar Handlin, *The Uprooted* (Boston: Little, Brown & Co., 1951).

[6] Cf. Talcott Parsons, *The Social System* (New York: The Free Press of Glencoe, Inc., 1951), Chapter V.

In dealing with racial, religious, and ethnic categories and collectivities, we need hardly stress, we are treating social phenomena of very considerable stability and continuity. Religious affiliations, for instance, are no mere preferences; very few associations constitute more durable marks of the identity of individuals in American society than membership in one of the three major religious faiths. It is estimated that probably 95 per cent of adults remain in the major religious grouping into which they were born.[7]

Relationships among individuals within these four social structures are mainly *ascribed* (fixed by birth or other involuntary membership), *diffuse* (covering a wide and open-ended range of rights and duties), and *particularistic* (based on particular relations to particular persons or statuses, not on generalized, impersonal rules). In modern complex societies, the four basic structures are interlaced and overlaid by economic and political systems that are organized in considerable part on radically different principles —the principles of achieved, competitive placement rather than ascription by birth, of impersonal universalistic norms, and of highly specific, narrowly defined relations among persons. Also, in our society, the major religious traditions all stress universalism in the ethical domain.

Primary relationships. In the primary structures of family, community, social class, and ethnic groupings lie the earliest attachments, the first relationships of trust in persons, the deepest dependencies, and the most important bases of emotional ambivalence. No child survives without these attachments. The early learning transforms the dependent and unformed child into a social being, capable of group loyalties and of outgroup rejection. It is evident that there must be early loyalties that are provincial and exclusive. In an emotionally secure child, taught to enlarge progressively his social capacities and loyalties and to generalize his ethical sensitivities, there can be a relatively straight-forward maturation into adulthood, relatively free from rigid outgroup prejudices. Some children do develop into mature persons who are realistic and adaptable and whose aggressive needs are constructively managed. It is possible, even if rare, to develop communities in which such personalities are nurtured and supported by the main institutional norms and group processes. But the development of mature personality is complex and difficult. Socialization is not easy or automatic. Most adult personalities represent the complicated outcome of many fierce internal battles and of imperfect compromises. Even the relatively secure and well-integrated personality may resort to irrational aggression against outgroups under certain conditions of extremely severe strain.

Furthermore, the person's basic securities usually are closely dependent upon his positions in the four social structures just described. To the degree

---

[7] J. Milton Yinger, "Social Forces Involved in Group Identification or Withdrawal," *Daedalus,* Proceedings of the American Academy of Arts and Sciences, XC, No. 2 (Spring, 1961), 249.

that the individual's developmental experience is constricted by rigidities and localisms bound up with family, community, class, and ethnic group, the individual will not acquire the knowledge, or the skill, or the positive motivations and values required for cooperative relationships with ethnic outsiders in a pluralistic society. At the same time, if people do depend for their security and satisfaction upon ascribed membership in family, community, and class, and if these memberships are rendered insecure and full of conflict, the individual is likely to attach great importance to the remaining ascribed statuses, such as those based on race, religion, or ethnic origin. Membership in a superordinate racial category, for example, can take on enormous emotional significance when it is felt to be the sole remaining social anchor for prestige-status and derivative self-evaluation.

In addition, the fact of social differentiation means that there are individuals and collectivities that may differ in their control of and their aspirations for power, wealth, prestige, and other scarce values. The realistic competition and struggle thus generated is an endemic source of intergroup tension and conflict. This basis for intergroup asperity would remain even in an unlikely world of completely sane, psychologically stable and mature adults who always sought their goals in a rational manner. In other words, there would be a basis for group conflict even in a world in which there were no sick individuals [8] or sick societies, provided only that groups or other collectivities are operating as distinct entities that are in competition or rivalry for scarce values.

Less personal relationship. In modern urban society, the relationships between individuals in occupational and organizational life outside of the family and of locality and congeniality groupings tend to emphasize norms quite different from those governing primary relationships. In terms of pattern variables, the worlds of work and of public life tend to be marked by emphases upon functional specificity, universalism, affective neutrality, and performance (achievement).[9] Although these normative principles may be, and are, inculcated in the diffuse ascribed settings of family and peer groups, it is likely that full capacity to function in terms of universalistic rules and

---

[8] We may well ponder the applicability of the observation of Kenneth M. Colby: "Now it does no good to criticize people in the hope of changing them. They are what they have to be, not what they want to be." [*A Skeptical Psychoanalyst* (New York: The Ronald Press Company, 1958), p. 5.]

[9] As Robert E. Park put it, this is the "great world" of business and politics as over against the "little world" of intimate relationships ". . . in which men were bound together by tradition, custom, and natural piety." Park went on to say: "On the other hand, it was and is in the market place where men from distant places come together to chaffer and bargain, that men first learn the subtleties of commerce and exchange; the necessity for cool calculation, even in human affairs, and the freedom to act, as individuals, in accordance with interests, rather than sentiments." ["Cultural Conflict and the Marginal Man" in Talcott Parsons *et al.,* eds., *Theories of Society,* II (New York: The Free Press of Glencoe, Inc., 1961), p. 945.]

performance norms is dependent upon extensive and intensive direct experience with them. An individual whose experience has been *only* in kinship and locality groups will have learned *primarily* the norms of functional diffuseness, particularism, affectivity, and quality (ascription). He will find it initially difficult to understand and to act in terms of the principles of specificity-universalism-neutrality-performance. He will tend to interpret specific relationships as implying total, diffuse relationships; he will expect (or will wish to enact) expressive actions when only instrumental emphases are institutionally called for; he will judge others by particular-relational criteria rather than by fixed, impersonal standards; and he will conceive of other persons more nearly in terms of qualities or essences rather than in terms of their demonstrated skills.

To the extent that the foregoing description is valid, it leads to implications that should be testable. In the first place, it implies that greatest difficulty and resistance to the acceptance of interaction across ethnic lines in situations that require the *gesellschaftliche* principles (specificity, neutrality, universalism, performance) are likely to appear among those persons who: (1) are of rural origin; (2) are women rather than men; (3) of lower socioeconomic position; (4) of lower educational level; (5) have experienced little geographic mobility; (6) have experienced little social mobility during their own occupational careers. These predictions, of course, would be expected to hold only if other relevant variables were constant in each instance. For example, higher education would be expected to offset sex-role differences; or, the stress of rapid and great downward social mobility would be expected to induce regressive tendencies that would more than undo the predicted effects of experience in contrasting social-class environments. But, other things being roughly comparable, the predictions should be supported by the facts of observed behavior.

Now, it is on the whole true that issues of discrimination and segregation in intergroup relations center upon the quality-performance dilemma—ascription versus achievement—and typically involve also the tendency to treat intergroup relations as implying *gemeinschaft* elements even in contexts such as occupation or higher education, otherwise normally characterized by specificity-neutrality-universalism.

Two further propositions immediately follow. First, the more nearly a situation into which an ethnic outgroup is attempting to enter is impersonal, the less the resistance. Second, the more nearly the experience of individuals (and especially of groups of individuals) has been confined to contexts of diffuseness, particularism, quality, and affectivity, the greater their resistance to and difficulty in accepting an ethnic outgroup even in functionally specific impersonal situations. The propositions just outlined are likewise consistent with the observation that some kinds of authoritarian reactions to intergroup relations are especially likely among lower-class groupings.[10]

Finally, as in the case of religious affiliations, all of these factors may be reinforced by real or imagined differences in beliefs and ultimate values. Thus, where actual differences in values and beliefs lead to patterns of behavior on the part of members of one religious body that adversely affect persons of a different religious faith, conflict and tension are not merely expressions of irrational prejudice but rather of reactions to genuine injury or threat. Differences in value orientations are of direct significance in inter= faith relations, in many political relations, and may sometimes be of importance in other concrete types of intergroup relations. For this reason, among others, it does not automatically hold that propositions that are valid for Negro-white relations, for example, will apply in the same way to Protestant-Catholic relations.[11]

Universality of differentiation. Each social relationship will in some measure call forth a unique set of interactions. But the demands on any given individual's sensitivity and time would quickly become immobilizing in large social networks unless some classifying, grouping, or standardizing could be accomplished. Networks must be limited, then, and persons must to some minimal degree be classified. The limiting and the classifying can be carried out in a great variety of ways. Universally the great biological landmarks of sex and age are used as reference points for the channelization and limitation of social interaction. Other bases for division lie in territorial community, in occupation, and in similarities and differences in language, religion, and a wide range of other sociocultural characteristics.

Social differentiation, then, is universal and inevitable. Categories, collectivities, and groups are universal and inevitable. Preferential association is universal and inevitable. But it is not universal and it is not inevitable that racial, or ethnic, or religious identifications will be the primary bases for any particular set of social relations. The point is vividly made when we find instances in which even well-established prejudices do not prevent interaction based on proximity, interdependence, common interests, and the like. In addition to our own studies, other research has found situations in which initial attitudes are less important in determining interaction than proximity and functional occasions for contact.[12] Thus, Wilner, Walkley,

---

[10] Jesse Pitts has suggested that the rigidities attributed to the syndrome of the authoritarian personality may be alternatively conceived as failure to differentiate performance from quality categories—a failure rooted in constricted social experience. (*Theories of Society,* II, p. 700.)

[11] Cf. the more extensive discussion in Robin M. Williams, Jr., "Religion, Value-Orientations, and Intergroup Conflict," *The Journal of Social Issues,* XII, No. 3 (1956), 12-20.

[12] See the summary in John Harding *et al.,* "Prejudice and Ethnic Relations," pp. 1032-33.

and Cook in a study of Negroes and whites in an integrated housing project showed that both proximity and prejudice were important, but that nearness to Negro neighbors was clearly the more influential condition in neighborly relations.[13] In other cases strong prejudices reinforced by ingroup sanctions take priority over proximity, convenience, comfort, economy, safety, good will, and a wide variety of other important considerations. We know also that group discrimination can remain at a high level even when the minority is too small and weak to be a realistic political or economic threat.[14] Some prejudice arises from intrapersonality processes only remotely connected with realistic threats. Some discriminatory behavior derives from the same sources. But both prejudice and discriminatory behavior require *objects* and can only be expressed through *interaction* (either within an ingroup, or with outgroup members).

Complexity of factors affecting intergroup relations. It cannot be repeated too often that both social and psychological factors are essential to adequate explanation of intergroup relations. To treat whole systems of discriminatory behavior—in all their extensiveness, complexity, regularity, and historical persistence—as if they were solely the outcome of the spontaneous expression of stereotyped beliefs and hostile feelings of separate individuals —this is now manifestly an untenable approach. To treat prejudice as if it were an automatic response to collective or societal structures and processes is likewise erroneous. The one gives too little place to the pervading influences of group properties and systemic effects. The other fails to see the imperatives of psyche and organism.

Staying close to the research evidence, it is possible to state in a fairly complete way several of the main classes of variables that repeatedly turn out to be importantly related to intergroup contact and interaction and to cooperation or conflict. These variables may be classified into these basic categories:

1. *Status attributes* of individual persons, for example, age, sex, marital status, education, generalized prestige ranking.

2. *Cultural values* held by individuals, for example, universalistic evaluations of competence in technical tasks.

3. *Stereotypes and prejudices* (definitions of ethnic objects).

4. *Personality* structure and dynamics of individuals (for example, sources of psychological energy).

5. Characteristics of the *situation of contact,* for example, nature of col-

---

[13] D. M. Willner, Rosabelle P. Walkley, and S. W. Cook, "Residential Proximity and Intergroup Relations in Public Housing Projects," *Journal of Social Issues,* VIII, No. 1 (1952), 45-69.

[14] Cf. H. M. Blalock, Jr., "A Power Analysis of Racial Discrimination," *Social Forces,* XXXIX, No. 1 (October, 1960), 57.

lective goals, if any; presence and role of third parties; number of participants and proportion of each significant social category represented; relative power.

6. *Collective properties emerging from interaction,* for example, awareness of attitudes shared with others; sense of group position; patterns of
concerted action (sit-ins, lynchings, passive resistance, boycotts); group
cohesion.

It is easy to see that *a priori* claims to raise one factor or set of factors
to a position of exclusive primacy cannot be accepted without fully taking
into account all the other possibly influential factors. Responsible judgments
therefore require detailed evidence concerning a considerable number of
factors. Further, the effects of any one factor are likely to vary according
to its varying combinations with other factors. Evidently there are a great
many possible combinations. We do not have to be overawed by this impressive complexity, but we do need to keep it in mind, especially when
we are confronted by single-factor explanations. Let us re-examine the
problem at the social level.

GROUP STRUCTURES AND INDIVIDUAL ATTITUDES

It is by now clear that intergroup relations never can be adequately
understood merely in terms of positive or negative attitudes of undifferentiated masses of individuals.[15] *Real societies are not made up of homogen-
ized aggregates of interchangeable and unattached psychological molecules.*
Societies are highly differentiated systems constituted by numerous subsystems. True as this is for our own society, the interplay of subsystems is perhaps easier to see in perspective in societies other than our own. It is evident,
for example, in the highly differentiated society of rural India, the classic
home of caste. Marriott [16] has pointed out the inadequacies of the conception
that in the Hindu case a caste's rank is determined by the ritual purity of its
behavior or attributes—its way of life, for example, vegetarianism, absti-
nence from alcoholic beverages, "pure" occupations. He proposes an interactional theory that holds that castes are ranked according to the structure
of interaction between them, especially the net flow of ritual honoring and
purification from others (for example, rank of foods transferred, of ritual
services). Dominance in the system of ritually significant exchanges is greatly

[15] Herbert Blumer, "Race Prejudice as a Sense of Group Position," *The Pacific
Sociological Review,* I, No. 1 (Spring, 1958), 6: "Historical records of major instances
of race relations, as in our South, or in South Africa, or in Europe in the case of the
Jew, or on the West Coast in the case of the Japanese show the formidable part
played by interest groups in defining the subordinate racial group."

[16] McKim Marriott, "Interactional and Attributional Theories of Caste Ranking,"
Man In India, XXXIX, No. 2 (April-June, 1959), 92-107.

affected by wealth and power (through money lending and control of land rights). Interactional ranking is thought to be more characteristic of the localistic villages; attributional ranking, of the urban, mobile, and educated sectors of the society.

Interrelations of social subsystems

As this case suggests, the term "intergroup relations" actually points to systems of relations built up of numerous interlocking and overlapping subsystems that connect in intricate and ever-changing configurations. A possibly useful way to think of these subsystems is to arrange them in classes defined by the two criteria of (1) size (number of members) and (2) demonstrated capacity for concerted, purposive collective action. The smallest subsystem consists of one individual from category A interacting with one individual from category B. Still at the small-group level are all those interpersonal aggregates of more than two parties that are nevertheless small enough so that each participant gains some direct and concrete impression of every other as a separate person upon each occasion of interaction. Millions of these interpersonal subsystems occur every day in the multiethnic society of the United States. So long as such small aggregates neither combine as subunits of larger and more definitely focalized organizations nor extend themselves beyond the established contexts of job, neighborhood, etc., in which they emerged, they may serve to bridge interethnic cleavages to some extent without having marked effects upon the basic structure of power within which ethnic categories have their life chances defined for them.

Intergroup or intercategory relations do not consist merely of isolated person-to-person relations or of diffuse linkages among small, informal groups. In addition to the diffuse point-to-point relations, there is the interplay of organized interest groups, the action of mass collective movements (boycotts, voting), and the representational and negotiating relationships of leaders and officials.[17] Furthermore, the various kinds of relationships existing among the ethnic groupings within a community or region form a system such that the relations of A to B are altered by changes in the relationship of B to C and so on.

An overview of intergroup processes

Here, then, is our summary view of intergroup relations at the community level, with which our own studies have been concerned: we find

---

17 See James Q. Wilson, *Negro Politics: The Search for Leadership* (New York: The Free Press of Glencoe, Inc., 1960); Herbert Garfinkle, *When Negroes March* (New York: The Free Press of Glencoe, Inc., 1959); Richard A. Schermerhorn, *Society and Power* (New York: Random House, 1961), Chapter V, "Countervailing Power."

certain historically created and culturally recognized social categories defined by reference to racial, ethnic, or religious identities. These categories are defined by more or less definite and more or less widely shared stereotypes and affective-evaluative attitudes. Given these definitions, the social categories begin to mark off real collectivities just to the extent that cumulative interaction, segregated intercourse, and differentiated behavior lead to awareness of collective differences, of common fate, and to identification with an ingroup and its symbols. Through these processes, what was originally a mere aggregate becomes a powerful functioning collectivity.

Given such structures existing side by side in the local community, intergroup relations involve several distinct sets of social processes. At the level of interpersonal relationships in specific situations of intergroup contact, behavior is importantly affected by the normative expectations each of the interacting parties has concerning his own reference group's probable reactions to his conduct in the situation, and his expectations and demands concerning the behavior of the other person. Because of the complex operation of *other* factors, the interacting parties typically modify their initial definitions of the situation, often quite markedly, in different concrete situations and in the same situation as it moves from initiation to termination.

But, at the same time, a second distinct set of relevant processes are going on, namely, those that occur exclusively within each of the collectivities taken separately. Here, within overlapping primary groupings marked by relations of trust, stereotypes are reinforced, awareness of group identity is sharpened, and ingroup solidarity is inculcated and strengthened. These processes are the more effective the greater the segregation of the socially recognized collectivities and the more intense the competition and conflict among them. Within the invisible walls of the collectivity, the expression of outgroup prejudice provides a legitimized mode for the management of otherwise disruptive or uncomfortable intragroup aggressions, supplies a common universe of discourse, reinforces a sense of belonging, and serves as a set of credentials of membership.

Still a third set of processes becomes evident when we turn our attention to the larger precedents for the basic patterns of intercollectivity relations. For some of the most decisive intergroup processes are those involving contact between representatives of formally organized groups, on the one hand, and those involving decisions about relations between the collectivities as such (not just among individuals who happen to be classified as members). Relations at this level cannot be easily or directly inferred from knowledge of interpersonal conduct at the level of the small group. Here we have the phenomena of the decisions leading to a Little Rock, or to the defiance of national law by the governor of Mississippi, the establishment of a policy of Apartheid, the perpetuation of segregation in publicly supported housing, the abolition of official segregation in the armed services. In such crucial precedent-setting public decisions, interpersonal relations of friendship or enmity or even the private attitudes of the decision makers often have surprisingly little to do with the outcome. These are decisions at a distance, which, by their very nature, tend to be categorical, that is, involving sharpening and leveling as well as the social imperatives of abstract generality, universal administrative applicability, and concrete definiteness of classification.[18]

Group properties and structural pluralism

At levels above the local community in power structures, the group properties of ethnic relations are clearly shown. Thus, in society after society during the past century, the emergence or intensification of nationalistic movements has been closely connected with discrimination against minority ethnic groupings within the society.[19] A striking case is the progressive worsening of Thai-Chinese relations since about 1910, as nationalistic movements gained strength in both the ethnic groupings, as economic competition intensified, and as the Chinese minority increasingly became socially self-sufficient, especially through the increased immigration of women. Some of the culturally assimilated descendants of immigrant Chinese are critics or even persecutors of unassimilated Chinese today. All these developments occurred against a background of considerable Thai-Chinese intermarriage and a long history of accommodation.[20]

A prevalent idea is that ethnic assimilation is a kind of natural or inevitable outcome of extended intercultural contact. Yet we know that distinct ethnic groups may live together in close contact for long periods without any really important borrowing or assimilation.[21] Also, rather complete overt assimilation may overlay the subtle retention of many of the characteristics of the original culture.[22] The melting pot does not always work.

---

[18] Robin M. Williams, Jr., "Continuity and Change in Sociological Study," *American Sociological Review*, XXIII (1958), 625-26.

[19] Cf. the analysis of Charles Wagley and Marvin Harris, *Minorities in the New World: Six Case Studies* (New York: Columbia University Press, 1958), pp. 241-43ff.

[20] Cf. G. William Skinner, *Chinese Society in Thailand: An Analytical History* (Ithaca, N.Y.: Cornell University Press, 1957).

[21] Cf. the summary and references in Brewton Berry, *Race Relations* (Boston: Houghton Mifflin Company, 1951), pp. 222-26. Also: John and Ruth Hill Useem, "Minority-Group Pattern in Prairie Society," *American Journal of Sociology,* L (March, 1945), 377-85; E. K. Francis, "The Russian Mennonites: From Religious to Ethnic Group," *American Journal of Sociology,* LIV (September, 1948), 101-07; B. W. Aginsky, "The Interaction of Ethnic Groups: A Case Study of Indians and Whites," *American Sociological Review,* XIV (1949), 288-93.

[22] F. L. K. Hsu, "The Chinese of Hawaii: Their Role in American Culture," *Transactions of the New York Academy of Science,* XIII (1951), 243-50; Mary Bosworth Trendley ["The Ethnic Group as a Collectivity," *Social Forces,* XXXI, No. 3 (March, 1953), 261-65] shows the retention of expressive culture and sense of membership in a highly adapted population of Syrians in Boston.

For example, Munch has shown some of the processes by which the original culture is defended against assimilation in the case of certain rural Norwegian groupings in Wisconsin, and he makes the very important point that *cultural* assimilation does not necessarily bring *social* assimilation.[23] This point has been developed by Milton M. Gordon, who makes a case for viewing our social structure as segmented or compartmentalized into relatively closed groupings defined by combinations of nationality background, racial, religious, class, and residence factors.[24] Acculturation to a common way of life has been extraordinarily complete in the United States. But, as our own studies suggest, separateness in primary social relationships has resulted in a society marked by structural pluralism.

Structural pluralism can persist for very long periods of time and need not be dissolved by urban-industrial modes of life. Examples are numerous. The lengths to which group separatism can go in an industrialized Western society are well illustrated in the vertical pluralism of the Netherlands. The society is divided into three basic columns, Catholic, Protestant, and humanistic (with small numbers of people who seek to be neutral), each of which encompasses the individual from the cradle to the grave.[25]

INTERDEPENDENCE OF SOCIAL SETTINGS AND PSYCHOLOGICAL PROCESSES

Importance of organized groups

We thus find that massive collective processes, eventuating in relatively enduring social structures, set the framework within which—and only within which—individual psychological factors can influence *group* (categorical) relations among persons.[26] It is apparent, for example, that in a complex urban society, intergroup relations *necessarily* transcend the level of small groups and interpersonal relations; they necessarily come to be regulated by law and organized action. Clashes of groups often, if not always, occur as a consequence of action in the service of incompatible interests—one group wants something that the other group has, or wants to act in a way that

---

[23] Peter A. Munch, "Social Adjustment Among Wisconsin Norwegians," *American Sociological Review,* XIV (1949), 780-87. See also: Douglas G. Marshall, "Nationality and the Emerging Culture," *Rural Sociology,* XIII (1948), 40-47; E. K. Francis, "The Adjustment of a Peasant Group to a Capitalistic Economy: The Manitoba Mennonites," *Rural Sociology,* XVII, No. 3 (1952), 218-28.

[24] Milton M. Gordon, "Assimilation in America: Theory and Reality," *Daedalus,* Proceedings of the American Academy of Arts and Sciences, XC, No. 2 (Spring, 1961), 279-83.

[25] David O. Moberg, "Social Differentiation in the Netherlands," *Social Forces,* XXXIX, No. 4 (May, 1961), 333-37.

[26] Cf. Stanley Lieberson, "A Societal Theory of Race and Ethnic Relations," *American Sociological Review,* XXVI, No. 6 (December, 1961), 902-10.

threatens the interests and values of the members of the other group, or is thought to have these wants or to do these things.[27] Quite without any unusual tendencies to use projection, displacement, or denial of reality, and without any unusual frustration or deprivation of group members, conflict may arise straightforwardly out of the fact that two social units are differently situated with regard to scarce values desired by both or differ with regard to beliefs and values upon which consensus is desired.[28]

How attitudes are related to intergroup behavior

Evidences from many sources point to the very loose relationship between opinions or attitudes (as expressed in interviews and questionnaires) and subsequent behavior with regard to the objects of these opinions or attitudes. This problematic relationship stands out sharply in situations of large-scale institutional processes [29] and social change. In the case of racial desegregation of public schools, it has been shown that, in terms of the particular question asked, slightly less than one-third of the white population in border states that had already desegregated their school system indorsed desegregation.[30] Yet desegregation had been largely accomplished without gross social conflict or disorder. Even apart from any immediate social influences, an initial generalized attitude before it actually issues in appropriate action may be turned in the direction of any of a range of possible behaviors depending upon time, place, persons, and other values and beliefs. A generalized attitude of social distance of a white person toward Negroes may be reshaped by many mediating and countervailing perspectives before it enters into a concrete policy judgment concerning local school desegregation.[31]

Furthermore, prejudice requires an object. Racial and ethnic prejudices require that prejudiced individuals be able to identify themselves as members of one distinct grouping set over against another or others. The group identities and the individual's sense of group positions and memberships are

---

[27] Jesse Bernard, "The Sociological Study of Conflict," in *The Nature of Conflict* (The International Sociological Association in collaboration with Jessie Bernard, T. H. Pear, Raymond Aron, Robert C. Angell) (Paris: UNESCO, 1957), p. 39.

[28] See, for an example: R. E. Murphy, "Intergroup Hostility and Social Cohesion, *American Anthropologist*, LIX, No. 6 (December, 1957), 1033.

[29] A detailed demonstration of this point is supplied by V. O. Key, Jr., *Public Opinion and American Democracy* (New York: Alfred A. Knopf, Inc., 1961); see especially chapters 5-8 and 19-21.

[30] H. H. Hyman and P. B. Sheatsley, "Attitudes toward Desegregation," *Scientific American*, CXCV (1956), pp. 35-39.

[31] See the discussion of countervailing perspectives in Melvin Tumin, Paul Barton, and Bernie Burrus, "Education, Prejudice and Discrimination: A Study in Readiness for Desegregation," *American Sociological Review*, XXIII, No. 1 (February, 1958), 41-49.

historical products derived from collective processes.[32] Through diffuse informal means as well as through mass communication, awareness of large-scale historical events is widely shared. Individuals acquire convictions that go far beyond their direct personal experience. Conceptions of group characteristics and positions are primarily developed and fixed by public discussions, especially as a result of acts and statements by conspicuous institutional leaders in connection with important and dramatic events and issues. In American history, the Southern Counterrevolution of *circa* 1895-1910 re-established white supremacy and fixed a pattern of racial segregation that was to last for nearly a half century. The regional political events that led to this crucial result cannot be adequately understood except by taking into account national political realities, which in turn were powerfully influenced by the flood tide of Western imperialism.[33]

Among many other studies that illustrate the point that attitudes are related to real intergroup events, not to mere fantasy, Prothro and Melikian's work shows that among students in the heterogeneous setting of Beirut there is a *general* reserve toward outgroups, a feeling of close relationships within the ingroup, and a tendency to emphasize national rather than religious social distance. Comparison with an earlier study by Stuart C. Dodd shows that changes in social distance reflect actual changes in the relationships among ethnic groupings, including the increased nationalism among Arab groupings.[34]

Relation of prejudice to personality affected by social settings

The extent to which prejudice is related to generalized personality characteristics will itself vary from one sociocultural setting to another. In American society, the idea of cultural assimilation is dominant, but group relations are seen in the context of an individually mobile and competitive system. Prejudices in such a setting probably are especially likely to reflect

---

[32] Herbert Blumer, "Race Prejudice as a Sense of Group Position," *The Pacific Sociological Review*, I, No. 1 (Spring, 1958), 3-7. Blumer says on p. 3 that ". . . race prejudice exists basically in a sense of group position rather than in a set of feelings which members of one racial group have toward the members of another racial group."

[33] "This was the era of Rudyard Kipling, of Manifest Destiny, of the White Man's Burden." William G. Carleton in H. D. Price, *The Negro and Southern Politics,* p. xi.

[34] E. Terry Prothro and Levon Melikian, "Social Distance and Social Change in the Near East," *Sociology and Social Research*, XXXVII, No. 1 (September-October, 1952), 3-11. See also: Wallace E. Lambert, "Comparison of French and American Modes of Response to the Bogardus Social Distance Scale," *Social Forces,* XXXI, No. 2 (December, 1952), 155-60. The data indicate that the scale-order of items differs as between French and American populations; for example, the French are more reluctant to admit ethnic outgroups as citizens, whereas acceptance as neighbor is relatively easy for them.

generalized dispositions toward rigidity, hostility, conformity, and so on. In more traditionalistic societies in which religious and ethnic groupings preserve clear identities, outgroup attitudes are less affected by personality variables. Thus Prothro and Melikian find essentially no association between F-scale scores and social-distance scores, and no tendency to generalize ethnocentrism to all outgroups, among students at American University in Beirut. They conclude that ". . . the more tradition-oriented, mosaic type of social structure found in the Near East encourages ethnocentrism but does not link it so closely to antidemocratic personality traits.[35]

If the continued existence of orderly human interaction depended upon the total absence of hostility, none of us would live in society as we now know it—if, indeed, we lived at all.[36] Hostility probably is deeply involved in the essential functioning of goal-seeking, symbol-using organisms, equipped with adrenal glands and related biochemical mechanisms, and subject to numerous important frustrations from other humans. Hostility is not a mere secondary manifestation of a basically serene organism, which needs only to be treated well to behave with loving care toward others. It it a universally important component of normal human social behavior in normal society. Its amount can be minimized under good conditions; it can be turned in constructive rather than destructive directions. But, to paraphrase Pareto, he who thinks to abolish hostility is cutting holes in the water.

Yet, even those intergroup relations that are most discriminatory are not explicable on the basis of hostile attitudes alone. Certainly there is ill will enough in ethnic and racial relations, but there may be less than at first appears to the eye. Actually there would seem to be little reason to doubt that much intergroup discrimination is a by-product of purposive action that is not primarily motivated by a need or desire to express hostility or to injure someone. This was one of the first great lessons impressed upon us in the field experience in the communities observed in the Cornell Studies. In the pursuit of personal goals and the satisfaction of personal interests, much instrumental action takes a discriminatory form. The most convincing evidence for this contention comes from the several studies indicating that intergroup behavior in the market or on the job is not closely related either to attitudes or to intergroup behavior in noneconomic contexts. Our own findings concerning situational variation and exemption provide much confirmatory evidence on this score.

---

[35] E. T. Prothro and L. H. Melikian, "Generalized Ethnic Attitudes in the Arab Near East," *Sociology and Social Research,* XXXVII, No. 6 (July-August, 1953), 379. The investigators add that students who express considerable social distance are not necessarily *hostile* toward the distant groupings.

[36] George C. Homans in *Social Behavior: Its Elementary Forms* (New York: Harcourt, Brace & World, 1961), p. 305, is willing to affirm that ". . . to make a man forego reward, no matter how small, is to arouse his hostility, no matter how little."

The case of religious affiliations in a multigroup society

Many of the general points just reviewed find concrete illustrations in the instance of interfaith relations in the United States. Most of our attention in the present volume has been directed to racial relations. But the basic concepts and the underlying model of a social system are adaptable to other types of intergroup relations. Let us illustrate the approach by examining briefly some of the main social features of interreligious relations in the United States.

A long-standing, if imprecise, hypothesis concerning social conflict has been that a society riven by many cleavages is in less danger of violent disruption than one in which a single massive division runs across the population.[37] Investigation of this notion takes on sharpened social relevance in view of our present understanding of the inevitability of *some* cleavages. Cleavages between groups exist in society as the simple "obverse of consensus within groups." This means that the question for analysis is not *why* is there cleavage, but *what* are the lines of potential cleavage in society, and what are the consequences of one configuration rather than another? [38]

Among the categorical bases for group formation in the United States are: race, religious affiliation, language, region, socioeconomic stratum, ethnic origin, political affiliation. Let us imagine that these attributes are invariably associated in such a way that only the following three clusters occur, with approximately the same numbers of persons in each:

	Clusters		
Category	I	II	III
Race	White	Negro	Chinese
Religion	Protestant	Catholic	Buddhist
Language	English speaking	Spanish speaking	Bilingual: Chinese-English
Region	New England	South	West
Class	Upper class	Middle class	Lower class
Ethnic origin	British	Gold Coast	China
Political party	Republican	Democrat	Socialist

What would be the outcomes of this situation? We may be sure that a society made up in this way would not be anything like the United States we now know. Nor would any of the major factors listed have its present significance.

Overlapping of religious membership with other social characteristics. Notice that in this hypothetical society there is *no overlapping of the several*

---

[37] *The Reduction of Intergroup Tensions,* Bulletin 57, Social Science Research Council, New York (1947), p. 59.

[38] James S. Coleman, "Social Cleavage and Religious Conflict," *Journal of Social Issues,* XII, No. 3 (1956), 53.

crucial social attributes. This characteristic makes for maximum likelihood of divergent interests and for maximum clarity of group membership. If groupings of this kind are in contact and *if* they are competitive, the likelihood is great that some form of conflict will emerge. Thus we may arrive at this hypothesis: "Group conflicts are at their strongest, are most likely to develop and least easily dissipated, when no conflict is felt within the person." [39] Another way of stating the point is to say that a major factor in reducing conflict *between* groupings is the maximizing of cross pressures within individuals through multiple, overlapping group memberships.

We may say, therefore, that:

1. Maximum potentiality of large-scale group conflict is present when the *major structural* categories of social differentiation coincide to form a small number of massive social categories, whose members nevertheless are competitively interdependent in economic and political subsystems.

2. Major structural categories of great importance in any society are (*a*) territorial community; (*b*) social class; (*c*) ethnic grouping; (*d*) race; (*e*) religion; (*f*) political affiliation.

3. A society faces maximum likelihood of massive conflict (or of political disruption) when the various lines of differentiation of values, interests, and collectivity memberships coincide among the same population aggregates. In contemporary United States, the various major bases for collectivity memberships crisscross in a most complicated fashion. Very different are the consequences to be expected from a cumulative coincidence of all these lines of differentiation.

If the points thus far made are valid, it is a reasonable supposition that differences in religion will be least disruptive in a multigroup society when they are not systematically associated with other important bases of divergence in values and interests.[40] In Underwood's study of an overwhelmingly Catholic city in northeastern United States,[41] it was observed that religious cleavage had been accentuated by the correlation of class and ethnic lines with religious affiliation, partly because this very association tended to reinforce stereotyped preconceptions and antipathies. Protestants were primarily of Yankee background and middle- and upper-middle-class position;

---

[39] *Ibid.,* 46.

[40] A conspicuous example of a modern religious sect that is radically alienated from the environing society is that of Jehovah's Witnesses. Like other alienated (proletarian) movements, it emphasizes a "cataclysmic end of the world with a millennium following," a system of esoteric knowledge, a doctrine of sharp rejection of the world, and a vision of a future utopia. Cf. Werner Cohn, "Jehovah's Witnesses as a Proletarian Movement," *The American Scholar,* XXIV, No. 3 (Summer, 1955), 284-88.

[41] Kenneth M. Underwood, *Protestant and Catholic* (Boston: The Beacon Press, Inc., 1957).

Catholics derived more largely from later immigration and tended on the whole to occupy the lower socioeconomic strata.

The hypotheses just discussed can be put into testable forms. Establishment of the conditions under which they are valid, would, presumably, be of great permanent interest.

A more positive source of social solidarity arises from the multiplicity of interests and values in the overlapping memberships that bind men together in a pluralistic society. Each man can have the security of diversified economic, political, and other socioemotional investments: he has not committed all his eggs to one basket. Conflicts of economic interest, of status aspirations, or even of religious views do not, therefore, have the desperate urgency that comes from staking everything on a single commitment.[42] This hypothesis is somewhat imprecise, and it will not hold without qualification under any and all circumstances. But the truth it contains becomes evident when we see the consequences of a threat to a single group membership upon which depends all the major values of a man's life. Whether the membership in question be that of clan, tribe, church, or nation, any severe threat to an all-inclusive bond of membership must necessarily arouse great fear. The most powerful and elemental reactions to great fear are two, namely, flight or attack. And if flight is impossible, fear can lead to the deepest rage and the most complete and merciless conflicts. These are underlying elements in the ferocity of blood feuds, religious wars, and totalitarian civil wars.

Conditions leading to conflict or accommodation among religious groupings. In all relations of members of one religious body to those of another, there is the possibility of active disagreement concerning genuine questions of ultimate values.[43] What we are increasingly discovering, however, is the great extent to which strictly religious differences need not interfere with peaceful coexistence, *if* certain other conditions are present. Again for illustration only, we cite a few additional hypotheses.

The likelihood of overt conflict between any two religious collectivities within a given social system would appear to be reduced by any one of the following conditions, or by any combination of them:

1. Low intensity or salience of belief in the exclusive validity of a highly specific, institutionalized belief system on the part of a high proportion of the members of both the religious groupings in question.[44]

---

[42] Cf. Margaret Mary Wood, *Paths of Loneliness* (New York: Columbia University Press, 1960), p. 194.

[43] Williams, "Religion, Value-Orientations, and Intergroup Conflict," *Journal of Social Issues,* XII, No. 3 (1956), 12-20.

[44] Commitment to *certain* theological tenets may reduce the likelihood of overt conflict. The complex problem posed by differing qualities and objects of faith and devotion cannot be treated here.

2. Frequent personal association of members of the religious collectivities in secular activities involving shared goals and cooperative action.[45]

3. Presence of an outside collectivity perceived as competing with or actively threatening the power position and other interests and values of both of the religious collectivities.

4. Multiple, overlapping membership (on the part of a large proportion of members of both religious groupings) in other collectivities.

5. A stable balance of power, which may be either a traditionalized situation of accommodation to marked inequality or a situation of such perceived equality that neither party sees any possibility of dominance save at prohibitive cost.

This limited examination suggests that further systematic and objective study of interreligious relations would be likely to produce results of great theoretical as well as practical importance.

STATUS AND STATUS CONGRUITY

Aspects of status congruity

The problems of the causes and consequences of status congruity and incongruity are found in two main forms. The first has to do with the combinations of positions that are normatively prescribed, preferred, permitted, and prohibited in a particular social system or part thereof. Certain combinations of statuses are both normatively disapproved and rarely found (say, a young, Negro woman construction boss who would supervise the work of crews of older white men).[46] The second form of congruity and incongruity concerns the combination of attributes associated with a given status. For example: ". . . each occupation and work position carries with it certain important status attributes or characteristics. Each has associated with it (1) a known level of *rewards,* both economic and psychological; (2) a social evaluation in terms of *prestige;* (3) a certain amount of control over the behavior of others—i.e., *authority* and (4) a certain *functional importance."* [47] Obviously, not only occupations and work positions but any kind of social position can be analyzed in these terms.

---

[45] Common participation in satisfying activities is not enough. Interdependence requiring cooperation to achieve goals seems essential. See Muzafer Sherif, "Superordinate Goals in the Reduction of Intergroup Conflict," *American Journal of Sociology,* LXIII, No. 4 (January, 1958), 354-56.

[46] See the classic essay by Everett C. Hughes, "Dilemmas and Contradictions of Status," *American Journal of Sociology,* L, No. 5 (March, 1945), pp. 353-59.

[47] Roland J. Pellegrin and Frederick L. Bates, "Congruity and Incongruity of Status Attributes within Occupations and Work Positions," *Social Forces,* XXXVIII, No. 1 (October, 1959), 24. See also: Emile Benoit-Smullyan, "Status, Status Types, and Status Interrelations," *American Sociological Review,* IX, No. 2 (April, 1944), 151-61; Ray Gold, "Janitors vs. Tenants: A Status-Income Dilemma," *The American Journal of Sociology,* LVII, No. 5 (March, 1952), 486-93; Gerhard E. Lenski, "Status Crystallization: A Non-Vertical Dimension of Social Status," *American Sociological Review,* XIX, No. 4 (August, 1954), 405-13.

In a society that has a quite elaborate division of labor, it may often happen that work positions carry status attributes that conflict with cultural prescriptions for appropriate behavior toward the persons who occupy these positions, who also occupy other statuses. It may happen that the young have greater authority than the old, women than men, ethnics than natives, newcomers than old-timers. It may also happen that well-educated and highly competent individuals find themselves, because of ethnic discrimination, deprived of the normal opportunities and prerogatives that ordinarily accompany the exercise of their training and talents.

Effects of status incongruity on intergroup relations

One of the most important things that can be said about ethnic discrimination in the United States is that both the moral uneasiness and the social tension it arouses are positively associated with the amount of status incongruity it occasions.[48] Upwardly mobile members of minority groupings feel incongruity between what they deserve by the criteria of achievement and what they actually get, under the depressing forces of prejudice and discrimination. Upper-status members of the dominant groupings often resist entrance of anomalous persons—those who represent status incongruity. The ragged and uneven accommodations of a mobile but discriminatory stratification system have been abundantly described in many community studies from Middletown on.[49]

In the United States the great emphasis upon individual economic advancement, rather than collective advancement through political means, has tended to maximize status incongruities and thereby to divide and weaken potential minority protest movements. To the extent that the environing society of a minority group is categorically discriminatory but at the same time allows for the social assimilation of individuals who (1) are culturally assimilable and (2) have attained high rank within the minority—to this extent the potential leadership of protest *tends* to be drawn away from the minority community.[50] Minorities based on national origin in the United

---

[48] Isidor Chein has dealt with some of the problems here under review as problems of inconsistency, and his conclusion is relevant: "For example, a man expresses certain attitudes toward Negroes, but in his contacts with Negroes acts in a manner seemingly inconsistent with these attitudes. Suppose, however, that further evidence clearly demonstrates that the fact that the individuals involved are Negroes is irrelevant to his manner of acting toward them; that all of the Negroes with whom he has contacts are among his subordinates; and that his actions toward his Negro subordinates are in no way different from his actions toward his other subordinates. With such evidence, the inconsistency obviously vanishes." ["The Problems of Inconsistency: A Restatement," *The Journal of Social Issues,* V, No. 3 (1949), 54.]

[49] Cf. W. Lloyd Warner and Leo Srole, *The Social Systems of American Ethnic Groups* (New Haven: Yale University Press, 1945), pp. 97-98.

[50] Note Sydney Collins' comment on the British scene: "The higher a coloured person rises in the social scale, the less he tends to associate closely with other coloured persons of lower social status and conversely the more he is drawn into white circles among people of his own status . . ." [*Coloured Minorities in Britain* (London: Lutterworth Press, 1957), p. 144.]

States obviously fit the description. The basic processes apparently have occurred many times elsewhere. As Orans has shown for the case of the some three million tribal Santals of India, an encysted society is especially subject to internal divisiveness and to assimilation toward the host culture of the dominant society once its members have begun to seek rank in that environing system *through economic improvement in a market economy*. Economic success produces internal differentiation and cleavage and encourages the partial assimilation of a minority elite to the surrounding culture.[51]

In American society, economic opportunity, political democracy, mass public education, and *relatively* fluid lines of social stratification not only create numerous incongruities but also make it impossible to stabilize a fixed caste-like order.

The place of education as an attribute of status

The role of education warrants special comment. Our own data have shown that level of education stands in complex relations to ethnic prejudice and interaction. Analysis of data from a large number of other studies indicates that better-educated white persons, as compared with the less well educated, are somewhat more often willing to give such tolerant or liberal responses as these: to accept Negroes as co-workers, to favor integration in the Armed Forces, to accept a Negro as a nurse, and to eat in a restaurant that serves Negroes. On the whole, however, the better educated are *less* willing to accept Negroes either as individual neighbors or as a substantial element in their residential area, and often fail to take a liberal position on the most highly controversial questions of interracial relations. The relationships between education and prejudices are quite complex, although the main effect appears to be the development of a more positive, accepting attitude. The effects are highly contingent upon general socioeconomic status and history of status mobility, upon initial ideology, and upon experience of interaction with members of minority groups, for example:

> The finding that education has more impact among those who have had contact with Negroes of their own status needs no special elucidation. We should note, however, that in the absence of such contact, schooling has little effect—a fact which points up how severely its potential is limited where segregation, formal or informal, continues to exist.[52]

Consistently it is found that high educational levels are associated with urbanism, liberalism, high level of information about minorities, and past

---

[51] Martin Orans, "A Tribe in Search of a Great Tradition: The Emulation-Solidarity Conflict," *Man in India*, XXXIX, No. 2 (April-June, 1959), 108-14.

[52] Charles Herbert Stember, *Education and Attitude Change* (New York: Institute of Human Relations Press, 1961), p. 178.

contact with minorities—all that which tend to go along with lesser prejudice. Beyond the elementary school level, the upper socioeconomic classes
within every educational level are the more often prejudiced in certain ways
against minorities (Jews and Negroes).[53] Thus, the relationships between
education and intergroup attitudes are not fully obvious, and certainly they
are not simple. In addition to the sources of variation already indicated, the
effect of educational level as compounded with socioeconomic status is modified by the relative status of the outgroup person to whom ego is oriented.

A great many other studies could be adduced here to fill in an extremely
complex picture of specific findings. Let us content ourselves with one additional factual note, followed by an attempt to state a rather far-ranging
hypothesis. Evidence has multiplied rapidly in recent studies that low socioeconomic position is correlated with high prevalence of psychological
anomie (or alienation) and of authoritarianism. The most severely deprived
strata of the population manifest an acceptance of or preference for external
leadership and control and for simple solutions of complex social issues.
These same strata tend to accept traditional stereotypes of outgroups and
to be unsophisticated in their global reactions to racial and ethnic categories.[54] Yet we also know that persons of high status can manifest strong
prejudice and act systematically to maintain systems of exclusion and discrimination. How may these findings best be interpreted?

We suggest that the relationship of educational levels to intergroup relations must be considered separately for attitudes (prejudice) as over against
actions (discrimination). In the first instance, higher levels of education in
our society tend generally to signify *greater complexity* and more *extended
perspectives*. The well educated tend to have more complex attitudes by
virtue of having access to more facts, to divergent opinions, to more subtle
distinctions. All other things being equal, educated persons react to a more
differentiated social world. At the same time, their horizons are larger in
terms of space, and time, and in the range of considerations taken in account in forming and expressing opinions. The prejudice of the well educated, when it does exist, may in some ways be harder, colder, more polite
and more thoroughly buttressed by rationalizations, but it is less likely to
be global, diffuse, and all-or-none in character.

---

[53] *Ibid.*, p. 176.

[54] Cf. Seymour M. Lipset, "Social Stratification and 'Right-Wing Extremism,' "
The British Journal of Sociology, X, No. 4 (December, 1959), 31: "Extremist movements have much in common. They appeal to the disgruntled and the psychologically
homeless, to the personal failures, the socially isolated, the economically insecure,
the uneducated, unsophisticated and authoritarian persons *at every level of the society*." [Italics added.] Cf. also: Melvin Tumin *et al.*, "Education, Prejudice and Discrimination: A Study in Readiness for Desegregation," *American Sociological Review*,
XXIII, No. 1 (February, 1958), 41-49, and Melvin Tumin, "Imaginary vs. Real
Children: Some Southern Views on Desegregation," *School and Society*, LXXXVI,
No. 2138 (October 11, 1958), 357-60.

It is likely that increased levels of formal education will, in the long run, serve to reduce ethnic/racial prejudice and discrimination. The effectiveness, however, will be crucially dependent upon the balance of gratifications in the stratification system, and upon all those events and processes that reduce a sense of threat in the movement toward the elimination of arbitrary segregation and discrimination. Thus, the reactions toward Negroes on the part of persons in the lower income strata in the white population are powerfully influenced by their own sense of integrity and well being. For example, the more these low-status white people themselves are disparaged and brought to feel that they are regarded as subordinate and of low worth, the greater will tend to be their demands for differential deference and prestige *vis-à-vis* racial and ethnic minorities, their resistance to equal interaction, and their resistance to changing stereotyped beliefs.

Social status and sense of threat

We are increasingly impressed with the importance of a sense of threat in intergroup relations, and with the peculiar potency of feared loss of social prestige. It has often been said that competition is responsible for antagonism of white workers toward Negroes. But individual competition obviously often is no greater (and may be less) than between any two of the white workers themselves. Furthermore, there may be just as much strictly interpersonal hostility and tension between individuals in the uniracial as in the biracial case. The crucial difference lies in the collective character of the relationships involved when racial categories are treated as socially real. Given the categorical definition of two social aggregates, the remarkable phenomena of group prejudice are intensified by the conjunction of (1) collective competition with (2) ingroup processes of conformity. The frequency of overt racial-ethnic conflict among the low-income, low-education strata of working-class Americans seems inexplicable on grounds of general differences in culture, but it seems understandable in view of the total constellation of factors reviewed in this section.

Numbers and sense of group position

In a similar way, we would suggest, the factor of numbers, or the proportion any particular racial, cultural, or religious minority constitutes of the total population, acquires causal significance through the compounding of outgroup threat and ingroup conformity. As already noted (in Chapter 7), a number of studies have shown that white persons' resistance to racial desegregation or, more generally, support of racial discrimination and segregation is often highly correlated with the proportion Negroes constitute of the total local population.[55] In an early study of a referendum in Virginia, it was found that the percentage favoring segregation correlated (by counties) +0.67 with the per cent Negro population.[56] A very similar result was found in Arkansas. The proportion of Negroes was negatively related to the pace of school desegregation in Kentucky (although, for special reasons, not in Missouri).[57] There was even a high correlation (+0.57) between per cent nonwhite and the 1955 vote of southern Presbyterians, by presbyteries, against union with the northern denomination.[58]

It is evident, of course, that the relation of race relations to proportion of Negroes in the population in different local areas in southern United States is confounded by several important correlated variables. Heaviest concentrations of Negro population still coincide with the slave states that formed the Confederacy. The local areas having high proportions of Negroes tend to be those that have had a history of most marked discrimination. The greater the discrimination, the more marked the cultural, for example, educational differences between the two populations. The greater the proportion of Negroes, the more important separate Negro institutions and organizations tend to be. And the greater the segregation, the greater the sense of separateness. Given the institutionalized dominance of the whites in such areas,[59] political and economic controls are systematically used to perpetuate Negro-white disparities in education, wealth, income, power, and prestige. Any proposed alteration in the control system tends to be reacted to as a threat.

CHANGE, CONFLICT, AND POLITICAL PROCESSES

The persistence of values and beliefs, formed in one period, into situations that no longer are the same is a common phenomenon, but no less important for that frequency. Present-day ethnic and racial relations in the

---

[55] See the summary in Thomas F. Pettigrew and M. Richard Cramer, "The Demography of Desegregation," *The Journal of Social Issues,* XV, No. 4 (1959), 61-71.

[56] W. F. Ogburn and C. M. Griff, "Factors Related to the Virginia Vote on Segregation," *Social Forces,* XXXIV, No. 4 (May, 1954), 301-8. See also D. M. Heer, "The Sentiment of White Supremacy: An Ecological Study," *American Journal of Sociology,* LXIV, No. 6 (May, 1959), pp. 592-98.

[57] T. F. Pettigrew, "Demographic Correlates of Border-State Desegregation," *American Sociological Review,* XXII, No. 6 (December, 1957), 683-89.

[58] S. M. Dornbusch and R. D. Irle, "The Failure of Presbyterian Union," *American Journal of Sociology,* LXIV, No. 4 (January, 1959), 352-55.

[59] Pettigrew and Cramer, "The Demography of Desegregation," p. 63: "Thus it is those counties with large percentages of relatively uneducated Negroes that form the core of racist political power in the South." See also Thomas F. Pettigrew and Ernest Q. Campbell, "Faubus and Segregation: An Analysis of Arkansas Voting," *Public Opinion Quarterly,* XXIV (Fall, 1960), 436-47.

United States provide many illustrations of the persistency of preformed modes of behavior after the basic situation that originally shaped the behavior has been greatly altered. A striking case in point is shown by Price's analysis of counties in the Deep South that have the political pattern of Black Belt areas even though they actually contain a low percentage of Negro population. His analysis shows that these anomalous counties usually are those that formerly had a large Negro population, now drastically reduced by out-migration.[60]

Under conditions of rapid technological change and economic expansion, fixed social classes tend to break down, and ethnic status prerogatives often are challenged. But the very processes of social fluidity in class position may intensify conflict over ethnic-racial distinctions, as when Negroes seek to purchase homes in restricted middle-class suburbs,[61] or strive for educational and political rights. Yet many of the fundamental social forces that are now powerfully shaping our national society are inimical to the grosser varieties of ethnic and racial prejudice and discrimination.[62]

Forces dissolving racial and ethnic discrimination

Nearly all of the most distinctive and definitive characteristics of the emerging twentieth-century American society are such as to place under strain the systems of racial and ethnic discrimination and segregation that had developed earlier. The international role of the nation renders arbitrary discrimination politically embarrassing, creates a considerable disadvantage in international persuasion and propaganda, and represents an economic liability and a military vulnerability. The needs of mass production for trained, reliable, and interchangeable labor-force units are to some extent inconsistent with racial discrimination, as are the needs of mass markets. The only principles upon which a political democracy can base and defend

---

[60] H. D. Price, *The Negro and Southern Politics* (New York: New York University Press, 1957).

[61] Kurt Mayer, "The Theory of Social Classes," *Transactions of the Second World Congress of Sociology,* II (London: International Sociological Association, 1954), p. 335: "An illuminating example of cross pressures between class and status systems can be seen in the use of residential restrictive covenants by which high status groups in American communities attempt to keep out 'undesirable' groups who have risen in the class structure to the point where they can afford to purchase high status symbols in the form of property in the best residential areas. Here class mobility is defined as a threat to their stability by the high status groups . . ."

[62] Cf. the eloquent statement of W. G. Carleton in his introduction to H. D. Price, *The Negro in Southern Politics,* p. xv: "The basic social trend of our time is the leveling of individual, group, class, racial, sectional, and local barriers, the trend to an integrated mass society . . . the American Dilemma . . . will be resolved in favor of democracy by the fusion of America's traditional ethos with . . . the forces that are diminishing scarcity, poverty, ignorance, and intolerance and spreading greater abundance, well-being, education, and opportunity."

itself make it difficult to justify denial of political liberties, political rights, or civil rights to any segment or class of the citizenry. Urbanization throws members of different racial, ethnic, and religious collectivities into unavoidable relationships. High levels of aspiration spread through the whole population in response to education, mass communication, advertising, and the experience of rising actual levels of consumption. Increasing commonality of culture and behavior patterns remove much of the previously accepted rationales for segregation and discrimination.

With decreased economic self-sufficiency and political autonomy, the smaller local areas are necessarily more and more exposed to population movements and mass communication. Both objective interdependence and the flow of information and evaluative opinions across community boundaries make it increasingly unlikely that any locality grouping can feel free to act without reference to outside reactions.[63] The limits of informal social control and personal mediation in situations of conflict are rather narrow. It is only in small social units with relatively stable membership, much interpersonal acquaintance, and relatively simple division of social functions, that diffuse sanctioning and informal justice will work well.[64] In structurally complex and culturally heterogeneous social systems, specialized agencies, roles, and personnel and formal rules (for example, laws) arise and are main avenues for dealing with conflict.[65] The increasing importance of legal and other formal means of regulating intergroup relations in modern society is, in large part, a special case of the more general tendency for political processes and structures to play a larger part in the control of behavior as a society or community becomes more highly differentiated in occupational structure and more diverse in values, beliefs, and interests.

The new importance of public policy in intergroup relations

It is likely that in coming years certain aspects of both racial and religious group relations will increasingly be recognized, explicitly, as normal objects of public policy in this country. Such intergroup relations always have been, *de facto,* dealt with to an important extent as matters of public policy—by segregation laws, real-estate practices, federal administration decisions

---

[63] Johan Galtung's study of segregationists, moderates, and integrationists in a Southern community indicates that: "For all three groups it would be hard in the long run to sustain a notion of the conflict as being in the hands of the community itself. . . . The most important causal factors are controlled from the outside." ["A Model for Studying Images of Participants in a Conflict: Southville," *The Journal of Social Issues,* XV, No. 4 (1959), 39.]

[64] Raymond Firth, "A Crisis in Tikopia," in Yehudi A. Cohen, ed., *Social Structure and Personality: A Casebook* (New York: Holt, Rinehart and Winston, Inc., 1961), pp. 461-68.

[65] E. Adamson Hoebel, *The Law of Primitive Man* (Cambridge: Harvard University Press, 1954), pp. 293ff.

(housing, military), and so on. But it has been maintained in many quarters that intergroup adjustments had best be left exclusively to the informal, natural processes of interpersonal dealings. It now seems quite evident that existing strains, tensions, and conflicts—that press imperatively for remedial action—cannot be contained or resolved by interpersonal contacts, private propaganda and education, voluntary groups, and informal negotiation and mediation.

The considerations that point to this crucial conclusion have been repeatedly encountered in earlier chapters. Paramount factors are these: (1) the fact of increased aspirations and claims on the part of previously less articulate and less well-organized racial and religious minorities; (2) the increased acknowledgment by the majority group, especially by its leadership, of the legitimacy of these aspirations and claims; (3) the increased political power and economic importance of these minorities (or of some segments of them); (4) the continuing and increasing massive segregation of the urban Negro population, North and South, with attendant frustrations, resentments, fears, and blocked communication between Negro and white citizens (interpersonal understanding ceases to be even a potential solvent of intergroup tension when no interpersonal communication is occurring); (5) continuing differences of beliefs and values in matters that are inherently objects of public policy; and (6) continuing large-scale differentials in economic returns and social rewards, differentials attributed by many minority-group persons to systems of categorical discrimination.

In the rapidly urbanizing and newly industrial South, social realities have outrun both traditional conceptions and the means of adequate intergroup communication. The conditions most conducive to status polarization— active discord between social strata—are conspicuously present: urbanization, weakness of bridging elements near the boundaries of white and Negro groupings, blocking of upward social mobility of Negroes, blockage of informal communication, and many others.[66]

Changes in public opinion

One of the great symptoms of impending social change is a shift in the respectability of dominant attitudes, beliefs, and values. When naïve ethnocentrism prevails in a society or a community, the support of existing patterns of discrimination and segregation takes the form of reference to unquestionable beliefs and values of the kind that everybody knows. These beliefs will be accepted and indorsed by the most prestigeful and respectable elements of the society—its leaders and pillars-of-normality in economic, religious, educational, and political affairs. It is always a sign of the possi-

---

[66] Cf. Angus Campbell, *et al., The American Voter* (New York: John Wiley & Sons, Inc., 1960), especially pp. 338-40 and 377.

bility of important changes when there is a break in the interlocking chain of consensus and support. The shift of a portion of the intellectual leaders and articulate commentators from full support to the expression of questions, doubts, and criticisms will, if long continued, spread a certain measure of alienation among the more highly educated, articulate—and often politically active—people. If the doubts and criticisms touch upon real vulnerabilities of inconsistency, maladaptations, and irreality—as judged in terms of *other* accepted values and beliefs—it may rather quickly happen that the criticized beliefs and values become divested of sanctity and prestige. A very great deal has already happened, for example, when people begin to refer to their own ethnocentric beliefs and feelings as prejudices, and their secure commitment to the old system has largely disintegrated by the time they say, "I can't help it, but I'm just prejudiced."

In the struggle of the groups seeking to eliminate racial segregation and those seeking to maintain it, especially since the *Brown* decision of the Supreme Court, it is clear that the top leaderships of both movements are concerned with public reactions of their followers and wish to have their organized efforts regarded as "respectable, legal, and nonviolent." [67]

Resolution of conflicts. Our society, like all others, represents a continuous process of communication through which numerous disagreements are formulated and numerous agreements reached. Differences of belief, of value, of interests are continually arising. Different individuals and groups develop divergent opinions concerning social policies. Conflicting evaluations emerge concerning the allocation or distribution of scarce values:

> Looking at these matters in a dynamic perspective, at a moment when change is visibly imminent or actually taking place, we see a vocal competition among different groups trying to make a case before a public tribunal that their point of view best serves the needs of society. Looking at the matter statically, one can say that every institution which makes a claim to public respectability is a settlement.[68]

Given a basis for group conflict, no matter what it may be,[69] the conflict may be prevented or resolved by definite social mechanisms, or it may develop in an uncontrolled manner to maximum disruptive effect. The possibilities of prevention, control, or resolution of conflict vary with the kinds of conflicting units (individuals, small groups, communities, associa-

---

[67] "Each seeks justification for its position in the same Constitution and in the same democratic and Christian tradition, and each seeks to discredit the other by accusing it of 'resorting to' or 'fomenting' violence." [Lewis M. Killian, "The Purge of an Agitator," *Social Problems*, VII, No. 2 (Fall, 1959), 153.]

[68] Howard Brotz, "Functionalism and Dynamic Analysis," *European Journal of Sociology,* II (1961), 9.

[69] ". . . there is ample evidence to say that, even today, the heart of Negro and white conflict is the effort to exclude the Negro from full and equal participation in the American economy." Wagley and Harris, *Minorities in the New World*, p. 276.

tions, nation-states, etc.), with the character of the superordinate or environing social structures within which the conflict-engendering situations arise, and with the specific nature of the mechanisms, if any, for dealing with conflict.

Modes of dealing with conflicts of individuals within relatively small and homogeneous ethnopolitical units are not the same as those likely to be found in the case of larger intergroup conflicts in structurally complex political societies.[70] Within the small local community, overt conflicts are minimized by close economic and social interdependence, shared beliefs and values, common socialization, a legitimate system of judging and sanctioning individuals who break the peace, beliefs in supernatural surveillance and punishment, and emigration or expulsion of deviant and recalcitrant members.[71] In modern America we have a *national* society, brief though its span may have been thus far.[72] It cannot do without very complex interwoven systems of political controls and many subtle and fluid balances of interests and influences that change from time to time. The less the society is held together by specific agreement on the norms regulating interpersonal conduct, the greater the tendency will be to rely on law and political structures to cope with the resulting tensions and overt conflicts.[73]

Conflict among men will continue to arise from time to time so long as there is not a more acceptable way of resolving disagreements. Disagreements will continue to arise so long as men differ in their interests, values, and beliefs. We foresee no way of totally avoiding disagreements, even should that outcome be thought desirable. But there are many disagreements that do not lead to conflict. If conflict does arise, it is not always violent. And whether or not it is violent, it does not have to be of a group character. If it is of a group character, it does not have to be polarized along ethnic lines.

Our conclusion, then, has to be that ethnic conflict is not inevitable. This means that we can conceive of realistic conditions under which ethnic conflict would be at such a low level of prevalence and intensity as to be of no serious concern in a given community or society at a particular time. Whether or not *other* kinds of conflicts would then arise we do not predict. Whether a high level of ethnic conflict is less desirable than a system of stable dominance is not a point at issue. It seems clear that the main cur-

---

[70] Cf. Robert A. LeVine, "Anthropology and the Study of Conflict: An Introduction," *The Journal of Conflict Resolution,* V, No. 1 (March, 1961), 10.

[71] *Ibid.,* 11.

[72] "The history of strong national loyalties for the masses is a history of less than two hundred years." [Morton Grodzins, *The Loyal and the Disloyal* (Chicago: The University of Chicago Press, 1956), p. 11.]

[73] Robert T. Holt has adduced much evidence to support these points in personal conversations at the Center for Advanced Study in the Behavioral Sciences, 1961-1962.

rents of American life do not point to either of the latter possibilities as a desirable destination.

Conclusion: On Integration

A human community or society exists as a complex structure of relationships. The main bases upon which a community or a society can function as a going concern are not too difficult to identify in a general way, no matter how hard it is to specify concretely how they work. The primary classes of factors in the coordination of behavior within social aggregates as *systems* are: [74]

1. Mutual advantage
    (*a*) internal protection, exchange, and facilitation
    (*b*) external defense and aggression
2. Consensus
    (*a*) on values
    (*b*) on goals
    (*c*) on norms
    (*d*) on interpersonal liking-disliking
3. Power
4. Technical capacities for communication
5. Various social mechanisms for settling conflicts, restricting conflict, and producing consensus

A multigroup society can continue to operate as a system with a low degree of consensus in some respects if it is a society with high mutual advantage, effective means of communication, and some minimal unitary exercise of order-maintaining power. It will be driven more and more toward reliance upon power, the less consensus there is concerning the distribution of rewards and concerning the basic rules for settling conflicts.

Ethnic relations represent problems of consensus and dissensus. To the extent that prejudice and discrimination are sources of tension, discord, and open conflict, to that extent there is a dissensus that raises the question of relative power to control the settlement of demands and claims. Conflicting claims in the absence of agreement on specific norms mean the exercise of power. Unless there is somewhere a stopping point at which *legitimacy* comes in—that is, where a source of power is invoked that represents a focus of value consensus—one can predict that there will be increasing disorder and the resort to increasing drastic means.

Once a specific conflict has been precipitated, many forces may be evoked

---

[74] We assume the presence of some resources, some motivation, some knowledge, and some skills adequate to survival of the system in an environment.

that were not a part of the original sources of the outbreak. Conflict is a vortex. Into it are drawn diverse elements not intrinsic to the initial causes of the conflict. The quality of this process is well suggested by Simmel's comment on the American Civil War:

> The moment, however, the situation took on the color of war, it itself turned out to be an accumulation of antagonisms, of attitudes of hatred, newspaper polemics, frictions between private persons, frictions at the borders, and reciprocal moral suspicions in areas outside the central point of conflict.[75]

The precipitating situation is permeated with a variety of latent conflicts of interests, of differences of values, of suppressed antipathies, of interpersonal alienation. Once the situation becomes one of open conflict, three things of decisive importance immediately occur: (1) the suppressive and repressive forces that have partially controlled tensions are weakened or removed; (2) latent threats become actual, and new threats emerge, both polarized along the cleavage of the conflicting groups; (3) the axis of social approval and disapproval shifts, so that acts which formerly were antisocial now become virtuous, thus placing the superego energies in direct alignment with a wide range of hostile and aggressive urges.

If a community or a society wishes (that is, if enough of its more powerful and responsible members wish) to control conflict, the time to do it is before the conflict starts, or at least before it begins to take on a breakaway momentum. In modern American society the relative lack in interethnic relations of social controls that derive either from personal reciprocities or from mutual dependence on the same concrete leaders, authorities, patrons, etc., removes an important network of containing and mediating relationships. The phenomena of race riots, juvenile gang warfare, vigilante activity, and diffuse terrorism illustrate the problem.

The most certain way to maximize conflict is to give one's opponent only the choice of conflict versus certain defeat, deprivation, or subordination; the most certain way to maximize violence is to leave to the opponent violence as the only alternative to his own destruction (or, to the same effect, the destruction of his most cherished objects of value).[76]

Furthermore, the greater the number of relationships affected by any

---

[75] Georg Simmel, trans. Kurt H. Wolff. *Conflict and The Web of Group-Affiliations* (New York: The Free Press of Glencoe, Inc., 1955), pp. 109-10.

[76] Cf. J. K. Zawodny, "Guerilla Warfare and Subversion as a Means of Political Change," paper given at the 1961 Annual Meeting of the American Political Science Association, St. Louis, Mo., September 6-9, 1961, p. 24. For a striking case in point: "The ebb and flow of membership in sabotage and guerrilla units is not related to the number of tactical victories of these units, to their losses, nor even to the prospects for success. The rate of recruitment is positively correlated with the intensity of terror applied by the enemy in suppressing the movement."

change in the relationships of two or more individuals, or two or more social roles, and the more important the values affected, the greater the likelihood that there will be intervention by some kind of third party. Considering the importance of ethnic relationships in a society like ours, it would be surprising were law and political authority generally not invoked to deal with conflicts of claims and breaches of order. Settlement of conflicts inevitably creates norms, and the creation and enforcement of legal norms is a decisive mode of securing consensus in complex sociocultural systems.[77]

In the American legal system, the Supreme Court occupies a unique and indispensable place. It represents the central arena of settlement of claims that cannot be settled at any lower level. It necessarily, therefore, works at the growing edges of the law—in the shadow zone of conflicting principles and semiformulated norms. Inevitably, then, many of its decisions will be controversial—otherwise the cases would not have reached the court in the first place.

Prior to the 1954 and 1955 decisions, which rendered unconstitutional forced racial segregation in the public schools, the NAACP already had won 34 of 38 cases before the Supreme Court. This record might seem to mean a transformation of race relations in this country. Actually the decisions leave vast areas of discrimination and segregation untouched. And the history of school desegregation since 1955 reveals a pace of change that seems glacier-slow to the proponents of integration. The rulings of the Supreme Court have been interpreted by lower courts in a large number of decisions in such ways as to permit delays, which promise to stretch on for many years, in implementing desegregation.

> Despite some on-the-surface appearances to the contrary, careful analysis of post-1954 decisions demonstrates that the patterns of judicial response parallel those of the pre-1954 decisions, for example, long delays before trial, affirmation of the constitutional right to be free of state-imposed segregation in the public schools but denial of immediate relief, rigid adherence to the exhaustion of the administrative remedies rule, and defense of inaction or reluctance to act by local school officials.[78]

Change through legal means under American conditions is typically a gradual and uneven process. Far from being revolutionary, it is the essence of established procedure and orderly development. Nevertheless, we would regard legal action through the courts and administrative action in business,

---

[77] Partly for this reason there is a tendency for the mere existence of central authority in a society to impose a central value system on that society. [Edward A. Shils, "The Macrosociological Problem: Consensus and Dissensus in the Larger Society," in *Trends in Social Science,* Donald P. Ray, ed. (New York: Philosophical Library, 1961), p. 70.]

[78] Butler A. Jones, "The Case Is Remanded," *Social Problems,* VII, No. 1 (Summer, 1959), p. 33.

education, government, and religious organizations as major avenues of realistic efforts to alter systems of discrimination and prejudice. These avenues are congruent with the dominant value systems and with the character of the complex social structure that has developed. And law and law enforcement are great agencies of public education.[79]

The slowness of change put up against the moral claims of minorities for equality of rights necessarily maintains high tension. Furthermore, it cannot be assumed that any and all types of industrialization and urbanization will lead to a decrease in discrimination or to a narrowing of occupational and income differentials between whites and Negroes. For instance, under conditions of plentiful labor and weak unions (or with segregated monopoly-oriented white unions), differential job and wage opportunities may be maintained even with large industrial growth. Blalock has presented data for Southern counties that suggest that Negro-white differentials in levels of living probably are not less in the highly urban areas than in the less urbanized, even though levels for both Negroes and whites are higher in the more urbanized counties.[80] In Northern and Western cities, segregation and discrimination in housing remain crucial areas of tension, not only in relation to Negroes but also in relation to Puerto Ricans, Jews, Mexicans, and others. Social exclusion and discrimination in education and employment affect large numbers of Jewish persons, and, in less well-known degree, Catholics in some areas and Protestants in others. Many political and civil rights are widely denied to members of ethnic minorities, especially to Negroes in the South.

Thus, the pluralism of American society continues to be a changing and conflictful condition. As a total social system, the political society of the United States has been unable to establish or guarantee political and civil equality of protection and opportunity to ethnic minorities. Yet it is equally unable to renounce the universalistic norms and democratic goals. It cannot settle for a caste system, nor for a mosaic society of separate cultural segments. Its nominal ideal is an emancipated order of low prejudice, and minimal segregation and discrimination. Resistances to changes in the direction of public equality and public integration often touch off overt conflict. Looking simultaneously at prejudice and at segregation, there are these possibilities:

---

[79] William Graham Sumner, often cited as a foe of purposive change through law and state action, held that in bringing about what he called arbitrary change it would be appropriate to deal with the ritual rather than the dogma—with prescribed *acts* rather than prescribed thoughts or feelings (in terms of our present interests, discrimination and segregation rather than prejudice). See: Harry V. Ball, George Eaton Simpson and Kiyoshi Ikeda, "Law and Social Change: Sumner Reconsidered," *American Journal of Sociology*, LXVII, No. 5 (March, 1962), 532-40.

[80] H. M. Blalock, Jr., "Urbanization and Discrimination in the South," *Social Problems*, VII, No. 2 (Fall, 1959), 146-51.

Segregation

Prejudice	Slight	Great
Low	Emancipated	Mosaic Pluralism
High	Mass Conflict	Stressful Caste-like

Great pressures exist to move the society toward social integration of ethnic minorities, the emancipated outcome. Great resistances are thereby aroused. One key to the understanding of resistance on the part of dominant ethnic groupings is the recognition that resistance derives from a sense of threat. One key to understanding a sense of threat is to be found in answers to the questions: what is threatened? And how? We already have suggested some partial and tentative answers. We would propose as especially important the following hypothetical propositions:

1. The extent and intensity of resistance to increased rights (or privileges) of any ethnic (racial, religious) segment of the society will increase directly with the degree to which the present or prospective change is perceived by persons in other ethnic categories as a direct threat to their own long-term future prestige ranking, as determined by the evaluations of other persons who are in a position to importantly affect that ranking.

In short, resistance will increase directly with perceived threat to prestige status.

2. More specifically, resistance will vary directly with the perceived threat from the reactions of others within the dominant ethnic segment who have economic or political power, religious authority, or other indirect sanctioning power (for example, the ability to influence community evaluations of the person). That is, anticipated sanctions from persons of power and authority are especially threatening.

3. Whatever the perceived threat to status, it will be the more powerful, the less possibility there is for alternative ways of maintaining status, once the prospective change has occurred. Feeling trapped tends to produce panic.

Although prestige status is the subject of these three propositions, they are expected to apply to any other threatened values.

What factors encourage a sense of threat in the first instance? We suggest, by way of examples, that under present conditions in the United States,[81] the sense of threat among persons in a dominant ethnic category facing potential change will be the greater: (1) the less the concrete knowl-

---

[81] The essential fact behind the qualifying phrase, "under present conditions in the United States" is that all the ethnic minorities have limited goals that are far short of those fantasied for them by uninformed members of dominant groupings. For instance, what Negroes actually want, at the level of realistic action, is much different from the social equality feared by some white people.

edge of the beliefs, values, and motivations of the aspirant or rising subordinates; (2) the less knowledge there is of the effects of the potential change in actual experience elsewhere; (3) the greater the *actual* likelihood that the potential change will damage the dominant group's interests.

We have suggested that political authority is one of the primary necessary and important factors in determining the balance of ethnic relations in our society. From any point of view the political element, in the widest sense, must be prominent in any appraisal of societal conflict and integration. As American Negroes become able to secure equal rights, including the vote, the possibility of protecting *other* rights will increase.[82]

The divisiveness of prejudices and the discontinuities of experience and communication that are generated by group segregation and discrimination are extensively documented by data presented at various points throughout this book. Inevitably, reflection upon the facts of ethnic separateness has raised the basic question: in the face of group divisiveness, how are pluralistic social systems maintained? To answer this question is one of the most important tasks of the entire body of the social sciences, not an assignment to be handily completed in a single work on intergroup relations. Nevertheless, we must perforce make a few additional observations dealing with the issue. At the risk of inappropriate simplification, let us list certain other major factors as we have sensed them in the communities here studied at first hand.

First, as we see Hometown or Southport, Valley City or Steelville at the point in time in which our surveys were conducted, the communities as units are crucially dependent upon the larger society in which they are embedded. However vaguely this interdependence may be sensed (actually it is sometimes recognized quite clearly by the man in the street), every major economic or political event brings it home to at least some of the community's members. Livelihood and safety—survival itself—depend upon the adequate functioning of a division of labor and of systems of communication and order extending far beyond the control or detailed comprehension of local residents. Such interdependence need not, and often does not, lead to sentiments of solidarity. Indeed, recognition of dependence on outside groups often provokes feelings of resentment and frustration. But the dependence is *there*—it is *objective*—in the sense that any real attempt to break the chain of linkages with the larger economic and political orders quickly and painfully shows the real and immediate costs of removal from the environing systems of relationships.

The impersonal network of trade and power relations exists also within

---

[82] And, of course, the result may have little to do with whites' "altruism." Cf. V. O. Key, Jr., with Alexander Heard, *Southern Politics in State and Nation* (New York: Alfred A. Knopf, 1950), p. 651: "When whites split among themselves and seek Negro support, the way may be opened for the Negro to vote."

the community. And at this local level also people may accept their interdependence, and the limited associations it necessitates, without developing sentiments of solidarity or diffuse reciprocities of concern and obligation. A man can say, "I don't like having those damn X's around here, but we need them as workers." A political worker can say, "I'd never invite one of them to my home—but their votes are always welcome."

At the local level, in common with the societal, there is, second, the community that is formed by the recognized sharing of common beliefs and values. The communities we studied may seem to have enough of antipathies and to be severely fragmented by differences in values and beliefs. They are, indeed, socially divided, when seen up close under the microscope. But from a more extended perspective each of the ethnic, racial, or religious groupings in each of the local communities tended to hold in common with all the other local groupings a vast store of shared culture. This commonality tends to be taken for granted and to be ignored in much of the intergroup relations of ordinary daily life. In the present studies we have very little direct evidence concerning its exact part in intergroup solidarity and conflict. We must note the possibility, however, that a wider comparative study would show this shared culture to be of decisive importance in setting the limits of group relations, in defining the terms of conflict (as well as those of cooperation), and in channelizing the possibilities of social change.

Third, the maintenance of a local social system extending across ethnic-racial-religious lines is affected profoundly by the kinds of arrangements that have developed for group insulation, through both psychological defenses and the restriction of the qualities of interaction, and for the resolution of frictions. To these arrangements or mechanisms we have repeatedly called attention in earlier discussions.

Fourth, there are sources of resiliency or tolerance of imperfection that result in the absorption by individuals and groups of frustrations, deprivations, and other stresses including those growing out of intergroup relations —stresses that would otherwise be more productive of conflict (and probably of social change). These sources of adjustive capacities are concretely very diverse, but consist primarily of adequate levels of gratifications secured in the total round of social life, on the one hand, and of socially induced capacities for affection and compassion, on the other, which cushion and mediate the harshness of systems of discrimination and segregation. We are here referring to personality resources of the social system, or to speak even more loosely, but perhaps more communicatively, to a surplus of affective capacities permitting toleration of others even in undesired roles. To say that this happens is not necessarily, of course, to unconditionally approve it.

Finally, we believe that the total body of evidence we have reviewed overwhelmingly supports the view that cooperation and solidarity among persons who differ in ethnic membership is fostered by any arrangements that produce joint action toward shared objectives. From a variety of approaches and theoretical suppositions one finds suggestions that *social solidarity among individuals or groups is enhanced by recognition of the sharing of a positive and noncompetitive regard for a common object of concern.*

Let us examine some examples of formulations that point to this conclusion.

> . . . Personal association of members of different groups is most effective in reducing hostility and increasing understanding when the focus of interaction is upon a common interest, goal, or task rather than upon intergroup association as such. . . . Prejudice is reduced by arranging for personal, intimate contacts of members of different groups who share important tastes and interests in common.[83]

Again, Sherif has laid considerable stress upon the sharing of superordinate goals as a mode of creating interindividual and intergroup cohesion.

> When individuals interact in a series of situations toward goals which appeal to all and which require that they co-ordinate their activities, group structures arise having hierarchical status arrangements and a set of norms regulating behavior in matters of consequence to the activities of the group.[84]

And commonality of interest in an object has been taken as the criterion for the existence of a social relationship in this statement by A. R. Radcliffe-Brown:

> While some measure of agreement about values, some similarity of interests, is a prerequisite of a social system, social relations involve more than this. They require the existence of common interests and of social values. When two or more persons have a common interest in the same object and are aware of their community of interest a social relation is established.[85]

There seems little doubt that in the communities we studied it was interaction with awareness of a congruent community of interest that minimized ethnic prejudice and encouraged the reduction of discrimination. As American society in the second half of the century experiences the struggle of minorities to end categorical ethnic discrimination and forced segregation,

---

[83] *The Reduction of Intergroup Tensions,* Bulletin 57, Social Science Research Council, New York (1947), p. 71.

[84] Muzafer Sherif, "Superordinate Goals in the Reduction of Intergroup Conflict," *American Journal of Sociology,* LXIII, No. 4 (January, 1958), 353.

[85] Reprinted from his *Structure and Function in Primitive Society* in Talcott Parsons *et al.,* eds., *Theories of Society,* II (New York: The Free Press of Glencoe, Inc., 1961), p. 953.

it will be a matter of urgency to determine what conditions, specifically, tend to produce cooperative rather than conflictful interaction, both at the level of person-to-person and of collectivity-to-collectivity. It will further be of great urgency to discover how conflict can be used to enhance understanding and social growth.

Particular importance attaches to the study of situations of change, for it is only there that we can observe variables in motion, with some possibility of discerning causal sequences. It is a genuine tragedy that we have had so little objective, systematic study of school desegregation or of the massive social changes in group relations now under way in the central cities of the large Northern metropolitan areas. It is a major source of hope that some excellent studies have been done and that the research horizon continues to attract the interest and effort of devoted students. Both science and public policy will have a great need for them in the years ahead.

There may be strangers next door, but we too are visitors in a world we did not make. Enrichment of our understanding of the others possibly will enrich our understanding of ourselves. It may even help us to make the most of our stay on this small planet.

A Complete Chronological List of Steps in Data-Collecting
for Cornell Studies in Intergroup Relations
(Hometown)

1948:

1. Participant-observers' reports on Negro, Jewish, Italian, Ukrainian, Polish, German, and Irish population elements.

2. Intensive study of local political organization and activity in 1948 presidential campaign.

3. Selection of area-probability sample for Voting Study and carrying out four interviews with each of the approximately 1,000 adults selected.

1949-1950:

1. Resurvey of 529 non-Jewish, white adults drawn from the basic panel-sample in Hometown.

2. Intensive observation of Hometown's intergroup patterns—in neighborhoods, factories, unions, organizations; in stores, taverns, restaurants; in sports; on the streets and in the homes.

3. Reconnaissance survey of Auburn, N.Y., searching out similarities to and differences from Hometown.

4. Special survey of Negro youths (conducted by Gloria May, under Sigmund Livingston fellowship).

5. Survey of samples of minority-group adults: 150 Negroes, 150 Italian-Americans, 150 Jews.

6. Special studies of high school youths.

7. Brief opinion survey of subsample of panel ("Wave VI").

8. First trials of active intervention in intergroup situations for purposes of diagnosing process.

1950-1951:

1. A special study of factory work groups in two Hometown plants in which Negro and white workers are integrated into the same departments and crews.

2. Reconnaissance surveys of intergroup relations in Lancaster, Pa., Norwalk, Conn., and Poughkeepsie and New Rochelle, N.Y.

3. A nationwide mail survey of selected informants in over 500 cities in order to obtain a preliminary inventory of certain patterns of intergroup relations in a representative sample of urban areas in the United States. (This survey developed into the nationwide study of 249 cities reported in Chapter 6.)

4. An intensive analysis of group membership and identification among Jewish youths in Hometown (conducted under a Sigmund Livingston fellowship by Bernard C. Rosen).

5. Continuation of a systematic study of Negro leadership in Hometown, utilizing survey techniques as well as unstructured interviews and participant observation.

6. Continuation of detailed study of the inception and functioning of local interracial and intercultural organizations. In particular, the research staff worked closely with the Hometown Mayor's Committee on Human Relations.

7. A survey of group processes in the upper-class elite of Hometown, designed to show similarities and differences in comparison with the studies of ethnic, racial, and religious groupings.

8. Detailed recording of new intergroup situations, e.g., the first Negro in a housing project, a court case involving charges of discrimination, the hiring of a Negro in the City Fire Department.

9. A resurvey of 450 individuals from the basic Hometown panel of 1,000 people.

10. Resurveys, on a reconnaissance basis, to secure evidence of changes in intergroup relations in Chester, Pa., and Montclair, N.J.

11. Resurveys of Steelville, Weirton, and of the Negro community in Hometown.

1951-1952:

1. A cross-section survey of intergroup attitudes and patterns of intergroup contact in Valley City. The study dealt with Negroes, Mexicans, majority group population, and special samples of the so-called Oakies and Arkies. This city represents a combination of new industrial patterns with a Southern system of race relations in a Far West setting.

2. Survey of youths in Phoenix. Six high schools were included: one segregated Negro school, one segregated white school, two white schools with Mexican children in attendance, one integrated school (including Mexicans and Negroes), and the Federal School for Indians.

3. A cross-section survey of both whites and Negroes in Southport, utilizing the standardized interview questionnaire developed in the preceding studies. (So far as known, this was the first study of this type in a city in the Deep South.)

4. Continuation of the intensive study of the Mayor's Committee on Human Relations in Hometown. The data provide materials for a detailed case study of processes of involvement and redefinition of problems in a group attempting to deal with intergroup relations at the local level.

5. Intensive interviews with 40 individuals selected from the Hometown panel. Previous interviews were drawn upon to select persons of high and low prejudice who scored high or low on an index of authoritarian personality.

6. Completion of a special study of changes since 1941 in Jewish participation in the larger community in Hometown (supported by the Anti-Defamation League of B'nai B'rith). Contrary to popular impressions, there was no evidence of withdrawal from intergroup participation by Jewish persons; on the contrary, civic and social intermingling have increased since the beginning of World War II.

7. Administration of a special questionnaire to meetings of intergroup relations practitioners (group workers, social workers, etc.) in Valley City, Steelville, Hometown, and at conferences in Buffalo, N.Y., and Chicago, Ill. In this activity the field staff helped to organize and operate workshops in three major conferences.

8. Completion of reconnaissance surveys of selected cities.

1952-1953:

1. Continuous collection of data and rechecking for accuracy of mail returns from special informants in a stratified national sample of 250 cities.

2. Experimental feedback presentations of research findings to local groups in Hometown.

1953-1954:

1. Complete resurvey of all youths in the schools of Phoenix previously studied in 1952.

1954-1956:

(Moratorium in data-collection. Staff engaged in analysis and writing.)

1956-1957:

Final resurvey of panel sample in Hometown, consisting of individuals who had previously been interviewed on six different occasions since 1948. The 200 persons interviewed included those who in the prior surveys had reported changes in both prejudice and intergroup contacts and a comparison group reporting no changes.

EXAMPLE OF INTERVIEW QUESTIONNAIRE USED
IN HOUSE-TO-HOUSE COMMUNITY SURVEYS

The illustrative guide that follows was used in the 1951 survey of the Hometown majority-group sample, constituting the panel population for the study of change. Many of the questions were used in each of the surveys in other cities, and parallel questions were asked by minority-group respondents. In addition, a subsample of the Hometown panel was resurveyed in 1956.

Hometown: 1951 Panel - Change

FACE SHEET (NAM)*

Identification no. _____ Sex: M F Age _____

Name _____ Marital status _____

Address _____ Residents in household:

Comments on previous interviews:

No	Relation	Sex	Age
___	___	___	___
___	___	___	___
___	___	___	___
___	___	___	___

RESULTS OF EACH VISIT:

Visit	Interviewer	Date	House	Community
1				
2				
3				
4				

* This code designated the white gentile sample (exclusive of Italian-Americans, who had been studied in a separate survey).

AA

We'd like to know something about your recent contacts with the different groups in town.

1. During the past month did you personally come in contact with any Jewish people?

    1949: ___ yes   1951: 1 ___ yes
        ___ no   2 ___ no

    With any Negroes?

    1949: ___ yes   1951: 4 ___ yes
        ___ no   5 ___ no

2. A. Are there any Jewish people living within a block or two of your home?

    1949: ___ yes   1951: 1 ___ yes
        ___ no   2 ___ no
        ___ don't know   3 ___ don't know

    IF "YES":

    B. Do you consider any of your neighbors that are Jewish:

	1949	1951
a) a close friend that you can talk over confidential matters with?	___ yes	___ yes 5
	___ no	___ no 6
IF "NO": b) a good friend to whom you can say what you really think?	___ yes	___ yes 7
	___ no	___ no
IF "NO": c) someone who calls you by your first name?		
IF "NO": d) someone you just know to speak to?	___ yes	___ yes 8
	___ no	___ no 9

    C. Have you ever done something social with this Jewish person, like going to the movies, or to a sports event, or visiting in each other's homes?

    1 ___ yes
    2 ___ no

    D. In general, how much do you like this Jewish person?

    4 ___ very much
    5 ___ fairly much
    6 ___ not so much
    7 ___ no special feeling

NOTE: This page was followed by the same set of questions under 2. A-D concerning Negro persons.

APPENDIX B

CC

A. Are there any Jews in a club or organization that you belong to?

1949: ___ yes 　　1951: 1 ___ yes
　　　 ___ no 　　　　　　 2 ___ no
　　　 ___ don't know 　　 3 ___ don't know
　　　 ___ no organization 　 4 ___ no organization

IF NO JEWS, SKIP TO NEXT PAGE.

IF "YES": What organization? _____

B. Do you consider any of the Jews in this organization:

	1949	1951
a) a close friend that you can talk over confidential matters with?	___ yes	___ 5
	___ no	___ 6
IF "NO": b) a good friend to whom you can say what you really think?	___ yes	___ 7
	___ no	
IF "NO": c) someone who calls you by your first name?	___ yes	___ 8
	___ no	___ 9
IF "NO": d) someone you just know to speak to?		

C. Have you ever done something social together with this Jewish person, like going to the movies, or to a sports event, or visiting in each other's homes?

1 ___ yes
2 ___ no

D. In general how much do you like this Jewish person?

4 ___ very much
5 ___ fairly much
6 ___ not so much
7 ___ no special feeling

NOTE: This page was followed by the same set of questions concerning Negroes.

EE

1. By the way, are you employed now or not?

1949: ___ employed 　　1951: 1 ___ employed
　　　 ___ not employed 　　　 2 ___ not employed

2. A. During the last month did you come in contact in your work with any Jewish people?

1949: ___ yes 　　1951: 4 ___ yes
　　　 ___ no 　　　　　　 5 ___ no

IF "YES":

B. Do you consider any of the Jews at your work:

	1949	1951
a) a close friend that you can talk over confidential matters with?	___ yes	___ 7
	___ no	
IF "NO": b) a good friend to whom you can say what you really think?	___ yes	___ 8
	___ no	
IF "NO": c) someone who calls you by your first name?	___ yes	___ 9
	___ no	
IF "NO": d) someone you just know to speak to?	___ yes	___ 0
	___ no	___ x

C. Have you ever done something social together with this Jewish person, like going to the movies, or to a sports event, or visiting in each other's homes?

1949: ___ yes 　　1951: 1 ___ yes
　　　 ___ no 　　　　　　 2 ___ no

D. In general, how much do you like this Jewish person?

4 ___ very much
5 ___ fairly much
6 ___ not so much
7 ___ no special feeling

NOTE: This page was followed by the same set of questions under 2. A-D concerning Negro persons.

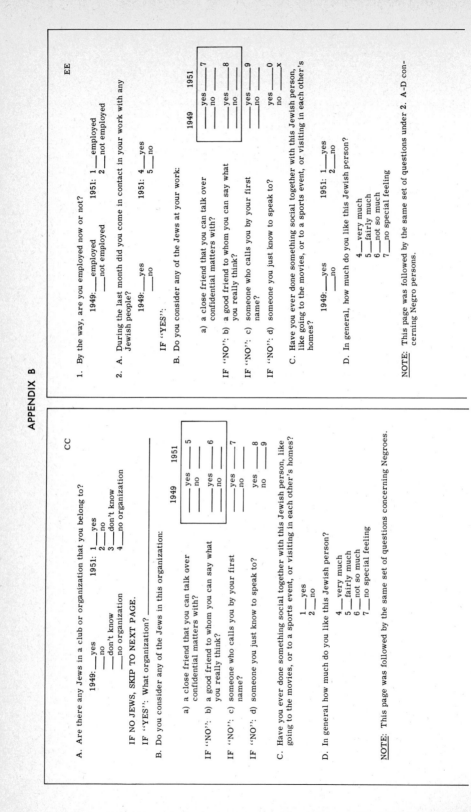

GG

A. Are there any Jewish persons you mix with socially in your home, in their home, or anywhere else?

1949: ___ yes   1951: 1 ___ yes
      ___ no   2 ___ no

IF "YES":

B. Do you consider any of these Jewish persons:

	1949	1951
a) a close friend that you can talk over confidential matters with?	___ yes ___ no	___ 4
IF "NO": b) a good friend to whom you can say what you really think?	___ yes ___ no	___ 5
IF "NO": c) someone who calls you by your first name?	___ yes ___ no	___ 6
IF "NO": d) someone you just know to speak to?	___ yes ___ no	___ 7 ___ 8

D. In general, how much do you like this Jewish person?

1 ___ very much
2 ___ fairly much
3 ___ not so much
4 ___ no special feeling

NOTE: These questions were repeated for the case of Negroes.

As you may remember, we interviewed you last year about your contacts with Jews and Negroes. If we have the record straight, the following changes have taken place. You now have a good friend who is a (Jew, Negro) in your _____.

	New Contacts	
	Jews	Negroes
neighborhood	1 ___	6 ___
organization	2 ___	7 ___
at work	3 ___	8 ___
social contact	4 ___	9 ___
other	___	
(what?)		

1. Could you tell me how you came to be good friends with him (her)? (PROBES: Who took the first steps to be friendly? What were the first situations in which you began to be good friends? What was it that drew you together as good friends?)

2. How has this contact affected your opinions about (Jews, Negroes)?

IF AFFECTED FAVORABLY: As a result of this experience, have you felt you would like to get to know other (Jews, Negroes)?

___ yes
___ no

3. Do you feel that your knowing this (Jew, Negro) has made you feel more friendly toward other (Jews, Negroes) as well?

___ yes
___ no

APPENDIX B

Now, if we have the record right, you no longer have a good friend who is a (Jew, Negro) in your

Lost Contacts	
Jews	Negroes
1 ___ neighborhood	___ 6
2 ___ organization	___ 7
3 ___ at work	___ 8
4 ___ social contact	___ 9
___ other	

1. Do you still see the (Jewish, Negro) person you used to know?

___ yes   Just as often as you used to, or
___ no

     ___ just as often
     ___ less often

IF "YES": Why is it that you no longer consider him a good friend?

IF "NO" or "LESS OFTEN": How is it that you no longer see this person (as often)?

IF STILL POSSIBLE TO SEE PERSON: Was there anything about this person that led you to draw apart? Anything in particular you disliked about (him, her)?

2. Do you think you feel different toward most other (Jews, Negroes) as a result of your contact with this one person?

___ yes
___ no

IF "YES": In what ways?

---

1. Do you think you would ever find it a little distasteful:

		1949:		1951:
a) to eat at the same table with a Jew?	yes	___	___	1
	no	___	___	2
b) to dance with a Jew?	yes	___	___	4
	no	___	___	5
c) to go to a party and find that most of the people were Jewish?	yes	___	___	7
	no	___	___	8
d) to have a Jewish person marry someone in your family?	yes	___	___	1
	no	___	___	2
e) to eat at the same table with a Negro	yes	___	___	4
	no	___	___	5
f) to dance with a Negro?	yes	___	___	7
	no	___	___	8
g) to go to a party and find that most of the people were Negro?	yes	___	___	1
	no	___	___	2
h) to have a Negro person marry someone in your family?	yes	___	___	4
	no	___	___	5

IF "YES" TO (e): Why do you think you would find it distasteful to eat at the same table with a Negro?

IF "YES" TO (g): Why do you think you would find it distasteful to go to a party and find that most of the people were Negro?

APPENDIX B

(Left panel)

LL

1. A. On the whole would you say you like or dislike Negro people?

1949:	1951:
___ like	1 ___ like
___ no special feeling	2 ___ no special feeling
___ dislike	3 ___ dislike

B. What about Jewish people?

___ like	6 ___ like
___ no special feeling	7 ___ no special feeling
___ dislike	8 ___ dislike

2. Do you agree or disagree with the following statements?

	1949:	1951:
a) This country would be better off if there were not so many foreigners here.	agree ___	agree ___ 1 / disagree ___ 2
b) Generally speaking, Negroes are lazy and ignorant.		agree ___ 4 / disagree ___ 5
c) Although some Jews are honest, in general Jews are dishonest in their business dealings.		agree ___ 7 / disagree ___ 8
d) Americans must be on guard against the power of the Catholic Church.		agree ___ 1 / disagree ___ 2
e) A Negro youth has as good a chance as any other youth to get ahead in life in Hometown.		agree ___ 4 / disagree ___ 5
f) The more contact a person has with Jewish people, the more he gets to like them.		agree ___ 7 / disagree ___ 8
g) Children are more prejudiced than adults.		agree ___ 1 / disagree ___ 2
h) There is almost no discrimination against Negroes in Hometown as far as getting jobs is concerned.		agree ___ 4 / disagree ___ 5
i) Strongly prejudiced people have warped or twisted characters.		agree ___ 7 / disagree ___ 8

(Right panel)

Since we last talked with you, your attitudes toward Jews seem to have become
___ more favorable
___ less favorable

1. Do you have any idea why that is? (PROBES: Has there been some particular experience you have had during the last year that has made you feel (more, less) favorable toward Jews?)

2. Have any of your recent contacts here in town affected your opinions about Jews?
___ no
___ yes (GET DETAILS)

IF "YES": What was there about this contact that affected your attitudes?

IF ATTITUDES MORE FAVORABLE:

3. Would you like to get to be good friends with more Jews?
___ no: Why is that?
___ yes: Have you had any chances during the last year to get to know any Jews you didn't know before?
___ no
___ yes

IF "YES": How is it that you did (not) get to know this Jewish person?

IF ATTITUDES LESS FAVORABLE:

3. Have you had any chances during the last year to get to know any Jews you didn't know before?
___ no: How would you feel about getting to know more Jews?
___ yes: How did you react to these situations? Did your feelings about Jews influence your reactions to this person(s)?

ATTITUDES TOWARD JEWS

	Unfavorable	Favorable
eat	up	down
dance	up	down
party	up	down
marry	up	down
like	down	up
dishonest	up	down

APPENDIX B

Since we last talked with you, your attitudes toward Negroes seem to have become
___ more favorable
___ less favorable

	ATTITUDES TOWARD NEGROES	
	Unfavorable	Favorable
eat	up	down
dance	up	down
party	up	down
marry	up	down
like	down	up
lazy & ignorant	up	down

1. Do you have any idea why that is? (PROBES: Has there been some particular experience you have had during the last year that has made you feel (more, less) favorable toward Negroes?)

2. Have any of your recent contacts here in town affected your opinions about Negroes?
___ no
___ yes (GET DETAILS)

IF "YES": What was there about this contact that affected your attitudes?

IF ATTITUDES MORE FAVORABLE:

3. Would you like to get to be good friends with more Negroes?
___ no: Why is that?
___ yes: Have you had any chances during the last year to get to know any Negroes you did not know before?
___ no
___ yes

IF "YES": How is it that you did (not) get to know this Negro?

IF ATTITUDES LESS FAVORABLE:

3. Have you had any chances during the last year to get to know any Negroes you did not know before?
___ no: How would you feel about getting to know more Negroes?
___ yes: How did you react to these situations? Did your feelings about Negroes influence your reactions to this person(s)?

NONCHANGER SHEET

1. Is there anything you recall about the past year or so that makes you continue to feel as you do about Jews or Negroes?

Jews Negroes
1 ___ 1 ___ yes: What is that?
2 ___ 2 ___ no

2. Do you remember ever feeling more or less favorable about Jews or Negroes than you now feel?

Jews Negroes
4 ___ 4 ___ yes, more favorable } How did you happen to change?
5 ___ 5 ___ yes, less favorable
6 ___ 6 ___ no

3. Have you had any chances during the last year to get to know any Jews or Negroes you didn't know before?

Jews Negroes
8 ___ 8 ___ no: How would you feel about getting to know some Jews or Negroes?

How is it that you didn't get to know them?

Jews Negroes
9 ___ 9 ___ yes

Did your feelings about Jews and Negroes in general influence your reactions to these (Jews, Negroes)?

4. Do you recall ever having had a good friend that was:

a Negro?
1 ___ yes: How is it that this Negro is no longer a good friend of yours?
2 ___ no

a Jew?
4 ___ yes: How is it that this Jew is no longer a good friend of yours?
5 ___ no

NONCHANGER SHEET   CP and C̄P̄

1. Is there anything you recall about the past year or so that makes you continue to feel as you do about Jews or Negroes?

   Jews Negroes
   1 ___ 1 ___ yes: What is that?
   2 ___ 2 ___ no

2. Do you remember ever feeling more or less favorable about Jews or Negroes than you now feel?

   Jews Negroes
   4 ___ 4 ___ yes, more favorable ⎫ How did you happen to change?
   5 ___ 5 ___ yes, less favorable ⎭
   6 ___ 6 ___ no

3. Last time we interviewed you, you had a good
   friend who was a

	Jew	Negro
neighborhood	___	___
organization	___	___
at work	___	___
social contact	___	___

   Was this the same person you told me about just now?

   1   2   3
   ___   ___   ___ yes
                          no: How did you come to be friends?

4. Would you say he (she) is typical of the (Jews, Negroes) or different in some respects?

   1   2   3
   ___   ___   ___ typical ⎫
   ___   ___   ___ different ⎬ In what ways?
   ___   ___   ___ don't know ⎭

   IF NEGATIVE: Why do you continue to see him (her)?

5. Do you think your feelings toward most other (Jews, Negroes) have changed as a result of your contact with this (these) person(s)?

   Jews Negroes
   ___   ___   no
   ___   ___   yes: In what ways?

B only

1. What would you say are your biggest problems and worries today?

2. How often do you express your ideas about Negroes and Jews to other people? (PROBE FOR LAST EXPERIENCE AND REACTIONS AMONG LISTENERS.)

3. Would you say you are less prejudiced or more prejudiced than other people you know?
   (PROBE: Why do you think that is?)

4. IF RESPONDENT HAS A CLOSE CONTACT WITH A NEGRO OR JEW, ASK:
   Since you feel the way you do about (Jews) (Negroes), what is there about the (Jewish) (Negro) person you told me about before which makes you like him (her)?

Which 4 or 5 of these things are most important to you? (Please make sure you read the whole list.)

HAND RESPONDENT CARD

1 _____ Getting ahead in a career
2 _____ Living an upright life
3 _____ Mixing socially with high type people
4 _____ Spending time with the family at home
5 _____ Participating in community affairs
6 _____ Having time to do the things one wants to outside the home
7 _____ Having time to oneself at home
8 _____ Visiting back and forth with close friends or relatives
9 _____ Always trying to learn new things to improve oneself
0 _____ Running an efficient household
x _____ Doing all one can for one's children
y _____ Working for causes of human betterment

1. Most of us know certain people we look up to and respect. What these people think is especially important to us. Who are the people in your case that you look up to and respect most—not their names, just who they are? (PROBE)

2. Could you tell me if (this person) feels the same way you do about Negroes or different? _____ About Jews? _____

3. Has (this person) had any especially pleasant or unpleasant experiences with Jews or Negroes during the last year or so?

4. Has (this person) changed his attitudes at all toward Jews or Negroes over the past year or two?

_____ (Relation to respondent)

2.
Negro	Jew	
1 ___	1 ___	different: In what ways?
2 ___	2 ___	same
3 ___	3 ___	don't know

3.
Negro	Jew	
5 ___	5 ___	pleasant (GET DETAILS)
6 ___	6 ___	unpleasant (GET DETAILS)
7 ___	7 ___	don't know
8 ___	8 ___	no

4.
Negro	Jew	
9 ___	9 ___	change favorable (GET DETAILS)
0 ___	0 ___	change unfavorable (GET DETAILS)
x ___	x ___	don't know
y ___	y ___	no

T only

1. How often do you express your ideas about Negroes and Jews to other people?

(PROBE FOR LAST EXPERIENCE AND REACTIONS AMONG LISTENERS.)

2. Would you say you are less prejudiced or more prejudiced than other people you know? (PROBE: Why do you think that is?)

I wonder if you have any idea what it is about your life experiences that has made you that way?

(PROBE FOR SPECIAL EVENTS OR PEOPLE THAT INFLUENCED RESPONDENT.)

MM

Here are some more statements which people have different opinions about. Please say whether you agree or disagree about each statement.

1. This country would be better off if the wealth were spread more evenly among the people.

   1 ____ agree
   2 ____ disagree

2. People with radical social and economic ideas should be allowed to run for public office.

   4 ____ agree
   5 ____ disagree

3. Young people today are too loose morally as far as sex goes.

   7 ____ agree
   8 ____ disagree

4. I usually feel rather uncomfortable about meeting people I have never seen before.

   1 ____ agree
   2 ____ disagree

5. In general, I think the Negroes have had a pretty hard time compared to other people.

   4 ____ agree
   5 ____ disagree

6. I am very much concerned with how I get along with other people.

   7 ____ agree
   8 ____ disagree

7. I feel a bit uneasy in the company of Negroes.

   1 ____ agree
   2 ____ disagree

8. People who break the law should be punished no matter how good their excuse is.

   4 ____ agree
   5 ____ disagree

9. Prison is too good for sex criminals; they should be publicly whipped or worse.

   7 ____ agree
   8 ____ disagree

10. Some say that you can't be too careful in your dealings with people, while others say that most people can be trusted. From your own experience, which would you agree with most?

   1 ____ can't be too careful
   2 ____ people can be trusted
   3 ____ don't know

   How strongly do you feel about this?

   5 ____ very strongly
   6 ____ fairly strongly
   7 ____ not strongly

---

1. Most of us know certain people we look up to and respect. What these people think is especially important to us. Who are the people in your case that you look up to and respect most — not their names, just who they are? (PROBE)

2. Could you tell me if (this person) feels the same way you do about Negroes or different? _____ About Jews? _____

3. Has (this person) had any especially pleasant or unpleasant experiences with Jews or Negroes during the last year or so?

4. Has (this person) changed his attitudes at all toward Jews or Negroes over the past year or two?

_____ (Members of immediate family)

2.
Negro		Jew	
1 ____	different: In what ways?	1 ____	different: In what ways?
2 ____	same	2 ____	same
3 ____	don't know	3 ____	don't know

3.
Negro		Jew	
5 ____	pleasant (GET DETAILS)	5 ____	pleasant (GET DETAILS)
6 ____	unpleasant (GET DETAILS)	6 ____	unpleasant (GET DETAILS)
7 ____	don't know	7 ____	don't know

4.
Negro		Jew	
9 ____	change favorable (GET DETAILS)	9 ____	change favorable (GET DETAILS)
0 ____	change unfavorable (GET DETAILS)	0 ____	change unfavorable (GET DETAILS)
x ____	don't know	x ____	don't know

_____ (Closest personal friends)

2.
Negro		Jew	
1 ____	different: In what ways?	1 ____	different: In what ways?
2 ____	same	2 ____	same
3 ____	don't know	3 ____	don't know

3.
Negro		Jew	
5 ____	pleasant (GET DETAILS)	5 ____	pleasant (GET DETAILS)
6 ____	unpleasant (GET DETAILS)	6 ____	unpleasant (GET DETAILS)
7 ____	don't know	7 ____	don't know

4.
Negro		Jew	
9 ____	change favorable (GET DETAILS)	9 ____	change favorable (GET DETAILS)
0 ____	change unfavorable (GET DETAILS)	0 ____	change unfavorable (GET DETAILS)
x ____	don't know	x ____	don't know

MM

1. Now think back to when you were a child. Did you spend most of your time with a bunch of other kids, just one or two others, or by yourself?
0 ___ with a bunch of others
x ___ with just one or two others
y ___ by myself

2. Think back now to how you felt when you were punished as a child. Did you feel you:
1 ___ always deserved it
2 ___ deserved it most of the time
3 ___ deserved it only part of the time

3. As a child how much were you afraid of being left alone?
5 ___ not at all
6 ___ a little
7 ___ fairly much

4. How afraid were you of not being liked by new friends?
9 ___ not at all
Q ___ a little
x ___ fairly much

5. Before you were married, did you have a good personal friend that was

Negro?
___ yes
7 ___ no
1 ___ never married

Jewish?
___ yes
2 ___ no

IF "YES": How often do you see this person nowadays?
3 ___ as often as you used to
4 ___ some, but not as often
5 ___ not at all

IF "YES": How often do you see this person nowadays?
8 ___ as often as you used to
9 ___ some, but not as often
0 ___ not at all

IF "SOME" OR "NOT AT ALL": Why is that?

IF "SOME" OR "NOT AT ALL": Why is that?

(PROBE WHETHER SPOUSE OBJECTED TO THIS ETHNIC FRIEND AND WHY.)

NN

1. Imagine you are in one of the restaurants where you often eat in town. A young, well-dressed Negro man comes in and sits down to have dinner and is refused service because of his race.
a) Would you approve or disapprove of his not being served?
1 ___ approve
2 ___ disapprove

IF "DISAPPROVE": What do you think you would do? (PROBE IF ANSWERED IN TERMS OF FEELINGS: Well what would you do?)

b) What do you think the Negro should do? (READ LIST)
4 ___ leave without saying anything
5 ___ protest to the manager
6 ___ try to sue the manager
___ something else: What?

c) Now suppose that instead of leaving, the Negro customer complains to the manager and the manager says: "Look fellow, I like your kind of people and I'd be glad to serve you, but my customers object. Be a good sport and try someplace else, will you?"
Would you:
1 ___ approve
2 ___ disapprove
How strongly?
4 ___ very strongly
5 ___ fairly strongly
6 ___ not strongly

d) Now suppose a well-known doctor who overhears the conversation between the manager and the Negro says: "I think you should serve this gentleman. He's entitled to service just like the rest of us. I think you're wrong about how your customers feel. This is America, you know, and we want to see that all people get treated fairly. If you don't serve him you'll lose my trade for good." So the manager agrees to serve the Negro.
Would you:
1 ___ approve
2 ___ disapprove
How strongly?
4 ___ very strongly
5 ___ fairly strongly
6 ___ not strongly

2. Suppose you were waiting in line for a table at a crowded restaurant. The headwaiter ushers some late arrivals directly to a table. The person standing next to you says: "Isn't that just like the Jews—never wait their turn, always pushing in."
a) Would you approve or disapprove of his saying that? 0 ___ approve
x ___ disapprove

IF "DISAPPROVE": What do you think you would do? (PROBE IF ANSWERED IN TERMS OF FEELINGS: Well, what would you do?)

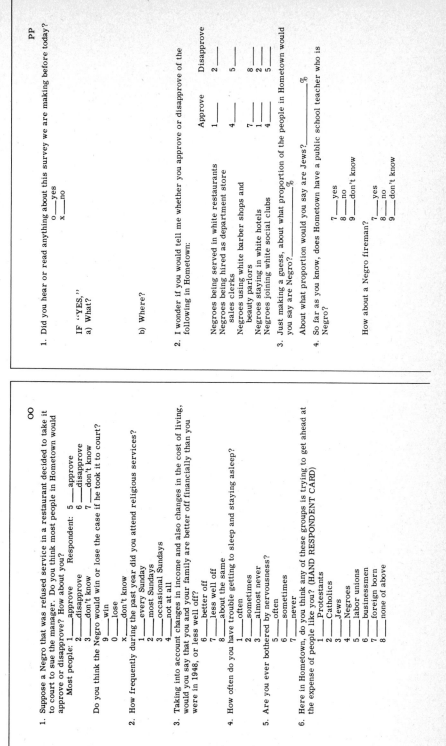

PP

1. Did you hear or read anything about this survey we are making before today?

   o ___ yes
   x ___ no

   IF "YES,"
   a) What?

   b) Where?

2. I wonder if you would tell me whether you approve or disapprove of the following in Hometown:

	Approve	Disapprove
Negroes being served in white restaurants	1 ___	2 ___
Negroes being hired as department store sales clerks	4 ___	5 ___
Negroes using white barber shops and beauty parlors	7 ___	8 ___
Negroes staying in white hotels	1 ___	2 ___
Negroes joining white social clubs	4 ___	5 ___

3. Just making a guess, about what proportion of the people in Hometown would you say are Negro? ___ %
   About what proportion would you say are Jews? ___ %

4. So far as you know, does Hometown have a public school teacher who is Negro?

   7 ___ yes
   8 ___ no
   9 ___ don't know

   How about a Negro fireman?

   7 ___ yes
   8 ___ no
   9 ___ don't know

OO

1. Suppose a Negro that was refused service in a restaurant decided to take it to court to sue the manager. Do you think most people in Hometown would approve or disapprove? How about you?

   Most people: 1 ___ approve   Respondent: 5 ___ approve
   2 ___ disapprove   6 ___ disapprove
   3 ___ don't know   7 ___ don't know

   Do you think the Negro would win or lose the case if he took it to court?
   9 ___ win
   0 ___ lose
   x ___ don't know

2. How frequently during the past year did you attend religious services?
   1 ___ every Sunday
   2 ___ most Sundays
   3 ___ occasional Sundays
   4 ___ not at all

3. Taking into account changes in income and also changes in the cost of living, would you say that you and your family are better off financially than you were in 1948, or less well off?
   6 ___ better off
   7 ___ less well off
   8 ___ about the same

4. How often do you have trouble getting to sleep and staying asleep?
   1 ___ often
   2 ___ sometimes
   3 ___ almost never

5. Are you ever bothered by nervousness?
   5 ___ often
   6 ___ sometimes
   7 ___ never

6. Here in Hometown, do you think any of these groups is trying to get ahead at the expense of people like you? (HAND RESPONDENT CARD)
   1 ___ Protestants
   2 ___ Catholics
   3 ___ Jews
   4 ___ Negroes
   5 ___ labor unions
   6 ___ businessmen
   7 ___ foreign born
   8 ___ none of above

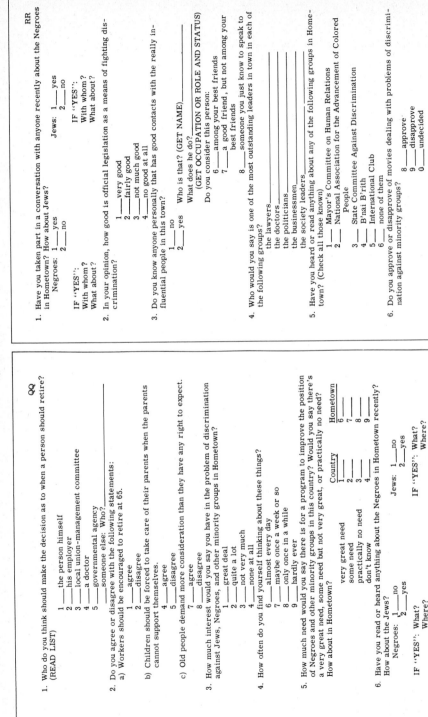

QQ

1. Who do you think should make the decision as to when a person should retire? (READ LIST)
   1 ___ the person himself
   2 ___ his employer
   3 ___ local union-management committee
   4 ___ a doctor
   5 ___ governmental agency
   ___ someone else: Who? _____

2. Do you agree or disagree with the following statements:
   a) Workers should be encouraged to retire at 65.
   1 ___ agree
   2 ___ disagree
   b) Children should be forced to take care of their parents when the parents cannot support themselves.
   4 ___ agree
   5 ___ disagree
   c) Old people demand more consideration than they have any right to expect.
   7 ___ agree
   8 ___ disagree

3. How much interest would you say you have in the problem of discrimination against Jews, Negroes, and other minority groups in Hometown?
   1 ___ great deal
   2 ___ quite a lot
   3 ___ not very much
   4 ___ none at all

4. How often do you find yourself thinking about these things?
   6 ___ almost every day
   7 ___ maybe once a week or so
   8 ___ only once in a while
   9 ___ hardly ever

5. How much need would you say there is for a program to improve the position of Negroes and other minority groups in this country? Would you say there's a very great need, some need but not very great, or practically no need? How about in Hometown?

	Country	Hometown
very great need	1 ___	6 ___
some need	2 ___	7 ___
practically no need	3 ___	8 ___
don't know	4 ___	9 ___

6. Have you read or heard anything about the Negroes in Hometown recently? How about the Jews?
   Negroes: 1 ___ no   2 ___ yes
   Jews: 1 ___ no   2 ___ yes
   IF "YES": What? Where?

RR

1. Have you taken part in a conversation with anyone recently about the Negroes in Hometown? How about Jews?
   Negroes: 1 ___ yes   2 ___ no
   Jews: 1 ___ yes   2 ___ no
   IF "YES": With whom? What about?
   IF "YES": With whom? What about?

2. In your opinion, how good is official legislation as a means of fighting discrimination?
   1 ___ very good
   2 ___ fairly good
   3 ___ not much good
   4 ___ no good at all

3. Do you know anyone personally that has good contacts with the really influential people in this town?
   1 ___ no
   2 ___ yes   Who is that? (GET NAME) _____
   What does he do? _____
   (GET OCCUPATION OR ROLE AND STATUS)
   Do you consider this person:
   6 ___ among your best friends
   7 ___ a good friend, but not among your best friends
   8 ___ someone you just know to speak to

4. Who would you say is one of the most outstanding leaders in town in each of the following groups?
   the lawyers _____
   the doctors _____
   the politicians _____
   the businessmen _____
   the society leaders _____

5. Have you heard or read anything about any of the following groups in Hometown? (Check all those known)
   1 ___ Mayor's Committee on Human Relations
   2 ___ National Association for the Advancement of Colored People
   3 ___ State Committee Against Discrimination
   4 ___ B'nai B'rith
   5 ___ International Club
   6 ___ none of them

6. Do you approve or disapprove of movies dealing with problems of discrimination against minority groups?
   8 ___ approve
   9 ___ disapprove
   0 ___ undecided

APPENDIX C

INDICES OF PREJUDICE: MAJORITY-GROUP, HOMETOWN

The three aspects of prejudice which received primary emphasis in the initial Hometown studies of the white majority-group population were social distance, threat, and stereotypes. Accordingly we had scores for each of these three facets. On the "threat" and "social distance" aspects of prejudice, we had separate scores for attitudes toward each of the three ethnic groups. In addition, a composite General Prejudice Score was devised, based on the three more specific types of prejudice scores.

General Prejudice Score

This was a composite score based on the Distasteful, Stereotype, and Threat ("Chicago Tension") Scores, which were dichotomized. One point was given for each of the following: Total Distasteful Score of 6 or more, Stereotype Score of 2 or more, and Tension Score of 2 or more.

Threat ("Chicago Tension") Score

This "threat" score was based on the following three questions, each followed by a question concerning intensity:

1. *As you see it, are (Negroes, Jews, Italians) today demanding more than they have a right to or not? (IF YES) Does this make you pretty angry, or a little angry, or don't you feel strongly about it?*

2. *Do you think (Ethnic Group) today are trying to push in where they are not wanted? (IF YES) Does this bother you a great deal, a little, or hardly at all?*

3. *On the whole, would you say that you like or dislike (Ethnic Group) people? Are your feelings about (Ethnic Group) very strong, pretty strong, not so strong, or not strong at all?*

On each question, the most favorable response counted zero, the least favorable (about which the respondent felt very strongly) counted two, and all other responses counted one, yielding a score ranging from 0 to 6.

A comparison of the distribution of the three tension scores showed as high a proportion of persons high on tension toward Jews as toward Negroes.

Tension Distribution

Score:		Toward Negroes	Toward Jews	Toward Italians
Low	0	22%	24%	48%
	1	34%	25%	32%
	2	19%	20%	9%
High	3	25%	30%	12%
	100% equals	(529)	(529)	(504)

409

Stereotype Score

The following four items were used in constructing the Stereotype Score, one point being given for agreement with each of the statements:

1. *This country would be better off if there were not so many foreigners here.* (One point for agree very strongly or fairly strongly.)
2. *Generally speaking, Negroes are lazy and ignorant.* (One point for any response BUT disagree very strongly or fairly strongly.)
3. *Although some Jews are honest, in general Jews are dishonest in their business dealings.* (One point for any response BUT disagree very strongly or fairly strongly.)
4. *Americans must be on guard against the power of the Catholic Church.* (One point for agree.)

As the distribution of this score in the total sample indicates, only about one-fifth of the sample endorsed all four or three of the four stereotype statements:

LOW	0	30%
	1	25
	2	24
	3	14
HIGH	4	7

Distasteful Scores

Essentially a type of social distance score, *the Distasteful Score indicated the number of situations in which respondents said they would find contact with ethnic individuals distasteful to them.* The following question was asked concerning each of the three ethnic groups (Negroes, Jews, Italian-Americans):

Do you think you would ever find it a little distasteful:
  to EAT at the same table with (Ethnic Groups)?
  to DANCE with (Ethnic Group)?
  to go to a PARTY and find that MOST of the people are (Ethnic Group)?
  to have a (Ethnic Group) MARRY someone in your family?

One point was given for agreement with each item, yielding a maximum score of 4, indicative of the greatest amount of discomfort about social contacts with that ethnic group.* The distribution in the total sample of these distasteful scores indicated that, unlike the Chicago Tension Score, on which there was as high a proportion of "threat" responses towards Jews as toward Negroes, on the social distance scores the score on attitudes toward Jews was more like that on

---

* More specifically, these scores were computed by counting one point for each of the following, with the abbreviations as noted:

D   . . . agree it would be distasteful
DK . . . don't know if it would be distasteful
NA . . . no answer to question

Jews: eat D; dance NA; party D or DK; marry D or NA; (maximum of 4 points). Negroes: dance D, NK or NA; party D, DK or NA; marry D or NA; (Maximum of 3 points). Italians: eat D; dance D; party D; marry D; (maximum of 4 points).

attitudes towards Italians. It was only on attitudes toward Negroes that a very large proportion of the sample was found clustered at the "high" end of the score:

Score:		Distasteful Distribution		
		Toward Negroes	Toward Jews	Toward Italians
Low	0	1%	41%	56%
	1	13%	30%	23%
	2	12%	15%	10%
	3	26%	8%	5%
High	4	48%	6%	6%
	100% equals	(529)	(529)	(504)

These scores were also combined into a Total Distasteful Score, indicating the total number of situations in which respondents said they would find contact with ethnic individuals distasteful to them. This score had a maximum of 11 rather than 12, since one item—"eat at the same table with Negro"—did not scale with the remainder.

INDEX OF SOCIAL-DISTANCE FEELINGS USED IN CHAPTER 8

In all cross-section samples of the populations in Hometown, Steelville, South-port, and Valley City, the respondents were asked a standard set of questions concerning social-distance feelings toward each relevant ethnic outgroup (white, Negro, Jew, gentile, etc.):

Do you think you would ever find it a little distasteful:
1. *To eat at the same table with a (Ethnic) person?*
2. *To dance with a (Ethnic) person?*
3. *To go to a party and find that most of the people are (Ethnics)?*
4. *To have a (Ethnic) person marry someone in your family?*

In the case of Negroes' attitudes toward white persons these four items were found to form a reliable score, conforming to a Guttman scale-pattern which a reproducibility of more than 90 per cent and a zero-cell in each box of the matrix (See Noel, p. 350). Items #2 and #3 resulted in very similar response patterns; analysis showed that Item #3 was preferable; and a three-item score (eliminating Item #2) finally was selected as the most efficient and least ambiguous score.

To categorize respondents as "prejudiced" or "not prejudiced," we divided those who scored zero (no distasteful response) from all others in Hometown, Steelville, and Valley City. In Southport, the division was made between those scoring 0-1 and those scoring 2-3 (for the reasons for this procedure, see Noel, p. 348).

Except as noted in the text, in using the scores just described we followed these conventions in terminology:

1. The term "prejudiced" (or "high prejudice") means indorsement of one or more of the social-distance responses ("distasteful") *except* in the case of Southport, in which it means that the individual accepts two or all of the three items.

2. If we say that some sample or subclass of the population is "more preju-diced" than another, this simply means that a higher proportion of that sample or subclass falls in the "prejudiced" category.

The following are a few examples of field guides and queries that were devised for field workers to use in reporting their participant-observations in interracial situations.

Instructions for Keeping Log of Contact Situations

For additional information, instructions, turning in reports, etc., call the office secretary of the Cornell Field Research Office, between 9 A.M. and 5 P.M. on weekdays.

In our intergroup relations study, we are interested in getting more information about the different kinds of contacts that whites and Negroes or Jews and gentiles have. We want to know the nature of these contacts, who the people are, what they say, how they seem to feel.

These pages are for recording a log of all contacts that you have with members of a different racial group. There are several kinds of forms here; *for each contact fill out one of the log sheets* that are at the front of the book. Select from the rest of the sheets those you need in order to give a full account of the contact situation. Which ones you select depend on what actually occurred in the contact situation. The different pages are for the following purposes:

Log Sheets (at the front of your notebook)

One of these sheets should be filled out for each contact situation. If an interracial contact is brief or casual, this one sheet may be enough. The word *Role* refers to the participant's function or part in the situation—sometimes his occupation or position (e.g. teacher, chairman, proprietor, minister's wife, president of the club, policeman, employer, etc.). In describing what happened, stress the details that have to do with the *interracial aspects* of the contact. Be brief about the rest. Write on the back if more space is necessary or select from the other sheets those you need to give a fuller account.

The list of words on the right-hand side describe the way you think each person felt in the situation. If none of them describes what you mean, substitute your own words in the blank spaces below. On some Log Sheets the list of adjectives are not numbered. You may find it easier to number them 1 to 23 (including blank spaces) and then, after a person's name, write only the number of the word that applies to him.

Under *Remarks* include any comments you have on the contact.

Chronology Sheets

These are for detailed description of especially important things that happened in the contact situation in the same time order as they occurred. Write the time in the left-hand columns. This sheet should give the word-for-word details of, for example, an amusing incident, an embarrassing comment, an illustration of prejudice or discrimination connected with race relations. The *Sym* in the upper right-hand corner means your initials or identifying symbol. Write as much detail as necessary, using blank sheets from the back of the book if more space is needed.

Try to get down direct quotations—phrases used or any especially good illustrations (e.g., Mrs. Patton patronizingly pointed out that "Some of my best friends are Jews"). Record any behavior that seems to be inconsistent with what is generally considered "proper," "right," or "conventional."

Spontaneous actions or reactions, especially those that are unexpected, should be noted.

Reflect on the contact situation *immediately afterwards*. The reflection will sensitize you to the impressions you want. When going into a contact situation, be sensitive to the things you want to watch for. In field work a few relevant details are worth carloads of general impressions.

Frequently it is best to put down pieces of conversations in the words the people used, as nearly as you can recall them:

Bill: (with rising inflection) Then they can just take their dough and beat it. I'm through with that sort of thing. I'm not going to do the dirty work for that crowd any longer!

Joe: (with whining tone) Aw, Bill, don't be that way. We've gotta work with them or we haven't a chance. If we don't help them on this thing, we haven't a chance of getting any favors from them.

In this sort of recording, put into parentheses the details that tell you what the person felt. In order to get down parts of conversations word-for-word, keep watching for the significant snatches of conversation that you will want to remember. Then, when a significant conversation occurs, you can memorize it better. If you wait until afterwards to decide what you want to put down word-for-word, you will probably find that you can't reconstruct it. Remembering word-for-word may be hard at first, but get down the important parts as near as you can; with a little practice you'll be surprised how closely you can reconstruct a conversation.

Analysis Sheet

On this sheet give your interpretation of the situation. Give your general impressions of the events that occurred. Put down your interpretation of any influence people have on each other (e.g. any orders given, directions laid down, requests, suggestions, signs of giving in, trying to impress, showing admiration, flattery, awe, etc.). *Try to analyze who impressed whom, and how.* You should include impressions about the things you can hardly remember or which are too fuzzy to report. Your impressions should reveal your understanding of the situation.

Participants Sheets

On these sheets, any persons, white or Negro, Jewish or gentile, who played an important part in the contact situation should be described. Give those descriptive details that most catch your attention, especially any features or be-havior that give clues to the person's personality. The more specific and less general your details are, the better: (e.g. "She kept dropping her eyes and evad-ing my questions. Finally she said with a shrug: 'I wouldn't know anything about that.'" Such a comment would be better than saying, "She seemed un-willing to talk freely with me.")

Get down your estimate of people's feelings in the contact situation; note anything important that was *not* said; record "how" things were said or done. The three sheets that describe the participant can be used for each person (some-times one sheet or two will suffice).

Projective Modification

This means what you think would have happened if some aspect of the situ-ation had been different. Just use your imagination and think how the contact situation would have ended if something else had happened instead of what did. This should be filled out for all situations when the Chronology is filled out.

Background Sheets

The diagram should show roughly the layout of the place where the contact situation occurred. It should also show where each of the people in the situa-tion were standing or sitting. In the second part, write down the important de-tails about what kind of place the contact situation occurred in, what kind of things usually happen there, what special things have happened in the past. The furnishings, upkeep, social class, or other relevant details will help. Include those details that will give the reader a mental picture of the setting, using spe-cific details rather than general words. This should be filled out for most con-tact situations that the Chronology is filled out for.

Special Note

If you have many recurring contacts on your job with persons of the other race, don't bother to put down each one of them. Instead fill out one complete set of sheets to cover these contacts on the job. On the Chronology Sheets put down some details about the different types of contact, if possible with a few sample conversations. Describe the main persons of the other race on the Par-ticipant Sheets, and so on.

CHRONOLOGY

Sym _____

For a chronological analytic account of what happened, including your impressions and the implications.

Approximate
time
_____

Date _____ Time: from _____ to _____ Initials _____

Place _____

Address _____

What was the occasion? (e.g. Was it a meeting? A social contact? A contact with a storekeeper? Or what?)

Draw line to each participant any word applies to:
friendly
amused
retiring
nervous
joking
indifferent
condescending
sarcastic
disapproving
reserved
helpful
uncomfortable
understanding
on edge
angry
irritable
distressed
hurt
annoyed
quarrelsome

Who were the Negro (or Jewish) participants?

Name _____ Role _____
Name _____ Role _____
Name _____ Role _____
Name _____ Role _____

Who were the white (or gentile) participants?

Name _____ Role _____
Name _____ Role _____
Name _____ Role _____
Name _____ Role _____

What happened? (Use back of sheet if need more space)

How did you feel in the situation? (Check words that apply)
___ amused   Why?
___ nervous
___ friendly
___ annoyed
___ indifferent
___ angry
___ uncomfortable
___ other:

Remarks:

APPENDIX E

Sym _____

ANALYSIS SHEET

1. What stands out especially in your mind?

2. What seemed most awkward or unusual?

3. What were the turning points in the situation and what might have happened at those points that might have made the outcome different?

Sym _____

Participant: _____

Physical Attributes:

Dress:
_____ expensive, well-groomed
_____ average
_____ shabby, inexpensive
_____ :

Speech and Social Graces:
_____ very refined
_____ average
_____ unrefined
_____ :

Role and Status: (What was P doing there? Any official capacity? How much authority did P have? What was P's place and standing in the structure of the situation?)

What did the way P behaved seem to indicate about his personality?

IMPRESSIONS

1. What stands out most in your impression of this individual?

2. Did he do anything that seemed especially friendly? (Note: this may duplicate your chronology in some cases)

3. Did he do anything that seemed especially unfriendly?

4. How did the P react after the contact situation?

5. What did the P then do? (dispose of him)

What was P's manner?   Toward whom?

ingratiating
friendly
joking
helpful
encouraging

compliant
approving
suggestful
understanding
receptive

submissive
retiring
contrite
reproachful
unattentive

dissenting
disapproving
reserved
dogmatic
self-righteous

condescending
sarcastic
authoritative
pompous
timid

disgusted
on edge
distressed
apologetic
on guard

hurt
contrary
sullen
flippant
resistant

irritable
hostile
quarrelsome
nagging
expansive

APPENDIX E

Projective modification of the circumstances, participants, their point of view:

A. "What do you think would happen if.......?"

B. "What if...?"

C. "What if...?"

INDEX